佐藤隆三
著作集

The Selected Works of
Ryuzo Sato

[第**7**巻]

Symmetry
and
Economic Invariance

日本評論社

佐藤隆三著作集刊行に寄せて

　この著作集（英語表記の通り正確には選集）は、米国流に言えば「四散していた子供たちを一堂に集めた」ようなもので、生みの親としてこれに優る喜びはない。

　何しろ著者は、昭和32年（1957年）にフルブライト留学生として氷川丸で2週間近くかけて米国留学をして以来、平成18年（2006年）に東京大学の客員教授として日本に専住するまで、50年間の日米両棲生活を送っていたのである。その間、両国の大学で博士号を取り、大学教授として、日本語と英語で多くの著書や論文を発表してきた。いわば子供たちたる作品が日米に散在している状態であった。

　当然のことながら、日本で発表したものは日本語、米国や欧州で出版したものは英語で書かれている。そのため、この著作集は、日本語と英語の双方でそのまま構成されている。こうしたかたちでの著作集はあまり例がないようだが、それにはこのような背景がある。

　まず、第1巻から第3巻までは、著者の専門分野である理論経済学というよりは、一般的な社会経済的諸問題を、米国との比較において日本の読者に提供しよう、との意図で書かれている。第4巻から第7巻までは、理論経済学の著作である。第4巻「経済成長の理論」は著者の一橋大学への博士号取得のために提出した著書であり、日経・経済図書文化賞を受けたものである。

　第5巻は、ニューヨークのアカデミック・プレス社から出版されたリー群の技術変化の理論への応用を試みた英文著書の日本語訳である。その後、英語版は、英国のE. エルガー社から拡大改訂版として出版されたが、今回収録した日本語版は、当時の訳書の出版社である勁草書房から出版されたものを同社とE. エルガー社の許可を得てそのままこの選集に加えたものである。両社の御厚意に深謝したい。

　第6巻は、この50年間に米大学の教授として執筆した著者の専門分野の研究の成果ともいうべき論文を集めたものである。周知の通り、米大学での正教授の座は、"Publish or Perish"（論文が発表できなければ消え失せろ）とされる

ほど熾烈な競争の下にある。年に5〜6本のオリジナル論文を、レフェリーによって精査を受ける国際的に著名な学術誌（例えば *American Economic Review* など）に発表し続けることが求められる。著者が好んで用いる譬えとして、メジャーリーグに留まるために、選手が平均打率3割を維持しようと努力し続けるのと似た状況である。

第6巻に収録されている論文は、E. エルガー社の20世紀経済学者シリーズの *Growth Theory and Technical Change: The Selected Essays of Ryuzo Sato, Volume One 1996, Production, Stability and Dynamic Symmetry, Volume Two 1999*（佐藤隆三選集、第1巻、および第2巻）と重複するものがあるが、最近の論文を含めるため、すべての論文について元の論文が出版されたジャーナルから本著作集の第6巻に入れることに関して改めて許諾を得ている。第6巻への序文において個別のジャーナルに対して感謝の意を述べている。

第7巻は、著者がいわば住の主軸を日本に移してから引き受けた世界屈指の出版社シュプリンガー・ネイチャー社の新企画 Advances in Japanese Business and Economics シリーズの編集主幹として出版した英語版の著書である。

この著作集に収集し切れなかった著作の中で、読者の興味の対象となり得る数冊を挙げたい。

1. Sato, Ryuzo and Gilbert S. Suzawa（1981）*Research and Productivity: Endogenous Technical Chage*, Engelska Auburn.
2. Sato, Ryuzo, Elias Grivoyannis, Barbara Byrne and Chengping Lian（1997）*Health Care Systems in Japan and the United States: A Simulation Study and Policy Analysis*, Kluwer.
3. 佐藤隆三（1982）『ニュー・マクロエコノミクス（現代経済学基礎シリーズ）』マグロウヒル出版

米国の親しい友人から、最近の日本の大学教授たちは名刺に「××大学大学院教授」と記しているが、日本の大学院は決して国際的に強力ではないのに、なぜ大学院を強調するのか、との質問をたびたび受ける。その答えとして、現在日本の大学は官立、私立の差別をなくし、学校法人になったので、大学院で教える資格の有無で差別化を図りたいのだろう、と答えた。筆者もこの著作集の肩書きに、日本式に大学院をつけた。

階級社会ではないはずの米国で、正教授職の中に三つのランクがあることを知る日本人はあまり多くない。すなわち「平(ヒラ)教授、冠(カンムリ)教授

(Chair Professor)、全学統括教授（University Professor）」である。ユニバーシティ・プロフェッサーは、ノーベル賞受賞学者でも必ずしも貰えない最高名誉の教授の座である。著名大学のすべての分野でもほんの数名である。（MITでは、サミュエルソン、ソローなどの数名。）

　冠講座は経済学部内でも特に業績のある教授数人に与えられる。米国式に「花（名誉）と団子（好待遇）」の両方を授けて、業績に報いようとする教授のポジションである。筆者は、ニューヨーク大学に在職した20年間、C. V. スター財団冠講座のチェアー・プロフェッサーのポジションを授与された。この財団はAIGの創始者であるスター氏の遺産をもとにしてつくられたもので、ロックフェラー財団と同規模である。AIGは中国、日本（AIU）から保険業を始め、世界最大の保険会社になった。

　筆者はこのニューヨーク大学の冠講座の支援で、日米での研究活動を続けることができた。この著作集もこの冠講座の支援がなければ出版は不可能であったろう。

　本著作集への転載に関しては、各巻の序文で謝意を記した。企画、編集、その他の業務については、日本評論社の小西ふき子、斎藤博の両氏の懇切な御協力とアドバイスを頂いた。この紙面を借りて深謝したい。

2016年6月　東京にて
佐藤　隆三

佐藤隆三著作集全7巻の概要

- ■第1巻　文化・社会の日米比較
- ■第2巻　米国から見た日本経済
- ■第3巻　日本企業と大学の実態
- ■第4巻　経済成長の理論
- ■第5巻　技術変化と経済不変性の理論：リー群論の応用
- ■第6巻　The Selected Scientific Papers of Ryuzo Sato on Production, Technical Change and Dynamics
- ■第7巻　Symmetry and Economic Invariance

第 7 巻「Symmetry and Economc Invariance」へのプロローグ

　本巻は2014年にSpringer社から出版された原書をそのまま再収録したものである。2年前に書いた「Preface」に特に追加することはないが、最近この分野における世界の専門家から、私信及び出版された論文の形で、筆者へのコンタクトがあった。それらは、本来ならばこの第7巻の第11章「A Survey on Recent Developments」の追加として、第12節（11. 12）に収録されるべきものである。

　これに触れる前に一つの体験的エピソードを紹介したい。ニューヨーク大学での国際シンポジウムに招待した日本の若手経済学者の一人が、筆者に「先生の理論は日本では無論のこと、国際的にも理解出来る人はいないのではないですか」とお世辞とも皮肉ともとれるコメントをした。彼の真意は「こんな難解な理論を発表しても、誰の興味も引きませんョ」と言うものではなかったか。

　この国際会議は筆者の研究所が主催したもので、ノーベル賞経済学者数人が参加した「動学・微分ゲーム」をテーマとしたものであった。日本からの学者数名のうち、このコメントをした学者を含む2、3名は、国際会議への参加は初めてらしく、晩餐会にＴシャツで出席しようとしていた。急拠サイズの合う上着をアメリカ人の同僚たちから借りるのに奔走したことを記憶している。つまり彼等が欧米のTPO（Time＝時間、Place＝場所、Occasion＝行事）のわきまえもないことに少々驚いた。

　「彼等はマルドメの経済学者なんですョ」と国際会議に馴れている同席の日本からの学者は苦笑していた。日本の企業の中では、「まるっきりドメスティック」の意味で、関心が国内の状勢にのみ向けられ、国際的空気の読めない人間を「マルドメ」と皮肉るらしい。彼によれば、それでもビジネスの世界ではこのマルドメたちが社長になる確率が高いそうである。

　ここで冒頭の説明に戻ろう。まず、本著のインターネット・ダウンロードが4000件を超えたことを出版社から知らされている。またこのマルドメ先生の「心配」に反して、筆者の「難しすぎる理論」を展開している本巻及び第5巻が引用されている一例として次の論文を紹介しよう。

最近、G. S. Perets（University of Lyon）及び E. Yashiv（Tel Aviv University and London School of Economics）の両教授から彼等の最新の論文が送られてきた。その論文（下記参照）は、筆者の Lie 群のアプローチを金融工学における Robert Merton（1969、1971）の消費と投資行動の最適分析に応用したものである。そこでは、HARA 効用関数が最も有効な型であることが証明されている。HARA（Hyperbolic Absolute Risk Aversion）型とは、「絶対的リスク回避度が総資産に反比例する」効用関数のことである。

本論文では、先ず微分方程式の Lie 群変換のもとでの不変性について議論が進められている（佐藤隆三著作集第 5 巻 pp.446～458のもとになっている英語論文、及びこの第 7 巻 pp.249～253が参照されている）。次に Merton モデルの分析が紹介され、消費・投資行動の最適微分方程式が導出され、それが、Lie 群変換の下で「富におけるスケール」の不変性を維持するために如何なる型の効用関数とコンパチブルか、が分析されている。答えは「HARA 型のみ」と結論づけられている（Lemma 1）。そして「経済的最適問題の分析用具として、Lie 群の対称性（Symmetry）と不変性（Invariance）の概念が最も有効である」と結論づけている。

本著作集第 5 巻へのプロローグにも記したが、ロシアの Cherkarshin Alexander 教授からこの第 7 巻の原本を入手したいとの要望があった。Springer 社が直接ネット上での購読を許可する扱いをして下さった。

また Springer 社からは原著をこの第 7 巻に再収録する許可が与えられた。本著の刊行にあたり、改めて Springer 社及び同社の河上自由乃氏に感謝の意を表したい。

2016年12月　東京にて

佐藤隆三

As stated in Japanese in my general introduction to this series, I wish to express my sincere thanks to NYU's Stern School and the C. V. Starr Foundation for the support given to my research endeavors.

Dec. 2016 Tokyo

Ryuzo Sato

・尚本巻の末尾には筆者の略歴及び著書・論文目録が記載されている。
・本プロローグに関する参考文献：

Merton, Robert C., [1969], "Lifetime Portfolio Selection under Uncertainty: The Continuous Time Case," *Review of Economics and Statistics* 51, 247-57.

Merton, Robert C., [1971], "Optimum Consumption and Portfolio Rules in a Continuous Time Model," *Journal of Economic Theory* 3, 373-413.

Perets, Gadi S. and Yashiv, Eran, [2016, May], "The Fundamental Nature of HARA Utility," Working paper dedicated to the memory of Bill Segal.

目　次

佐藤隆三著作集刊行に寄せて……………………………………………………iii
佐藤隆三著作集全7巻の概要……………………………………………………vi
第7巻「Symmetry and Economic Invariance」へのプロローグ …………vii
初出一覧……………………………………………………………………………xiii

Symmetry and Economic Invariance ……………………………………xii

RYUZO SATO Biographical and Bibliographical Data ………………… 275

初出一覧

　この巻におさめた著書の出所は以下のとおりである。本文は原文の通りに収録することを原則とした。

Symmetry and Economic Invarians, by Ryuzo Sato and Rama V. Ramachandran, Supringer Japan, 2014

Advances in Japanese Business and Economics

Editor in Chief:
RYUZO SATO
C.V. Starr Professor Emeritus of Economics, Stern School of Business,
New York University

Senior Editor:
KAZUO MINO, Professor Emeritus, Kyoto University

Managing Editors:
HAJIME HORI, Professor Emeritus, Tohoku University
HIROSHI YOSHIKAWA, Professor Emeritus, The University of Tokyo
KUNIO ITO, Professor Emeritus, Hitotsubashi University

Editorial Board Members:

TAKAHIRO FUJIMOTO
Professor, The University of Tokyo

YUZO HONDA
Professor Emeritus, Osaka University
Professor, Kansai University

TOSHIHIRO IHORI
Professor Emeritus, The University of Tokyo

TAKENORI INOKI
Professor Emeritus, Osaka University
Special University Professor,
Aoyama Gakuin University

JOTA ISHIKAWA
Professor, Hitotsubashi University

KATSUHITO IWAI
Professor Emeritus, The University of Tokyo
Visiting Professor, International
Christian University

MASAHIRO MATSUSHITA
Professor Emeritus, Aoyama Gakuin University

TAKASHI NEGISHI
Professor Emeritus, The University of Tokyo
The Japan Academy

KIYOHIKO NISHIMURA
Professor, The University of Tokyo

TETSUJI OKAZAKI
Professor, The University of Tokyo

YOSHIYASU ONO
Professor, Osaka University

KOTARO SUZUMURA
Professor Emeritus, Hitotsubashi University
The Japan Academy

Advances in Japanese Business and Economics showcases the research of Japanese scholars. Published in English, the series highlights for a global readership the unique perspectives of Japan's most distinguished and emerging scholars of business and economics. It covers research of either theoretical or empirical nature, in both authored and edited volumes, regardless of the subdiscipline or geographical coverage, including, but not limited to, such topics as macroeconomics, microeconomics, industrial relations, innovation, regional development, entrepreneurship, international trade, globalization, financial markets, technology management, and business strategy. At the same time, as a series of volumes written by Japanese scholars, it includes research on the issues of the Japanese economy, industry, management practice and policy, such as the economic policies and business innovations before and after the Japanese "bubble" burst in the 1990s.

Overseen by a panel of renowned scholars led by Editor-in-Chief Professor Ryuzo Sato, the series endeavors to overcome a historical deficit in the dissemination of Japanese economic theory, research methodology, and analysis. The volumes in the series contribute not only to a deeper understanding of Japanese business and economics but to revealing underlying universal principles.

Ryuzo Sato • Rama V. Ramachandran

Symmetry and Economic Invariance

Second Enhanced Edition

Ryuzo Sato
Stern School of Business
New York University
New York, USA

Rama V. Ramachandran
Pebble Brook Lane
Plano, Texas, USA

ISSN 2197-8859 ISSN 2197-8867 (electronic)
ISBN 978-4-431-54429-6 ISBN 978-4-431-54430-2 (eBook)
DOI 10.1007/978-4-431-54430-2
Springer Tokyo Heidelberg New York Dordrecht London

Library of Congress Control Number: 2013950104

© Springer Japan 1998, 2014
This work is subject to copyright. All rights are reserved by the Publisher, whether the whole or part of the material is concerned, specifically the rights of translation, reprinting, reuse of illustrations, recitation, broadcasting, reproduction on microfilms or in any other physical way, and transmission or information storage and retrieval, electronic adaptation, computer software, or by similar or dissimilar methodology now known or hereafter developed. Exempted from this legal reservation are brief excerpts in connection with reviews or scholarly analysis or material supplied specifically for the purpose of being entered and executed on a computer system, for exclusive use by the purchaser of the work. Duplication of this publication or parts thereof is permitted only under the provisions of the Copyright Law of the Publisher's location, in its current version, and permission for use must always be obtained from Springer. Permissions for use may be obtained through RightsLink at the Copyright Clearance Center. Violations are liable to prosecution under the respective Copyright Law.
The use of general descriptive names, registered names, trademarks, service marks, etc. in this publication does not imply, even in the absence of a specific statement, that such names are exempt from the relevant protective laws and regulations and therefore free for general use.
While the advice and information in this book are believed to be true and accurate at the date of publication, neither the authors nor the editors nor the publisher can accept any legal responsibility for any errors or omissions that may be made. The publisher makes no warranty, express or implied, with respect to the material contained herein.

Printed on acid-free paper

Springer is part of Springer Science+Business Media (www.springer.com)

"This reprint has been authorised by Springer Science & Business Media for distribution Worldwide."

Reprint from the English language edition:
Symmetry and Economic Invariance
by **Ryuzo Sato and Rama V. Ramachandran**
Copyright © Springer Japan 2014
Springer Japan is a part of Springer Science+Business Media
All Rights Reserved

Preface

This book provides an introduction to the application of group theory, a mathematical tool, to examine the structure of economic models. Even for models that can be analyzed by mathematical methods now standard in economics, group theory provides better intuition. Complex conditions that characterize the equilibrium path of a dynamic model can be expressed as a simple conservation law. Reflecting recent developments and a broadening interest among economists, this new enhanced edition has two parts. The first part reproduces the chapters from the 1998 edition of *Symmetry and Economic Invariance* and the second consists of four chapters (Chapters 8 – 11) and a mathematical appendix (Chapter 12). The appendix supplements a survey of mathematical techniques in Chapter 1.

We first met symmetry in the philosophy of Pythagoras, who used it to attribute mythical properties to some numbers and geometric figures. In contrast, the twentieth-century physicists under the influence of analytical philosophy used it to expunge classical physics of concepts that have no observable consequences! Sophus Lie showed how continuous groups can be used to determine the integrability of differential equations while his contemporary Felix Klein used discrete groups to codify Euclidean and non-Euclidean geometries. Today mathematicians relate group theory to differential topologies while simultaneously developing geometric methods that provide visual interpretation of analytical results. We have adopted in Part I, whenever possible, the geometric approach so as to relate our discussion to diagrammatic analysis in economics; the interpretations we provide are consistent with the positivist traditions now prevalent in our science.

Chapter 1 provides a heuristic introduction to group theory. Basic mathematical techniques are introduced and the use of group theory to determine the symmetric invariance of economic models is explained.

Chapter 2 uses group theory to analyze the controversy over whether productivity growth can be decomposed into that arising from technical progress and that from scale economies. We argue, following Sato (1981), that certain types of technical progress are indistinguishable from scale economies generated by particular types of production functions. In the process we develop additional analytical concepts in group theory.

Chapter 3 asks the inverse question: Given any production function with scale economies, is there any type of technical progress that generates the same pattern of productivity growth? In this chapter we discuss group theoretic properties of differential equations.

Chapter 4 uses group theory to discuss some well-known equations in consumer theory. We derive the Slutsky equation from group transformations and then examine the integrability conditions in utility theory.

Chapter 5 examines duality and self-duality using methods developed earlier. The result of empirical study that uses self-duality to compare the price elasticities in Japan and the United States is reported.

In Chapter 6 we use group theory to consider the properties of index numbers. Further, the invariance of Divisia index numbers is used to relate the discussion here to that of Chapter 2.

Finally, in Chapter 7, group properties of optimal dynamic models are used to derive "conservation laws."

The first chapter in Part II discusses the history of conservation laws in economics and then derives the conservation law for a model of heterogeneous capital goods. The law is interpreted as establishing the constancy of the income/wealth ratio along the trajectory. Its validity for the one-good model of Ramsey and the one of Liviatan and Samuelson and for the many goods models of von Neumann is demonstrated.

Chapter 9 using the Noether theorem, divides the continuous dynamic models into five groups: (1) zero discount; (2) fixed discount; (3) variable discount; (4) technical and taste change; and (5) local conservation laws (laws valid in the neighborhood of the stationary point). It also discusses conservation laws for discrete models: The conservation law for a firm arising from value maximization is developed. A section of the chapter develops laws for discrete models.

Chapter 10 explains how technological change plays an important role in economic growth by increasing the productivity of inputs. This chapter examines how input market conditions create differential growth in the productivity of inputs which is important as growth in efficiency of inputs can alleviate shortages of specific inputs in an economy. A technical problem in examining biased growth is that the elasticity of substitution between inputs must be determined and shown to be less than unity. Empirical analysis shows that Japan compensated for its lower population growth and for aging by increasing productivity.

Chapter 11 is a survey of recent developments. First, it establishes the extension of the conservation laws derived by Weitzman and Sato. Further extensions consider markets with distortions due to externalities and policy intervention and when income is stochastic. The two following sections examine alternative mathematical techniques to derive conservation laws and assess their comparative advantages. The next section considers investment that meets criteria for sustainability and intergenerational equity allocation when some resources are exhaustible. A discussion of considering technical change as a magnification type of Lie group follows. The final section reports on studies using differential geometry, exterior algebra and stochastic calculus.

Preface

Chapter 8 is a revised version of "The Invariance Principle and Income–Wealth Conservation Laws: Application of Lie Groups and Related Transformations," *Journal of Econometrics*, Vol. 30, pp. 365–389. Chapter 10 is a revision of "Quantity or Quality: The Impact of Labour Saving Innovation on US and Japanese Growth Rates, 1960–2004," *Japanese Economic Review*, Vol. 60, No. 4, pp. 407–434. We are grateful to the publishers of the journals, Elsevier and Wiley, respectively, for permission to reprint the material.

We thank Paul A. Samuelson for many discussions we had over the years. A conference organized in the Center for Japan–U.S. Business and Economic Studies led to the publication of a book entitled *Conservation Laws and Symmetry: Applications to Economics and Finance*, Springer (originally published by Kluwer Academic Publishers in 1990). We thank the participants for exploring many new applications in group theoretic methods. The first edition of this book was the fourth in a series, Research Monographs in Japan–U.S. Business and Economics, sponsored by the Center and published by Kluwer.

We thank Springer for their support in bringing out this revised and enhanced edition of *Symmetry and Economic Invariance*.

Tokyo, Japan Ryuzo Sato
Plano, Texas, USA Rama V. Ramachandran

Contents

Part I Introduction

1 Introduction 3
    1.1   Group Theory and Classification of Mathematical Structure 4
    1.2   Lie Groups and Invariance 8
    1.3   Economic Applications of Lie Groups 12

2 Technical Progress and Economies of Scale: Concept of Holotheticity 13
    2.1   A Reformulation of the Problem 13
    2.2   Lie Groups 22
    2.3   Holotheticity 24
    2.4   Conclusion 28

3 Holothetic Production Functions and Marginal Rate of Technical Substitution 29
    3.1   Types of Technical Progress Functions and Holotheticity 30
    3.2   Marginal Rate of Transformation and Extended Transformation 34
    3.3   Holotheticity and Lie Bracket 37
    3.4   Conclusion 41

4 Utility and Demand 43
    4.1   Integrability Conditions 47
    4.2   Conclusion 53

5 Duality and Self Duality 55
    5.1   Duality in Consumer Theory 55
    5.2   Separability and Additivity 59
    5.3   Self-Duality in Demand Theory 62
    5.4   A Method of Deriving Self-Dual Demand Functions 66
    5.5   Empirical Estimation of Self-Dual Demand Functions 68

	5.6	Implicit Self-Duality of Production and Cost Functions	69
	5.7	Conclusion	72
6	**The Theory of Index Numbers**		73
	6.1	Statistical Approach	73
	6.2	Test Approach	74
	6.3	Economic Index Numbers	79
	6.4	Divisia Index	82
7	**Dynamics and Conservation Laws**		87
	7.1	The Variational Problem and the Ramsey Rule	88
	7.2	Steady State and the Golden Rules	93
	7.3	The Hamiltonian Formulation and Control Theory	94
	7.4	Noether Theorem and Its Implications	98
	7.5	Conservation Laws in von Neumann Model	101
	7.6	Measurement of National Income and Income-Wealth Ratios	104
	7.7	Conclusion	105
	References to Part I		107

Part II Recent Developments

8	**The Invariance Principle and Income-Wealth Conservation Laws**		113
	8.1	Introduction	113
	8.2	Brief Summary of the Literature	114
	8.3	A Model with Heterogeneous Capital Goods	115
	8.4	Noether'S Theorem (Invariance Principle)	116
	8.5	Income-Wealth Conservation Laws	119
	8.6	Special Cases	124
	8.7	Generalized Income/Wealth Conservation Laws	125
	8.8	Income-Capital (Wealth) Conservation Law in the von Neumann Model	128
	8.9	The Total Value Conservation Law of the Firm	132
	8.10	Empirical Applications	133
	8.11	Summary	138
	Appendix		139
	References		141
9	**Conservation Laws in Continuous and Discrete Models**		143
	9.1	Introduction	143
	9.2	Continuous Models	144
		9.2.1 Review of the Noether Theorem	144
		9.2.2 Model 1: Zero Discount Rate	146
		9.2.3 Model 2: Fixed Discount Rate	148
		9.2.4 Model 3: Variable Discount Rate	150

		9.2.5	Model 4: Technical and Taste Change	151
		9.2.6	Model 5: "Local" Conservation Laws	152
		9.2.7	Total Value Conservation Law of the Firm	153
	9.3	Discrete Models (2012 Version) by Shigeru Maeda		154
		9.3.1	Introduction	154
		9.3.2	Model 6: Discrete Growth Models	154
		9.3.3	Quadratic Conservatives: A Mathematical Digression	157
		9.3.4	Economic Conservation Laws	163
	9.4	Summary		167
	Appendix			169
	References			175
10	**Quantity or Quality: The Impact of Labour Saving Innovation on US and Japanese Growth Rates, 1960–2004**			**177**
	10.1	Introduction		177
		10.1.1	Recent Studies	179
	10.2	A Model of Biased (Labour Saving) Technical Change		179
		10.2.1	Importance of the Elasticity of Factor Substitution	180
		10.2.2	Why Do We Need Biased Technical Change?	183
		10.2.3	Equilibrium Growth and Stability Under Biased Technical Change	185
	10.3	Applications to the US and Japanese Data		187
		10.3.1	Tests of Non-unity of σ	187
		10.3.2	Estimates of Production Functions	189
		10.3.3	Simulation Results	193
		10.3.4	Biased Technical Change of Japan and the USA	195
		10.3.5	Contrast in Response to Oil Crises	197
		10.3.6	Economic Performance Revisited	199
	10.4	Conclusion		202
	Appendices			204
	References			207
11	**A Survey on Recent Developments**			**209**
	11.1	Introduction		209
	11.2	Extensions of the Income-Wealth Conservation Law		209
	11.3	Externalities and Policy Interventions		211
	11.4	Stochastic Income and Wealth Conservation Law		213
	11.5	Warning		214
	11.6	Conservation Laws and Helmholtz Conditions		215
	11.7	Comparisons: Three Approaches		218
	11.8	Hartwick Rule and Conservation Laws		218
	11.9	Factor-Augmenting Technical Changes as the Magnification Type of Lie Group Transformations: Justification for Biased Technical Change		222

	11.10 Empirical Estimation of Biased Technical Change and Aggregate Production in Function............................	225
	11.11 More Abstract Applications of Group Theory to Economics and Finance..	226
	References...	228

12 Appendix to Part II. Symmetry: An Overview of Geometric Methods in Economics 231
    12.1   Introduction 231
    12.2   Toolbox 236
            12.2.1   Mapping 236
            12.2.2   Charts and Manifolds 237
            12.2.3   Curves and Functions 238
            12.2.4   Vectors and Tangents 239
            12.2.5   1-Forms.. 242
            12.2.6   Tensors 244
            12.2.7   Vector Field, Connections and Covariant Derivatives.. 247
            12.2.8   Groups in Differential Equations...................... 249
            12.2.9   Calculus of Variation and the Hamiltonian Formulation 253
            12.2.10 Conservation Laws and Noether Theorems 255
    12.3   Holotheticity: Symmetry of the Isoquant Map 258
    12.4   Examples of Conservation Laws in Economics 261
    12.5   Conclusion 264
    References... 265

Biographies 267

Index 269

Ryuzo SATO Biographical and Bibliographical Data...................... 275

Part I
Introduction

Chapter 1
Introduction

Samuelson (1947, p. 3) argued that seemingly diverse fields in economics possessed formal similarities and that the same inequalities and theorems appeared again and again in these theories. He recognized that each field involved interdependent unknowns determined by presumably efficacious equilibrium conditions but argued that there exists identically meaningful theorems in other fields, each derived by essentially analogous methods. Consider microeconomic theory. The interaction between consumers and firms is studied using two major analytical techniques—optimization and equilibrium (Varian 1984, pp. 1–3). The characterization of the optimum behavior requires specification of the actions that the unit can take, the constraints to such actions and the objective function that the unit has. In examining the equilibrium of the model, we are considering whether the actions of all units are compatible. Equilibrium is modeled as the solution of a set of equations.

The analysis is then used to predict how the unit will respond to a change in its economic environment. If we give some specific forms to the objective functions or constraints, then we can ask what restrictions are implied by the model and then check it against the observed behavior. On the other hand, we can use a set of data satisfying a list of observable restrictions to construct the hypothetical model and then check if it can generate the data. This is the question of recoverability.

In dynamic economics, we examine the trajectory of system over time. Descriptive models assume pre-determined behavioral relations, like given savings rate, and derive the dynamics of the model; steady-state represents the dynamic equilibrium. As in comparative statics, the effect of changes in the behavioral constants on the path and steady state can be examined. In contrast, the optimal models assume that the parameters are chosen so as to maximize some objective function.

The formal similarities of economic models arise from the common mathematical structures that underlie them. Linear algebra, multivariable calculus, and difference/differential equations are among the mathematical techniques used in the formulation and analysis of the models. In these discussions of "formal similarities" of economic models, the model and its mathematical structure are taken as given and the question is whether the methods used to derive the theorems are similar. There is a deeper sense in which we can examine the similarity of mathematical models (Olver 1995, pp. 1–3). We can ask whether differential equations characterizing two different economic models are the same equations written in terms of different independent and dependent variables. It is not a theoretical curiosity; since both models fit a given data equally well, it affects the interpretation of data and choice decisions that are based on them. Sato (1981) showed that the differential equations characterizing the productivity growth from certain types of technical progress (assuming that the production function exhibit constant returns to scale) can be transformed into differential equations of scale economies (for the same series of inputs and outputs) for a production function with no technical progress. If the goal of social policy is to increase productivity, should it invest more in developing new technologies or in increasing the scale of operations?

Symmetry of a geometric object is merely a self-equivalence of a geometric object. This is the sense in which we use symmetry in non-technical discussions; when we say a painting, pattern or building is symmetric, we mean that we can rotate it or mirror image the object and it will look the same. The ordinal revolution can be viewed as deriving the law of demand from the symmetry of the level sets (indifference curves) of a utility surface. The solution of the equivalence problem of differential equations will include the determination of the symmetries of a given differential equation. Symmetry leads to conservation laws; all conservation laws in physics can be related to the underlying symmetry of the model. In economics, the first explicit derivation of a conservation law was by Samuelson (1970); he showed that aggregate capital output ratio in a von-Neumann economy is constant.

Equivalence, symmetry and conservation laws are the core of this book. In this chapter will introduce the concept of a group and then use it to derive equivalence and symmetry. In the subsequent chapters, we will examine the insights it provides in various branches of economics.

1.1 Group Theory and Classification of Mathematical Structure

Introduction to Group Theory

Economists are quite familiar with sets, real number system, and vector analysis and use them frequently in their modeling. A set is a collection of objects with no further structure imposed on it. The properties of the real number system, that we learned though our intuitive introduction to integers, have the structure of a field. The vector space is even more complex, though we look upon it as a generalization of the familiar Euclidean space.

The simplest structure that can be imposed on a set is to make the elements form a group; it has only one operation conveniently called multiplication compared to the field which has addition and multiplication. A set of objects or operators G form a

1.1 Group Theory and Classification of Mathematical Structure

group if the elements $a_i \in G$ and multiplication operation denoted by a dot, $\cdot$, satisfy the following relations.

(i) $a_i, a_j \in G \Rightarrow a_i \cdot a_j \in G$ \qquad Closure
(ii) $a_i \cdot (a_j \cdot a_k) = (a_i \cdot a_j) \cdot a_k$ \qquad Associativity
(iii) There exists an $a_0 \in G$ such that $\forall a_i \in G$, \qquad Identity
$a_0 \cdot a_i = a_i = a_i \cdot a_0 a_0 \cdot a_i = a_i = a_i \cdot a_0$
(iv) There exists an $a_j \in G \forall a_i \in G$ \qquad Inverse
such that $a_i \cdot a_j = a_i = a_j \cdot a_i$

The set of integers with group multiplication defined as addition form a group; identity is zero and inverse is subtraction. But they do not from a group if the group operation is defined as multiplication; the identity can be defined as unity but inverses of integers are not integers and so are not elements of the set.

The elements of the set need not be numbers; they can be operators. A simple example is the set of one-to-one functions which maps the elements of the finite set, $(x_1, x_2, \ldots, x_n)$ into itself. Let $f(\cdot)$ be a function that maps x_i to x_{i+1} with x_n mapped to x_1. The identity is the function $i(x_i) = x_i$. The inverse of f, f^{-1}, maps x_i to x_{i-1}. The set G of these one-to-one functions form a group.

We indicated earlier that our objective is to reveal the underlying symmetry of the mathematical structures of our economic models and that groups provide the tool that enables us to explore it. Yet, as defined above, groups seem to impose minimal structure on the underlying sets, much less than that of fields and vector spaces that are used in economic modeling. One may wonder what such a structure can contribute to any discussion of physical or social phenomena, over and above the results that are already derived using more elaborate ones? Research in mathematics and physical sciences have established the usefulness of group theoretic methods as a tool of scientific analysis; the study properties of objects that are invariant to a given group of transformations have resulted in the discovery of many important results. A quick review some of these well-established results will provide an understanding of potentialities of group theory.

Going Beyond Elementary Mathematics: Felix Klein and the Erlanger Program

Mathematics curricula all around the world begins a correspondence between numbers and space. Children are taught to express distance in numbers and directions in a set of numbers—two miles to the east and one to the northeast— that constitute vectors. This correspondence is the core of Euclidean geometry that for eleven centuries, from around 300 B.C. and well into the nineteenth century, scientists considered were a correct idealization of the properties of physical space. Conversely, that the correct approach to scientific formulation of real world phenomena is the axiomatic method of Euclid.

The one source of concern was that the parallel axiom of Euclid seemed to be less self-evident than the others. Since no one was willing to doubt its validity, attempts to resolve the doubt about its appropriateness followed one of two approaches:

replace the axiom with another more self-evident one or derive the parallel axiom from other nine axioms. Neither approach proved to be fruitful.

By 1799, Carl Gauss was convinced that the parallel axiom cannot be deduced from the remaining Euclidean axioms but non-Euclidean geometries were logically possible. Still the renowned a mathematician did not dare to publish his results during his life-time fearing, as he admitted in a letter to a contemporary mathematician Friedrich Bessel, ridicule. The intellectual world was still dominated by adherents of Kantian philosophy (Klein 1972, pp. 871–872). The first formal theses on non-Euclidean geometry are attributed to Nikolai Lobatchevsky and John Bolyai.

Even though Gauss, Lobatchevsky and Bolyai had proved many theorems in what is now known as hyperbolic geometry, they could not offer a proof of consistency. By mid-eighteenth century, other non-Euclidean geometries were developed and intensively studied. It was more a matter of faith to believe that no contradictions would ultimately be found in any of these geometries. This situation changed in the third quarter of the century, when contemporary mathematicians were convinced by proofs using projective geometry that the new geometries were logically consistent if Euclidean geometry was consistent.

For the first time, the monolithic dominance of Euclidean geometry was shaken. Felix Klein who had contributed to the development of the new geometries tried, in his 1872 inaugural address at Erlanger University, to reestablish order by developing a hierarchy among the geometries. The approach he proposed was to characterize geometries as the science which studies the properties of figures preserved under a certain group of transformation (Yoglam 1988, p. 115; Klein 1972, pp. 917–921). In Klein's scheme, the groups associated with Euclidean, hyperbolic and elliptic geometries were subgroups of the one associated with projective geometry. Euclidean geometry, in particular, was identified with a group of transformation that leaves invariant length, angle, and the size and shape of a figure.

Klein's emphasis on invariants under transformations was carried into mechanics and mathematical physics. Traditionally Newtonian physics is defined in Euclidean space but it is not essential for its formulation. There is no experiment that an observer subject to Newtonian laws of motion can make within a spaceship, say, which would permit him to decide whether the spacecraft is at rest and one moving with constant velocity. The new approach would define Newtonian physics as dealing with physical properties that are invariant to a wider group of transformations than the Euclidean group, namely, the Galilean group.

The Erlanger program, like all grand schemes in mathematics, was found to be less than all encompassing but the program had a profound influence in geometry and mathematical physics during the next half-century. It was one of the first major achievements of group theory.

The Reality of Non-Euclidean Space: Group Theory in New Physics

Inspite of the proofs of consistency of non-Euclidean geometries and the development of a classificatory scheme for various geometries, Klein and other leading

1.1 Group Theory and Classification of Mathematical Structure

mathematicians of his time did not doubt that the space around us was Euclidean. They treated the new geometries as logical constructs without physical relevance.

We have already observed that Newton's laws of motion are invariant to the Galilean transformation. Why is it then necessary to assume the physical space around is Euclidean in which you can define absolute position and velocity? Gottfried Leibniz, mathematician and philosopher, made this objection against Newtonian physics. Maxwell's electrodynamic equations published in 1864 seemed to resolve this controversy in favor of absolute space; it assumes that light had a constant absolute velocity as it propagates through empty space.

The Michelson–Merely experiment of 1887, intended to establish the validity of Maxwellian assumption, actually undermined it. The relative velocity of light with respect to earth was constant even though earth was moving through space! In 1905, Albert Einstein recognized the source of this paradox when he showed that Maxwell equations are invariant to Lorentz transformation. Of course, the Newtonian equations of motion were not invariant to Lorentz transformation but the problem could be solved by a modification of momentum. Hermann Minkowski showed in 1908 that Einstein theory can be interpreted as describing a four dimensional manifold where the distance element is preserved by the Lorentz transformation. The young Einstein under the influence of Leibniz and Mach was committed to expunging from Physics all non-observable quantities and, unlike Gauss, made a frontal assault on the Kantian notions of space; "... the twentieth-century philosophy of science, and logical positivism in particular, is almost inconceivable without relativity, for relativity theory was second only to Principia Mathematica as an intellectual model for the positivists." (Friedman 1983, p. 3).

The development of quantum mechanics radically changed our understanding of the physical relations at sub-atomic level. It was originally formulated in two very different and seemingly incompatible formulations—Heisenberg's matrix mechanics and Schrodinger's wave mechanics. Paul Dirac showed that the two formulations are equivalent by proving that the variables in one system can be transformed into that of the other using unitary group.

In 1835, William Hamilton had introduced the concept of action and stated Hamiltonian principle of least action which asserted that motions derived in classical dynamics were shown to be the ones that made the action stationary. As long as we are in Newtonian mechanics, analytical dynamics was just an alternate formulation. But quantum mechanics denies the possibility of defining position and momentum at the same time and the Hamiltonian formulation with its duality between momentum and space, and between energy and time became the preferred formulation. It is possible to exploit the symmetries of the Hamiltonian system, using the continuous groups of transformations developed by Sophus Lie, to derive many result s including conservation laws.

In summary, as Dirac wrote in the preface to his well-known textbook on quantum mechanics: "The growth of transformation theory, as applied first to relativity and later to quantum theory, is the essence of the new methods of theoretical physics." (Dirac 1958, p. vii).

1.2 Lie Groups and Invariance

Lie Groups and Their Infinitesimal Generators

Consider an open region of $\Re^2$; $\bar{x} = (\bar{x}_1, \bar{x}_2)$ is a point in the region. Now we can use a simple algebraic equation to map this point to another point in the region. The simplest example would be a translation of the point in the direction of one of the axes: $\bar{x}'_1 = \bar{x}_1 + \varepsilon$; $\bar{x}'_2 = \bar{x}_2$.

More generally, the displacement in the direction of a given vector, **a**, is given by equation (Fig. 1.1): $x' = \bar{x} + \varepsilon \mathbf{a}$. Here we are considering ε to be a parameter; the transformation can depend on many parameters but we will confine in the first five chapters to the case of one parameter.

Having defined transformation, can group properties be imposed on the transformation? Of particular interest are continuous groups of (point) transformation (also called Lie group) in which the variables and parameters have group structure and the functions that define the transformations are smooth. If $x'_i = x + \varepsilon_1 \mathbf{a}$ and $x''_i = x' + \varepsilon_2 \mathbf{a}$; then there should exist a parameter ε_3 such that $x''_i = x + \varepsilon_3 \mathbf{a}$; in this specific case $\varepsilon_3 = \varepsilon_1 + \varepsilon_2$. In addition there should exist a value of the parameter ε_0, such that $x_i = x_i + \varepsilon_0$ and there should be another value of the parameter ε_{-1}, for which $x_i = x'_i + \varepsilon_{-1}$. The requirement that the parameters should satisfy group properties can be stated in terms of the four properties of the group stated earlier. In much of our subsequent discussion, the parameter will be time represented by a scalar t. Since $\Re^1$ satisfies the group properties for "group multiplication" defined as simple addition, we will not state it formally.

In the examples above, the transformation mapped the point $\bar{x}$ to another point, $\bar{x} + \varepsilon \mathbf{a}$. If we follow it with second transformation, with parameter value ε', then

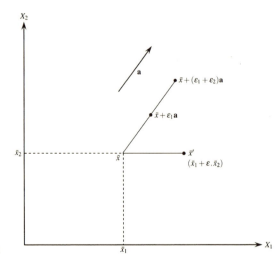

Fig. 1.1 Translation of a point as group transformation

1.2 Lie Groups and Invariance

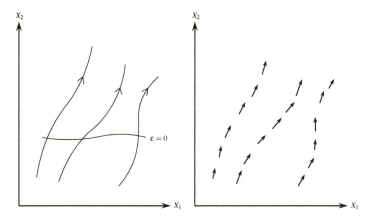

Fig. 1.2 Orbits of one parameter group of transformations and field of tangent vectors associated with them

we get a new point, $\bar{x} + (\varepsilon + \varepsilon')\mathbf{a}$. The three points will lie along a straight line; the straight line is the group-invariant subset of the two dimensional space in the sense that applying any element of the group of transformation to any point on the line will map it another point on the line; the line is the orbit of this transformation. Through any other point of the open region, not on the above orbit, we can draw another orbit and it will be another straight line (Fig. 1.2). More formally, the orbit of a transformation group is a minimal nonempty group-invariant subset of the open region over which the transformation is defined.

Having defined the orbit, we can define a tangent to the orbit at any point; the tangent is a vector.[1] Additional tangent vectors can be drawn at other points of the curve and now it is possible to reverse our perspective and look at the orbit as the flow generated by those vectors. At every point of the open region, there is a vector and the set of vectors, one at each point in the space, is said to form a vector field. The set of orbits is completely characterized by the vector field and, in turn, vector fields by its orbits (Olver 1986, pp. 24–31; Stephani and MacCullum 1989, pp. 5–11).

The concept of vector fields arises naturally in economics though it may not have been formally stated as above. In neo-classical growth theory, take x_1 and x_2 to be capital, K and labor, L respectively. The production function gives the output at each point of the space (K, L). Given the output, the savings out of the income is given by a behavioral function and that in turn determines the rate of growth of capital.

The growth of labor is given by another behavioral function. Here the orbits are the dynamic path of the system from any given initial value of capital and labor. In turn the vector field gives the rate of growth of the inputs, for given values of inputs

---

[1] In the case of the two examples discussed in the text, the orbits are straight lines and so the tangent vectors are collinear with them.

as determined by the behavioral rules. Here the dynamic paths (orbits) and the rate of growth of inputs at different points (the vector fields) determine one another.

Invariance, Symmetry and Conservation Laws

In the previous section we developed the notion of a Lie group. In this subsection we consider its applicability to determining the symmetries, a property that made transformation theory so central to modern physical sciences. In the next section we will summarize the analysis of economic models using group theoretic methods as developed in subsequent chapters. In popular discussion an object is symmetric if different parts of it can be interchanged without making it different. A building is symmetric if each half looks a mirror image of the other, so that we can replace any half with the other and not affect the appearance of the building. The theory of transformation generalizes this idea by extending it to abstract systems; symmetry is the invariance of the system to a transformation.

Consider a function $F(x,y) = x - cy$. Now consider a translation given by an element of the group of transformations $G : (x,y) \to (x+c\varepsilon, y+\varepsilon)$. Substituting, we see that $F(x,y) = F(g \cdot (x,y)) = F(x+c\varepsilon, y+\varepsilon)$. If $F(\cdot)$ is the equation for an indifference curve or an isoquant, the transformations would map *each of these curves* into itself. In applications, we are more interested in symmetry defined in a weaker sense, where one of the curves is mapped into another. Now the family of curves is invariant to the transformation even though individual curves are not. Consider the Cobb–Douglas function, $F(x,y) = (xy)^{0.5}$. The level sets of this function (indifference curves if the equation is a utility function and an isoquant if the function is a production function) is given by the equation, $(xy)^{0.5} = c$; they are the set of points (x,y) such that the function $F(\cdot)$ has a constant value. Consider the transformation corresponding to a Hicks neutral change $F(x,y;t) = e^{\alpha t}(xy)^{0.5}$; the value of the function along any level set, $F(x,y) = $ a constant, at time t will depend only on the value of a and t and not on the specific values of x and y. For a production function, the isoquant at time t corresponding to $z_1 = e^{\alpha t}(xy)^{0.5}$ will be mapped to the isoquant $z_0 = (xy)^{0.5}$ as the output z_1 will now produced by inputs combinations that used to produce z_0 at time $t = 0$.

Mathematical systems are associated with geometric objects like curves or surfaces and the discussion of symmetry extended to them. We can take this approach to analyzing the symmetry of differential equations. A differential equation is first related to a geometric object in a space defined for it; the dimensions of this space is determined by adding to the number of dependent and independent variables one dimension each for the (partial) differential coefficients. Thus the Laplace equation $u_{xx} + u_{yy} = 0$ can be thought as defining a "hyperplane" in the 8 dimensional space $(x,y;u;u_x,u_y;u_{xx},u_{xy},u_{yy})$. $u = f(x,y) = x - 3xy^2$ is a solution for its graph lies in that hyperplane ($u_{xx} = 6x; u_{yy} = -6x$). Then the symmetry of the differential equation is characterized by a group of transformations that leaves the geometric object invariant (Olver 1986, pp. 92–104).

This is another approach to relating the symmetry of differential equations to our previous discussion. A single infinity of curves involving an arbitrary constant (like

1.2 Lie Groups and Invariance

the family of indifference curves or isoquants) is equally determined by a unique differential equation of the first order, of which the equation involving the arbitrary constant is the general solution. The differential equation can be written as:

$$Mdx + Ndy.$$

Now we can use the symmetry to determine the integrating factor for this first order differential equation; if the differential equation is multiplied by the integrating factor, it can be written as the total differential of a function and we have integrated the equation. In consumer theory, the equation has special relevance as, for indifference curves $N/M = R$ is the marginal rate of transformation; in production theory, it is the rate of technical transformation. On many occasions, we want to know whether a differential equation characterizing the underlying relationship is invariant to a transformation of the space of inputs without having to integrate differential equation. The basic difference in dealing with differential equations is that, in addition to the variables x and y, we have theirs differential coefficients. As will be shown in Chap. 3, we can associate an operator U' such that the condition for the integral curves of the differential equation, $w(x,y,R) = 0$, to map to one another is that $U'w = 0$.

Finally, when we consider optimal growth models in Chap. 7, we are interested in the symmetry of the Hamiltonian. Economists use optimal control to solve different problems that involve intertemporal maximization. The dynamics of the model depends not only on the coordinates of the system but also on the values of a control variable whose value must lie within given bounds. Hence the problem is expressed as

$$\max \int_0^t (x, u, t) ds$$

$$\text{subject to } \dot{x} = f(x, u, t), \quad x(0) = \bar{x}.$$

Here x is the state variable whose values change only as the system evolves over time and u is the control variable whose value is to lie in a given interval. The problem is first restated in terms of the Hamiltonian written as (refer to Chap. 7 Eq. (7.13)):

$$H = -L + pf.$$

Maximizing the value of H with respect to u at every point of time and writing the maximized value as H^*, the rates of change of the two variables are written as

$$\dot{p} = -\frac{\partial H^*}{\partial x},$$

$$\dot{x} = \frac{\partial H^*}{\partial p}.$$

The integral curves of these equations, given by the phase diagrams, define the optimal dynamic path for any given initial conditions.

If the Hamiltonian has symmetries, that is if it is invariant to transformations of the state space x, then, for each of these transformations, we can identify a scalar function that would remain constant over the optimal trajectory. The constant value of that function completely characterizes the path and so it provides another way of characterizing the trajectory of a dynamic model. In Physics, the symmetry of the Hamiltonian with respect to time is related to the conservation of energy. Other conservation laws can be derived from other symmetries. In economics, the famous Ramsey rule can be interpreted as a conservation rule. The first conservation law was explicitly derived for the von-Neumann model when he showed that income/capital ratio is conserved along the optimal path. Conservation laws are discussed in Chap. 7.

1.3 Economic Applications of Lie Groups

In the previous section, we showed how a group of continuous point transformations can be represented by its infinitesimal generators and how the symmetry of mathematical model to a set of transformations helps us derive the mathematical properties of the model and give physical interpretations to them.

In Chap. 2, we reexamine the controversy whether the growth in productivity is explained by increasing returns to scale or technical progress. This controversy is as old as the exchange between Clapham and Pigou and as recent as the latest estimate of growth in total factor productivity. It will be argued that there are one-to-one mappings between types of technical change and corresponding types of economies of scale. These mappings are derived using Lie group of transformations.

In Chap. 3, the inverse quest ion whether, given a technical progress function there is a production function that is "holothetic" to it will be discussed.

Chapter 4 looks at two questions. First, treating price change as a transformation, it examines whether the Slutsky equations can be derived using infinitesimal generators. Next the infinitesimal transformation is used to derive "integrability conditions," in utility theory. Duality theory has found to be useful for theoretical and empirical work in economics. In Chap. 5, an elegant reformulation of self-duality is achieved using continuous transformations. The results of using self-dual demand functions for comparing price elasticities in U.S. and Japan are reported. Then the conditions for self-duality of production and cost functions are stated.

In Chap. 6, the infinitesimal generators are used to derive the conditions that must be satisfied by economic index numbers. Further the invariance of Divisia index used in estimating productivity growth is examined and related to the group properties of technical progress in Chap. 2.

Finally the invariance of dynamic systems is used to derive the conservation laws associated with Ramsey and Samuelson and the new ones derived in Sato (1990) are reviewed. Empirical ongoing work on testing the conservation laws are reported.

Chapter 2
Technical Progress and Economies of Scale: Concept of Holotheticity

Economists are interested in returns to scale for three reasons. First, the equilibrium of an industry is dependent on the nature of its technology. Next, growth theorists, while attributing most of the growth in per capita output to factors other than the increase in capital intensity, are not able to agree whether productivity increases should be modelled as arising from technological change or scale effects. Finally, econometricians recognize the problems in identifying the two sources of productivity in any empirical study.

These debates can be traced back to the beginning of marginal economics. Mathematical formulations facilitated clarification of various concepts of equilibria and of the role of time in economic analysis. Following Alfred Marshall, price theory recognizes the distinction between internal and external economies. Production function theory identifies technologies as homothetic or non-homothetic and classifies technical change as neutral or biased. Building on these mathematical formulations, Sato (1981) showed, using Lie groups, that specific types of technical change and corresponding types of scale economies may not have observationally distinct implications. This chapter examines the contribution of Lie group analysis to this debate.

2.1 A Reformulation of the Problem

On Empty Economic Boxes

As Sraffa (1926) pointed out, the laws of returns were antecedent to neoclassical economics. The law of diminishing returns was, to paraphrase his arguments, formulated in the context of rent in agriculture. The law of increasing returns played a much less prominent part and was treated merely as an important aspect of the division of labor; it was considered as arising from general economic progress than from an expansion of production. One of the major contributions of the neoclassical economies was the elimination of the asymmetric treatment of the two laws. They are amalgamated into a single law of variable proportions, a process requiring increase in the scope of one and reduction in that of the other.

The law of diminishing returns was released, without difficulty, from the confines of agricultural operations and universalized in its domain. The reformulation of the law of increasing returns, however, posed some serious conceptual challenges. The efforts of Marshall to establish the existence of equilibrium of firms in an industry under increasing returns generated controversies that continue to this day.

Following Whitaker (1990), we can distinguish four cases: (a) industry output is homogeneous and firms have internal economies; (b) output heterogeneous and there are no internal economies; (c) output is homogeneous and internal economies are absent; and (d) output heterogeneous and sustained internal economies are present. It is widely agreed that perfect competition is not consistent with the first case. Case (b) was to be discussed in second volume of *Principles* in the context of retail trade but the volume was never written.

The case (c) corresponds to the static model in price theory. Firms enter or exit only in the context of changing size of the industry; otherwise there is no reason for the firms to change. While Marshall was not clear on the functional dependence of marginal and average costs on output of a firm, he argued that the output is determined by equality of marginal cost to price. Differential endowments of firms imply that industry supply curves slopes upwards to the right and that intra-marginal firms enjoy a surplus.

If economies were external to a firm but internal to the industry, the effect can be illustrated using "particular expense curves". Unlike cost curves, they are drawn on the assumption that the output of the industry is fixed; this output, Y, enters parametrically the marginal cost of a firm, $c_i(w, r, y_i; Y)$, where w and r are input prices and y_i is the output of the ith firm (Fig. 2.1).

The supply curve slopes upwards to the right because of the scarcity of inputs of superior quality. SS, unlike P_E, is drawn assuming that, at any output Y, external economies are those corresponding to Y_1. Hence SS will be above P_E to the left of Y; P_E will shift down if Y increases. If there were no external economies, the two curves will coincide. It is generally agreed that Marshall did not come up with any convincing example of economies that are external to the firm but internal to the industry.

Marshall's treatment of the fourth case created most of the controversies. He lacked Chamberlain's method of analysis of a large group with selling costs and modern game theoretic analysis of strategic interaction among small groups. But he tried to retain the concept of price and output for an industry consisting of many firms producing differentiated products. He argued that the demand curve facing each firm is not given to it but can be influenced by the investment in internal organization and external networking. He visualized the process as time consuming and also needing continuous maintenance. It is in this context that he introduced the controversial concept of representative firm.

2.1 A Reformulation of the Problem

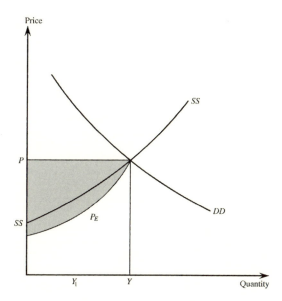

Fig. 2.1 Particular expense curve and supply curve

But he also qualified his definition of increasing returns, as follows:

> "An increase in labor and capital leads generally to improved organization, which increases the efficiency of the work of labour and capital." (Marshall 1920, p. 318)

This definition precludes from economies of scale any economies "that may result from new innovations." (*ibid.*, p. 460). It is this restriction that Clapham (1922a, p. 314) found objectionable.

> "As to Increasing Returns: if we are to restrict the conception as, I believe, Dr. Marshall does, to increased efficiency resulting from improved organization which generally accompanies an increase of capital and labor in any industry, or to industries in general, to exclusion of the efficiency flowing from invention and a very good case can be made for such restriction—then , I think, we should on principle avoid even the suggestion that we know that particular industries come into increasing returns category, because we never know what proportion of their efficiency is due to organization resulting from mere size and what to invention."

Pigou (1922, p. 461) argued that the distinction between increasing and diminishing returns is fundamental to the theory of value:

> "To take the categories of increasing and diminishing returns out their setting and to speak of them as though they were a thing that could be swept away without injury to the whole *corpus* of economics is a very perverse proceedings."

Clapham (1922b, p. 502) pointed out that Pigou did not directly address the question whether or not inventions could be excluded from increases in efficiency attributed to increasing returns. A more direct answer seems to come from Robertson (1924, p. 18).

"But (II) decreasing average cost may accompany expanded output for another reason, namely, because, *given time*, methods of techniques and of organization are capable of improvement in anyone of the myriad different groups, so that ultimately, a larger output can be produced at a lower cost per unit than that at a smaller output previously produced. . . . But the differences between the classes can be seen by reflecting that nothing but a *raising of the demand schedule* can be relied upon to establish a lowered cost in class (I), while the progress of time, and the enterprises of producers and the occurrences of inventions are expected, without necessarily any alteration of normal demand, to provide this result of class (II)."

Economies of scale are, in short, time independent and reversible while technological change is time dependent and irreversible; this view provides the rationale for using cross-sectional analysis to identify scale economies.

Scale Elasticity and Homotheticity

Production functions enable us to quantify the relation between quantities of inputs and outputs. When all inputs are varied simultaneously and in the same proportion, the output varies, through not necessarily in that proportion. The comparison between two proportional variations suggests that it may be useful to define their ratio as an elasticity in line with the analysis prevalent in demand theory. Various authors come upon this concept independently and termed it differently.

Johnson (1913) calls it "elasticity of production" while Schneider (1934) terms it "*Engiebigkeitsgrad der Production*." Carlson (1939) uses the expression "function coefficient" while Frisch (1965, p. 65) christens it "*passus coefficient*."

"The *Passus Coefficient* is the elasticity of the product quantity withrespect to one of the factors, when all factors vary proportionately."

"The Passus Coefficient $\varepsilon = \dfrac{d^{pr}x}{d^{pr}v_k} \cdot \dfrac{v_k}{x} = \dfrac{d^{pr}x/x}{d^{pr}v_k/v_k}$ where $d^{pr}v_i$ ($i = 1, 2, \ldots, n$) represents infinitesimal *proportional* factor increments (pr = proportional) and $d^{pr}x$ indicates increase in product quantity."

Frisch's treatment is of special interest as he carries the arguments well beyond the points of definition. Beginning with a given input vector, he considers the (half) ray in factor space corresponding to all (positive) multiples of that output. If isoquants are drawn in factor spaces, then each point on the factor ray will correspond to a level of output (Fig. 2.2).

Let V_0 be an input vector and let the output be $Y_0 = Y(V_0)$. The input ray can be defined as μV_0 ($0 < \mu < \infty$) and output at various points of this ray, can be written as

$$Y^\mu = Y(\mu \cdot V_0) = g(\mu).$$

The scale elasticity (as passus coefficient will henceforth be referred to) along the factor ray is given by the equation

$$\varepsilon(\mu) = \frac{dg}{d(\mu \cdot V_0)} \cdot \frac{\mu \cdot V_0}{g} = \frac{dg}{d\mu} \cdot \frac{\mu}{g} = \frac{d\log g}{d\log \mu}. \tag{2.1}$$

2.1 A Reformulation of the Problem

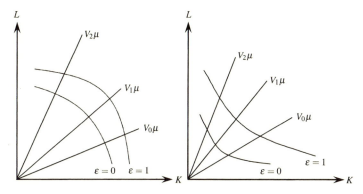

Fig. 2.2 Scale contours

Frisch next considered the change in output as μ varies within limits. Considering the above equation as a differential equation in μ, one can easily show that the value of output for $\mu = m$

$$Y^m = g(m) = g(1)\exp\left(\int_{\mu=1}^{m} \varepsilon(\mu)\, d\log\mu\right)$$

where $g(1)$ is the output for $\mu = 1$. So, along a ray, the output can be expressed as a solution of a differential equation relating the scale elasticity to the scale of operation. As shown below, Zellner and Revanker (1969) use a generalization of this relation for the econometric estimation of homothetic production functions.

Frisch assumes that the scale elasticity decreases monotonically along a factor ray; this is consistent with the traditional assumption that long-run cost curve is U-shaped. He then draws the scale contours consisting of all points in factor space at which the production function has the same scale elasticity. He shows (1965, p. 121) that the scale contours will slope downwards to the right but can be convex or concave.

The scale contour corresponding to $\varepsilon = 0$ is called "the curve for the technically maximal scale" as there is no point beyond this curve at which both marginal productivities (in two factor case) are positive. This conclusion follows from another relationship derived by Frisch (1965, p. 77) called the passus equation. The equation states that the scale elasticity equal the sum of the partial elasticities of output with respect to inputs. This together with the assumption that the scale elasticity is monotonically decreasing, ensures that the economic region of production is bounded by the curve for technically maximal scale.

Functional forms of production functions widely used in econometric work, like Cobb–Douglas or CES, can be made, at best, linearly homogeneous. This implies that scale elasticity is independent of output; for example, the scale elasticity of a Cobb–Douglas function, $Y = K^\alpha L^\beta$, is $\alpha + \beta = $ a constant. This does not match with the standard assumption about average cost curves which assumes that scale elasticities decrease with output.

The simplest functional form that incorporates variable scale elasticity is homothetic production function. Shepherd (1953, p. 41) defines a homothetic production function as a monotone continuous transformation of a homogeneous function. $Y = g(f(K,L))$ is a homothetic production function if f is homogeneous and g is continuous positive monotone increasing function of f. Under these assumptions, g has an inverse function, q; $q(Y) = f(K,L)$. Consider an input vector, $V_0 = (K_0, L_0)$ and let the corresponding output be Y_0. For the input vector $(\mu K_0, \mu L_0)$, one gets the relation $q(Y_1) = \mu \cdot f(K_0, L_0)$ and $\mu = \dfrac{q(Y_1)}{q(Y_0)}$. Consider another input vector (K_1, L_1) corresponding to the output Y_0. Let $(\lambda K_1, \lambda L_1)$ be the input vector corresponding to Y_1. Then Shepherd (1953, p. 42) showed that for a homothetic production function, $\mu = \lambda$. Every isoquant can be obtained by a radical expansion of the canonical isoquant. It follows from (1) that scale elasticity is constant along an isoquant and that homothetic production functions are a special class of functions for which the isoelastic curves are congruent with isoquants. Shepherd's assumption that $\dfrac{dg}{df} > 0$ is equivalent to assuming that $\varepsilon > 0$ for the entire factor space.

As noted earlier, the value of output along any factor ray can be expressed as the solution of the differential equation, expressing scale elasticity as a function of the distance along that factor ray from a chosen isoquant. For any homothetic function, the scaling of the isoquant is independent of the factor ray, and the differential equation generates the production function (without constraining to a ray). The definition of homothetic function as a monotone increasing transformation of a homogeneous function fails to stress this.

It is left to Zellner and Revanker (1969) to exploit this property for the econometric estimation of homothetic functions. They showed that, if $f(K,L)$ is a neoclassical production function homogeneous of degree α, a constant, then the production function $Y = g(f)$, for preassigned returns to scale $\varepsilon(F)$, can be obtained by solving the differential equation

$$\frac{dY}{df} = \frac{Y}{F} \frac{\varepsilon(f)}{\alpha}. \tag{2.2}$$

It is easy to show that $Y = g(F)$ is a homothetic production function when $\varepsilon(Y) > 0$. Thus the concept of scale elasticity can be exploited for econometric estimation of production functions.

On the Relative Significance of Technical Progress and Scale Economies

Solow (1957) tried to differentiate, in an elementary way, changes in output per head that is due to changes in availability of capital per head from that due to technical

2.1 A Reformulation of the Problem

progress. He assumed constant returns to scale and Hicks neutral technical progress. Under these assumptions, the production function can be written as

$$Q = A(t)F(K,L)$$

where Q is the output, $A(t)$ is the index of technical efficiency at time t, and K and L are the quantities of labor and capital respectively. Because of the assumption of linear homogeneity, this can be written as

$$\frac{\dot{q}}{q} = \frac{\dot{A}}{A} + \theta_K \frac{\dot{k}}{k}$$

where $q = \frac{Q}{L}$, $k = \frac{K}{L}$, and θ_K is the share of capital in national income and $\frac{\dot{q}}{q}$, $\frac{\dot{A}}{A}$ and $\frac{\dot{k}}{k}$ are growth rates in q, A and k respectively. If the increases in output per head were due to increase in capital per head, $\frac{\dot{A}}{A}$ would vanish. But applying the equation to American data for 1909–1949, Solow established that eighty-seven and a half percent of the increase in output per head was attributable to technical progress defined as *any kind of shift* in the production function.

Partly because this destroyed the traditional view of Western industrialization as increasing standards of living through use of more capital-intensive methods and partly because of discomfort with this umbrella concept of technical progress, various attempts were made to "explain away" the residual productivity, $\frac{\dot{A}}{A}$. One such attempt of particular interest to us, was that by Stigler (1961); he sought to attribute a sizable port ion of the productivity growth to increasing returns to scale.

Using US and British data, Stigler attempted to estimate a Cobb–Douglas production function, $K^\alpha L^\beta$: using international data avoided some of the problems in cross-sectional estimation using national data. He concluded that $\alpha + \beta$ was 1.27 and that the effect of technical progress is reduced to one sixth of what it would be if a constant- returns production function was used.

While agreeing with Stigler that scale economies can be important, Solow in his comment on Stigler's paper, argues that using international data does not solve all the problems related to cross-sectional analysis. He continues to hold that increasing returns are best captured using time series. He concluded by saying that the problem of measuring economies of scale and distinguishing it from those of technical progress is an econometric puzzle worthy of anybody's talents.

Correspondence Between Homotheticity and Hicks Neutral Technical Progress

Sato and Ramachandran (1974) uses the idea of defining homothetic production function as primitive of a differential equation in scale elasticity to provide a partial answer to the question the separability of economies of scale and technological progress. We show that, for an expanding production process, the scale elasticity of a homothetic production function completely accounts for the residual productivity attributable to Hicks neutral technical progress. Consider a firm whose inputs and outputs are increasing over time. Assume that the production technology of the firm can be represented by a homothetic production function, $Y = g(f(K,L))$, $g' > 0$. Differentiate it totally with respect to time to get

$$\dot{Y} = \frac{\partial g}{\partial L}\dot{L} + \frac{\partial g}{\partial K}\dot{K}.$$

The proportionate growth rate in output is given by

$$\begin{aligned}\frac{\dot{Y}}{Y} &= \frac{L}{Y}\frac{\partial g}{\partial L}\frac{\dot{L}}{L} + \frac{K}{Y}\frac{\partial g}{\partial K}\frac{\dot{K}}{K} \\ &= \frac{L}{Y}\frac{\partial g}{\partial L}\frac{\dot{L}}{L} + \frac{K}{Y}\frac{\partial g}{\partial K}\frac{\dot{L}}{L} + \frac{K}{Y}\frac{\partial g}{\partial K}\left(\frac{\dot{K}}{K} - \frac{\dot{L}}{L}\right).\end{aligned} \quad (2.3)$$

But from the definition of scale elasticity

$$\varepsilon(Y)Y = L\frac{\partial g}{\partial L} + K\frac{\partial g}{\partial K}. \quad (2.4)$$

Substituting (2.4) into (2.3), we get

$$\frac{\dot{Y}}{Y} = \varepsilon(Y)\frac{\dot{L}}{L} + \theta_K\frac{\dot{k}}{k}. \quad (2.5)$$

Now consider a homogeneous production function with Hicks neutral technical progress, $Y = A(t)f(K,L)$; by differentiation as above, it can be shown to lead to the familiar growth equation,

$$\frac{\dot{Y}}{Y} = \frac{\dot{A}}{A} + \frac{\dot{L}}{L} + \theta_K\frac{\dot{k}}{k}. \quad (2.6)$$

Equating (2.5) and (2.6),

$$\varepsilon(Y)\frac{\dot{L}}{L} = \frac{\dot{A}}{A} + \frac{\dot{L}}{L},$$

$$\varepsilon(Y) = 1 + \frac{\dot{A}/A}{\dot{L}/L}. \quad (2.7)$$

Here $\dot{L}/L$ is an index of the expansion of economy, when netted for changes in factor proportions; it substitutes for μ in our discussion in Sect. 1.2 of this chapter. Equation (2.7) shows that a homothetic production function with scale economies

2.1 A Reformulation of the Problem

$\varepsilon(Y)$ will have the same residual productivity as a linear homogeneous production function with Hicks neutral growth rate given by (2.6), provided the labor is growing at the rate $\dot{L}/L$. This shows the problems in identifying the role of scale economies and technological change alluded to in the previous section.

It is instructive to see why growth in residual productivity due to other types of technical progress cannot be absorbed by the scale economies of a homothetic production function. Assume that technical progress is Harrod-neutral, $Y = f(K, AL)$. It is easy to show by mathematical manipulations similar to that leading to Eq. (2.7) that

$$\varepsilon(Y) = 1 + \frac{\theta_L \dot{A}/A}{\dot{L}/L}$$

where θ_L is the share of wages. Except for Cobb–Douglas production function, θ_L will depend on the capital-labor ratio and from the above equation so would the scale elasticity. But the scale elasticity of a homothetic function depends only on output and not capital-labor ratio. Hence, Harrod-neutral technical progress cannot be equivalent to homotheticity. It is this restrictiveness which makes our result interesting.

There is another way of looking at the problem. Hicks-neutral technical progress increases the efficiency of each input at the same proportionate rate. Hence, the quantities of input required to produce a given out put declines proportionately. The point Q on isoquant Y_2 in Fig. 2.3 (corresponding to a homothetic production function) moves down in time $(t_2 - t_1)$ to P. The point S, in the same time moves by a proportional amount to R. Hence the net effect of the passage of time is to renumber the isoquant PR as Y_2.

Now assume that technical progress is Harrod-neutral. Labor increases in efficiency but capital does not. During the period Δt in which Q moves to P', let us assume that S moves to R'; the exact position of R' and the output can be determined by techniques discussed later in Sect. 2.3 and in the next chapter. From the discussion in the previous section, we know that if the production function is CES, then R' cannot be on the isoquant Y_1. So Harrod-neutral technical progress cannot lead to a renumbering of the isoquants of a homothetic production function. It is natural to ask whether there is any other production function whose isoquants are renumbered by Harrod-neutral technical progress. If there is such a production function, then we say it is holothetic (holo = whole, thetic = transformation) with respect to Harrod-neutral technical progress. In Sect. 2.3, we will discuss the general idea of a holothetic production function and in Chap. 3 we will discuss methods of finding it for a given type of technical progress.

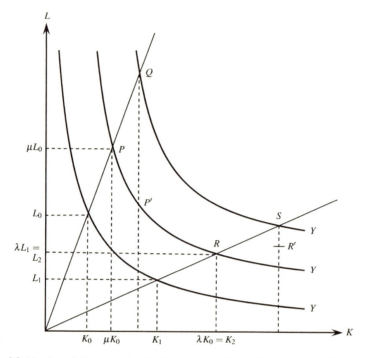

Fig. 2.3 Mapping of the isoquants of a homothetic production function under Hicks neutral technical progress

2.2 Lie Groups

The Idea of a Transformation Group

In Chap. 1, Sect. 1.1, a group was defined as a set whose elements satisfy 4 properties: closure, associativity, identity and inverse.

Consider a region of 2-dimensional space (x_1, x_2).

Consider the two differentiable functions

$$x'_1 = f^1(x_1, x_2; \varepsilon),$$
$$x'_2 = f^2(x_1, x_2; \varepsilon) \tag{2.8}$$

These functions can be interpreted as mapping of a point $P(x_1, x_2)$ in the 2-dimensional space to the point $P'(x'_1, x'_2)$; for the present we confine to the case where the parameter ε is a scalar (Fig. 2.4 below). We assume without loss of generality, that for $\varepsilon = 0$, the transformation is an identity and the smoothness assumption assures that, by a proper choice of the value of the parameter ε, P' can

2.2 Lie Groups

Fig. 2.4 Group transformation as translation of a point

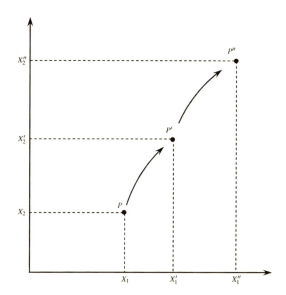

be made to be as close to P as desired. By taking (x'_1, x'_2) as the new values of the independent variable, we can substitute it into a function, with the parameter taking the value δ (not necessarily different from ε) and obtain another point P''; this is the law of composition of the transformation.

P'' can also be obtained by applying the transformation to P with the value of the parameter equal to $\phi(\varepsilon, \delta)$; the function ϕ is assumed to satisfy group properties. When the parameter is a scalar, we will take $\phi(\varepsilon, \delta) = \varepsilon + \delta$.

Together with continuity, it implies that, for any discrete change, we can find a series of transformations that differ infinitesimally from each other and yet sequentially take us from P to P'. Groups of transformation that have these properties are special case of Lie groups.

We define a continuous function $F(x_1, x_2)$ whose value varies as x_i ($i = 1, 2$) are transformed as in (2.8) above. In the particular expense curves of Marshall, the parameter is output of the industry.

Consider the transformation of a point $x = (x_1, x_2)$ to x' as in (7.8); the change in value of a function $F(x)$ can be obtained by a Taylor series expansion of $F(x)$

$$F(x') = F(x) + \varepsilon \sum_{i=1}^{2} \frac{\partial F}{\partial x_i} \frac{\partial f^i}{\partial \varepsilon}. \tag{2.9}$$

This indicates that we can define an operator

$$U = \sum_{i=1}^{2} \frac{\partial f^i}{\partial x_i} \frac{\partial}{\partial x_i} \tag{2.10}$$

that will determine the change in the value of $F(\cdot)$ for an infinitesimal change in the parameter. It follows from the group properties discussed earlier that any discrete transformation can be considered as a series of infinitesimal transformations.

2.3 Holotheticity

Taxonomy of Technical Progress

Hicks-neutral technical progress increases the efficiency of capital and labor proportionately so that it is equivalent to a movement along the ray *OP* or *OR* in Fig. 2.3. The system acts as if it is at Q even though the physical inputs correspond to P. The reason for this is that each unit of input has become more efficient and acts as if it has multiplied itself. It is natural to ask two questions. First, in what ways can the Hicks-neutral concept be generalized? Second, are there any common restrictions which we want to impose on these concepts, even as we seek to generalize them?

If K' and L' are inputs in efficiency units, as a result of Hicks-neutral technical progress, then

$$K' = A(t)K = \lambda_1(t)K, \quad L' = A(t)L = \lambda_2(t)L$$

with $\lambda_1 = \lambda_2$ and both depending on t only. If technical progress is factor augmenting and biased,

$$K' = \lambda_1(t)K, \quad L' = \lambda_2(t)L \quad (\lambda_1 \neq \lambda_2).$$

But there is no reason why λ_i should depend on t only. The next step in generalization would be to make it a function of K/L; rate of technical progress on different rays are different but the rate is constant on each of them. We can go further and make it a function of K and L, $\lambda_i(K,L,t)$. Then the rate of technical progress will not only be different on different rays but will differ along a ray. These considerations suggest the following scheme:

Case 1. $\lambda_1 = \lambda_2$

     1a $\lambda_1(t) = \lambda_2(t)$

     1b $\lambda_1\left(\dfrac{K}{L},t\right) = \lambda_2\left(\dfrac{K}{L},t\right)$

     1c $\lambda_1(K,L,t) = \lambda_2(K,L,t)$

Case 2. $\lambda_1 \neq \lambda_2$

     2a $\lambda_1(t) \neq \lambda_2(t)$

     2b $\lambda_1\left(\dfrac{K}{L},t\right) \neq \lambda_2\left(\dfrac{K}{L},t\right)$

     2c $\lambda_1(K,L,t) \neq \lambda_2(K,L,t)$

2.3 Holotheticity

Consider the restrictions that must be placed on the functions, λ_i, we like to have the impact of technical change in period $(t_2 - t_0)$ to be equal to sum of the changes in the two subperiods, $(t_2 - t_1)$ and $(t_1 - t_0)$. Otherwise we cannot speak unambiguously of the efficiency of inputs at time t_2 relative to that at time t_0. Further we want $\lambda_i(K, L, 0)$ to be equal to one. Finally if the efficiency increases from 1 at time t_0 to $\lambda_i(\cdot)$, $i = 1$ or 2, at time t_1, then we should be able to say that, as we go back in time from t_1 to t_0, the efficiency decreased from λ_i to 1. These considerations suggest that the technical progress functions must be a transformation group.

Hicks Neutrality and Holotheticity

Consider a case where the technical progress functions or transformation rules are

$$K' = e^{\alpha t} K, \quad L' = e^{\alpha t} L.$$

It is easy to show that the rules of transformation of K and L satisfy group properties with $t_3 = \phi(t_1, t_2) = t_1 + t_2$.
Now define an infinitesimal operator[1] as:

$$U = \alpha K \frac{\partial}{\partial K} + \alpha L \frac{\partial}{\partial L}. \tag{2.11}$$

Note that $UK = \alpha K$ and $UL = \alpha L$. Expanding K' by Taylor series

$$\begin{aligned} K' &= K + UK \cdot t + U^2 K \cdot \frac{t^2}{2!} + \cdots \\ &= K + \alpha K \cdot t + \alpha^2 K \cdot \frac{t^2}{2!} + \cdots \\ &= K \left(1 + \alpha t + \frac{t^2}{2!} + \cdots \right) \\ &= e^{\alpha t} K. \end{aligned} \tag{2.12}$$

Similarly $L' = e^{\alpha t} L$.

An economic interpretation of this transformation can obtained from the isoquant diagram. A firm employs an input vector (K_1, L_1), given by the point P_1 in Fig. 2.5;

---

[1] We can think of differentiation of a function $f(x)$ with respect to x as application of an operator $\frac{d}{dx}$ to the function $f(\cdot)$; $f' = \left(\frac{d}{dx} \right) f(x)$. Then second and higher order differentiation of the function can be viewed as repeated application of the operator to the function; $f'' = \left(\frac{d}{dx} \right) \left(\frac{d}{dx} \right) f(x)$. Notice that the infinitesimal operator is here the linear combination of two partial differential operators.

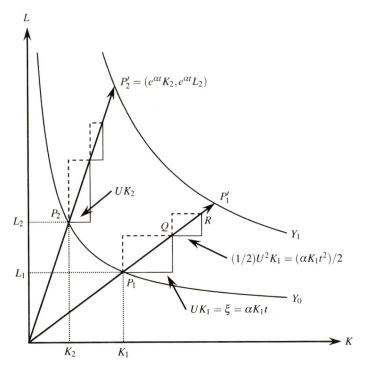

Fig. 2.5 Geometric representation of virtual expansion path

to produce an output $Y_0 = F(K_1, L_1)$ at time 0. Over a period of time t, the factors increase in efficiency so that, in old efficiency units they are equal to $(e^{\alpha t} K, e^{\alpha t} L)$ and output becomes $Y_t = F(K', L')$; even though the firm is hiring only (K, L), it is acting as if the inputs have been increased to (K', L'). We can think of this as a *virtual expansion* in the input space occurring in increments corresponding to the terms of the Taylor series in (2.12). In short, output is thought as increasing in steps from (K, L) to $(K + UK \cdot t, L + UL \cdot t)$, from $(K + UK \cdot t, L + UL \cdot t)$ to $\left(K + UK + UK^2 \dfrac{t^2}{2!}, L + UL \cdot t + UL^2 \dfrac{t^2}{2!}\right)$, and so on till it reaches (K', L') given by P'_1. The output increases from Y_1 to Y_t.

Now consider the process as starting from another input combination (K_2, L_2) given by P_2 in Fig. 2.5; technical progress will transform it in time t to $(e^{\alpha t} K, e^{\alpha t} L)$. If the point corresponding to this input combination, P'_2 lies on the isoquant Y_2, then the effect of the technological change is to renumber the isoquant Y_1 to Y_2. This, as we saw in Sect. 2.1, is the definition of holotheticity and we say that the production

2.3 Holotheticity

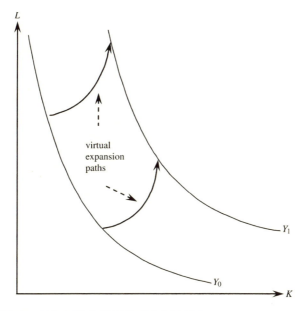

Fig. 2.6 Virtual expansion path for biased technical progress

function is holothetic to Hicks-neutral technical progress. The technical change is indistinguishable from a scale economy that achieves the same renumbering of isoquants.

Sato and Ramachandran (1974) derives a scale elasticity from the rate of Hicks-neutral technical progress, assuming a given rate of expansion along a ray and then integrates the resulting differential equation to get a homothetic production function. Lie group approach derives the correspondence between Hicks-neutrality and homotheticity by considering the infinitesimal transformation at a point.

Biased Technical Progress

One simple generalization of Hicks-neutral technical progress assumes that efficiencies of capital and labor grow at constant but unequal rates, α and β. The output Y_t is $F(e^{\alpha t}K, e^{\alpha t}L)$ and it can be easily shown that $UK = \alpha K$ and $UL = \beta L$.

The effect of such technical progress is that the virtual expansion curve will be curved as in Fig. 2.6. We saw that other than Cobb–Douglas, no homothetic production function will be holothetic to non-neutral technical progress. Sato (1981, pp. 31 & 398) showed that the production function holothetic to biased technical progress is $Y = F(K^{1/\alpha}Q(L^\alpha/K^\beta))$. The inverse problem of deriving production functions holothetic to any particular technical progress will be discussed in the next chapter.

2.4 Conclusion

Consider a production technology given by a linear homogenous production function. Its isoquants are evenly spaced in the input space; the distance from the origin to an isoquant $2Y$ along any isoquant is twice that to the isoquant corresponding to unit output. Now assume that increasing returns come into operation, the isoquants will collapse in the input space with the one for $2Y$ coming closer to the origin. What we saw in Figs. 2.5 and 2.6 is that a similar effect can occur if the technology undergoes certain types of technical change. The collapse in input space under technical change and returns to scale will be the same if there is compatibility between the production function and technical progress. Holotheticity gives the needed condition for such compatibility.

Chapter 3
Holothetic Production Functions and Marginal Rate of Technical Substitution

In the last chapter we examined the question whether the increases in efficiency of inputs due to technical progress can be explained by economies of scale. Economies of scale can be considered as resulting in a transformation of the production function which in turn leads to a renumbering of the isoquants. The condition for technical progress to have the same effect is that it should also map one isoquant to another. This was shown in Fig. 2.5 by constructing virtual expansion paths based on the coefficients of $\frac{\partial}{\partial K}$ and $\frac{\partial}{\partial L}$ in the operator U in Eq. (2.10); there we indicated, without deriving, that the production function holothetic to Hicks neutral technical progress is a homothetic production function and that the one for biased technical progress has to be non-homothetic. In this chapter, we will discuss the derivation of production functions that are holothetic to given technical progress functions and show the types of technological changes that are holothetic to some well-known production functions.

Over and beyond specifying combinations of inputs that produce the same output, isoquants, through their slopes at each point, determine an important economic variable: the marginal rate of technical substitution. If the transformations map one isoquant to another, the question arises how the slopes of the isoquants that are mapped relate to each other. Comparison of slopes of two curves is meaningless unless it is predetermined which point on the second curve is being compared to any specific point on the first curve. From our discussion in the last chapter, it seems natural to pair points mapped by the virtual expansion path and we derive a method for comparing the change in slope along the path. This discussion then leads to an alternate derivation of the holotheticity condition where we express movements along the isoquant and the expansion path as parametric shifts.

3.1 Types of Technical Progress Functions and Holotheticity

Consider a general neoclassical production function, $Y = f(K,L)$. We will now assume that technical progress functions which transforms the natural units of K and L into efficiency units, are functions of K, L and t.

$$\overline{K} = \phi(K,L,t), \quad \overline{L} = \psi(K,L,t). \tag{3.1}$$

Using (2.10), we can write the operator U as:

$$U = \xi \frac{\partial}{\partial K} + \eta \frac{\partial}{\partial L} \tag{3.2}$$

where

$$\xi = \left.\frac{\partial \phi}{\partial K}\right|_{t=0} \quad \text{and} \quad \eta = \left.\frac{\partial \psi}{\partial L}\right|_{t=0}.$$

The output $\overline{Y}_t$ is now a function $\overline{f}(K,L,t)$ with $\overline{f}(K,L,0) = f(K,L)$ (Sato 1981, pp. 22–32).

The production function is holothetic to the technical progress functions if there is a transformation of $F_t(\cdot)$ such that

$$\overline{Y}_t = \overline{f}(K,L,t) = f(\overline{K},\overline{L}) = F_t(f). \tag{3.3}$$

The second and third terms from the left indicates that the output measured by the original neoclassical function has increased not from increases in inputs measured in physical units but from increases in efficiency of each unit of the input or increases in inputs measured in efficiency units.

The last term indicates that, for any input combination that produced an output $f(K,L)$ at time 0, the output at time t is $F_t(f)$; the isoquant, $Y = f(K,L)$ has been renumbered to $Y = F_t(f)$. So Eq. (3.3) reiterates the condition for holotheticity, that the technical progress functions should map one isoquant to another.

If we draw a three dimensional diagram with output on the vertical axis, then the production function will be a surface. We already associated ξ and η with the virtual expansion path in the input space. In Fig. 3.1, they are vectors in the tangent space to the production function and technical progress represents a move along the surface defined by the tangent vectors (Fig 3.1).

Holotheticity requires that the points on the surface which are at a given height (points that correspond to one isoquant) should be mapped, in a given interval of time, to points of equal height on the surface; the output level at any input combination is changed from the one corresponding to the original neoclassical production function, $f(K,L)$ to one corresponding to $F_t(f)$. The transformation of f to $F(f)$ can be viewed as a distortion of the production surface and we shall now construct a measure of the distortion, $G(f)$. In Eq. (3.5), we will establish that the condition for the two transformations, one viewed as movement along a given

3.1 Types of Technical Progress Functions and Holotheticity

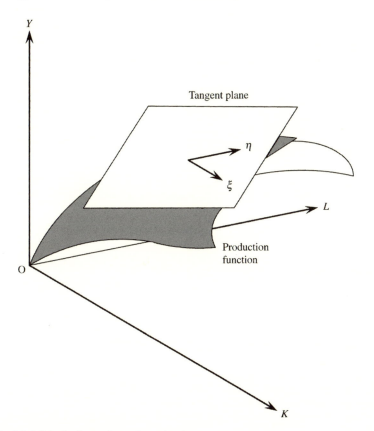

Fig. 3.1 Infinitesimal generators as tangent vectors

surface and the other as a distortion of the surface, to lead to the same output change. Just as we expressed the $f(K,L,t)$ as the sum of an infinite series using the operator U generated by the technical progress functions, we can expand $F_t(f)$ in terms of infinite series involving only a factor $G(f)$ and its derivatives. Here $G(\cdot)$ plays a role in Eq. (3.4) similar to U in Eq. (2.11) above (see Sato (1981, pp. 30–31)).

$$f(K,L,t) = F_t(f) = f + G(f)\frac{t}{1!} + G'(f)G(f)\frac{t^2}{2!} + \cdots . \tag{3.4}$$

Since the production function is holothetic to the technical progress only if the transformations of the production function by $U(f)$ and $G(f)$ leads to the same change:

$$Uf = \xi\frac{\partial f}{\partial K} + \eta\frac{\partial f}{\partial L} = G(f) \tag{3.5}$$

Fig. 3.2 Virtual expansion path as integral curve of a system of differential equations

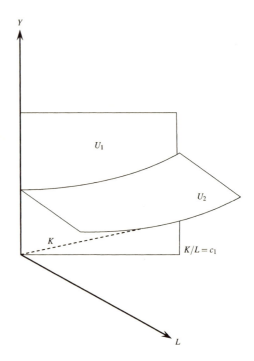

where ξ and η are as defined in Chap. 2. This formulation of the holotheticity condition has the advantage that it enables us to solve for a holothetic function corresponding to any given type of technical progress.

Equation (3.5) can be shown to lead to a system of ordinary differential equations,

$$\frac{dK}{\xi} = \frac{dL}{\eta} = \frac{df}{G(f)}. \tag{3.6}$$

For Hicks neutral technical progress, $\overline{K} = e^{\alpha t} K$ and $\xi = \alpha K$; similarly $\eta = \alpha L$. The first two equations of (3.6) lead to the relation, $d \log K = d \log L$. So the solution of the differential equation $\dfrac{d \log K}{dt} = \dfrac{d \log L}{dt}$ indicates that the virtual expansion path has K/L to be a constant as we saw in Fig. 2.5.

In a three dimensional diagram, it corresponds to a vertical plane (Fig. 3.2),

$$u_1(K, L, Y) = \frac{K}{L} = c_1. \tag{3.7}$$

To determine $G(f)$, let us examine whether $G(f) = \beta Y$ is consistent with $\xi = \alpha K$ and $\eta = \alpha L$. If there is a value of β that satisfies the system of equations (3.6),

3.1 Types of Technical Progress Functions and Holotheticity

this means that the production function holothetic to constant rate of Hicks neutral technical progress is a non-linear homogeneous production function; from Eq. (2.7) we know this to be true.

Substituting in Eq. (3.6), we get that $\dfrac{d\log Y^\beta}{dt} = \dfrac{d\log L^\alpha}{dt}$ or

$$u_2(K,L,Y) = \frac{Y^\beta}{L^\alpha} = c_2. \qquad (3.8)$$

This in turn gives a surface in the three dimensional space and we see that the scale elasticity is $\dfrac{\beta}{\alpha}$. The intersection of the two surfaces, $u_1 = c_1$ and $u_2 = c_2$ gives one of solutions or integral curves of the system of differential equations in (3.6) above.

Now consider biased technical progress with constant rates of factor augmentation. Then $\xi = \alpha K$ and $\eta = \beta L$; reasoning as earlier, we find that the virtual expansion path is given by the curve, $\dfrac{K^\alpha}{L^\beta} = $ a constant. The virtual expansion path is not a straight line which agrees with what we saw in the last chapter; homothetic functions cannot be holothetic to biased technical progress.

Sato (1981, pp. 33 & 398) has shown that a production function holothetic to biased technical progress is $Y = F(K^{1/\alpha}Q(L^\alpha/K^\beta))$ where the functions F and Q must satisfy some regularity conditions. The almost homogeneous production function proposed by Lau (1978) and the almost homothetic function of Sato (1977a) are special cases of this function.

Lau (1978, p. 163) considers a generalization of the case of fixed inputs where one set of inputs is increased by a factor of λ and another by λ^{k_2}. If the output increases by a factor of λ^{k_1} so that

$$F(\lambda L, \lambda^{k_2} K) = \lambda^{k_1} F(K,L) \quad (\lambda > 0).$$

Then the production function is taken to be almost homogeneous of degree k_1 and k_2 in input L and K respectively.

Lau shows that this is true for continuous differentiable function if and only if it satisfies the following differential equation (compare it with Eq. (3.5)).

$$L\frac{\partial F}{\partial L} + k_2 K \frac{\partial F}{\partial K} = k_1 F(K,L).$$

Sato (1981) explores some of the properties of almost-homogeneous and almost-homothetic CES functions. In the case of homogeneous or homothetic CES, the capital-labor ratio, k, is independent of output for a given value of the wage-rental ratio ω and the expansion path is a straight line.

$$\log k = \log a + \sigma \log \omega.$$

If the production function is not homothetic, then the capital-labor ratio will depend not only on the wage-rental ratio but also on the level of output.

The most general class of Cobb–Douglas or CES functions can now be written as (i) or (ii) where a is the elasticity of substitution and $\rho = \dfrac{1-\sigma}{\sigma}$.

(i) $F(K,L,Y) = \log K + C(Y) \log L - H(Y) = 0$ $(\sigma = 1)$
(ii) $F(K,L,Y) = K^{-\rho} + C(Y) L^{-\rho} - H(Y) = 0$ $(\sigma \neq 1)$

This can be written together as

$$X_1 + C(Y) X_2 = H(Y)$$

where $X_1 = \log K$ or $K^{-\rho}$ and $X_2 = \log L$ or $L^{-\rho}$ depending on the value of σ. $\dfrac{dC}{dY}$ reflects non-homotheticity as it is zero for homothetic functions. The almost-homogeneous production function is a special case of this where $C(Y) = \dfrac{\beta_2}{\beta_1} Y^{\beta - \alpha}$ and $H(Y) = (\beta_1 Y^\alpha)^{-1}$. Integrating we get the non-homothetic CES function given earlier.

The derivation of production functions holothetic to Hicks neutral and biased technical progress leads to the question whether this approach can be extended to more general types of technical progress. Sato (1981, pp. 52–54) shows that all known types of technical progress can be encompassed under the projective type; here ξ and η are both polynomials of second degree in K and L.

3.2 Marginal Rate of Transformation and Extended Transformation

We saw that, under holothetic transformation, the isoquants of the production function are mapped into one another. The slope of the isoquants is the marginal rate of technical substitution; it measures the rate at which one input can be substituted for another and, if the input markets are competitive, the rate equals the price ratio. When inputs are mapped into another under holothetic transformations, the question arises as to what the relation between the slopes of the isoquants at corresponding points is.

From Eq. (3.1), $\overline{Y} = F_t(f(K,L)) = F_t(Y)$, so that under hoalotheticity,

$$\tilde{R} = \frac{\overline{Y}_L}{\overline{Y}_K} = \frac{\frac{\partial \overline{Y}}{\partial L}}{\frac{\partial \overline{Y}}{\partial K}} = \frac{Y_L}{Y_K} = R.$$

3.2 Marginal Rate of Transformation and Extended Transformation

The holothetic transformation one is such that the marginal rate of technical substitution at the output $\overline{Y}$ measured in the *original units* of inputs is the same for the transformed production function as it is for the original production function. In terms of Fig. 2.5, not only are all points on the lower isoquant mapped to points on the higher isoquant but each point is mapped to one where the slopes of the two curves are equal. For a homothetic function, the slopes of the isoquants are the same along a ray from the origin and the virtual expansion path should coincide with it; we see in Fig. 2.5 that this happens only if technical progress is Hicks-neutral.

Another interpretation of the equality can be obtained by relating it to the concept of separability (Sato 1981, p. 24). The idea is that the function $\tilde{f}(K,L,t)$ takes the form $g(f(K,L),t)$ and that

$$\frac{\partial\left(\left(\frac{\partial g}{\partial L}\right)/\left(\frac{\partial g}{\partial K}\right)\right)}{\partial t} = 0.$$

In the Hicks-neutral case, the separability takes a special form, $A(t)f(K,L)$.

Care should be taken not to fall into the confusion of equating $\tilde{R}$ to the ratio of the marginal product of the transformed function in terms of efficiency units $\overline{R} = (d\overline{Y}/d\overline{L})/(d\overline{Y}/d\overline{K})$; when we change the units from natural units in Fig. 2.5 to efficiency units, the slope of the isoquant will change.

Now define $p = \dfrac{dL}{dK}\bigg|_{y=c} = -\dfrac{1}{R}$ and $\overline{p} = \dfrac{d\overline{L}}{d\overline{K}}\bigg|_{\overline{y}=\overline{c}} = \dfrac{1}{\overline{R}}$ so that

$$\overline{p} = \frac{\frac{\partial \psi}{\partial K} + \frac{\partial \psi}{\partial L}\frac{\partial L}{\partial K}}{\frac{\partial \phi}{\partial K} + \frac{\partial \phi}{\partial L}\frac{\partial L}{\partial K}} + \frac{\frac{\partial \psi}{\partial K} + \frac{\partial \psi}{\partial L}p}{\frac{\partial \phi}{\partial K} + \frac{\partial \phi}{\partial L}p}. \tag{3.9}$$

Since R or p is a differential coefficient, any relation involving K, L and R (or p) would be a differential equation. Minhas (1963, pp. 35–42) estimated, using international cross-sectional data, the relation between capital-labor ratios and wage-rental ratios, p; the interpretation of the coefficient of the regression equation led to the derivation of the CES production function. Sato (1977) used a generalization of this approach to define and estimate the non-homothetic CES functions. Another example of the use of a differential equation to derive a production relationship is Zellner and Revanker (1969).

The isoquants themselves can be expressed as the integral curves of a differential equation

$$M(K,L)dK + N(K,L)dL = 0 \tag{3.10}$$

where $N/M = R$. Since a holothetic transformation maps the isoquants of a production function to itself, the question arises as to how the differential equation (3.10) is affected by the transformation. One solution, of course, is to integrate the differential equation and examine the isoquants. It turns out that the existence of an operator U corresponding to the holothetic transformation gives us a means to integrate the differential equation. If the family of the integral curves of the differential equation $Mdx + Ndy = 0$ is left unaltered by the group $Uf \equiv \xi \frac{\partial f}{\partial K} + \eta \frac{\partial f}{\partial L}$, then $\frac{1}{\xi M + \eta L}$ is an integrating factor of the differential equation.

But it is desirable to be able to analyze the transformation of a production relation characterized by a differential equation without having to integrate the equation. In short, we want to examine whether the transformation of the inputs can be extended to analyze the variables of the differential equation, K, L and p. From (3.1) and (3.9), we see how the three variables are transformed:

$$\overline{K} = \phi(K,L,t), \quad \overline{L} = \psi(K,L,t) \quad \text{and} \quad \overline{p} = \frac{\frac{\partial \psi}{\partial K} + \frac{\partial \psi}{\partial L} p}{\frac{\partial \phi}{\partial K} + \frac{\partial \phi}{\partial L} p}. \quad (3.11)$$

As we associated a group operator U with the first two equations above, so we can associate with an extended group operator with the triplet.

$$U' = \xi(K,L)\frac{\partial}{\partial K} + \eta(K,L,t)\frac{\partial}{\partial L} + \eta'(K,L,p)\frac{\partial}{\partial p}. \quad (3.12)$$

η' is obtained by differentiating p partially with respect to t (Cohen 1931, p. 43 and Sato 1981, p. 401). While we follow notation standard in the literature on Lie group, it is worth mentioning, to avoid any terminological confusion, that η' is not a differential, partial or total, of $\eta(K,L)$ with respect to K or L but is given by the relation:

$$\eta' = \frac{\partial \eta}{\partial K} + \left(\frac{\partial \eta}{\partial L} - \frac{\partial \xi}{\partial K}\right)p - \frac{\partial \xi}{\partial L}p^2. \quad (3.13)$$

A differential equation, $h(K,L,p) = 0$, is invariant under the transformation U' if and only if $U'h(K,L,p) = 0$; if this is true then, the integral curves of the differential equation are mapped into themselves by the transformation. Again as we associated a system of ordinary differential equations (3.6) with U, so we can associate the following system with U':

$$\frac{dK}{\xi} = \frac{dL}{\eta} = \frac{d(dL/dK)}{\eta'}. \quad (3.14)$$

As we saw from (3.6), the first two terms give us the virtual expansion path in the input space; given the initial amount of capital and labor, it tells us the increase in output from increased efficiency. The last equation taken together with the first two allows us to derive how p will vary along the virtual expansion path given by the first two; it gives rise to an expression involving the differential coefficient, termed *differential invariant*, that remains constant along the virtual expansion path.

Consider Hicks-neutral technical progress. As before, $\xi = \alpha K$, and $\eta = \alpha L$. Substituting in the Eq. (3.13) for η', it can be easily shown that η' is zero. This implies that p or R does not change along the virtual expansion path. We have already seen that the virtual expansion path for Hicks-neutral technical progress is a ray through the origin and that the holothetic production function corresponding to this type of technical change is a homothetic production function; for this function, R is indeed constant along a ray.

It is more interesting to consider biased technical progress. Here $\xi = \alpha K$, and $\eta = \beta L$ and $\eta' = (\beta - \alpha)p$. The first two equations lead to the conclusion we derived earlier that the equation for virtual expansion path for biased technical progress is $L^\alpha / K^\beta = c_1$, a constant. The last and middle equation leads to the condition

$$\frac{p^\alpha}{K^{\beta-\alpha}} = c_2.$$

For an almost homothetic CES, the share ratio under competition can be shown to be

$$-\frac{dL}{dK}\frac{K}{L} = R(e^{(1/\beta)\log L} - e^{(1/\alpha)\log K})$$

so if capital and labor are growing at an exponential rate α and β then the share ratio will be a constant; the share ratio is the differential invariant. This agrees with our earlier statement that the almost homothetic functions are holothetic to biased technical progress.

Following the procedure outlined for the two types of technical progress, we can calculate η' and the differential invariant for any other type of technical progress that satisfy the group property.

3.3 Holotheticity and Lie Bracket

In Chap. 2, we saw that the production process can be characterized by an algebraic function or as the integral curve of a differential equation. We can write an isoquant as the graph of an algebraic function $F(K,L) = $ a constant or as the integral of a differential equation involving the marginal rate of technical substitution, R.

$$M(K,L) + R \cdot N(K,L) = 0. \tag{3.15}$$

Recollecting that $R = -\dfrac{F_K}{F_L} = -\dfrac{M}{N}$, this can be written as

$$AF = N(K,L)\frac{\partial F}{\partial K} - M(K,L)\frac{\partial F}{\partial L} = 0. \tag{3.16}$$

Just as the symbol or operator U is associated with the tangent vector to the virtual expansion path, so the symbol or operator, A, can be associated with the tangent to

Fig. 3.3 Tangent vectors to isoquant and expansion path

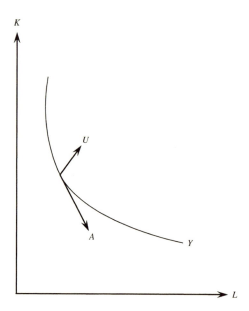

the isoquant (Fig. 3.3):

$$A = N(K,L)\frac{\partial}{\partial K} - M(K,L)\frac{\partial}{\partial L}. \tag{3.17}$$

We know that a production function is holothetic if and only if every isoquant is mapped to another. Since the isoquants are the integral curves of (3.15), the condition for holotheticity can be stated using (3.12) as

$$U'(M+NR) = \xi(K,L)\frac{\partial(M+RN)}{\partial K} + \eta(K,L)\frac{\partial(M+RN)}{\partial L}$$
$$+ \eta'(K,L,R)\frac{\partial(M+RN)}{\partial R}$$
$$= 0. \tag{3.18}$$

Using the definitions of U', η', A from Eqs. (3.12), (3.13) and (3.17) above, it can be shown that (3.18) can be written as

$$U'(M+NR) = (UN - A\xi)\frac{\partial F}{\partial K} - (UM + AN)\frac{\partial F}{\partial L} = 0. \tag{3.19}$$

3.3 Holotheticity and Lie Bracket

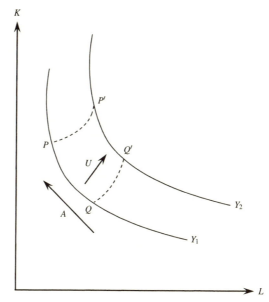

Fig. 3.4 An interpretation of holotheticity using the operators A and U

Since (3.16) and (3.19) must be satisfied simultaneously, the coefficients of $\dfrac{dF}{dK}$ and $\dfrac{dF}{dL}$ must be proportional. So

$$\frac{UN - A\xi}{N} = \frac{UM + AN}{M} = \lambda(K,L). \tag{3.20}$$

We saw that we can associate with technical progress functions a virtual expansion path and that the coefficients, ξ and η, in the operator U define the tangent vector to the virtual expansion path. Similarly we saw that the tangent to the isoquants can be associated with the coefficients $M(K,L)$ and $N(K,L)$ in the operator A. Since holotheticity requires that the technical progress functions map one isoquant to another, it is obvious that there should be some relation between the vectors tangent to the technical progress functions and those tangent to the isoquants.

Figure 3.4 provides a simple diagrammatic illustration of this relationship. Intuitively, U represents the rate of movement along the virtual expansion path and A along the isoquant. Consider any two points of an isoquants, P and Q. If the technical progress functions are holothetic to the production function, the virtual expansion paths defined by the tangents associated with U will map points P and Q on one isoquant to P' and Q' on another isoquant. In other words, for any parametric shift that takes P to P' a parametric shift equal in magnitude but opposite in sign will take Q' to Q. If we now think of the movement from Q to Q' as due to a parametric shift operating through A, then an inverse shift should take P' to P.

Holotheticity requires that they can be compounded so that equal and opposite shifts in the two parameters end up in the same point, as seen in Fig. 3.4. Algebraically this is written as (Sato 1981, pp. 44–45)

$$(U,A)F = UAF - AUF = \lambda(K.L)AF = 0. \tag{3.21}$$

Notice that for the first time we combined the two operators, U and A; we formed a Lie bracket (U,A). The middle equation can be thought of as a definition of Lie bracket, the third one a condition for holotheticity and the last equality follows from (3.16).

Finally we show that any differential equation representing isoquants has technical progress functions holothetic to it. From the holotheticity condition, we obtain after a normalization of $G(\phi)$,

$$U(\phi) = \xi \frac{\partial \phi}{\partial K} + \eta \frac{\partial \phi}{\partial L} = G(\phi) = 1.$$

But

$$A\phi = N \frac{\partial \phi}{\partial K} - M \frac{\partial \phi}{\partial L} = 0.$$

Hence we obtain by solving these equations,

$$\frac{\partial \phi}{\partial K} = \frac{M}{\xi M + \eta N}, \quad \frac{\partial \phi}{\partial L} = \frac{N}{\xi M + \eta N}.$$

Hence, we can show that $(\xi M + \eta N)^{-1}$ is an integrating factor of (3.6) for multiplying both sides by the integrating factor we get

$$\frac{M}{\xi M + \eta N} dK + \frac{N}{\xi M + \eta N} dL = \frac{\partial f}{\partial K} dK + \frac{\partial \phi}{\partial L} dL = 0. \tag{3.22}$$

Hence $\phi = c$ is an integral curve of (3.22). The converse, that if $(\xi M + \eta N)^{-1}$ is an integrating factor, then the technology is holothetic to the technical progress function, was stated earlier. We can now state the following theorem (Sato 1981, p. 34): *Given any isoquant map, there exists at least one Lie type of technical change under which the production function is holothetic.*

But it must be remembered that if there exists one integrating factor, then there may exist many others. In the case of (3.21) it can be shown that there are an infinite number of integrating factors, each corresponding to a different type of technical progress.

3.4 Conclusion

In this chapter we elaborated on the analysis of holotheticity in Chap. 1. We showed how to derive production functions that are holothetic to given types of technical progress. In particular, we derived the production functions holothetic to Hicks neutral and biased technical progress functions. We asserted the generality of this procedure by indicating without proof that all technical progress functions are special cases of projective type.

Since the slope of the isoquant has a specific economic meaning, we examined how this slope varies with the mapping of isoquants under a holothetic technology. We showed that the slope must be a constant along the expansion path. Further we derived the differential invariant that will remain constant along the expansion path. Again we considered the two special cases of Hicks neutral and biased technical progress and showed that the differential invariants for these two types are the marginal rate of substitution and the share ratio.

Finally we considered the relationship between the tangent to the isoquant and the tangent to the virtual expansion path and restated the condition for holotheticity in terms of the Lie bracket.

Chapter 4
Utility and Demand

Microeconomic theory recognizes that the allocation of resources in economy is driven forces of demand and supply. Supply is determined by technology and the cost of inputs. In previous chapters, we discussed how group theoretic method allows us to examine the effects of technological change on supply. In this chapter, we look how the traditional results of demand theory can be reinterpreted using group theoretic methods.

In his review of demand theory, Katzner (1970, p. 5) notes:

> "The historical origins of demand theory lie in the discovery of two concepts: utility and demand. For a long time these appeared only in separate contexts; focusing on one seemed to preclude consideration of the other. However, during the second half of the nineteenth century a link between them became apparent, and at this point theoretical contents were given to the study of demand."

This interlinking of the concepts was first achieved in the pioneering works of Dupuit and Gossen and further developed by Jevons, Marshall, Menger and Walras. Since then, the theory has "marched steadily towards greater generality, sloughing off the successive stages unnecessarily restrictive conditions" (Samuelson 1938, p. 61). The ordinal formulation of utility beginning with Edgeworth and Pareto and developed, in the middle of this century, by Allen, Hicks and Samuelson has expunged from the theory all the hedonist implications of the Benthamite utility theory. Individuals are now assumed to maximize an objective function whose value depends on their ability to use scarce resources while the scarcity of the resources itself is defined in terms of a constraint.

The constraint can take many forms. The decision today can affect the level of an objective function contemporaneously as in static consumer theory. But it might also affect the levels of constraint in the future in which case the objective becomes the maximization of a functional, generally an integral, of the instantaneous objective functions over the consumer's time horizon. The intertemporal problem can be expressed in terms of optimal control models and group theoretic methods help us identify the properties of the optimal path, like the conservation laws discussed in Chap. 7 that are not evident otherwise.

In this chapter we apply group theory to the simpler problem that is at the core of traditional microeconomic theory, namely comparative statics. The method of Lagrange multipliers allows us to examine the effects of a one time shift in the constraint. The shift in the constraint is modelled through a change in the parameter and that suggests that group theoretic methods which also depend on parametric methods can be applied to study the problem. But the use of transformation groups to solve the comparative statics does not lead to new results; the object is to demonstrate the consistency of the classical and group theoretic methods and to pave the way for discussion of duality in the coming chapters.[1]

The constrained maximization problem can be formulated as follows:

$$\max z = f(x; \alpha), \quad x = (x_1, \ldots, x_n) \tag{4.1}$$

subject to the constraint

$$g(x; \alpha) \leq b. \tag{4.2}$$

The corresponding Lagrangian is

$$h(x, \lambda; \alpha) = f(x; \alpha) + \sum \lambda [b - g(x; \alpha)]. \tag{4.3}$$

The first order conditions, assuming interior solution, can be stated as:

$$h_i(x, \lambda; \alpha) = \frac{\partial h}{\partial x_i} = f_i(x; \alpha) - \lambda g_i(x; \alpha) = 0 \quad (i = 1, \ldots, n), \tag{4.4}$$

$$h^{n+1}(x) = \frac{\partial h}{\partial \lambda} = b - g(x; \alpha). \tag{4.5}$$

In the traditional comparative static analysis, these equations are differentiated with respect to the r parameters. Then the effect of the changes of any one parameter can be derived using the Cramer's rule (Silberberg 1990, pp. 180–187) or any standard graduate microeconomic textbook). To derive the comparative static results using group theoretic methods, we have to transform the variables, x_i as entering the first order conditions and then derive their infinitesimal transformations.

In general, the transformations of the variable x_i as entering one of these $n+1$ equations may not be the same as in another and, since x is an n-vector, there are in total $n(n+1)$ transformations (Sato 1981, p. 135):

$$\bar{x}_s^i = \phi^{is}(x_1, \ldots, x_n; \alpha) \quad (i = 1, \ldots, n), \tag{4.6}$$

$$\bar{x}_s = \phi^s(x_1, \ldots, x_n; \alpha). \tag{4.7}$$

---

[1] The notation in this chapter is more complex than in the previous chapters. A reader, if not interested in the technical issues discussed here, can skip the chapter.

4 Utility and Demand

The first set of equations refers to transformations of the n-variables in Eq. (4.4) and the second to the transformations of variables in Eq. (4.5). Keeping but one of the parameters constant, we examine the effect of a change in that parameter; for economy of notation, we will write the parameter also as α. Totally differentiating Eqs. (4.4) and (4.5), we get

$$\begin{bmatrix} f_{11} - \lambda g_{11} & \cdots & f_{1n} - \lambda g_{1n} & -g_1 \\ \vdots & \ddots & \vdots & \vdots \\ f_{n1} - \lambda g_{n1} & \cdots & f_{nn} - \lambda g_{nn} & -g_n \\ -g_1 & \cdots & -g_n & 0 \end{bmatrix} \begin{bmatrix} \frac{\partial x_1}{\partial \alpha} \\ \vdots \\ \frac{\partial x_n}{\partial \alpha} \\ \frac{\partial \lambda}{\partial \alpha} \end{bmatrix} = \begin{bmatrix} -h_{1\alpha} \\ \vdots \\ -h_{n\alpha} \\ -h_\alpha^{n+1} \end{bmatrix}. \tag{4.8}$$

Since in this chapter, we are interested in the derivation of the Slutsky equation, we assume that the objective function representing the utility level of the consumer is concave and that the constraint is linear. We further specialize to the case in which the objective function is not affected by the transformation. For the $n+1$ parameters, p and I and for λ, the Lagrangian is:

$$L = u(x_1, \ldots, x_n) - \lambda \left(I - \sum_{i=1}^{n} p_i x_i \right). \tag{4.9}$$

Without loss of generality, we can write the price vector as $p = (e^{\alpha_1}, \ldots, e^{\alpha_n})$ and we can introduce a dummy variable x_{n+1} identically equal to unity so that $I = e^\beta x_{n+1}$. In addition, we can normalize the system, by choosing the appropriate units for the commodities and the numeraire, such that $\alpha_1 = \cdots = \alpha_n = \beta$ in the initial state. The first order conditions can now be written as:

$$h_i = u_i - \lambda e^{\alpha_i} = 0, \tag{4.10}$$

$$h_{n+1} = e^\beta x_{n+1} - \sum_{i=1}^{n} e^{\alpha_i} x_i = 0. \tag{4.11}$$

Following Sato (1981, p. 16) assume that the infinitesimal transformations of variables in (4.11) are

$$V = \sum_{s=1}^{n+1} x_s \frac{\partial}{\partial x_s} \tag{4.12}$$

while for Eq. (4.10), the n operators are

$$X_i = \lambda \frac{\partial}{\partial \lambda}. \tag{4.13}$$

46   4 Utility and Demand

Now consider, as we did in deriving Eq. (4.8), that all parameters except one corresponding to the kth price are constant. For economy of notation we will continue to represent this parameter as α. Totally differentiating Eqs. (4.10) and (4.11) we get

$$\begin{bmatrix} u_{11} & \cdots & u_{1n} & -p_1 \\ \vdots & \ddots & \vdots & \vdots \\ u_{n1} & \cdots & u_{nn} & -p_n \\ -p_1 & \cdots & -p_n & 0 \end{bmatrix} \begin{bmatrix} \frac{\partial x_1}{\partial \alpha} \\ \vdots \\ \frac{\partial x_n}{\partial \alpha} \\ \frac{\partial \lambda}{\partial \alpha} \end{bmatrix} = \begin{bmatrix} -\frac{\partial h_1}{\partial \alpha} \\ \vdots \\ -\frac{\partial h_{n+1}}{\partial \alpha} \end{bmatrix} = \begin{bmatrix} 0 \\ \vdots \\ \lambda \\ \vdots \\ 0 \\ \vdots \\ x_k \end{bmatrix}. \quad (4.14)$$

For this specific case, the role of the infinitesimal transformation is in evaluating the vector on the right hand side of Eq. (4.14). The vector $\left[\frac{\partial x_1}{\partial \alpha}, \ldots, \frac{\partial x_n}{\partial \alpha}, \frac{\partial \lambda}{\partial \alpha} \right]^T$ can be evaluated by both sides of Eqs. (4.14) by the inverse of the matrix on the left hand side.

Similarly, totally differentiate Eqs. (4.10) and (4.11) with respect to β. The matrix equation after inversion of the matrix will be

$$\begin{bmatrix} \frac{\partial x_1}{\partial \beta} \\ \vdots \\ \frac{\partial x_n}{\partial \beta} \\ \frac{\partial \lambda}{\partial \beta} \end{bmatrix} = \begin{bmatrix} u_{11} & \cdots & u_{1n} & -p_1 \\ \vdots & \ddots & \vdots & \vdots \\ u_{n1} & \cdots & u_{nn} & -p_n \\ -p_1 & \cdots & -p_n & 0 \end{bmatrix}^{-1} \begin{bmatrix} 0 \\ \vdots \\ -1 \end{bmatrix}. \quad (4.15)$$

From the above equations, we can derive, using Cramer's rule, the Slutsky equation which decomposes the effect of price change into income effect and substitution effect.

$$\frac{\partial x_i}{\partial p_k} = \frac{\partial x_i}{\partial \alpha} = \frac{\lambda \Delta_{ki}}{\Delta} + \frac{x_k \Delta_{n+1,i}}{\Delta} = \frac{\partial x_i}{\partial p_k}\bigg|_{u=\bar{u}} + x_k \frac{\partial x_i}{\partial I}\bigg|_{p_i=\bar{p}}. \quad (4.16)$$

As noted earlier, the group theoretical arguments which are very powerful in discussion of dynamic problems, do not contribute any new results to comparative static analysis. But in reproducing the familiar results in the new format, an insight into the logic of the method can be obtained.

4.1 Integrability Conditions

In the previous section, we derived the demand curve from the utility theory. But what we observe in the market is not utility but demand for commodities at various prices and incomes. This provides the motivation to analyze the inverse problem: can the demand functions we observe in market possibly be derived from the maximization of the utility function? The solution of the inverse problem gives us greater confidence on the validity of the utility maximization approach even if we cannot directly verify the axioms of consumer behavior.

Consider the familiar two commodity case. If the utility function can be assumed to exit, then the inverse demand function, taking the second commodity as numeraire, can be expressed as the slope of the indifference curve: $f^1(x_1,x_2) = -g^1(x_1, u(x_1,x_2))$. The budget constraint is written as $m = x_2 + f^1(\cdot)x_1$ and the two equations together give the demand function. If, on the other hand, the demand function is given, then we can obtain f^1 at any point on the commodity space where the function is defined; it generated vectors that originate at all such points of the $x_1 - x_2$ space. The question then is whether the field of vectors can be integrated to form a one-parameter family of curves that we can identify with the indifference surface of a utility function.

If the slope of the indifference curve is expressed as a function of the quantities of the two commodities,

$$\frac{dx_1}{dx_2} = -r^1(x_1,x_2) \qquad (4.17)$$

or as a total differential expression,

$$R^1 dx_1 + R^2 dx_2 = 0 \qquad (4.18)$$

then the differential equation has a solution if there exists a $w(x_1,x_2)$ such that

$$\frac{dw(x_1,x^0)}{dx_1} = -r^1(x_1,w(x_1,x^0))$$

and

$$x_2^0 = w(x_1^0,x^0).$$

$w(\cdot)$ is the equation for the indifference curve in terms of the parameter x^0. The first equation gives the slope of the indifference curve and the second equation determines the point at which we are measuring the slope (Katzner 1970, pp. 65–74 & 117–133). The theory of ordinary differential equations shows that the condition for the existence of a solution in the neighbourhood of x^0 is that r^1 be continous and that for its uniqueness is that the Lipschitz condition be satisfied. These are accepted as fairly weak conditions.

The integrability problem really arises when we move to higher dimensions. From a pure economic point of view, the need for additional restrictions to ensure the existence of such a fundamental concept as the utility surface when there are more than two commodities is counterintuitive and created much confusion in the early years of theory. Jevons, Marshall, and Walras did not have to deal with it since they assumed that the utility of any commodity depends on its quantity alone. Even though Antonelli provided the solution to integrability question, it had to be rediscovered by Fisher; even then Pareto did not discuss it in the first edition of his book published in 1906. Samuelson (1950, pp. 355–356), in his survey of the earlier discussion, point out that even writers like E.B. Wilson who recognized the problem, considered it to be a theoretical nicety not relevant for economics. It was left to the ordinal revolution in the middle of this century to recognize its importance and to derive the integrability conditions rigorously.

Two approaches were used to provide economic justifications for the integrability conditions. We can derive them using Antonelli or Slutsky matrices and then examine their implications. Or we can examine the nature of preferences when integrability fails (Samuelson 1950; Katzner 1970). Today the conditions for integrability are considered to have been so satisfactorily solved that most graduate microeconomics textbooks delegate them at best to a footnote. Its main relevance seems to be in estimation of specific functional forms of demand curves. In contrast to this neglect, we will examine the integrability problem from two viewpoints: constructive and conceptual. First, we will show how to derive the conditions using the Lie groups and provide economic interpretation for the reformulated conditions. Next we will examine the general nature of the restrictions required to ensure integrability and enquire how the utility theory fits into it.

For the first approach, we shall, following Samuelson (1950, pp. 376–379), assume that there are single valued and continuous differential functions, $x_k D^k(p_1,\ldots,p_n,I)$, which are homogeneous of degree zero in the variables. After setting the nth good as the numeraire and inverting the functions, we get

$$\frac{p_i}{p_n} = f^i(x) \quad (i = 1,\ldots,n-1) \tag{4.19}$$

and

$$\frac{I}{p_n} = x_n + \sum_{i=1}^{n-1} \frac{p_i}{p_n} x_i = f^n(x) \tag{4.20}$$

where $x = (x_1,\ldots,x_n)$. If the D^k are derived from the utility maximization, then f^i should equal the slope of the indifference surface and f^n should reflect the budget constraint. But to claim that (f^i)'s are the negative of the partial derivatives of a constant utility (indifference curve) function, is to associate with (4.19) the following $(n-1)$ partial differential equations:

$$\frac{\partial x_n}{\partial x_i} = r^i(x) \quad (i = 1,\ldots,n-1) \tag{4.21}$$

4.1 Integrability Conditions

or the total differential expression,

$$R^1(x_1,\ldots,x_n)dx_1 + \cdots + R^n(x_1,\ldots,x_n)dx_n = 0. \tag{4.22}$$

Integration of the expressions implies that we can find a function, $u(x)$, such that its indifference surface at a point x_0 has slopes in the $x_i - x_n$ planes (for different i's) given by equations of the form (4.21). The problem is that Eq. (4.21) is in general not integrable.

For illustrative purposes, we will consider a model of three commodities, with commodity 3 as numeraire. If Eq. (4.22) is the total differential of a function $u(x_1,x_2,x_3)$, there has to be an integrating factor, G, such that

$$du = GR^1 dx_1 + GR^2 dx_2 + GR^3 dx_3$$

but for G to be the integrating factor, the following must hold:

$$\frac{\partial (GR^i)}{\partial x_j} = \frac{\partial (GR^j)}{\partial x_i} \quad (i \neq j, \; i,j = 1,2,3).$$

Expanding the above expressions and after some simplification, it can be shown that the conditions for the existence of a total differential for the three commodity case reduce to one condition (See Evans (1930, pp. 118–121) for details):

$$R^1 \left[\frac{\partial R^3}{\partial x_2} - \frac{\partial R^2}{\partial x_3}\right] + R^2 \left[\frac{\partial R^1}{\partial x_3} - \frac{\partial R^3}{\partial x_1}\right] + R^3 \left[\frac{\partial R^2}{\partial x_1} - \frac{\partial R^1}{\partial x_2}\right] = 0.$$

We shall now derive the integrability condition for the n-commodity case using Lie groups. Reverting to the notation of Eq. (4.21), define the infinitesimal transformations (Sato 1981, p. 150),

$$X_i = \frac{\partial}{\partial x_i} - r^i \frac{\partial}{\partial x_j} \quad (i,j = 1,\ldots,n-1). \tag{4.23}$$

If there is a function that is invariant under these transformations, that is, if the value of the function is not changed with the transformation, then

$$X_i u = \frac{\partial u}{\partial x_i} - r^i(x) \frac{\partial u}{\partial x_j} = 0 \quad (i,j = 1,\ldots,n-1). \tag{4.24}$$

Equations (4.23) and (4.24) can be interpreted using Fig. 4.1. The intersection of the indifference surfaces of a function u with the plane $x_i - x_n$ defines a set of indifference curves. We can then intuitively define $\frac{\partial u}{\partial x_i}$ and $\frac{\partial u}{\partial x_n}$ as the rate of increase of u along the two directions shown and $X_i u$ as the increase in the direction

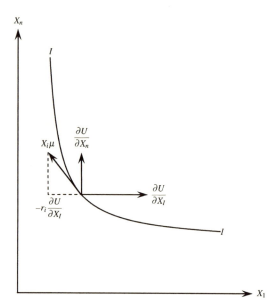

Fig. 4.1 The indifference curve in one plane

obtained by combining the two rates using the parallelogram law. But along the direction X_i, the rate of change of the function is zero and so it must be the direction of the tangent, at that point, to the indifference curve; in this two dimensional section of the n-space, we get a condition similar to that for the 2-commodity case.

We can now derive the standard condition for constrained utility maximization:

$$\frac{\frac{\partial u}{\partial x_i}}{\frac{\partial u}{\partial x_n}} = r^i(x) = \frac{p_i}{p_n}. \tag{4.25}$$

But these conditions are not in themselves adequate as we are just looking at a series of sections of the space. A further condition that is needed for integrability is to interrelate the various X_i's using Lie bracket (See also Sect. 2.3 for discussion of Lie bracket). It is defined as

$$(X_i, X_j) = X_i X_j - X_j X_i \quad (i, j = 1, 2, \ldots, n-1). \tag{4.26}$$

The condition for integrability is then:

$$(X_i, X_j) \equiv 0. \tag{4.27}$$

Figure 4.2 gives a geometric interpretation of the condition. Consider the planes $x_1 - x_n$; following Fig. 4.1, we can think of X_a as a tangent vector and the curve AB

4.1 Integrability Conditions

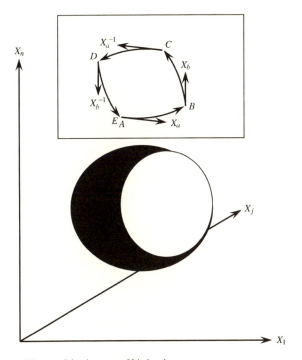

Fig. 4.2 Integrability condition in terms of Lie bracket

as created by a shift ε in the parameter, α_1. Similarly X_b is a tangent vector and the curve BC is generated by a shift ε in the parameter, α_2. Beginning with the new point on the indifference surface, consider the reverse changes in the two parameters represented by the curves CD and DE; then the condition that the Lie Bracket should be identically zero, requires that the curves should form a closed loop or E coincide with A (Olver 1986, p. 37); compare Fig. 4.2 with Fig. 4 of Samuelson (1950, p. 368). Another interpretation is offered by expanding the expression on the right hand side of Eq. (4.26); substituting for X_i's in Eq. (4.23), it can be shown that the condition for the bracket to be equal to zero is (Sato 1981, p. 152):

$$\frac{\partial r_i}{\partial x_j} - r_j \frac{\partial r_i}{\partial x_n} = \frac{\partial r_j}{\partial x_i} - r_i \frac{\partial r_j}{\partial x_n} \quad (i,j = 1,2,\ldots,n-1). \tag{4.28}$$

We now test whether these conditions are satisfied by a specific form of the inverse demand functions, the non-homothetic CES functions for three commodities (Sato 1981, p. 215). Normalizing to make income equal to 1, write the functions as:

$$p_i = \alpha_i^{-a} x_i^{-a} \quad (i=1,2)$$

and

$$p_3 = \frac{[1 - \alpha_1^{-a} x_1^{1+a} - \alpha_2^{-a} x_2^{1+a}]}{x_3}.$$

Then

$$r_1 = \frac{\alpha_1^a x_1^{-a} x_3}{1 - \alpha_1^{-a} x_1^{1+a} - \alpha_2^{-a} x_2^{1+a}}$$

and

$$r_2 = \frac{\alpha_2^a x_2^{-a} x_3}{1 - \alpha_1^{-a} x_1^{1+a} - \alpha_2^{-a} x_2^{1+a}}.$$

By substitution of the r_i's in the expression on the left and right hand sides of Eq. (7.26), it can be shown easily that they equal $r_1 r_2 / \beta x_3$ where $\beta = 1/a =$ the own price elasticity of demand = the elasticity of substitution of the CES functions. Hence the integrability condition is satisfied for these functions. Sato (1981, p. 215) has shown that the corresponding utility function is

$$U(x) = \log x_3 + \frac{\beta}{1+\beta} \log\left[1 - \sum_{i=1}^{2} \alpha_i^{1/\beta} x_i^{1/\beta}\right].$$

This utility function reduces to the Cobb–Douglas when $\beta = -1$.

The equality conditions given by (7.26) can be related to the traditional symmetry conditions of the Antonelli matrices. Sato (1981, pp. 151–152), shows that, in the general case of n commodities, the condition reduces to the well-known equations, $u_{rs} = u_{sr}$ $(r,s = 1,\ldots,n)$. We saw that the integrability of differential equations (14a) can be reduced to finding conditions under which (14b) describes one parameter surfaces. We now examine the general mathematical conditions for this to be feasible and show how it is related to utility theory. Expressions like $\sum R^i dx_i$ involving dx_i are called 1-forms and the requirement for the integrability of the differential equation $\sum R^i dx_i = 0$ can be expressed as $C_2^{n-1} = \frac{(n-1)!}{2!(n-3)!}$ conditions on the coefficient functions, R's (Edwards 1994, pp. 313–329). In the case of utility theory, the $(n-1)(n-2)/2$ conditions are formulated as those required for the symmetry of the Slutsky matrix (Samuelson 1950, p. 378). A well-known special case is when $n = 2$; then the differential equation is always integrable. As dimension of the space increases, the number of conditions increases: 1 for 3 commodity case, 6 for 4 commodity case, etc. Hence the integrability requirements in utility theory are but special cases for the conditions needed for a 1-form in n-space to represent a set of one parameter family of surfaces.

4.2 Conclusion

Here we are expressing the traditional comparative statics in terms of Lie groups. It provides insights into the integrability conditions. It brought out clearly the relation between the geometric analysis of constrained maximization and the solution of differential equations underlying the integration process.

While new results were obtained in the discussion of comparative statics in demand theory, by showing where the transformations are entering the equations, it showed the relation between the traditional analysis and group theoretic methods.

Chapter 5
Duality and Self Duality

The wide use of duality in economics arises from the theoretical insights that it provides and from its usefulness for empirical work. The economic implications of the optimization problem and the restrictions that have to be imposed on functional relations to enable econometric estimation become more transparent in the dual than in the original formulation.

In consumer theory, we assume that the consumer is maximizing a nonlinear objective function (the utility or preference function) subject to linear constraint. Consider an economy with 2 goods, X_1 and X_2, (in vector form, x) with given prices p_1 and p_2 (in vector form, p). The utility derived from the consumption is given by a scalar function, $u(x)$. The budget constraint can be expressed in terms of the dot product of the price and quantity vectors, $p \cdot x \leq M$ ($\sum p_i x_i \leq M$), where M is the maximum expenditure in the numeraire commodity that is permissible under the constraint. With appropriate restrictions on the utility function, it corresponds to the textbook case of linear budget line and convex indifference curve. A similar analysis can be made of the production decisions of a firm.

5.1 Duality in Consumer Theory

In the standard Lagrangian formulation the consumer is assumed to maximize $L = u(x) - \lambda(p \cdot x - M)$. The necessary conditions are known to be

$$\frac{\partial L}{\partial x_i} = \frac{\partial u}{\partial x_i} - \lambda p_i = 0 \quad (i = 1, 2), \tag{5.1}$$

$$\frac{\partial L}{\partial \lambda} = p \cdot x - M. \tag{5.2}$$

For a given value of M, the three equations can be solved for the demand functions

$$x_i = x_i(p) \quad (i = 1, 2). \tag{5.3}$$

This can be illustrated for a consumer with Cobb–Douglas utility function, $u = x_1^\alpha x_2^{1-\alpha}$ and income M facing a market where prices p_1 and p_2 are given. The Lagrangian can be written as

$$L = x_1^\alpha x_2^{1-\alpha} + \lambda(M - p_1 x_1 - p_2 x_2).$$

The first order conditions above lead to the equations

$$\frac{\alpha}{x_1} x_1^\alpha x_2^{1-\alpha} = \lambda p_1,$$

$$\frac{1-\alpha}{x_2} x_1^\alpha x_2^{1-\alpha} = \lambda p_2,$$

$$p_1 x_1 + p_2 x_2 = M.$$

Dividing the first equation by the second, substituting in the third and by some further manipulations, we get the demand functions as

$$x_1 = \frac{\alpha}{p_1} M$$

and

$$x_2 = \frac{1-\alpha}{p_2} M.$$

Substituting Eq. (5.3) into the utility function, the maximized utility function $v(p, M) = u(x^*(p, M))$ is a function of prices and income when there is no ambiguity, we will suppress the constant budget constraint, M. For the Cobb–Douglas utility function, $v(p) = \alpha^\alpha (1 - \alpha)^{1-\alpha} p_1^{-\alpha} p_2^{-(1-\alpha)} M$. Under certain conditions (Diewert 1982), $v(p)$ was used to construct $u(x)$ just as, the original optimization problem $u(x)$ can be used to construct $v(p)$. The correspondence between u and v is the essence of duality.

Geometrically the level sets of the indirect utility function can be derived from the indifference curves associated with the direct utility function, as in Fig. 5.1 (Darrough and Southey 1977).

The upper right hand quadrant traces the traditional indifference curve. The utility maximizing basket of goods is given by the point of tangency of the budget line and the indifference curve. Each end point of the budget line shows what the consumer can purchase if he spends all his budget on one commodity.

5.1 Duality in Consumer Theory

Fig. 5.1 Direct and indirect utility functions

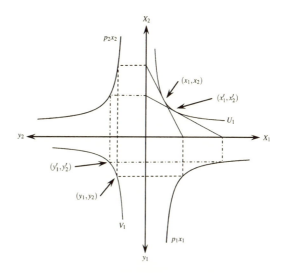

It is convenient to normalize the prices by dividing by the fixed income; in other words, we define new prices, $y_i = p_i/M$. Hence, by definition, the basket corresponding to the end point of the budget line is $x_i = 1/y_i$. On the upper left quadrant and in the lower right quadrant, two special rectangular hyperbolas are drawn. Since the equations for hyperbolas are $x_i y_i = 1$ $(i = 1, 2)$, the other coordinate corresponding to x_i, in these quadrants, is y_i. Drawing points corresponding for other baskets along the indifference curves, we get the set of prices, (y_1^j, y_2^j) that, if prevailing, would lead to utility maximizing baskets (x_1^j, x_2^j) along the indifference curves. The set of indifference curves along the left lower quadrant then defines the indirect utility function. If the regularity conditions stated by Diewert (1982) are satisfied, then the process can be reversed and the direct utility function derived from the indirect utility function, establishing a one-to-one relationship between them.

One may ask what is achieved by representing the same choice problem of the consumer in two different ways. Cornes (1992, p. 36) compares the strengths and weaknesses of two approaches. In comparative statics, we are interested in changes in the quantity demanded of one commodity as a function of changes in the parameters, prices and income. The Lagrangian approach that we described above starts with the utility function whose arguments are quantities and not prices. Hence it does not directly give an expression for the uncompensated demand curve in terms of the parameters; first we have to derive a set of equations and then invert it to get an expression for the dependent variable, change in quantity, in terms of the independent variables, the prices. This is what makes the economics of the process obscure. If we start with indirect utility function, the Marshallian demand function can be obtained directly by differentiating it with respect to the price; this result follows from the Roy's identity,

Fig. 5.2 Cost functions (Deaton and Muelbauer 1980, p. 38)

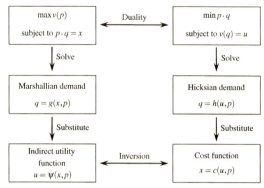

$$x_i(p,M) = -\frac{\partial v(p,M)/\partial p_i}{\partial v(p,M)/\partial M}. \tag{5.4}$$

It is a simple exercise to substitute the indirect utility function for the Cobb–Douglas case that we derived earlier into (5.4) and obtain the Marshallian demand functions.

Lau (1969) proved a number of useful properties of the indirect utility functions which we state without proof.

1. *A direct utility function is a homogeneous function of degree k if and only if the indirect utility function is homogeneous of degree −k.*
2. *A direct utility function is positively homothetic if and only if the indirect utility function is negatively homothetic.* (A function is homothetic if it is a monotonic function of a homogeneous function; a transformed function is positively or negatively homothetic depending on whether the underlying function is homogeneous of degree k or $-k$ respectively.)
3. *The Lagrange multiplier λ equals ku if and only if, the direct utility function is homogeneous of degree k.*
4. *A utility function is homothetic if and only if $\lambda = f(u)$ where f is a function of one variable.*
5. *A function with at least one strictly non-zero partial derivative is homothetic if and only if the ratio of first partial derivatives is a homogeneous function of degree zero in all pairs.*

The dual of utility maximization subject to budget constraint is a minimization problem: minimize $M = p \cdot x$ subject to $u^*(p,1) = \bar{u}$. From the geometric point of view, the original problem can be thought of as a search for the highest indifference curve along a budget line while the dual problem is a search along a given indifference curve for the point of lowest cost. The relation between direct and indirect utility functions, Marshallian and Hicksian demand functions, and cost functions is summarized in Fig. 5.2 due to Deaton and Muelbauer (1980, p. 38).

5.2 Separability and Additivity

In these days where a grocery store is stocking in excess of ten thousand individual products, it is not realistic to assume that each and every differentiated brand should be treated as a separate product with its own price. The dimensions of the system of equations (5.3), when extended from the two goods case to the more realistic one, will become very large. In spite of the elegant formulation of consumer theory, its empirical estimation poses the problem that the parameters to be estimated are too numerous, given the data that is generally available.

Additional theoretical structures that reduce the dimensions of the parameter space have been proposed and widely used in applied econometric work.

In every econometric study of consumer behavior, many "related" commodities are treated as a group and price index used in place of individual prices. One approach is to resort to the composite commodity theorem. Consider an economy with n commodities. If one of the n prices and the income M vary in an arbitrary manner but relative prices of the other $(n-1)$ goods remain constant, then Hicks (1946, pp. 312–313) suggested that the $(n-1)$ commodities $X_2,\ldots,X_n$ can be treated as one good and the problem reduces to one in which the consumer chooses between two goods. Construct an index number of prices (Chap. 6 will discuss index numbers) and then divide the expenditures on the group to obtain a quantity index.

On the other hand, if commodities are consumed in fixed proportions, then the normalized vector of these commodities can be treated as a unit of the composite commodity and the expenditure on the normalized vector as the composite price. But most economists have reservations about assuming that price ratios or quantity ratios remain constant. Another approach to reducing the number of parameters that have to be estimated is to assume separability or additivity.

Separability, as the word indicates, implies that a group of commodities enter the utility function in a manner that separates them from other group of commodities. These groups are formed by dividing or partitioning the commodity space: each of the n commodities belongs to one and only one of the m groups, $G_1,\ldots,G_m$. The utility function $u(x) = u(x_1,\ldots,x_n)$ can now be written as $u(g_1,\ldots,g_m)$ where g_i is a particular basket from the group G_i. The extent of the separation between groups depends on the exact formulation adopted.

Weak Separability

The utility function $u(x_1,\ldots,x_n) = u(g_1,\ldots,g_m)$ is said to be weakly separable with respect the partitioning of the commodity space to m groups, $G_1,\ldots,G_m$, if the marginal rate of substitution between any two goods x_i and x_j within a group is independent of the quantities of commodities in other groups.

$$\frac{\partial\left(\frac{\partial x_i}{\partial x_j}\big|_{u=\bar{u}}\right)}{\partial x_l} = 0 \qquad (5.5)$$

Fig. 5.3 Indifference curve between X and Y in the case of separable utility

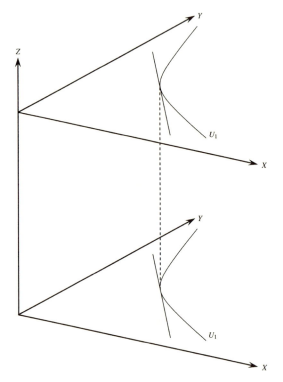

where x_i and x_j *belong to the same group*, G_r, while x_l belongs to any other group. In other words, the indifference curves for commodities within a group are, in shape and position, independent of commodities outside the group (Fig. 5.3).

Consider a three commodity space, with commodity Z measured along the vertical axis and X and Y along the other two axes. Let X and Y belong to a group; then, by rules of partitioning, Z forms a (singleton) group by itself. Under these assumptions, the indifference curves between X and Y in any plane perpendicular to the Z axis will be identical to that in any other horizontal plane; the quantities of Z in the baskets do not affect their shape.

Goldman and Uzawa (1964) proved that the utility function in the weakly separable case can be written as

$$u(x) = f(u^1(g_1), \ldots, u^m(g_m)) \tag{5.6}$$

where f is a scalar function of m variables and each u^a is a scalar function of the commodities constituting group G^a. In the case of a strictly concave function, the Slutsky term $\left(\text{the substitution term, } \left.\dfrac{dx_1}{dP_k}\right|_{u=\bar{u}}\right)$ can be written as

5.2 Separability and Additivity

$$s_{1k} = s_{ab}(x)\frac{\partial x_1}{\partial M}\frac{\partial x_k}{\partial M} \qquad (5.7)$$

where x_1 is a commodity in group G^a and x_k is a commodity in G^b, $a \neq b$. The number of Slutsky terms to be estimated is reduced as s_{1k} depends only on the groups, G^a and G^b, and not on the individual commodities, x_1 and x_k.

Pearce Separability

The marginal rate of substitution between any two commodities belonging to a group is independent of the quantity of any other commodity (including those in the same group). Thus Eq. (5.6) is valid even if x_1 and x_k belong to the group G^a.

Strongly Separable (Block Additive) Utility Functions

For such utility functions, the marginal rate of substitution between any two commodities *from different groups*, G^a and G^b, is independent of the quantities consumed outside of the two groups from which they came. If $x_i \in G^a$, $x_j \in G^b$, and $x_1 \in G^c$ then

$$\frac{\partial \left(\frac{\partial x_i}{\partial x_j}\Big|_{u=\bar{u}}\right)}{\partial x_1} = 0. \qquad (5.8)$$

Goldman and Uzawa (1964) demonstrated that when $m > 2$, this definition implies that

$$U(x) = f(u^1(g_1) + u^2(g_2) + \cdots + u^m(g_m)). \qquad (5.9)$$

Further, if $u(\cdot)$ is strictly quasi-concave, then the assumptions imply that the substitution terms can be written as

$$k_{ij}(x) = k(x)\frac{\partial x_i}{\partial M}\frac{\partial x_j}{\partial M}. \qquad (5.10)$$

Thus all substitution terms can be written in terms of m income effects and one additional function.

Houthakker's Directly Additive Preferences

This is a special case of strongly separable utility function where *each group consists of one good only*. The marginal rate of substitution between any two goods is independent of the consumption of a third commodity. The importance of additive preferences for demand estimation is that the estimate of income elasticity is more reliable than that of price elasticities. If we are willing to make the assumption of direct additivity, then the substitution effect is proportional to the product of the income effects of the two commodities and the constant of proportionality $k(x)$ is independent of the pair of commodities. The cost, of course, is the strong restriction on the shape of the utility function. These characteristics of the direct utility function can be related to similar properties of the indirect utility function.

5.3 Self-Duality in Demand Theory

The relations between the properties of the direct and indirect utility functions are brought out by the above results. An interesting question raised by the study of duality is whether there exist utility functions whose direct and indirect forms have the same functional forms. The theory of "self-dual preferences" was developed by Hicks (1969), Houthakker (1960, 1965), Lau (1969), Samuelson (1965, 1969), Samuelson and Swamy (1974) and Sato (1976). Originally it was thought that only Cobb–Douglas functions exhibit self-duality but it was later shown that a wider class of functions has this property.

Even if the demand system is well-behaved in the sense that the Slutsky matrix satisfies all symmetry and negative semi-definiteness conditions, we may not be able to obtain the underlying direct utility function of the representative individual. The indirect utility function, by theorems stated above, will identify many of the properties of the direct utility function but, for certain purposes, we only want to recover the direct utility function. Systems of demand functions can in general be integrated to obtain the underlying indirect utility function. The estimation of direct utility functions from a system of demand equations is facilitated if we can assume self-duality. What is more, almost all of the known types of demand systems used in empirical analysis fall into this category.

Exactly (or Strongly) Self-Dual Preference Ordering

Samuelson (1965) defined preference ordering as (exactly) self-dual if its direct utility function $u(x)$ is identically equal to its indirect utility function $-v(y)$, where y equals $\left(\frac{p_1}{M}, \ldots, \frac{p_n}{M}\right)$ the price vector normalized with respect to income. This

5.3 Self-Duality in Demand Theory

requires that the indifference curves in the quantity and price spaces in Fig. 5.1 are mirror images of one another.

The relationship between the demand, x, and the vector of normalized prices, y, is given by the demand and inverse demand curves

$$x = f(y) \geq 0, \quad y = g(x) \geq 0 \tag{5.11}$$

and self-duality imposes the restrictions on $f(\cdot)$ and $g(\cdot)$ that would require them to satisfy the following conditions:

$$x \equiv f(f(x)), \quad y \equiv g(g(x)). \tag{5.12}$$

Consider, for example, the linear demand functions and its inverse functions together with the budgetary constraint, $x_1 y_1 + x_2 y_2 - 1 = 0$.

Demand Functions	Inverse Demand Functions
$x_1 = b - y_1$	$y_1 = b - x_1$
$x_2 = (y_1^2 - by_1 + 1)/y_2$	$y_2 = (x_1^2 - bx_1 + 1)/x_2$

We see that the demand function, $f(x)$, and inverse demand function, $g(y)$, have the same functional form and satisfy $f(f(x)) \equiv x$ and $y \equiv g(g(y))$. Sato (1981, p. 206) shows that the direct and indirect utility functions for this system of demand curves are

$$u(x) = -\frac{1}{2}\log(x_1^2 - bx_1 + 1) + \frac{b}{\sqrt{B}}\tan^{-1}\left(\frac{2x_1 - b}{\sqrt{B}}\right) + \log x_2,$$

$$-v(x) = -\frac{1}{2}\log(y_1^2 - by_1 + 1) + \frac{b}{\sqrt{B}}\tan^{-1}\left(\frac{2y_1 - b}{\sqrt{B}}\right) + \log y_2$$

and shows that they satisfy the Samuelson condition, $u(x) = -v(y)$.

An elegant reformulation of self-duality is achieved by considering the system of demand functions, together with the budget constraint, as a (continuous) transformation of y to x. Let the transformations be:

$$T^1 : x_i = f^i(y_1, \ldots, y_n),$$
$$T^2 : x'_i = f^i(x_1, \ldots, x_n)$$
$$(i = 1, 2, \ldots, n).$$

Then the system of demand functions is "exactly" self-dual if

$$T^2 : x'_i = f^i(x_1, \ldots, x_n) \equiv y_i = f^i(f^i(y)),$$
$$T^2 = I \tag{5.13}$$

where I is the identity transformation.

This implies that the demand function is an *involution*, a transformation that is its own inverse as required by (5.12) above.

Intuitively, self-duality seems to let us switch the variables x and y and yet satisfy the economic constraints of the system. This can be formally stated using the concept of set-symmetric functions. Before considering the general case, take the example of the demand system given above. We can form two independent equations: $F^1 = x_1 + y_1 - b = 0$ and $F^2 = x_1 y_1 + x_2 y_2 - 1 = 0$. The Jacobian of the system is

$$\begin{vmatrix} 1 & 0 \\ y_1 & y_2 \end{vmatrix} = y_2 > 0.$$

The switching of x_i and y_i leaves F^i invariant.

In general there will be n functions of the n quantities, $x_1, \ldots, x_n$, and n normalized prices, $p_1, \ldots, p_n$. This can be written in vector form as

$$F(x,y) = 0. \tag{5.14}$$

A function is set-symmetric if the variables can be permuted without affecting the function. Self-duality can be elegantly defined in terms of set-symmetric functions. We state the result without proof (Sato 1981, p. 204).

The necessary and sufficient condition for a preference ordering to be "exactly" or "strongly" self-dual is that $F(x,y) = 0$ be set-symmetric in absolute value with respect to quantity and (real) price vector (absolute value of $F(x,y)$ is invariant):

$$F(x,y) \mp F(y,x). \tag{5.15}$$

Homotheticity of a utility function is advantageous in that it permits the aggregation of commodities into composite commodities; this will be discussed in detail in Chap. 6. Note that for a homothetic function, the ratios of quantities demanded is a function of the marginal rates of substitution. The necessary and sufficient condition for self-duality of a homothetic utility function follows from the general result:

The necessary and sufficient conditions for a homothetic utility function to be exactly self-dual is that the $(n-1)$ implicit functions relating y_i/y_j (the marginal rates of substitution) and x_i/x_j (demand ratios) be set-theoretic in absolute value with respect to

$$\frac{x}{x_i} = \left(\frac{x_1}{x_i}, \ldots, \frac{x_n}{x_i} \right)$$

and

$$\frac{y}{y_i} = \left(\frac{y_1}{y_i}, \ldots, \frac{y_n}{y_i} \right)$$

5.3 Self-Duality in Demand Theory

for at least one i $(i = 1,\ldots,n)$; i.e.

$$\left|F\left(\frac{x}{x_i}, \frac{y}{y_i}\right)\right| \equiv \left|F\left(\frac{y}{y_i}, \frac{x}{x_i}\right)\right| \tag{5.16}$$

subject to $x'y = 1$.

Weakly Self-Dual Functions

A weaker definition of self-duality (Houthakker 1965; Russell 1964) is more interesting from an empirical point of view. But Houthakker (*ibid.*, p. 797) noted, the "same form of a function" is an elusive concept. Lie group theory allows us to define the concept more rigorously.

To do so we must make an extension of the theory of continuous transformation that we discussed in Chap. 2. There we considered a function, relating inputs in natural and effective units, that is shifting with the change of one parameter, t. It is not hard to think of a function that depends on more than one parameter and shifts as any one of them changes. While this looks like some simple extension of the one parameter case, there are some mathematical niceties that need to be considered; the most important of it is that none of the parameters should be redundant which would happen, for example, if we have two parameters measuring time in different calendars. A set of r parameters, $a_1,\ldots,a_r$, are said to be *essential* if it is not possible to choose $r-1$ functions of them, $A_1,\ldots,A_{r-1}$ such that

$$f^i(x_1,\ldots,x_n;a_1,\ldots,a_r) = F^i(x_1,\ldots,x_n;A_1,\ldots,A_{r-1}).$$

We now use this transformation to define weakly self-dual functions. Earlier we wrote the demand and inverse demand functions as $x = f(y)$ and $y = g(x)$; consider that each of them are functions of r parameters, $a = (a_1,\ldots,a_r)$ and $b = (b_1,\ldots,b_r)$. It is also assumed that b is a function of a; $\pi : a \to b$. If the functions, f and g and the mapping, π, are such that the demand and inverse demand functions are inverses of each other, i.e.,

$$T_a : x_i = f^i(y;a),$$
$$T_b : y_i = g^i(x;b) = f^i(x;b) \tag{5.17}$$

with $T_a^{-1} = T_b$ or $\pi^2 =$ identity, then the system of demand functions is said to be weakly self-dual. Many empirical demand functions satisfy the additional restriction that there exists a set of essential parameters such that $\pi : a \to b$, $\pi(\bar{a}) = \bar{a}$, and $x_i = f^i(y,\bar{a})$ and $y_i = f^i(x,\bar{a})$; if this is satisfied then the functions are said to be *weakly self-dual in the strict sense*. Again we state the necessary and sufficient condition for weak self-duality without proof.

A system of demand functions is weakly self-dual in the strict sense if and only if there exists $F^i(x,y;a) = 0$ $(i = 1,\ldots,n-1)$ and $F^n = x'y - 1 = 0$ such that

$$F^i(x,y;\overline{a}) = \pm F^i(y,x;\pi(\overline{a})) \tag{5.18}$$

for some involution $\pi : a \to b$ and $\pi(\overline{a}) = \overline{a}$.

A related concept is uniform demand functions. A system of demand functions can be said to be weakly uniform if a demand function for the ith good, $x_i = f^i(y_1,\ldots,y_n;a)$ becomes a demand function for x_j by interchanging x_j and y_j for x_i and y_i respectively, for some value of the parameter a. The homothetic CES utility functions have a system of demand functions that are both weakly self-dual and weakly uniform.

$$x_i = \frac{\alpha_i y_i^\beta}{\sum \alpha_k y_k^{1+\beta}}, \quad y_i = \frac{\alpha_i^{-1/\beta} x_i^{1/\beta}}{\sum \alpha_i^{-1/\beta} x_k^{1+1/\beta}}. \tag{5.19}$$

Thus the condition for uniform demand functions is met by the CES family of functions that are widely used in empirical work.

5.4 A Method of Deriving Self-Dual Demand Functions

It was believed earlier that Cobb–Douglas functions are the only ones that exhibit self-duality. Consider the Cobb–Douglas utility function, $U = x_1^{0.5} x_2^{0.5}$; substituting into the equation for demand curves, we get $x_i = 0.5/p_i$. The demand curve is a rectangular hyperbola and so is the inverse demand curve; the mapping from one of them to the other is an involution as shown in Fig. 5.4.

Here we outline a method to develop a wider class of self-dual demand functions through a continuous transformation of the unitary elastic demand functions associated with the Cobb–Douglas type of preference ordering. Let $z_i = 1/ny_i$ ($i = 1,\ldots,n$) where, as before, x_i, is the quantity of the commodity i, and $y_i = p_i/M$ is the price of the commodity normalized with respect to income. Then the demand function with one parameter

$$x = f(y;t) = f(z^{-1};t) = \phi(z;t) \tag{5.20}$$

may be considered as a continuous transformation, $T : z \to x$, where the variables satisfy the budget constraint $x'/z = n$. Further we restrict ϕ such that

$$x = z \quad \text{at} \quad t = t_0,$$
$$z = \phi(x;t) \quad \text{at} \quad t = \overline{t},$$
$$x = \phi((x;\overline{t});t) = \phi(x;b(t,\overline{t})),$$
$$x/z' = n. \tag{5.21}$$

5.4 A Method of Deriving Self-Dual Demand Functions

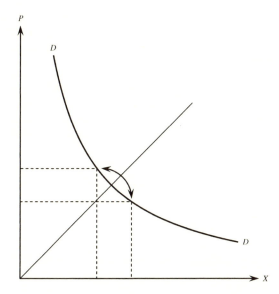

Fig. 5.4 Marshallian and inverse demand curves for Cobb–Douglas utility function

In this system of equations, we have used the fact that the first one corresponds to the Cobb–Douglas utility function with identical exponents ($\alpha = 1 - \alpha = 1/2$ for the Cobb–Douglas utility function for the two commodity case that we considered earlier). So the self-dual demand functions generated by the system are continuous transformations of this special case.

Writing the infinitesimal transformations associated with (5.21) as

$$U = \sum_{i=1}^{n} \xi_i(z) \frac{\partial}{\partial z_i}. \tag{5.22}$$

Consider an example where $\xi_i = a_i z_i$. Then the invariants derived form the first $(n-1)$ terms of

$$\frac{dx_1}{a_1 x_1} = \frac{dx_2}{a_2 x_2} = \cdots = \frac{dt}{1}$$

are

$$\frac{x_i^{1/a_i}}{x_j^{1/a_j}} = \frac{z_i^{1/a_i}}{z_j^{1/a_j}} \quad (i \neq j,\ i,j = 1,\ldots,n). \tag{5.23}$$

Finally, combining $(1/a_1) \log x_1 = (1/a_1) \log z_1 + t$ (from the first and the n-th equation) with the system of equations (5.23), we get the self-dual demand functions, $x_i = e^{a_i t} z_i = e^{a_i t}/n y_i$; together with the budget constraint, they define a system of demand functions associated with Cobb–Douglas preferences with unequal exponents.

Thus, using the infinitesimal transformations, we generalized the class of self-dual demand functions from those associated with Cobb–Douglas preferences with equal exponents to those with unequal exponents. Infinitesimal transformations will give methods for deriving other types of weakly self-dual demand functions like the Bergson (Homothetic CES) family of weakly self-dual demand functions stated in Eq. (5.19) (Sato 1981, pp. 219–221). Sato and Matsushita (1989) fitted one set of linear demand functions and ten sets of log-linear demand functions (all of them are weakly self-dual) to the data for urban consumers in the United States and Japan. The study showed that a system of non-homothetic CES type functions gave good empirical results (*ibid.*, p. 273).

5.5 Empirical Estimation of Self-Dual Demand Functions

As noted above, Sato and Matsushita (1989) estimated eleven sets of self-dual demand functions. For sake of brevity, we confine the discussion in this section to the estimation of the non-homothetic CES type demand functions. They used Japanese annual data on personal consumption expenditure of an average household for the period 1963 to 1975 and of those in cities with population of 50,000 or more for the period 1947 to 1975. For the United States, they used the annual data series from 1956 to 1975. Since the Japanese data were classified into five groups, the US data were also adjusted to form five comparable groups. Because OLS estimators are not unbiased, Beach–MacKinnon estimators were estimated.

Food: The estimation showed that there is no significant difference in own price elasticity for food between the two groups (all households and households in cities) in Japan. Differences between dietary life of US households and that of Japanese households were reflected in these own elasticities. Demand was much less elastic in the United States.

Housing: The demand for housing is elastic. USA and all households in cities have the almost the same pattern of demand though confidence interval for households in cities is large, the own price elasticity for all households in less than in USA; Japanese had a less elastic demand for houses, conjecturally because households move less than in the United States.

Fuel and Light: The own price elasticity of demand for fuel and light was the same for the three groups. This is surprising as the per capita energy consumption in Japan is substantially less than in United States.

Clothing: The own price elasticity for all households is slightly larger than that of the USA but for it is much larger than for others.

5.6 Implicit Self-Duality of Production and Cost Functions

The role of separability, homogeneity and uniformity assumptions in utility and demand theory is to reduce the number of parameters that needs to be estimated in an empirical study. The similarity between optimization problems in consumer theory and in production theory is well-known: consumers seek the basket of goods where the budget line is tangent to the indifference curve while producers choose the input combination corresponding to the tangency of an isoquant and an isocost curve. However, there is one important difference. The consumer maximizes a non-linear function (utility function) subject to a linear constraint (budget line) while the producer minimizes a linear function (isocost curve) subject to a non-linear constraint (isoquants). Further, we are not interested in comparing direct and indirect production functions (as we were with utility functions); rather we contrast production and cost functions.

We can assume that production and cost functions are explicitly separable as in utility analysis. But it would imply many strong restrictions not justified by empirical evidence. For example, in the case of an explicitly homothetic production function, the elasticity of substitution between all pairs of inputs would have to be the same. A less restrictive approach imposes implicit separability (Hanoch 1975; Sato 1974, 1977b). We can proceed to examine, as we did for utility functions, the necessary and sufficient conditions for homothetic, self-duality and uniformity but we will confine the discussion below to the results needed in the next chapter on index numbers.

In Chap. 3, we showed that production functions can be viewed as primitive of differential equations generated from empirical analysis. The CES functions were first identified from regression of wage-rental ratios on capital-labor ratios. If, as in equilibrium, the wage-rental ratio equals the marginal rate of substitution, then we can write the differential equation

$$-\frac{dK}{dL} = a\left(\frac{L}{K}\right)^{-1/\sigma}$$

or

$$K^{-1/\sigma}dK + aL^{-1/\sigma}dL = 0.$$

The following equation can be shown, by simple differentiation, to be the primitive of the differential equation given above:

$$\alpha K^{-1/\sigma} + \beta L^{1-1/\sigma} = C(Y)$$

where $C(Y)$ is an arbitrary function independent of K and L. Solving for Y, we obtain the family of homothetic CES functions

$$Y = C^{-1}(\alpha K^{-1/\sigma} + \beta L^{1-1/\sigma}) = F(\alpha K^{-1/\sigma} + \beta L^{1-1/\sigma}). \qquad (5.24)$$

As noted in Sato (1977a), empirical observation, particularly time-series data, suggests (L/K) ratios vary even when the marginal rate of substitution is constant. One solution is to assume that technical progress is biased (see discussion in Chap. 3) but it leads to the well-known problem regarding the estimation of the elasticity of substitution and bias simultaneously. The other solution is to relax the assumption of homogeneity. Consider second order differential equation stating that the elasticity of substitution, in a two commodity case,

$$\sigma = \frac{x_1 f_1 + x_2 f_2}{x_1 x_2 \left(-\dfrac{f_1 f_{22}}{f_2} + 2 f_{12} - \dfrac{f_2 f_{11}}{f_1}\right)} = \frac{x_1 + x_2 \omega}{x_1 x_2 \left(\dfrac{\partial \omega}{\partial x_1} - \dfrac{\partial \omega}{\partial x_2} \omega^{-1}\right)} \quad (5.25)$$

is constant. The solution of this equation will involve two arbitrary functions and can be written as

$$F(C_1(Y), C_2(Y), K, L) = 0. \quad (5.26)$$

The relation between $C_1(f)$, $C_2(f)$ and a function $H(f)$ of f determines whether the function is homothetic or non-homothetic and separable or non-separable. The condition for homotheticity is that $\dfrac{dC_i}{df} \equiv 0$ $(i = 1, 2)$ and $\dfrac{dH}{df} \neq 0$.

In the general case of n inputs, the production function in implicit form can be written as

$$F(C(Y); x) = 0 \quad (5.27)$$

where $C(Y) = \{C_1(Y), \ldots, C_n(Y)\}$ and $x = (x_1, \ldots, x_n)$. A multi-factor form of implicitly homothetic technology can be written as (Sato 1981, p. 170)

$$F(C_1(Y), \ldots, C_{n-1}(Y), x) = C_n(Y).$$

From the duality theory, we can show that the production function (Eq. (5.27)) has a normalized cost function

$$G(B(Y), p) = 0 \quad (5.28)$$

where $B(Y) = (B_1(Y), \ldots, B_n(Y))$ and $p = (p_1, \ldots, p_n)$ are normalized to make the total cost $C = 1$. Sato (1981, p. 223) shows that, if and only if the production function is implicitly homothetic, the cost function can be written as

$$C = g(C_1(Y), \ldots, C_{n-1}(Y); p) C_n(Y). \quad (5.29)$$

Further it can be shown that if and only if the production function is explicitly homothetic can the cost function be written as

$$C = g(p) C_n(Y) \quad (5.30)$$

5.6 Implicit Self-Duality of Production and Cost Functions

with $g(\cdot)$ a linear homogeneous function. Only if the product function is explicitly homothetic, can it be written as

$$f(x) = C_n(Y); \quad f(\lambda x) = \lambda C_n(Y).$$

Self duality in implicit form is best given in terms of factor demand and inverse demand functions. Moreover, these functions are homogeneous of degree zero and hence they can be expressed in terms of ratios of factor demand functions or marginal rate of substitution functions. Let the marginal rate of substitution between x_i and x_j in (5.26) be

$$\frac{p_i}{p_j} = R^i_j\left(C_1(Y),\ldots,C_{n-1}(Y); \frac{x_1}{x_j},\ldots,\frac{x_i}{x_j},\ldots,\frac{x_n}{x_j}\right)$$

where $i, j = 1,\ldots,n$.

Similarly the inverse demand function can be written as

$$\frac{x_i}{x_j} = S^i_j\left(C_1(Y),\ldots,C_{n-1}(Y); \frac{p_1}{p_j},\ldots,\frac{p_i}{p_j},\ldots,\frac{p_n}{p_j}\right).$$

These can be written more compactly as

$$P = R(D(Y),X), \tag{5.31}$$

$$X = S(D(Y);P). \tag{5.32}$$

Then the production and cost functions are self-dual if

$$P = R(D(Y);R(D(Y);P)), \quad X = S(D(Y);S(D(Y);X)) \tag{5.33}$$

that is, if P and X are exactly the same mathematical functions in terms of $D(Y)$, X, and P. We can state the conditions for implicit self-duality (compare with the conditions for self-duality of utility functions).

The necessary and sufficient conditions for implicit self-duality of production and cost functions are that there exist $(n-1)$ *functions satisfying the conditions*

$$H(X,P;D(Y)) = |H(P,X,D(Y))| = 0$$

where $H = (H^1,\ldots,H^{n-1})$.

Further, if and only if there exist $(n-1)$ *functions satisfying*

$$H(X,P) = |H(P,X)| = 0$$

are the production and cost functions explicitly self-dual.

The effect of uniform factor augmenting technical progress on the cost function (of a production function $F(x,t)$) is to shift it down by a factor of proportionality. Thus, if the production function with technical progress is written as

$$Y = F(e^t x)$$

then the cost function is of the form

$$C = e^{-t} g(p, y).$$

In particular, if the production function has constant returns to scale,

$$Y = e^t f(x)$$

then the cost function takes the form

$$C = e^{-t} g(p) Y.$$

There is perfect symmetry between the primal and dual returns to scale in Y and C.

5.7 Conclusion

Historically economic theory began with the assumption of a given set of preferences or production relations and proceeded to derive the demand or cost functions. We saw that each of these functions possesses certain properties and that they are useful in uncovering information about market behavior. Self-duality imposes additional restrictions that the functional form of both the direct and indirect functions must be same. The paper by Sato and Matsushita (1989) applied it to empirical estimation in demand theory.

Chapter 6
The Theory of Index Numbers

The theory of index numbers has a long and distinguished history. The quantity theory of money asserts that the value of money, which in itself is a function of the general level of prices, varies with its supply. If the change in the money supply is followed by a proportionate change in all prices, then the measurement of the changes in the price level will not constitute any problem. Scholars like Edgeworth and Bowley were quick to recognize that the difficulties in quantifying fluctuations in purchasing power of money arose from the absence of such proportionality (Allen 1975, p. 2). As Frisch (1936, p. 1) noted:

> "The index number problem arises whenever we want a quantitative expression for a complex that is made up of individual measurements for which no common physical unit exists. The desire to unite such measurements and the fact that this cannot be done by using physical or technical principles of comparison only, constitute the essence of the index-number problem and all the difficulties center here".

Surveys by Frisch (1936), Samuelson and Swamy (1974) and Diewert (1987) have identified three approaches to index numbers: (i) statistical approach; (ii) test approach; and (iii) the functional approach.

6.1 Statistical Approach

The statistical or stochastic approach assumes that the change in the price level ought to manifest itself as a proportionate change in all prices (Frisch 1936, p. 4). In the real world, prices do not move in unison but deviate in all directions due to the interplay of the markets. Bowley (1928) showed that neither the price ratios nor their logarithms were symmetrically distributed around the mean. He and Keynes (1930) argued that prices were not independently distributed as they were interrelated: real factors, instead of affecting each price in a random fashion, will alter them systematically as required by the general equilibrium of the markets. Keynes also argued that the price level should be defined relatively to groups of individuals in a particular situation and that it had no clear meaning unless this reference was given.

These objections were considered definitive and unweighted averages ceased to be used in theoretical or empirical studies.

6.2 Test Approach

Index numbers are constructed to compare levels across time and space; for brevity of exposition, we shall consider only inter-temporal comparisons. Under this assumption, the price index compares the prices at two inst ants of time using weighted averages. The weights involve quantities; hence, in an n commodity world, the price or quantity index in its most general form, is a scalar function of the n prices and n quantities at each of the two points of time. Most economists will agree that meaningful measures of the absolute level of prices and quantities do not exist and the indices are generally used to measure changes in the levels rather than the level itself.

By the end of the nineteenth century, a large number of index numbers were suggested by different authors including those by Laspeyers and Paasche. It was necessary to have some criteria to choose from this plethora of formulae, and tests were proposed to establish superiority of one index over others. As Afriat (1984, p. 39) comments:

> "Irving Fisher, with his book The Making of Index Numbers, represents a culmination of this phase, which is not yet quite dead. In the beginning were the formulae, each with as much right as any even though they were subject to favouritism. Fisher classified them and gave tests for judging their legitimacy, to bring order and discrimination to the prolific host. Though by the standard she laid down they are all illegitimate, he settled for one as his ideal index. The reasons he gave for this choice are still to some extent arbitrary. But theoretical properties have been discovered for it that give it an interest."

Fisher (1922) discusses five tests, but in a recent survey, Diewert (1987) lists nine. One could also treat some of the tests as axioms; in that case we exclude from consideration index numbers that do not satisfy them. Samuelson and Swamy (1974, p. 566) notes that Fisher, by making an index number satisfy certain properties of real numbers, sought to make it act like an individual price or quantity. Real numbers satisfy group properties and further these tests are intrinsically restrictions on the change in an index as one or more of its components change. So it is not surprising that these tests can be expressed as group invariances; Sato (1981, pp. 292–326) exploited this property when he reformulated the theory of index numbers using Lie groups.[1]

---

[1] This section of the chapter is more abstract than other sections and readers who are not interested in index number theory can skip to Sect. 6.4: Divisia Index without loss of continuity. Banerjee (1975) provides an overview of the theory and practise of index numbers and complements (Allen 1975).

6.2 Test Approach

Traditional index number theory concentrates on the effect of a price change on an index but does not examine the dynamics of the price change. To use group theory, we want a mechanism by which we can postulate the changes in individual prices as group transformations and examine how they affect the price index; if we have such a methodology, we can build into it the restrictions needed to meet various tests proposed in the literature. To simplify the exposition we will, *for the present*, make the restrictive assumption that quantities are fixed. We have then two price vectors, P^0 and P^1, for the time period 0 and 1, as well as the constant quantity vectors, $\overline{X}^0$ and $\overline{X}^1$. An efficient way to do this is to assume that all observed prices are first transformed into "efficiency prices" by a one-parameter transformation and second examine how the changes in the parameter would affect the index. So first we define a set of $2n$ functions, ϕ_i^j ($i = 1,\ldots,n$, $j = 0,1$) which are taken to be, in their most general form, functions of the two price vectors, P^0 and P^1 as well as a parameter, λ (λ_0 is the identity in the group operation). The transformation can be thought as affecting the efficiency prices ϕ_i^j entering the price index. Then the changes in the price index, as prices change, can be expressed in terms of the infinitesimal variation of the index with λ and the properties that the price index must satisfy as restrictions on the infinitesimal generators.

The index or aggregator is now a function from a $2n$ (non-negative real) vector to a non-negative real number, $\mathcal{R}_+$.

$$p: (P^0, P^1; \overline{X}^0, \overline{X}^1) \longrightarrow p(\phi_\lambda) \longrightarrow p(P^0, P^1). \tag{6.1}$$

We can now define the infinitesimal transformation for the group operation as

$$U = U^0 + U^1 = \sum_1^n \xi_i^0 \frac{\partial}{\partial p_i^0} + \sum_1^n \xi_i^1 \frac{\partial}{\partial p_i^1} \tag{6.2}$$

where $\xi_i^0 = \left.\frac{\partial \phi_i^0}{\partial \lambda}\right|_{\lambda=\lambda_0}$ and $\xi_i^1 = \left.\frac{\partial \phi_i^1}{\partial \lambda}\right|_{\lambda=\lambda_0}$.

If we apply U to p, then Up will show how the price index changes when the prices change as a result of the change in the parameter λ. Desired properties of the index numbers are now constraints on the infinitesimal variation.

The following four axioms must be satisfied by all index numbers.

A1. *Monotonicity axiom.* If the price increases in period 1, the price index must increase; if the price in period 0 increases, the index should decrease. A change in λ that increases the base year prices alone must lead to decrease in the index and one that increases the second year price must result in an increase in the prices. Setting $\xi_i^0 > 0$ and $\xi_i^1 = 0$, this requires that all $\frac{\partial p}{\partial p_i^0} < 0$ and similarly that $\frac{\partial p}{\partial p_i^1} > 0$.

A2. *Identity axiom.* If all prices remain constant, then the value of p equals unity: $p(P^0,P^0) = 1$. Setting $\xi_i^0 = \xi_i^1$, it follows that, for all i, $\dfrac{\partial p}{\partial p_i^1} = -\dfrac{\partial p}{\partial p_i^0}$.

A3. *Homogeneity Invariance Axiom.* If all prices in the year 1 is to increase λ-fold, then p also increases λ-fold. For this property, the functions ϕ_i^j form a uniform magnification group; then $\xi_i^1 = p_i^1$ for all i (See Chap. 2 for definition of uniform magnification). In terms of the infinitesimal operator, this implies that $U^1 p - p = 0$.

A4. *Dimensional Invariance Axiom.* A change in the unit of currency should not affect the value of p. This requires that ϕ_i^0 is also a magnification group. So $\xi_i^0 = p_i^0$ and $Up = U^0 p + U^1 p = 0$. Using the infinitesimal operators, it is easy to show that these axioms are independent and consistent in the sense that an index number can satisfy one or more of them without any logical inconsistency or redundancy but we will leave the proof out. Notice that these tests are satisfied by the Laspeyers and Paasche indices.

The other tests of Fisher can be derived from these axioms.

T1. *Proportionality test.* If the prices in year 1 is λ-fold the base year price, then the price index is λ. This follows directly from the homogeneity invariance axiom.

T2. *Homogeneity-Of-Degree-Minus-One test.* Any aggregator that satisfies (A3) and (A4) must also have the property that a λ-fold increase in the base year prices will be λ^{-1}-fold change in the index.

$$p(\lambda P^0, P^1) = p(P^0, \lambda^{-1} P^1) = \lambda^{-1} p(P^0, P^1).$$

T3. *Mean Value test.* As we noted at the beginning of this chapter, if all prices change in the same proportion, then the price index will change by that factor. The idea of the mean value test is that, if prices change by different proportions, then the price index is a measure of the average change and so the value of p must lie between the smallest and the largest of these price changes.

Since

$$\min\{p_1^1/p_1^0,\ldots,p_n^1/p_n^0\} \leq p \leq \max\{p_1^1/p_1^0,\ldots,p_n^1/p_n^0\}$$

set

$$\min\{p_1^1/p_1^0,\ldots,p_n^1/p_n^0\} = \lambda.$$

Then,

$$\min\{p_1^1/p_1^0,\ldots,p_n^1/p_n^0\} = \lambda = \lambda p(P^0,P^0) = p(P^0,\lambda P^0) \leq p(P^0,P^1)$$

as $\lambda P^0 \leq P^1$. By setting $\mu = \max\{p_1^1/p_1^0,\ldots,p_n^1/p_n^0\}$, it can be shown that $p(P^0,P^1) \leq \mu$.

6.2 Test Approach

T4. *Circular Reversal Test.* If over the first time period, all prices change from P^0 to P^1 and over the next period from P^1 to P^2, then the price indices for the various periods must satisfy the following:

$$p(P^0, P^1) \cdot p(P^1, P^2) = p(P^0, P^2).$$

T5. *Time Reversal Test.* This follows from (T4); by setting $p^1 = p^2$ and $p^2 = p^0$, we get that

$$p(P^0, P^2) \cdot p(P^2, P^0) = p(P^0, P^0) = 1.$$

The circular reversal test is very powerful; we state below, without proof, the proposition that indices that satisfy the test must be of ratio of two functions. The numerator should be a function only of the price in the current year and the denominator a function of the base year prices.

Any price index which satisfies the circular test must have the form

$$p(P^0, P^1) = g(P^1)/g(P^0) \qquad (6.3)$$

where $g(P)$ is a homogeneous function of degree one in P such that
$$\frac{\partial g(P)}{\partial p_i} > 0.$$

The proof is given in Sato (1981, p. 298) but the idea is quite simple. From (T4), we see that $p(P^1, P^2)$ must equal $p(P^0, P^2)/p(P^0, P^1)$; as this must hold for all values of P^0, the right hand side must be independent of P^0. This requires that $p(P^0, P^2)$ are products of functions in P^0 and P^2 respectively and $p(P^0, P^1)$ is the product of functions of P^0 and P^1 so that the function involving P^0 cancels out in the ratio. The proposition follows immediately. It can also be proved that any price index that satisfies the four axioms (A1) to (A4) must be of the ratio form as Laspeyers and Paasche indices indeed are.
Now we will remove the restrictive assumption we made earlier, that quantities are constant. The price index in all generality can be written as a function from n vector to the scalar, p.

$$p : (P^0, X^0, P^1, X^1) \longrightarrow p(P^0, X^0, P^1, X^1) \qquad (6.4)$$

If the n quantities are changing, there is a need to construct a measure of the change in quantity, a quantity index. As in the case of a price index, the quantity index should be a measure of "the average" change in quantities and should satisfy the same types of tests. Samuelson and Swamy (1974) argue, in a passage that we will quote later, that quantity indices are more important to economic analysis than price indices. But, for the moment, let us consider their interrelationship.

T6. *Commensurability Invariance test.* A change in the units of measurement of commodities does not change the value of p. When quantities are changed by a factor $1/\lambda$, prices change by the factor λ.

$$p(\lambda_1^0 p_1^0, \ldots, \lambda_n^0 p_n^0, X_1^0/\lambda_1^0, \ldots, X_n^0/\lambda_n^0,$$
$$\lambda_1^1 p_1^1, \ldots, \lambda_n^1 p_n^1, X_1^1/\lambda_1^1, \ldots, X_n^1/\lambda_n^1)$$
$$= p(P^0, X^0, P^1, X^1).$$

Notice that the infinitesimal generators that was defined in Eq. (6.2) where only prices where changing, has to be generalized to take into account the changes in prices and quantities. For the case of changes in prices and quantities, we will define it as:

$$U = \sum_{i=1}^{n} \alpha_i^0 \left(p_i^0 \frac{\partial}{\partial p_i^0} - x_i^0 \frac{\partial}{\partial x_i^0} \right) + \sum_{i=1}^{n} \alpha_i^1 \left(p_i^1 \frac{\partial}{\partial p_i^1} - x_i^1 \frac{\partial}{\partial x_i^1} \right)$$

for all i. For most applications, $\alpha_i^0 = \alpha_i^1$. Then the test can be written as

$$Up = 0.$$

T7. *Factor Reversal test.* This requires that, on changing P^0 with X^0 and p^1 with X^1, we obtain the quantity index, q:

$$p(X^0, P^0, X^1, P^1) = q(X^0, P^0, X^1, P^1). \tag{6.5}$$

Since this implies that the same formula is used for price and quantity indices, it can be called "strong" self-duality condition. We can impose another condition that the product of price and quantity index should equal the ratio of the expenditures.

$$p(X^0, P^0, X^1, P^1) q(X^0, P^0, X^1, P^1) = \frac{P^1 X^1}{P^0 X^0}. \tag{6.6}$$

Any price index that satisfies Eq. (6.3) and the invariance condition $Up = 0$ will satisfy (6.6). The economic intuition behind this condition is that the price and quantity indices should account for the value change.

In conventional definition, the price index $p(\cdot)$ is a weighted average of price ratios while $q(\cdot)$ is the weighted average of quantity ratios. Thus, in the Laspeyers price and quantity indices, the expenditure in base year, $p_i^0 q_i^0$ is used as weights for the price ratios, p_i^1/p_i^0, and the quantity ratio, q_i^1/q_i^0 respectively. Paasche indices can be take to be harmonic means of price and quantity ratios with weight, $p_i^1 q_i^1$ or the arithmetic mean of the same ratios with weights $p_i^0 q_i^1$ and $p_i^1 q_i^0$ respectively. The resulting formulae can be summarized as follows:

Laspeyers:

$$p_L = \frac{\sum p_i^1 q_i^0}{\sum p_i^0 q_i^0}, \quad q_L = \frac{\sum p_i^0 q_i^1}{\sum p_i^0 q_i^0}.$$

Paasche:

$$p_P = \frac{\sum p_i^1 q_i^1}{\sum p_i^0 q_i^1}, \quad q_P = \frac{\sum p_i^1 q_i^1}{\sum p_i^1 q_i^0}.$$

Notice that both Laspeyers and Paasche indices are strongly self-dual though they do not satisfy (6.6). However, as Allen (1975, p. 46) points out, (6.6) is satisfied by crossing Laspeyers and Paasche indices.

$$p_P q_L = p_L q_P = \frac{\sum p_i^1 q_i^1}{\sum p_i^0 q_i^0}. \tag{6.7}$$

This property played a crucial role in Irving Fisher's definition of an ideal index number, $\sqrt{p_L p_q}$. Even though it did not have the theoretical significance that Fisher gave it, it makes economic sense. But note that it does not satisfy the circular reversal test.

6.3 Economic Index Numbers

The test approach to index numbers looked on them as mapping from $4n$ vector to positive real numbers with tests providing criteria for choosing between the many possible mappings. But prices and quantities are related through the market behaviour of the individuals. It is therefore natural to ask whether it is possible to examine the economics underlying an index number. We are also interested in the welfare-theoretic question whether an individual or group of individuals are better off or not from a price change after they have adjusted the quantities to maximize their utilities at the new prices. Frisch (1936, p. 10) called this "the functional approach" and wrote that the index is "in point of principle, appear as observable with the same sort of precision as the price of an individual commodity, provided the necessary data are available."

In reality, we run into two types of problems. First, the statistics of prices are easier to collect those on quantities and as a result, information on quantities are available only after considerable lag. Recollect that one of the advantages of the Laspeyers index is that only base year quantities need be known.

Second, even if all the prices and quantities are available, the criteria for determining the welfare of the individuals would pose problems. Before we construct the index, we have to identify a reference group whose economic welfare is being compared. Then we have to justify the assertion that their welfare depends only on expenditure. As long as we are dealing with one consumer, we are on solid grounds. "To go from these limiting confines to wider problems requires an act of faith rather than an application of economic theory ... To make economic-theoretic sense here we need to take on trust the existence of a group or average preference map, to permit interpersonal utility comparisons." (Allen 1975, pp. 47–48). Third, we have to identify the level of utility which we take as the reference for comparison between the two situations.

If we can somehow ascertain that an individual or group of individuals spending e_1 in period 1 are as well as off as the person or group of persons who spend e_0 in period 0, then we can define the economic price index as

$$P_E = \frac{e_1}{e_2}. \tag{6.8}$$

William Fleetwood, in 1707, compared the cost of living of an Oxford student then and 260 years earlier. The widely used Consumer Price Index (CPI) is constructed on the basis of a sample survey of households. For the rest of this section, it will be assumed that a well-defined representative group has been agreed upon.

Speculation along these lines led Konus (1939) to define an index number on the basis of the minimum cost of achieving a reference utility, $u(X)$, where X is a vector of n commodities, at the price P^1 (a n-vector) as compared to the price P^0. The consumption baskets for which $u(\cdot)$ is constant form an indifference surface in the n dimensional space. The price index is then the ratio of the two bundles of goods at which the budget planes before and after the price change are tangent to the indifference surface. Reinterpreting e_0 and e_1 of (6.8) as the minimum costs at prevailing prices to attain a constant utility level u, we see that p_E is the Konus index.

Price Index (Samuelson and Swamy 1974, p. 567): This must equal the ratio of the (minimum) costs of a given level of living in two price situations.

$$p_E = \frac{e(u(X) = \bar{u}, P^1)}{e(u(X) = \bar{u}, P^0)} \tag{6.9}$$

where by definition $e(u(X) = \bar{u}, P^j)$ is the minimum expenditure $\sum p_i^j x_i^j$ ($i = 1,\ldots,n, j = 0, 1$) that is required to archive the utility level, $\bar{u}$. Notice that the budget surfaces corresponding to $e(u(X) = \bar{u}, P^j)$ are tangent to the indifference surface $u(x)$. Samuelson and Swamy (1974, pp. 567–578) note: "Although most attention in the literature is devoted to price indexes, when you analyze the use to which price indexes are generally put, you realize that the quantity indexes are actually most important. Once somehow estimated, price indexes are in fact used, if at all, primarily to "deflate" nominal or monetary totals in order to arrive at estimates of underlying "real magnitudes"." Their definition of quantity index (*ibid.*, p. 567) is:

Quantity Index: This measure for two presented quantity situations X and X, the ratio of the minimum expenditure needed, is the face of reference price situation P, to buy their respective levels of well-being.

6.3 Economic Index Numbers

$$q_E = \frac{(e(X^1), \overline{P})}{(e(X^0), \overline{P})} \tag{6.10}$$

where $e(\cdot)$ is as in (6.9). Diewert (1987) calls q_E the Allen index.

Another approach takes the ratio of expenditures in the two periods and deflates it by a price index. If there is only one commodity, the deflation would give the correct ratio of quantities, $(p_1^1 x_1^1 / p_1^0 x_1^0)/(p_1^1/p_1^0) = x_1^1/x_1^0$ and this provides the intuition to use the index as deflator in the general case. We could either take the Laspeyers or Paasche index and Diewert (1987) calls the resulting quantity indices Laspeyers–Konus and Paasche–Konus indices.

Consider a situation where $e(\cdot)$ is the product of two functions $g(u)h(P)$; Shepherd (1953) showed that this will be true if $u(\cdot)$ is homothetic. In (6.9), u is constant and $g(u)$ will cancel, making P_E a function of P^0 and P^1 only. We can now ask what is the most general condition under which P_E is independent of X and q_E is independent of P. Following Samuelson and Swamy (1974), we can show that this would be true if and only if the preferences are homothetic.

If and only if preferences are homothetic, p in Eq. (6.9) and q in Eq. (6.10) are invariant in the sense that

$$\frac{\partial p}{\partial \overline{x}_i} = 0, \quad \frac{\partial q}{\partial \overline{p}_i} = 0. \tag{6.11}$$

This result follows directly from the discussion of duality in Chap. 4.

There exist "no" price and quantity indices which are self- dual if preference orderings are explicitly non-homothetic. As Sato (1981, p. 306) shows, this follows from the fact that p is always linear and non-homogeneous in P^1 but q is not homogeneous in X^1, by assumption. This violates the condition for self- duality.

We may ask whether the economic index numbers can be defined using the indirect utility functions instead of the direct utility functions. Define the indirect utility index function v as in Chap. 4. In the Allen index, q_E, was defined earlier (Eq. (6.10)) as the ratio of two expenditure functions, $e(P^i : u = \overline{u}) = \min_x PX$ ($i = 0, 1$). Dual quantity index, q^*, is defined as the ratio of two expenditure functions, $e^*(X : v = \overline{v}) = \min_P XP$ and so is completely dual to q_E with P and X, and u and v interchanged.

Dual Quantity Index: The dual quantity index q^* of X^0 and X^1 is defined as the ratio of the minimum expenditure, given P, needed to attain their respective highest standards of living at a given cost condition.

$$q^* = \frac{e^*(X^1 : v = \overline{v})}{e^*(X^0 : v = \overline{v})}. \tag{6.12}$$

The dual quantity index satisfies (T1) to (T5) and further we can show that it is invariant under changes in P if and only if preference orderings are explicitly homothetic. The latter follows as the product e^* can be written in product form only if the condition is satisfied (Sato 1981, p. 309).

q^* is homogeneous of degree one with respect to X^1 for any preference ordering while q is so if an only if the preference ordering is homothetic. Two interesting consequences of this property is that q^* equal to q only for homothetic preferences but p and q^* satisfy the weak form of factor reversal test for all preferences.

Another question that arises in the economic theory of index numbers is the invariance of the index under taste change. If utility function is defined as $u(X.t)$ where t represents an index of exogenous taste change, then the price index is invariant if

$$\frac{\partial p}{\partial t} \equiv 0 \quad \text{at} \quad u = \bar{u}. \tag{6.13}$$

Again the condition is that preferences be homothetic.

6.4 Divisia Index

When the price index number is used for a binary comparison between the current year t and base year 0, the information about the prices and quantities for the intermediate years are ignored. One way to look at the Divisia index is to view it as an index that makes a more efficient use of the data for the intermediate years. It would be continuous time equivalent of the chain index (Allen 1975, pp. 177–180).

Assume that there exists a continuous price index, $p_D(t)$, and a quantity index, $q_D(t)$, such that the following relation holds continuously over time:

$$e(t) = p_D(t)q_D(t) = P(t)Q(t) = \sum_{i=1}^{n} p_i(t)q_i(t). \tag{6.14}$$

Take the differential of the first two terms in (6.14) and divide them by $e(t)$ to get:

$$\frac{de(t)}{e(t)} = \frac{dp_D(t)}{p_D(t)} + \frac{dq_D(t)}{q_D(t)}. \tag{6.15}$$

Repeating the process with the first and last terms in (6.14) leads to

$$\frac{de(t)}{e(t)} = \frac{\sum q_i(t)dp_i(t)}{\sum p_i(t)q_i(t)} + \frac{\sum p_i(t)dq_i(t)}{\sum q_i(t)p_i(t)}. \tag{6.16}$$

From the definitions of $p_D(t)$ and $q_D(t)$, components of (6.15) and (6.16) must be equal to each other and so must the other two terms. Hence we get the differential equations

$$d(\ln p_D) = \frac{\sum q_i(t)dp_i(t)}{\sum p_i(t)q_i(t)} \tag{6.17}$$

6.4 Divisia Index

and

$$d(\ln q_D) = \frac{\sum p_i(t)dq_i(t)}{\sum q_i(t)p_i(t)}. \tag{6.18}$$

The existence of the Divisia indices amount to the condition that these differential equations are integrable. But this does not imply that, for all paths of prices and quantities that result in the same difference $e(t) - e(0)$ of the indicies—the integrals of (6.17) and (6.18)—have the same values; if this condition is satisfied then the index is said have the path independence property. This property will hold if the two differential equations are exact differential or if there exists scalar functions $\psi(P)$ and $\phi(Q)$ such that

$$d\psi(P(t)) = \dot\psi(t)dt = \frac{\sum q_i(t)d\dot p_i(t)dt}{\sum p_i(t)q_i(t)} \tag{6.19}$$

and

$$d\phi(Q(t)) = \dot\phi(t)dt = \frac{\sum p_i(t)d\dot q_i(t)dt}{\sum q_i(t)p_i(t)}. \tag{6.20}$$

In that case,

$$d(\ln p_D(t)) = \dot\psi(t)dt, \quad d(\ln q_D(t)) = \dot\phi(t)dt$$

and

$$p_D(t) = p_D(0)e^{\psi(t)}, \quad q_D(t) = q_D(0)e^{\phi(t)} \tag{6.21}$$

(see Allen (1975, p. 180), Samuelson and Swamy (1974, p. 579), and Sato (1981, p. 315)).

If the path invariance condition is not satisfied, then two economies that had the same price and quantity vectors in times 0 and t will have different price and quantity indices which goes against economic intuition. But, if we assume path invariance the motivation of the Divisia index suggested by Allen (1975, p. 178), then the condition indices do not take into consideration all the information on prices and quantities. It again shows that there cannot be an ideal index number that meets all the economically-motivated criteria that can be imposed on it.

So far we have followed purely mathematical considerations in defining the Divisia indeed. Naturally we are led to wonder whether it has any economic properties like those defined in the previous section. It can be shown that if the consumer or producer is continuously minimizing a well behaved linearly homogeneous aggregator function subject to budget constraints at all points of time from 0 to t, the Divisia price (quantity) indeed equals a true Konus price (quantity) index (Diewert 1981, pp. 195–196).

Richter (1966) showed that the Divisia indices are the only ones that satisfy a set of axioms that he stated. One of the axioms was that, as long as the path of the system was along an indifference curve or isoquant, the quantity index ϕ should be constant. If we are moving along an indifference curve, this condition implies that the index should be a measure of the real income; this reinforces the point that Samuelson and Swamy (1974, pp. 567–568) makes regarding the greater importance of the quantity index.

We can now ask whether there is an transformation that leaves the Divisia quantity index invariant. This requires that the transformation should leave the differential equation (6.20) invariant and the condition for that is that one indifference curve should be mapped to another (Chap. 3); in other words, it should leave the real income constant. For this to hold, the changes in quantity along the virtual expansion paths (the infinitesimal generators of the transformation) multiplied by the price ratios should be the same at all points along the indifference curve. This is in fact the condition derived in Sato (1981, pp. 318–320) using the Noether theorem:

$$\sum_{i=1}^{n} \left(\frac{\partial \phi}{\partial q_i}\right) \xi^i = \sum_{i=1}^{n} \left(\frac{p_i}{\sum p_j q_j}\right). \tag{6.22}$$

Divisia indices are not used in calculation of price and quantity indices. Its most common use is in estimation of total factor productivity change, a measure of the change in output over and above that due to the increase in inputs. As we saw in Chap. 2, much effort has been devoted to measuring and interpreting total factor productivity after Solow (1957) estimated it to be the main determinant in the growth of per capita income in the United States. In fact, the motivation that we provided in Chap. 2 for the representation of technology by Lie groups is that the efforts to decompose the changes in total factor productivity to technical progress and increasing returns were futile. The Divisia index is a summary measure of the total factor productivity growth over a period of time. Since we have argued that the technical progress that could be the source of productivity growth has group properties, it is valid to ask whether the Divisia index has properties that reflect them.

The Divisia index is generally written as

$$D(t) = \exp \int_0^t \left(\frac{\dot{Y}}{Y} - \frac{\sum w^i \dot{x}_i}{\sum w^i x_i}\right) dt$$

where x_i is an input and w_i is its price. Let us assume that the technical progress is of Lie type, $U = \sum \xi^i \partial/\partial x_i$; then, under assumptions of constant returns to scale, we have

$$\frac{\dot{Y}}{Y} - \frac{\sum w^i \dot{x}_i}{\sum w^i x_i} = \frac{\sum \xi^i \partial Y/\partial x_i}{Y} = \frac{\sum w^i \xi^i}{\sum w^i x_i}. \tag{6.23}$$

6.4 Divisia Index

But, by Richter's axiom, the right hand side of (6.22) should be a constant along an isoquant. Along an isoquant, the denominator of the middle term is a constant. The numerator is, using the interpretation of Chap. 2, the increase in output along the virtual expansion path. For the equality of the two terms of the equation it follows that the numerator of the central term must be constant. So the transformation maps one isoquant to another. This line of argumentation shows that the Lie group interpretation of Divisia index (commonly used in empirical work to measure residual productivity due to technical progress) is consistent with the discussion of the identifiability of its sources in Chap. 2.

Chapter 7
Dynamics and Conservation Laws

In dynamic analysis, we examine the movements of a system over time. From the infancy of their science, economists were interested in the microeconomic and macroeconomic adjustment processes. As for long-term trends, classical economists assumed that would tend towards a stationary state. Modern growth theory, as developed in the second half of this century, indicated the possibility of a non-stationary equilibrium and provided strong impetus to appropriate and adopt for study of economic dynamics the mathematical tools developed in physical sciences.

There are three well-tested and time-honored methods for modeling dynamic phenomena in physical sciences. The first approach defines the movement of the system at each value of its variables; given the values of the variables and their rate of change at a specific time, a differential equation defines the future movement of the system for all time. The vector approach was first used by Newton in his study of mechanics and hence is called Newtonian dynamics. The second approach considers the whole path instead of a point on it and claims that the system will choose the path that minimizes or maximizes the integral of a function along the path; this leads to Lagrangian dynamics. The third approach is due to the Irish mathematician, William Rowen Hamilton, who developed a geometric method for modeling the dynamic system. In this approach, a phase space is defined and the state of the system is specified by a point of the phase space which in turn completely specifies its future states. In addition to providing greater intuition into the dynamic process, Hamiltonian mechanics is able to conceptualize complicated systems that are intractable in the Newtonian approach. Another advantage of the Hamiltonian method is that, in many instances, it is easy to identify a scalar function that is constant along the external; such functions are called first integrals. However, for classical problems in mechanics, the three methods are different ways of modeling the same phenomena and dynamic paths derived are the same irrespective of the approach.

The situation in economics is more complicated. The Harrod–Domar model and Solow–Swan model are considered descriptive models for they take some behavioral and institutional parameters as given. If these values are set at levels observed in any economy, we can derive using the model the path that will be followed by the economy. But the path may not correspond to the maximization of the integral of that society's social valuation function. The question then arises whether the parameters can be changed so as to move the economy along an "optimal path" defined as that which maximizes the social valuation function. Then, obviously, different social valuation functions will give different dynamic paths so that there is no one-to-one correspondence between descriptive and optimal models.

Pioneering work in deriving a model that maximizes an intertemporal utility function was done by Ramsey (1928) when he examined the question of optimal savings. Even though Keynes in his obituary note on Ramsey called the paper one of the most remarkable contribution to mathematical economics, it did not have any immediate impact on the profession. This is due partly to the novelty of the question and partly due to the special assumptions that Ramsey used to make his problem tractable. Further his conclusion that optimal savings rate could be well above the observed ones seemed to have little relevance in the inter-war years. In the 1960s, many development economists believed that the savings rate that existed under prevailing institutional arrangements in developing countries was far below the optimal level needed to achieve self- sustaining growth and that the government should adopt policies to increase the savings rate. In this intellectual climate, Ramsey's analysis had a short spurt of popularity.

Soon the discussion moved to consideration of optimality in the framework of Solow–Swan model. Among the many directions in which the model was developed was the examination of the maximal consumption path that is infinitely sustainable under different assumptions; these discussions led to the so-called "golden rules". The path of an economy outside the steady-state needs to be examined and the one approach that turned out to be very productive was the application of Hamiltonian dynamics to intertemporal problems.

7.1 The Variational Problem and the Ramsey Rule

Mathematically, calculus of variations is concerned with the determination of the extremum of a definite integral. But the clear distinction between determining the extremum of a function and the extremum of an integral is itself the product of modern methods. Earlier discussions, like Hero's derivation of law of reflection, solved variational problems using geometric method. Euler used *method of finite differences* to reduce the variational problem to that of finding the extremum of a function of n variables. A short discussion of that method would be very useful as an introduction of the Euler equation (Gelfand and Fomin 1963, pp. 4 & 27–29).

Consider a functional of the form,

$$J(y) = \int_a^b F(x, x', t)\, dt, \quad x(a) = a, \quad x(b) = b. \tag{7.1}$$

7.1 The Variational Problem and the Ramsey Rule

Fig. 7.1 Geometric interpretation of variational derivative

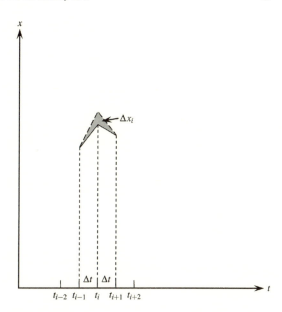

The integral assigns a number to each curve. To use the finite difference, divide the interval $[a,b]$ into $(n+1)$ equal parts with $t_0 = a$ and $t_{n+1} = b$ and then replace the curve $x = x(t)$ by a polygonal line,

$$(a; x(t_0)), (t_1, x(t_1)), \ldots, (t_n, x(t_n)), (b, x(t_{n+1})).$$

The functional $J(x)$ can be approximated by the sum

$$J(x_1, \ldots, x_n) = \sum_{i=0}^{n} F\left(x_i, \frac{x_{i+1} - x_i}{\Delta t}, t_i\right) \Delta t \qquad (7.2)$$

where $x_i = x(t_i)$ and $\Delta t = t_{i+1} - t_i$ (Fig. 7.1).

Notice that $J(\cdot)$ is a function of n variables, $t_1, \ldots, t_n$, as the two end-points, $(a, x(t_0))$ and $(b, x(t_{n+1}))$ are fixed. We now introduce the concept of *variational* or *functional derivative* which plays the same role for functionals as partial derivatives do for functions of n variables. Each variable x_i appears twice in sum on the right hand side—in $F[x_i, (x_{i+1} - x_i)/\Delta t, t_i]$ and $F[x_{i-1}, (x_i - x_{i-1})/\Delta t, t_{i-1}]$—and so the differentiation of (7.2) partially with respect to x_k gives the expression

$$\frac{\partial J}{\partial x_k} = F_x\left(x_k, \frac{x_{k+1} - x_k}{\Delta t}, t_k\right)\Delta t + F_{x'}\left(x_{k-1}, \frac{x_k - x_{k-1}}{\Delta t}, t_{k-1}\right)$$
$$- F_{x'}\left(x_k, \frac{x_{k+1} - x_k}{\Delta t}, t_k\right).$$

This expression goes to zero as $\Delta t \to 0$; dividing both sides by Δt, we get

$$\frac{\partial J}{\partial x_k \Delta t} = F_x\left(x_k, \frac{x_{k+1} - x_k}{\Delta t}, t_k\right) + \frac{1}{\Delta t}\left(F_{x'}\left(x_{k-1}, \frac{x_k - x_{k-1}}{\Delta t}, t_{k-1}\right)\right)$$
$$- \frac{1}{\Delta t}\left(F_{x'}\left(x_k, \frac{x_{k+1} - x_k}{\Delta t}, t_k\right)\right).$$

The expression gives the rate of change of the integral as the curve is marginally shifted at t_k by Δx_k. In fact, the expression on the denominator on the left hand side is the shaded area between the two curves. Notice that as Δt decreases, the number of divisions of the interval (a, b) increases and the polynomial approximation comes closer to a smooth curve. As we set Δt to zero, the expression attains a limit called the *variational* derivative. If the curve $x(t)$ corresponds to the extremum of the integral, then the directional derivative should be zero.

$$\frac{\partial J}{\partial x} = F_x(x, x', t) - \frac{d}{dt} F_{x'}(x, x', t) = 0. \qquad (7.3)$$

The second and third terms together form the Euler equation for a variational problem. Notice that it is a second order partial differential equation.

The proof depended on the "localization property" of the functional, that if the curve is divided into parts and the functional is calculated for each part, then the sum of these should equal the value of the functional for the whole curve. It is only such functionals that are considered in calculus of variations (Gelfand and Fomin 1963, p. 3).

When Ramsey set out to prove the optimal rate of savings using calculus of variations, he had to solve a number of conceptual problems. He considered one-good economy where output was produced using labor and capital; what is saved was invested resulting in an increase in the capital stock. He assumed no population growth so that per capita output and gross output had the same trend. The instantaneous utility was expressed as a function of total consumption, $U(C)$, and the disutility of labor, $V(L)$.

The localization property implied that the instantaneous utility as a function of current consumption must be a cardinal measure which could be summed or integrated over the time interval and that there is no complementarity in consumption over time. Assuming such integral converges, the objective function was to maximize the integral.

The question then arises as to the time horizon over which the consumers were planning to use in the maximization problem; this corresponds to the interval (a, b) in the variational problem. It is natural to take the present time as the beginning of the interval but any finite endpoint would be arbitrary. So Ramsey assumed that the optimization is over an infinite time interval.

For the problem as formulated above the indefinite integral does not converge and so comparisons of the integral for different consumption paths are meaningless. He solved the problem by assuming that there is a maximum to the level of enjoyment

7.1 The Variational Problem and the Ramsey Rule

possible, either because of production or consumption saturation. He argued that it is desirable to attain bliss in a finite time or move to it asymptotically as otherwise a finite shortfall over an infinite time horizon can be very costly in utility terms. In short, he used the bliss as a reference path (Samuelson later used it as the turnpike) and converted the objective function to one of minimizing the integral of shortfall of the actual path from this reference one.

Incremental consumption at a future date may be valued differently from that today for two set of reasons. First, the level of consumption at the subsequent date may be different from that today and so marginal utility at two points of time can differ. Second, even if the consumption levels were the same, the individuals could discount future utility for what Ramsey called "want of imagination."

A two-period model will bring out the economics of the Ramsey model (Dixit 1976, pp. 98–103) for a detailed treatment of the two period model). In the two period model, the capital in the beginning, K_0, and the capital that must be left for the future, K_2, are given. The capital in the second period depends on the initial capital plus savings. The savings in the second period is then determined by the condition that capital in the next period should be equal to K_2. The consumption in each period is output minus savings and output will depend on the constant labor and the current level of capital. Mathematically these conditions can be written as

$$C_0 = F(\overline{K}_0, \overline{L}) - (K_1 - \overline{K}_0),$$
$$C_1 = F(K_1, \overline{L}) - (K_2 - \overline{K}_1).$$

The only choice variable is K_1; so differentiating both equations with respect to K_1 and taking ratios we get,

$$-\frac{dC_1/dK_1}{dC_0/dK_1} = 1 + F_1 = 1 + i \qquad (7.4)$$

as, for in a single commodity model, the marginal product of capital has to equal the interest rate, i. Now we postulate an intertemporal utility function,

$$U(C_0, C_1) = u(C_0) + \frac{1}{1+\rho} u(C_1)$$

where ρ is the discount rate. The marginal rate of substitution is then,

$$\frac{\partial U/\partial C_0}{\partial U/\partial C_1} = \frac{u'(C_0)}{u'(C_1)/(1+\rho)}. \qquad (7.5)$$

Equating (7.4) and (7.5) under the usual assumption that the slope of the transformation function should equal the slope of the indifference curve, we get

$$\frac{u'(C_0)}{u'(C_1)(1+\rho)} = 1 + i.$$

Ramsey argued that ρ should be equal to zero in which case the above equation can be written as

$$\frac{u'(C_0) - u'(C_1)}{u'(C_1)} = i. \tag{7.6}$$

Thus the rule is that the proportionate change in marginal utility should equal interest rate; it is a variant of the Keynes–Ramsey rule. Ramsey's original problem can be restated as

$$\min \int_0^\infty (B - (U(C) - V(L))) \, dt \tag{7.7}$$

such that

$$\frac{dK}{dt} + C = F(K, L).$$

Here $U(x)$ is the instantaneous utility from consumption and $V(L)$ the disutility of labor. Ramsey then noticed that he could change the variable of integration from t to K using the second equation in (7.7) above and so the problem became

$$\min \int_{K_0}^\infty \frac{B - (U(C) - V(L))}{F(K, L) - C} \, dK. \tag{7.8}$$

Since C and L are arbitrary function of K, the condition for the minimum can be calculated by differentiating it with respect to C and setting it equal to zero. This gives the condition in the form

$$\frac{dK}{dt} = S = F(K, L) - C = \frac{B - (U(C) - V(L))}{U'(C)}. \tag{7.9}$$

The Ramsey–Keynes rule states that savings times marginal utility of consumption equals the shortfall in current level of utility from the bliss. Suppose savings, S, decreases by \$1, then the time to make the same increase in capital, $\dot{K}$, will increase by $1/S$. The attainment of bliss will also be delayed that much. So the cost in terms of utility is $S^{-1}[B - (U(C) - V(L))]$. The benefit of the reducing savings by \$1 is the marginal utility. Equation (7.8) equates the two.

In general the savings rate is not constant but, as the system tends towards bliss, it will also move to a classical stationary state with zero savings. Much of the work in the late fifties and early sixties was directed at removing this limitation of the model. This is achieved by assuming that labor was growing at an exogenous rate and that the equilibrium is a steady state in which relevant variables are growing at a fixed rate so that their ratios remain constant. Discounting and technical progress were also introduced into these models. Samuelson and Solow (1956) extended the model to heterogeneous capital goods. Economists became also more willing to accept the summation of cardinal utility as a measure of welfare though Arnold (1973) examined the implications of replacing it with the Rawls' principle.

7.2 Steady State and the Golden Rules

Modern growth theory escapes from the classical stationary state by assuming that population grows at an exponential rate and that the production function has the needed degree of concavity to achieve a steady state. If we postulate a linear homogeneous production function, $Y_t = F(K_t, L_t)$, where K_t and L_t are the quantities of capital and labor at time then the output per unit of labor can be written as $y_t = f(k_t)$, where k_t is capital per unit of labor. The Solow model then gives us a differential equation for the growth of k_t

$$\dot{k} = sf(k_t) - nk_t \tag{7.10}$$

where s is the institutionally given savings rate. This has a steady state at the capital labor ratio, k^* given by $sf(k^*) = nk^*$. The consumption per person in steady state (fudging distinction between population and employment) is $c^* = f(k^*) - nk^*$.

The assumption of constant population that Ramsey used is more than a mathematical simplification for there is "many possible integrals that might be maximized when L grows and choosing among them is not easy." (Samuelson 1965, p. 494). The earliest attempt to solve this problem was to maximize the consumption per person in steady state which led to the golden rule.

As with the Ramsey problem, we can approach it at two levels: mathematical and economic. Mathematically, the solution is obtained by noticing that c^* is a function of k^* and determining the value of k^* that maximizes c^*. For this simple growth model, the value is given by the well-known condition that $f'(k^{**}) = n$. Since, in this golden rule steady state, $sf(k^{**}) = nk^{**} = f'(k^{**})k^{**}$, it can be shown by simple expansion that total savings and investment in the economy is equal to total income earned by capital.

The question then arises what type of value judgment is involved in choosing this criteria. The papers by Pearce (1962) and Samuelson (1967) point out to the dangers of seeing the golden rule as a social optimum as other paths can dominate the golden rule one in terms of consumption and utility. As Phelps (1987) writes in a survey of the golden rules, one can give maxmin rejoinders to these refutations, but an unambiguous way to think of the problem was the one suggested by Koopmans. Assume that an international organization like the World Bank offers an economy any amount of capital on the condition that once they accept the offer, they are bound to keep the capital-labor ratio at the post-gift level. What is the amount of capital that the society should accept? Given that we are strictly steady-states, each of which could be painlessly attained, the condition is that it should choose the capital needed to attain the golden rule. It is a rule that forces the future generations to sacrifice to the interests of succeeding generations what they accept out of the present generation. This then is the value judgment underlying the rule and it forewarns against the dangers of oversaving.

The next extension was to establish a criterion to choose between paths outside the steady state. This led to the voluminous literature on optimal control models which are best discussed using the Hamiltonian formulation.

7.3 The Hamiltonian Formulation and Control Theory

In the discussion of Ramsey's formulation of the optimal savings problem, we saw how he simplified the problem by a very clever change of variables. The coordinates in which it is natural to formulate a problem may not be the one that is most appropriate for solving it. One of the advantages of the variational approach is that we could use any system of coordinates that assists us in solving the problem, provided that they are finite, single valued, and differentiate with respect to time.

So formulated the problem is said to be expressed in terms of generalized coordinates, q_i ($i = 1, \ldots, n$) where n is the dimension of the configuration space. The evolution of q over time is over the extremal of the integral

$$\int L(q, \dot{q}, t) \, dt$$

where $L(q, \dot{q}, t)$ is called the Lagrangian and the extremal satisfies the Euler–Lagrange equations. The ability to solve problems in analytical dynamics frequently depends on finding an appropriate coordinate system to solve the equations,

$$\frac{d}{dt}\left(\frac{\partial L}{\partial \dot{q}_i}\right) = \frac{\partial L}{\partial q_i} \quad (i = 1, \ldots, n). \tag{7.11}$$

From its roots in mechanics, it is traditional to refer to q_i as generalized velocities and $\partial L / \partial \dot{q}_i = p_i$ (by definition) as generalized momenta. There is one change of co-ordinates that is so useful and so widely used that the transformed coordinates are called the *canonical coordinates*. We will follow Arnold (1989, pp. 61–65) in deriving the canonical coordinates from the Legendre transformations. Confining to scalar functions for convenience, the Legendre transformation of a convex function, $z = f(x)$, is a new function g of a new variable p, constructed from f as follows. Draw the curve of f in the $x - z$ plane as in Fig. 7.2. If p is any number, draw the straight line $z = px$. We define $x(p)$ as the point at which the curve is farthest from the straight line in the vertical direction. For each p, the function $F(p, x) = px - f(x)$ has a maximum with respect to x at $x(p)$. We can now set $g(p) = F(p, x(p))$. The point $x(p)$ is defined by the extremal condition, $\dfrac{\partial F}{\partial x} = 0$ or $f'(x) = p$. An interesting property of this transformation is that, if we take the Legendre transformation of $g(p)$ we will get $f(x)$; in other words, the transformation is involutive as its square (transformation applied twice) is identity (Fig. 7.3).

7.3 The Hamiltonian Formulation and Control Theory

Fig. 7.2 Steady state and golden rule for a neo-classical growth model

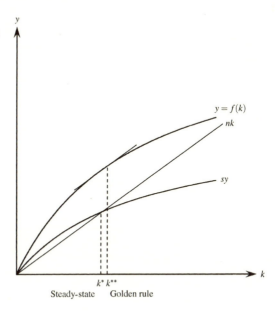

Fig. 7.3 Legendre transformation

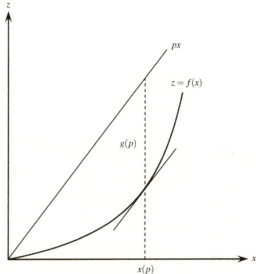

In terms of canonical coordinates of our variational problem, we can write the Euler–Lagrangian equations as $\dot{p}_i = \partial L/\partial q_i$ where $p_i = \partial L/\partial \dot{q}_i$ with the given Lagrangian L assumed to be convex with respect to $\dot{q} = (\dot{q}_1, \ldots, \dot{q}_n)$. Then the

Legendre transformation of the Lagrangian function, viewed as a function of q is $H(p,q,t) = p\dot{q} - L(q,\dot{q},t)$ where $p = (p_1,\ldots,p_n)$ and $q = (q_1,\ldots,q_n)$.

We can then conclude that *the system of n Euler–Lagrange equations* (7.11) *is equivalent to the system of 2n first order equations*

$$\dot{p}_i = -\frac{\partial H}{\partial q_i}, \tag{7.12}$$

$$\dot{q}_i = -\frac{\partial H}{\partial p_i} \tag{7.13}$$

where the Hamiltonian

$$H(p,q,t) = \sum_{i=1}^{n} p_i \dot{q}_i - L(q_1,\ldots,q_n,\dot{q}_1,\ldots,\dot{q}_n,t) \tag{7.14}$$

is the Legendre transformation of the Lagrangian function.

One of the advantages of the Hamiltonian formulation is that we are only dealing with first order partial differential equations; this is to be contrasted with the Euler–Lagrange equations which we know to be of second order. Another advantage of this approach is that, even where exact analytical solutions cannot be found, qualitative results can be derived and stability of particular solutions examined; this is particularly useful in economics where we can only define the functions as belonging to certain general classes.

One extension of the Hamiltonian approach that has found wide use in economics is to make the dynamics of the model depend not only on the coordinates of the system but also on a variable (policy instrument) whose value can be controlled within bounds. This formulation leads to the optimal control models. The position in the state space as given by its coordinates cannot be changed, unlike the control variable, except through the evolution of the system and so the coordinates are called state variables. Here the problem is formulated as

$$\max \int_0^T L(x,u,t)\,ds + B(x(T),T) \tag{7.15}$$

subject to

$$\dot{x} = f(x,u,t), \quad x(0) = \bar{x}. \tag{7.16}$$

Here x is the state variable whose rate of change is given by (7.16) and u is a control variable which is chosen at any instant of time. The Hamiltonian can now be written as

$$H = -L + pf. \tag{7.17}$$

We first maximize the Hamiltonian with respect to the control variable. Assuming that the maximization problem has an interior solution, this is given by the condition,

7.3 The Hamiltonian Formulation and Control Theory

$\partial H/\partial u = 0$. Substituting for the value of u from this condition in (7.17), we get the maximized Hamiltonian, H^*. The co-state equations give the rate of change of x and p

$$\dot{p} = -\frac{\partial H^*}{\partial x} \quad \text{and} \quad \dot{x} = \frac{\partial H^*}{\partial p}. \tag{7.18}$$

The system must also satisfy (bequest) conditions at time T called the transversality conditions,

$$H^*(x,T) = B(x,T), \quad p(T) = B_x(x,T). \tag{7.19}$$

If T is infinite, then the transversality condition becomes

$$\lim_{T \to \infty} p(T)x(T) = 0. \tag{7.20}$$

The differential equations (7.18) are already familiar. If we think of p as a shadow price, then (7.19) and (7.20) have obvious interpretations; the first states that the Hamiltonian should have the value of the required bequest and that the shadow price at T is the marginal contribution to the bequest value of an increase in x while the second states that at infinite time the value of the state variable should be vanish. If the Lagrangian has time entering in an exponential manner, the model can be easily modified to get equations of motion similar to (7.18) above but we will show it with an example (see (7.24) below).

We can apply these models to Solow type growth model. We already recognized that there are problems in choosing a Lagrangian in the case where labor is growing but let us assume that we want to maximize the integral of the utility of per capita consumption.

$$\max \int_0^\infty e^{-\rho t} u(c)\, ds \quad \text{s.t.} \quad \dot{k} = f(k) - nk - c \tag{7.21}$$

where the Hamiltonian is written as

$$H = u(c) + p(f(k) - nk - c). \tag{7.22}$$

The value of c is chosen to maximize H at any instant of time and setting $\partial H/\partial c = 0$, we get $u'(c) = p$. From this we can get the value of c as $g(p)$. Substituting for c in the Hamiltonian, we get the differential equations as

$$\dot{p} = \rho p - \frac{\partial H^*}{\partial k} = \rho p - p(f'(k) - n) \tag{7.23}$$

and

$$\dot{k} = \frac{\partial H^*}{\partial p} = u'g' - (f(k) - nk - g - pg') = f(k) - nk - c. \tag{7.24}$$

We can examine the condition for steady state where $\dot{k}$ and $\dot{p}$ are zero. From (7.24), we get that $\dot{k}$ is zero when $nk = f(k) - c$ which is the same as for the simple Solow–Swan model if we make the substitution $c = (1-s)f(k)$. From (7.23), we get the condition for $\dot{p} = 0$ when $f'(k) = \rho + n$. This is called the modified golden rule in comparison with the earlier golden rule where there was no discounting.

The Hamiltonian formulation can also be used to reformulate the Ramsey model. Since the Lagrangian is $[B - U(C) - V(L)]$, the Hamiltonian can be written as

$$H = -[B - U(C) - V(L)] + p(t)\dot{K}$$

with C and L as the control variables. From the first order conditions, we get

$$\frac{\partial H}{\partial C} = U'(C) - p(t) = 0; \quad -V'(L) = 0.$$

Writing the values of C and L that satisfy the above equations as C^* and L^*, we can write the maximized Hamiltonian as

$$H^* = -[B - U(C^*) - V(L^*)] + U'(C^*)[F(K) - C^*].$$

Notice that H^* is not explicitly a function of t; since $\partial H/\partial t = dH/dt$, we see that H^* is a constant over time. The constant value can be obtained from considering the case of utility saturation. Then $U(C) = B$ and $U'(t) = 0$ and, by substitution, the constant value of the Hamiltonian is zero. So the Hamiltonian itself is a first integral of the Lagrangian, that is a function that remains constant on the integral curves of the system.

The first integrals are called, for historical reasons, conservation laws. In this case we discovered it by examination but in the next section we state a systematic method for deriving such laws.

7.4 Noether Theorem and Its Implications

We saw that Lagrangian can be expressed in generalized variables. Suppose we transform the configuration space of these variables. We saw that, if the Lagrangian is not an explicit function of time, then a transformation of t to a new variable $\bar{t} = t + \varepsilon$ does not affect the value of the Lagrangian or the Hamiltonian. Another possible transformation is to multiply variables, q_i, by a constant.

The effect of the transformation is to shift the integral curves of the Lagrangian system. Following Arnold (1989, pp. 88–89), we show the shift of $q(t)$ under a transformation h^s to $h^s(q(t))$ in Fig. 7.4 and q changes to $h_*^s(q)$; here s is a parameter representing the transformation. The point q is shifted to $h^s(q)$ and the point $q(t)$ along the original integral curve to $q(s,t) = h^s(q(t))$.

7.4 Noether Theorem and Its Implications

Fig. 7.4 Noether's theorem (Arnold 1989, p. 89)

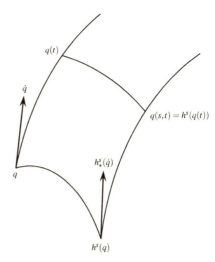

A functional $J(q)$ (see Eq. (7.1)) is invariant under the transformation if $J(q) = J(h^s(q))$ or the functional has the same value along both curves. If we can identify such a transformation, then Noether theorem gives a constructive method to derive the first integrals or conservation laws.

The transformation of the configuration space can be modeled as we did in Chap. 2. In the Fig. 2.4, the shift of the curve is dependent on one parameter, s. In the discussion of the Ramsey model, the parameter was t as we saw how the Lagrangian is invariant to a shift in the origin of time. In other models, we may shift, in addition to t, the origin and units of the other economic variables. Thus, in general, the transformation of the configuration space may depend on r parameters, $\varepsilon = (\varepsilon_1, \ldots, \varepsilon_r)$.

The transformed variables can be expressed as

$$\bar{t} = \phi(x,t,\varepsilon); \quad \bar{x}_k = \psi^k(x_1,\ldots,x_n).$$

As we did in Chap. 2, we can associate an infinitesimal generator with each of the above transformations,

$$\tau_s(x,t) = \frac{\partial \phi}{\partial \varepsilon_s}\bigg|_{\varepsilon=0}; \quad \xi_s^k(x,t) = \frac{\partial \psi_k}{\partial \varepsilon_s}\bigg|_{\varepsilon=0}. \tag{7.25}$$

The curve $x(t)$ is mapped to $\bar{x}(\bar{t})$. The functional

$$J(x) = \int_a^b L(x,\dot{x},t)\,ds$$

is said to be *absolutely invariant* under the transformation if $J(x) = J(\bar{x})$.

The Noether theorem states: *If the functional $J(x)$ is invariant under the r parameter transformations then,*

$$\sum_{i=1}^{n} L_{\dot{x}_i}\xi_s^i + \left(L - \sum_{i=1}^{n} \dot{x}_i L_{\dot{x}_i}\right)\tau_s = 0 \quad (s = 1,\ldots,r) \tag{7.26}$$

is r constants along any extremal of $J(x)$. They provide the r first integrals. Note that the term in parenthesis is the Hamiltonian, $-H$, of the problem.

Consider the special case where $L(x,\dot{x})$ is not an explicit function of t. Then consider a parameter transformation, $\bar{x} = x$, and $\bar{t} = t + \varepsilon$. Now, with $s = 1$, $\xi^i = 0$ and $\tau = 1$. Substituting in (7.26), it is evident that H is a constant. As an application of this special case, consider the problem in mechanics where $L = T - U$ where T, kinetic energy, is a quadratic function in velocity and U, potential energy, is function of position. Then as the Lagrangian is not an explicit function of t, the Hamiltonian is constant along the extremal and, because kinetic energy is a quadratic function, it can be shown that $H = T + U$. So we have derived the classical conservation of energy. Other conservation laws of classical mechanics, like conservation of linear momentum, can also be derived from the symmetry of the system.

In classical physics, the Hamiltonian formulation is one of three possible formulations and the laws like the conservation of energy and momentum are derived independently of this formulation even if it provides further intuition into the problem.

The situation with regard to modern physics—relativistic and quantum dynamics—is different. Some theories have no other formulation; others may have alternate formulations but the Hamiltonian formulation makes explicit the consistency of a theory with other accepted models. So the Hamiltonian formulation and Neother theorem have found extensive applications in modern physics.

But energy as interpreted in these theories is different from its eighteenth century conceptualization just as utility in modern economics is different from what it meant to the utilitarian philosophers. Richard Feynman et al. (1964, Vol. 1, p. 4-2), who received a Nobel prize for his work in this area, is very emphatic: "It is important to realize that in physics today, we have no knowledge of what energy is. We do not have a picture that energy comes in little blobs of a definitive amount. It is not that way. However, there are formulas for calculating some numerical quantity, and when we add it all together it gives "28"—always the same number. It is an abstract thing in that it does not tell us the mechanism or the reasons for various formulas." Further, there is no definite method to arrive at the Lagrangian to begin with. Feynman et al. (1964, Vol. 2, p. 19-8) comments: "You just have to fiddle around with the equations that you know and see if you can get them into the form of the principle of least action."

As we noted earlier, the situation in economics is more complicated than in physics. "Scratch an economist and you find a moralist underneath," began Koopmans' review (1967, p. 96) of intertemporal distribution and optimal growth. We cannot "fiddle around" with the Lagrangians because each of them incorporates a specific intertemporal valuation. In static theory, the utilitarian tradition is to redistribute the consumption stream from the rich to the poor, balancing the gains in social welfare against the costs of productive inefficiency that the process may generate. The basic problem with growth financed by savings and investment is that consumption stream is shifted from the present poor to the future rich; the contemporaneous costs can be easily formulated but the benefit of growth to those who make the sacrifice now is harder to evaluate. We already saw how the skepticism in the interwar years towards the Keynes–Ramsey savings formula and how optimal savings became once more fashionable during the postwar period when the development economists were skeptical of the ability of the local institutions to finance adequate growth. The more recent concern about the exhaustibility of some resources reverses the ethical dilemma once again, as the present generation impoverishes the future ones.

Further, unlike in physics, we cannot assume that the system is moving along an extremal and only along an extremal. Among others, this is one of the issues debated in the theories of business cycles.

7.5 Conservation Laws in von Neumann Model

Consider a consumptionless von Neumann economy where a flow of n goods is produced using stocks of the same n goods. Incremental increase in the stock of each commodity equals output of that commodity as there is no consumption; this assumption also saves us from the moral dilemmas of intergenerational distribution. The vector of capital goods at time t is $\hat{K}_t = (K_t^1, \ldots, K_t^n)$ and the vector of capital formation at time t is $\dot{K}_t = (\dot{K}_t^1, \ldots, \dot{K}_t^n)$ where the dot represents differentiation with respect to time. The transformation relating K_t to $\dot{K}_t$ is

$$F(K_t, \dot{K}_t) = 0. \tag{7.27}$$

We assume that F is homogeneous of degree one, concave and smoothly differentiable. The process is considered to have begun at time $t = 0$, with a capital vector K'_0, and terminates at time T (Fig. 7.5).

If a "truncated" terminal capital vector, $K'_T = (K_T^2, \ldots, K_T^n)$, is specified, then we can define a criterion for intertemporal efficiency in terms of the maximization of K_T^1 subject to K_0 and K'_T.

A diagrammatic representation of a von Neumann model in discrete time, adapted from Dorfman et al. (1958) and Vanek (1968) will give a visual picture of the dynamics. Consider a two good economy with an initial endowment (K_0^1, K_0^2). Depending on the allocation of this resource among the two industries which produce K^1 and K^2, the economy produces a specific output vector $(\dot{K}_0^1, \dot{K}_0^2)$ which in turn gives the capital vector for period 1 as $(K_1^1, K_1^2) = (K_0^1 + \dot{K}_0^1, K_0^2 + \dot{K}_0^2)$.

There are two separate concepts of efficiency involved here: static efficiency and inter-temporal efficiency. Static efficiency requires that the allocation of two

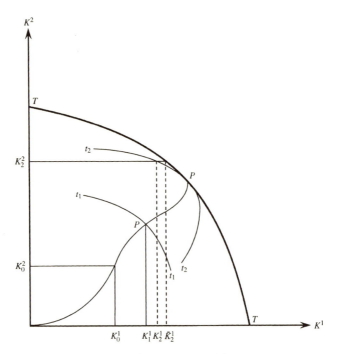

Fig. 7.5 Diagrammatic representation of von-Neumann model

inputs K_0^1 and K_0^2 between two industries should be along the contact curve of the production box diagram. But there are many allocations which will satisfy this condition; each of them will give a different vector $(\dot{K}_0^1, \dot{K}_0^2)$ and hence a different capital vector for period 1. Let the possible capital vectors for period 1 be given by the curve $t_1 t_1$.

Suppose the economy chooses to attain a point P_1 on $t_1 t_1$. Repeating the arguments above, we notice that the possible outputs in the period 1 that meets static efficiency generate a curve $t_2 t_2$ of possible capital stocks in period 2. But the economy need not be at P_1 in period 1; if it was at another point on $t_1 t_1$, then the new K_1 would in turn generate a new curve $t_2' t_2'$ (not shown on diagram) of all capital stocks in period 2. The envelope of all such curves is $T_2 T_2$. The curve $t_2 t_2$ is tangent to $T_2 T_2$ at P_2.

The objective is to maximize K_2^1, given that $K_2^2 = \overline{K}_2^2$. If the economy has chosen K_1^1 in period 1, it would end up in K_2^1. But the diagram shows that there is another point of $t_1 t_1$ that would have a higher capital $\overline{K}_2^1$ which dominates K_2^1. Hence, choice of P_1 in period 1 is appropriate if the objective was to attain the terminal capital stock P_2. Given initial capital, the transformation function (7.27), the truncated terminal vector K_T' and the objective of maximizing K_T^1 the unique intertemporal efficient path can be derived analytically.

7.5 Conservation Laws in von Neumann Model

The variational problem in continuous time can be written as:

$$\max \int_0^T \dot{K}_t^1 \, dt$$

subject to $F(K_t, \dot{K}_t) = 0$ and the boundary condition.

The Lagrangian is $K_t dt + \lambda F(K_t, \dot{K}_t)$ and, from the previous analysis, we know that the Hamiltonian is a constant along the extremal. So, by substitution and expansion,

$$-H = L_t - \sum_{j=1}^n \dot{K}_t^1 \frac{\partial L_t}{\partial \dot{K}_t^j}$$

$$= -\lambda_t \sum \frac{\partial F}{\partial \dot{K}_t^j} = \text{constant}.$$

Samuelson points out that $-\dfrac{\partial F}{\partial \dot{K}_t^j}$ can be thought of as the price of the jth commodity; since the output of that commodity in the economy is $\dot{K}_t^j$, it follows immediately that the sum of their products is the national income, Y_t. Hence from the constancy of the Hamiltonian, we get the first conservation law:

$$\lambda_t Y_t = \text{constant}. \tag{7.28}$$

Samuelson then goes on to derive a second conservation law relating to wealth. He argues, following Dorfman, Samuelson, and Solow (1958) that $\partial F / \partial K_t^j = R_t^j$, the rental of capital; note that $Y_t = \sum R_t^j K_t^j$. Writing out the Euler equations and simplifying, he shows that

$$-\frac{\dot{\lambda}_t}{\lambda_t} = \frac{R_t^j}{P_t^j} + \frac{\dot{P}_t^j}{P_t^j}.$$

Since this is true for all j, it shows that the right hand side is independent of j. Differentiating wealth, $W_t = \sum P_t^j K_t^j$ and through some simple algebraic manipulation, he shows that

$$r_t = \frac{\sum \left(\dfrac{R_t^j}{P_t^j} + \dfrac{\dot{P}_t^j}{P_t^j}\right) P_t^j K_t^j}{\sum P_t^j K_t^j} = -\frac{\dot{\lambda}_t}{\lambda_t}.$$

So the wealth at time t equals

$$W_t = W_0 \int_0^t e^{rs} \, ds = \frac{W_0 \lambda_0}{\lambda_t}.$$

It follows that the second conservation law is

$$\lambda_t W_t = \text{constant.} \quad (7.29)$$

Dividing (7.29) by (7.28), we find that the capital output ratio is a constant.

$$\frac{W_t}{Y_t} = \text{constant.} \quad (7.30)$$

In deriving the second conservation law, Samuelson did not directly use the symmetry of the system as he did for the derivation of the first. Sato (1981) showed, using a more general formulation of the Noether theorem, that it arises from transformations whose infinitesimal generators are constant multiples of the inputs.

7.6 Measurement of National Income and Income-Wealth Ratios

In the national income accounts, the value of current investment is added to current consumption to arrive at a measure called the net national product. We then make intertemporal and international comparisons. Yet when we enquire into the welfare theoretic interpretation of national income, we run into many problems. Samuelson (1961, p. 51) pointed out some of them: "Our rigorous search for a meaningful welfare concept has led to a rejection of all current income concepts and has ended up with something close to wealth." This comes about because investment is not an end in itself but only valued for future consumption that it facilitates.

Weitzman (1976, p. 156) argues that Samuelson's pessimism must be moderated as "the welfare justification of net national product is just the idea that in theory it is a proxy for the present discounted value of future consumption." Kemp and Long (1982) has generalized the result to a model with less restrictive assumptions than that of Weitzman.

Define k_t as an n-vector representing the stock of n capital goods and $\dot{k}_t$ as the vector of investments. The utility that the society can attain is a function of k_t and $\dot{k}_t$. So the welfare functional can be written as

$$J = \int_0^\infty e^{-\rho t} U(k, \dot{k}) \, dt$$

subject to appropriate initial conditions. We write the Lagrangian as $e^{-\rho t} U(k_t, \dot{k}_t)$. From the Euler–Lagrange equations, we get (Sato 1985, p. 368) that

$$\dot{p}_i = -\frac{\partial U}{\partial k_i} + \rho p_i \quad \text{where} \quad p_i = -\frac{\partial U}{\partial \dot{k}_i}. \quad (7.31)$$

Assume that t and k_i are subject to a one parameter (ε) transformation, with τ and ξ^i as before, the infinitesimal generators. To derive the conservation laws, we have to use the more general version of the Noether theorem that we mentioned in the last section. Instead of assuming that $L(k,\dot{k},t)$ is invariant, we will assume, for the one parameter case, that

$$L\left(\bar{k},\frac{d\bar{k}}{d\bar{t}},\bar{t}\right)\frac{d\bar{t}}{dt} - L(k,\dot{k},t) = \sum_i^n \varepsilon \frac{d\phi_s}{dt}.$$

The conservation law is then

$$\Omega = -H\tau + \frac{\partial L}{\partial \dot{k}_i}\xi^i - \phi \quad \text{where} \quad H = -L = \sum \dot{k}\frac{\partial L}{\partial \dot{k}_i}. \tag{7.32}$$

Though it does not involve any concepts that we have not already discussed, the derivation of the conservation law is rather long and the reader is referred to Sato (1985) for details. In the end we get, assuming $\tau = 1$ and $\xi^i = 0$, that

$$U(t) - \sum \dot{k}^i \frac{\partial U}{\partial \dot{k}} = \rho \int_t^\infty e^{-\rho(s-t)} U(s)\,ds. \tag{7.33}$$

Given our social valuation function, the left-hand side is the utility measure of income and the right hand side the utility measure of wealth. So for the standard case where $\rho > 0$,

$$\frac{\text{income}(t)}{\text{wealth}(t)} = \rho.$$

7.7 Conclusion

In this chapter we have examined the development of intertemporal optimization in economics. From the publication of the pioneering paper by Ramsey, the economic profession has attempted to grapple with the problem of equitable intertemporal distributions. While the Solow–Swan models were originally descriptive models, it permitted calculation of optimal growth paths based on specific social valuation functions. The Hamiltonian formulation provides an intuitive interpretation of the qualitative properties of these models. What was not obvious even then was that there are simple scalar functions that remained constant along the optimal trajectory and that these functions can be derived using Noether theorem. Further, it was found that they have simple interpretations in terms of the utility of income and wealth. Assuming that the measures of income and wealth that we have corresponds closely to the theoretical concepts, then we can examine the optimality of the system by checking the constancy of the ratios of income to wealth.

References to Part I

Arnold, K.J. (1973). Rawls' principle of just saving. *Swedish Journal of Economics*, 75, 323–335.
Afriat, S.N. (1984). The true index. In A. Ingham, & A.M. Ulph (Eds.), *Demand, equilibrium and trade: essays in honor of Ivor Pearce*. London: McMillian.
Allen, R.G.D. (1975). *Index numbers in theory and practice*. London: Macmillian.
Arnold, V.I. (1973). *Ordinary differential equations*. Cambridge, MA: MIT Press.
Arnold, V.I. (1989). *Mathematical methods of classical mechanics*. New York: Springer.
Banerjee, K.S. (1975). *Cost of living index numbers*. New York: Marcel Dekker.
Bowley, A.L. (1928). Notes on index numbers. *Economic Journal*, 38, 216–237.
Carlson, S. (1939). *A study on the pure theory of production*, Stockholm economic studies, no. 9. London: P.S. King & Sons.
Clapham, J.H. (1922a). Of empty economic boxes. *Economic Journal*, 32, 305–314.
Clapham, J.H. (1922b). The economic boxes: a rejoinder. *Economic Journal*, 32, 560–563.
Cohen, A. (1931). *An introduction to the Lie theory of one-parameter groups*. Boston, MA: Heath.
Cornes, R. (1992). *Duality and modern economics*. Cambridge: Cambridge University Press.
Darrough, M.N., & Southey, C. (1977). Duality in consumer theory made simple: the revealing of Roy's identity. *Canadian Journal of Economics*, 10, 307–317.
Deaton, A., & Muelbauer, J. (1980). *Economics and consumer behavior*. Cambridge: Cambridge University Press.
Diewert, W.E. (1981). The economic theory of index numbers: a survey. In A. Deaton (Ed.), *Essays in the theory and measurement of consumer behaviour in honour of Sir Richard Stone*. London: Cambridge University Press.
Diewert, W.E. (1982). Duality approaches to microeconomic theory. In K.J. Arrow, & M.D. Intriligator (Eds.), *Handbook of mathematical economics*, vol. II (pp. 535–599). Amsterdam: North Holland.
Diewert, W.E. (1987). Index numbers. In J. Eatwell, M. Milgate, & P. Newman (Eds.), *The new palgrave: a dictionary of economics*. London: Macmillian.
Dirac, P.A.M. (1958). *The priniciples of quantum mechanics*. Oxford: Clarendon Press.
Dixit, A.K. (1976). *The theory of equilibrium growth*. London: Oxford University Press.
Dorfman, R., Samuelson, P.A., & Solow, R.M. (1958). *Linear programming and economic analysis*. New York: McGraw Hill.
Edwards, H.M. (1994). *Advanced calculus: a differential forms approach*. Boston: Birkhauser.
Evans, G.C. (1930). *Mathematical introduction to economics*. New York: McGraw-Hill.
Feynman, R.P., Leighton, R.B., & Sands, M. (1964). *Feynman lectures in physics*. Massachusetts: Addison-Wesley.
Fisher, I. (1922). *The making of index numbers*. Boston: Houghton.
Friedman, M. (1983). *Foundations of space-time theories: relativity physics and philosophy of science*. NJ: Princeton University Press.

Frisch, R. (1936). Annual surveys of general economic theory: the problem of index numbers. *Econometrica*, *4*, 1–38.
Frisch, R. (1965). *Theory of production*. Chicago: Rand-McNally.
Gelfand, I.M., & Fomin, S.V. (1963). *Calculus of variations*. Englewood Cliffs, NJ: Prentice-Hall.
Goldman, S.M., & Uzawa, H. (1964). A note on seperability in demand analysis. *Econometrica*, *32*, 387–398.
Hanoch, G. (1975). Production or demand models with direct or indirect implicit addictivity. *Econometrica*, *43*, 395–420.
Hicks, J.R. (1946). *Value and capital*, 2nd edn. Oxford: Clarendon Press.
Hicks, J.R. (1969). Direct and indirect addictivity. *Econometrica*, *37*, 353–354.
Houthakker, H.S. (1960). Addicitive preferences. *Econometrica*, *28*, 244–257.
Houthakker, H.S. (1965). A note on self-dual preferences. *Econometrica*, *33*, 797–801.
Johnson, W.E. (1913). The pure theory of utility curves. *Economic Journal*, *23*, 483–513.
Katzner, D.W. (1970). *Static demand theory*. New York: McMillian.
Kemp, M.C., & Long, N.V. (1982). On evaluation of social income in a dynamic economy: variations on the Samuelsonian theme. In G.R. Feiwel (Ed.), *Samuelson and neoclassical economics*. Boston: Kluwer-Nijhoff.
Keynes, J.M. (1930). *A treatise on money*. London: McMillian.
Klein, M. (1972). *Mathematical thought from ancient to modern times*. New York: Oxford University Press.
Konus, A.A. (1939). The problem of the true index of the cost of living (English translation of 1924 article). *Econometrica*, *7*, 10–29.
Koopmans, T.C. (1967). Intertemporal distribution and 'optimal' aggregate economic growth. In *Ten economic studies in the tradition of Irving Fisher*. New York: Wiley.
Lau, L.J. (1969). Duality and the structure of utility preferences. *Journal of Economic Theory*, *1*, 374–396.
Lau, L.J. (1978). Applications of profit functions. In M. Fuss, & D. Mc-Fadden (Eds.), *Production economics: a dual approach to theory and applications*, vol. 1. Amsterdam: North-Holand.
Marshall, A. (1920). *Principles of economics: an introductory volume*. London: McMillian.
Minhas, B.S. (1963). *An international comparison of factor costs and factor use*. Amsterdam: North-Holland.
Olver, P.J. (1986). *Applications of Lie groups to differential equations*. New York: Springer.
Olver, P.J. (1995). *Equivalence, invariants, and symmetry*. Cambridge: Cambridge University Press.
Pearce, I.F. (1962). The end of the golden age in Solovia. *American Economic Review*, *52*, 1088–1097.
Phelps, E.S. (1987). Golden rule. In J. Eatwell, M. Milgate, & P. Neuman (Eds.), *New pelgrave: a dictionary of economics*. London: McMillian.
Pigou, A.C. (1922). Empty economic boxes: a reply. *Economic Journal*, *32*, 16–30.
Pollak, R.A. (1971). Additive utility functions and linear engel curves. *The Review of Economic Studies*, *37*, 401–413.
Ramsey, F. (1928). A mathematical theory of saving. *Economic Journal*, *38*, 543–559.
Richter, M.K. (1966). Invariance axioms and economic indexes. *Econometrica*, *34*, 739–755.
Robertson, D.H. (1924). Those empty economic boxes. *Economic Journal*, *34*, 16–30.
Russell, R.R. (1964). *The empirical evaluation of theoretically plausible demand functions*, Ph.D. Dissertation. Harvard University, Cambridge, MA.
Samuelson, P.A. (1938). A note on the pure theory of consumer's behavior. *Economical*, *5*, 62–71.
Samuelson, P.A. (1947). *Foundations of economic analysis*. Cambridge, MA: Harvard University Press.
Samuelson, P.A. (1950). The problem of integrability in utility theory. *Economica*, *17*, 355–385.
Samueslon, P.A. (1961). The evaluation of social income: capital formation and wealth. In F.A. Lutz, & D.C. Hague (Eds.), *Theory of capital*. London: McMillian.
Samuelson, P.A. (1965). A catenary turnpike theorem involving consumption and the golden rule. *American Economic Review*, *55*, 486–496.

Samuelson, P.A. (1967). Turnpike refutation of the golden rule in the welfare-maximizing many year plan. In K. Shell (Ed.), *Essays in the theory of optimal economic growth*. Cambridge: MIT Press.

Samuelson, P.A. (1969). Corrected formulation of direct and indirect additivity. *Econometrica, 37*, 355–359.

Samuelson, P.A. (1970). Law of conservation of capital-output ratio in closed von Neumann systems. *Proceedings of the National Academy of Science, Applied Mathematical Science, 67*, 1477–1479.

Samuelson, P.A., & Solow, R.M. (1956). A complete capital model involving heterogeneous captial goods. *Quarterly Journal of Economics, 70*, 537–567.

Samuelson, P.A., & Swamy, S. (1974). Invariant economic index numbers and canaoncial duality: survey and synthesis. *American Economic Review, 64*, 566–593.

Sato, R. (1974). On the separable class of non-homothetic CES functions. *Economic Studies Quarterly, 25*, 42–55.

Sato, R. (1976). Self-dual preferences. *Econometrica, 44*, 1017–1032.

Sato, R. (1977a). Homothetic and non-homothetic CES functions. *American Economic Review, 67*, 559–569.

Sato, R. (1977b). The implicit formulation and non-homothetic structure of utility functions. In H. Albach, E. Helmstadter, & R. Henn (Eds.), *Qualitative wirtshcaftsfors chung: W. Krelle zum 60. Geburstag*. Tubingen: Mohr.

Sato, R. (1981). *Theory of technical change and economic invariance: application of Lie groups*. New York: Academic Press.

Sato, R. (1985). The invariance principle and income-wealth conservation laws. *Journal of Econometrics, 30*, 365–389. Reprint (1990) In R. Sato, & R. Ramchandran (Eds.), *Conservation laws and symmetry: applications to economics and finance* (pp. 71–106). Norwell, MA: Kluwer.

Sato, R. (1990). The invariance principle and income-wealth conservation laws. In R. Sato, & R. Ramachandran, *Conservation laws and symmetry*. Boston:Kluwer

Sato, R., & Matsushita, M. (1989). Estimation of self-dual demand functions: an international comaprison. In R. Sato, & T. Negishi (Eds.), *Developments in Japanese economics*. Tokyo: Academic Press.

Sato, R., & Ramachandran, R. (1974). Models of optimal endogenous technical progress, scale effect, and duality of production functions, Discussion Paper, Department of Economics, Brown University, Providence, RI

Schneider, E. (1934). *Theorie der production*. Vienna: J. Springer.

Shepherd, R.W. (1953). *Cost and production fucntions*. Princeton, NJ: Princeton University Press.

Solow, R.M. (1957). Technical change and the aggregte production function. *Review of Economic Statistics, 39*, 312–320.

Silberberg, E. (1990). *The structure of economics: a mathematical analysis*. New York: McGraw Hill.

Sraffa, P. (1926). The laws of return under competitive conditions. *Economic Journal, 36*, 535–550.

Stephani, H, & MacCullum, M. (1989). *Differential equations: their solution using symmetries*. Cambridge: Cambridge Unviversity Press.

Stigler, G.J. (1961). Economic problems in measuring changes in productivity. *Output, input, and productivity, measurement, conference on research in income and wealth* (pp. 47–63). Princeton, NJ: Princeton University Press.

Vanek, J. (1968). *Maximal economic growth*. Ithaca, NY: Cornell University Press.

Varian, H.R. (1984). *Microeconomic analysis*. New York: W.W. Norton & Co.

Weitzman, M.L. (1976). On the welfare significance of national product in a dynamic economy. *Quarterly Journal of Economics, 90*, 156–162.

Whitaker, J.K. (1990). Marshall's theories of competitive price. In R.M. Tullberg (Ed.), *Alfred Marshall in retrospect* (pp. 29–48). Vermont: Edward Elgar.

Yoglam, I. (1988). *Felix Klein and Sophus Lie: evolution of the idea of symmetry in the nineteenth century*. Boston: Birkhauser.

Zellner, A., & Revanker, N.S. (1969). Generalized production functions. *Review of Economic Studies, 36*, 241–250.

Part II
Recent Developments

Chapter 8
The Invariance Principle and Income-Wealth Conservation Laws*

8.1 Introduction

In the early part of the nineteenth century William Rowan Hamilton discovered a principle which can be generalized to encompass many areas of physics, engineering and applied mathematics. Hamilton's principle roughly states that the evolution in time of a dynamic system takes place in such a manner that integral of the difference between the kinetic and potential energies for the system is stationary. If the "action" integral is free of the time variable, the sum of the kinetic and potential energies, the Hamiltonian, is constant—the conservation law of the total energy.

In the early part of this century Emmy Noether (1918) discovered the fundamental invariance principle known as the *Noether Theorem*.[1] This principle not only extended the idea of Hamilton and the conservation law of total energy, but also provided the formal methodology to study the general "invariance" problem of a dynamic system. Influenced by the work of Klein (1918) and of Lie (1891) on the transformation properties of differential equations under continuous (Lie) groups, Noether had the ingenious insight of combining the methods of the formal calculus of variation with those of Lie group theory. Since the first application of the Noether invariance principle to particle mechanics by Bessel-Hagen (1921), this new area of mathematics has exhibited remarkable development in the last 50 years (Klein 1918, Lie 1891, Logan 1977, Moser 1979, Nôno 1968, Rund 1966, Sagan 1969, Whittaker 1937, Gelf and Fomin 1963, Lovelock and Rund 1975, Nôno and Mimura 1975, 1976, 1977, 1978).

---

*This chapter is a revised and expanded version of Sato (1985) and the author wishes to express his appreciation to Paul A. Samuelson, William A. Barnett, Hal R. Varian, Gilbert Suzawa, Takayuki Nôno, Fumitake Mimura, and Shigeru Maeda for their helpful comments on an earlier version of this chapter.

[1] Her paper has recently been translated into English by Tavel, who also supplies a brief motivation and historical sketch (see Noether (1918)).

The study of economic conservation laws is still in its infancy compared with its counterparts in physics and engineering. Yet this is an area where rapid progress is being made. In economics the conservation law has its roots in Ramsey (1928). But it was Samuelson (1970a,b) who first explicitly introduced conservation laws to theoretical economics. The recent work by Weitzman (1976), Sato (1981, 1982), Kemp and Long (1982), Samuelson (1982), Sato, Nôno, and Mimura (1984) and Kataoka (1983) provide an indication of the rapid progress being made in this field and the great interest shown in the analysis of economic conservation laws. In Ramsey (1928), Samuelson (1970a,b, 1982), Weitzman (1976) and Kemp and Long (1982), the authors used the standard invariance condition of the calculus of variation, which is a special case of the Noether invariance principle, while in Sato (1981, 1982) and Sato, Nôno, and Mimura (1984) we employed the Noether invariance principle and, thus, were able to obtain the more general results of "hidden" conservation laws.

The purpose of this paper is to extend the work on economic conservation laws in the direction of uncovering more "hidden" conservation laws. We shall briefly discuss the application of the conservation laws to the econometric estimation of the optimal growth models. However, before we do so, we shall begin with a brief summary of the literature.

In this chapter, the summation convention common in linear algebra and physics according to which an index variable appearing twice in a single term implies summation of that term over all the values of the index is adopted: $a_i x^i = \sum a_i x^i$ ($i = 1, 2, \ldots, n$).

8.2 Brief Summary of the Literature

Ramsey's (1928, p. 547) famous rule of optimal saving is the first reference (implicit) to a conservation law in economics. His rule states that

$$\dot{c} = \frac{dc}{dt} = f(a,c) - x = \frac{B - (U(x) - V(a))}{u(x)} \tag{8.1}$$

where f = production function, a = labor, c = capital, x = consumption, $U(x)$ = utility of consumption, $V(a)$ = disutility of labor, $u(x) = \partial U/\partial x$ = marginal utility of consumption. This rule is an economic version of the law of conservation of energy. Letting L(Lagrangian) $= -(U(x) - V(a))$ and Bliss $B = H$(Hamiltonian), the Ramsey rule is derived from the conservation law,

$$H = B = u(x)\dot{c} + (U(x) - V(a)) = u(x)\dot{c} - L. \tag{8.2}$$

Samuelson (1970a) is the first economist to explicitly introduce conservation laws in theoretical economics. From the analogy of the law of conservation of (physical) energy, kinetic energy + potential energy = constant, Samuelson obtained the *conservation law of the aggregate capital-output ratio* in a neoclassical von Neumann economy, where all output is saved to provide capital formation for the system's growth.

A typical optimization model in modern economics deals with the problem of maximizing

$$\int_0^T L(t,k,\dot{k})\,dt = \int_0^T D(t)U(f(t,k,\dot{k}))\,dt \tag{8.3}$$

where $D(t)$ = discount rate factor, U = utility function, f = consumption possibility function, k = capital-labor ratio and $\dot{k}$ = time derivative of k. Here, we also assume that U and f are neoclassical functions satisfying all the regularity conditions. In his recent work, Weitzman (1976) has derived the invariance condition of the income-wealth ratio in a neoclassical model (8.3) when the welfare of the society is discounted at a constant rate for $T \to \infty$ and f is free of technical progress. A similar result is obtained by such authors as Kemp and Long (1982), Samuelson (1982) and Sato (1982).

The first derivation of economic conservation laws via the application of Noether's theorem and Lie groups is contained in Sato (1981), where some of the existing known results are confirmed, and also several new hidden laws are uncovered. For instance, it is shown (Sato 1981, p. 279) that Samuelson's (1970b) two conservation laws are the only laws globally operating for the von Neumann system of optimal growth. Also in studying the Ramsey and general neoclassical growth models, it was discovered that there exist several new conservation laws operating in the vicinity of the steady state. For example, in the Liviatan–Samuelson model (1969), *the discounted welfare measured in terms of the modified income, which is the sum of production income and rental income is constant* (Sato 1981, p. 264). The problem of how various types of technical progress will affect the conservation laws was studied by Sato, Nôno, and Mimura (1984). By redefining income and supply price of capital, we were able to uncover several "hidden" conservation laws.

In earlier works (e.g. Sato (1981, 1999)), an attempt was made to discover conservation laws which are *independent of the forms of production and utility functions*. In the present paper we intend to incorporate these functions in conservation laws, which will enable us to uncover more hidden invariances.

8.3 A Model with Heterogeneous Capital Goods

Let utility depend on consumption of many goods which in turn depend on a vector of capital goods, $k = (k^1, \ldots, k^n)$, and a vector of investment, $\dot{k} = (\dot{k}^1, \ldots, \dot{k}^n)$, so that

$$U = U(\dot{k}, k). \tag{8.4}$$

Let $U(\dot{k}, k)$ be a strictly concave function with existent partial derivatives, for which

$$U(0,k) < U(0,\bar{k}) = 0 \quad (k \neq \bar{k}),$$

$$U_i(0,\bar{k}) \neq 0, \quad U_i = \frac{\partial U}{\partial \dot{k}^i} \quad (i = 1, \ldots, n). \tag{8.5}$$

The society's problem is to maximize the welfare functional

$$J = \int_0^\infty e^{-\rho t} U(\dot{k}(t), k(t)) \, dt \quad (\rho > 0) \tag{8.6}$$

subject to the appropriate initial conditions. For simplicity we shall write

$$L(t, k, \dot{k}) = e^{-\rho t} U(\dot{k}(t), k(t)). \tag{8.7}$$

The necessary condition for the optimal solution is that the Euler–Lagrange equations vanish:

$$E_i = \frac{\partial L}{\partial k^i} - \frac{d}{dt}\left(\frac{\partial L}{\partial \dot{k}^i}\right) = e^{-\rho t}\frac{\partial U}{\partial k^i} - \frac{d}{dt}\left(e^{-\rho t}\frac{\partial U}{\partial \dot{k}^i}\right)$$

$$= e^{-\rho t}\left[\frac{\partial U}{\partial k^i} + \rho\frac{\partial U}{\partial \dot{k}^i} - \frac{d}{dt}\left(\frac{\partial U}{\partial \dot{k}^i}\right)\right] = 0 \tag{8.8a}$$

which implies that

$$E_i = 0 \iff \frac{\partial U}{\partial k^i} + \rho\frac{\partial U}{\partial \dot{k}^i} - \frac{d}{dt}\left(\frac{\partial U}{\partial \dot{k}^i}\right) = 0 \quad (i = 1, \ldots, n). \tag{8.8b}$$

If we define the supply price of the ith capital as $p^i = -\partial U/\partial \dot{k}^i$, (8.8) states that the time derivative of p^i is equal to

$$\dot{p}^i = -\frac{\partial U}{\partial k^i} + \rho p^i \quad (i = 1, \ldots, n). \tag{8.8c}$$

8.4 Noether'S Theorem (Invariance Principle)[2]

Before we present the analysis of economic conservation laws (hidden or unhidden) associated with the above model, we briefly discuss the mathematical properties of

---

[2] A comprehensive treatment of Noether's theorem and invariance identities is given in Sato (1981, pp. 236–251). Those who are familiar with this aspect of the mathematics can skip this section.

8.4 Noether'S Theorem (Invariance Principle)

Noether's theorem and invariance identities. As this theorem is relatively unknown to economists, we shall begin with the definitions of dynamic symmetry (or invariance).

Let us consider a Lagrange function L, which is twice continuously differentiable in each of its $2n + 1$ arguments. We then have the variational integral

$$J(x) \int_a^b L(t, x(t), \dot{x}(t))\, dt, \tag{8.9}$$

where $x =$ the set of all vector functions $x(t) = (x^1(t), \ldots, x^n(t))$ ($t \in [a,b]$). The type of invariance transformations that will be considered are (technical change) transformations of configuration space, i.e., $(t, x^1, \ldots, x^n)$-space, which depend upon r real, independent (essential) parameters $\varepsilon^1, \ldots, \varepsilon^r$. To be more precise, we require here that the transformations are given by

$$\bar{t} = \phi(t, x, \varepsilon), \quad \varepsilon = (\varepsilon^1, \ldots, \varepsilon^r),$$
$$\bar{x}^i = \psi^i(t, x, \varepsilon) \quad i = 1, \ldots, n. \tag{8.10}$$

In economic terms, ϕ can be considered as "subjective" time (Samuelson 1976), while ψ^i represent "technical" or "taste" change. We assume that

$$\phi(t, x, 0) = t, \quad \psi^i(t, x, 0) = x^i \quad (i = 1, \ldots, n). \tag{8.11}$$

Expanding the right-hand sides of (8.10) in Taylor series around $\varepsilon = 0$, we obtain

$$\bar{t} = t + \tau_s(t, x)\varepsilon^s + O(\varepsilon),$$
$$\bar{x}^i = x^i + \xi_s^i(t, x)\varepsilon^s + O(\varepsilon) \quad (i = 1, \ldots, n),$$
$$s = 1, \ldots, r, \text{ summation convention in force}[3]. \tag{8.12}$$

The principal linear parts τ_s and ξ_s^i are called the *infinitesimal generators* (or *transformations*) of the transformational (8.9) given by[4]

$$\tau_s(t, x) = \frac{\partial \phi}{\partial \varepsilon^s}(t, x, 0), \quad \xi_s^i(t, x) = \frac{\partial \psi^i}{\partial \varepsilon^s}(t, x, 0). \tag{8.13a}$$

---

[3] We adopt the so-called Einstein summation convention (Young (1978, pp. 333–334)). When a lower case Latin index such as $j, h, k, \ldots$ appears twice in a term, summation over that index is implied, the range of summation being $1, \ldots, n$. For example, $a^i x^i$ means $\sum_{i=1}^{n} a^i x^i$.

[4] In many cases the transformations (8.10) may be Lie groups and, hence, (8.13) may be the infinitesimal transformations of a group. However, to study Noether's invariance principle the group property is not necessary. We simply assume the existence of the infinitesimal transformations.

Using the customary symbol of the infinitesimal transformations, we write (8.13a) as

$$X_s = \tau_s(t,x)\frac{\partial}{\partial t} + \xi_s^i(t,x)\frac{\partial}{\partial x^i} + \left(\frac{d\xi_s^i}{dt} - \dot{x}^i\frac{d\tau_s}{dt}\right)\frac{\partial}{\partial \dot{x}^i}. \qquad (8.13b)$$

Definition 8.1 (Dynamic invariance or dynamic symmetry).

(a) The fundamental integral (8.9) is absolutely invariant under the r-parameter family of transformations (8.10) if and only if we have

$$\int_{\bar{t}_1}^{\bar{t}_2} L\left(\bar{t},\bar{x}(\bar{t}),\frac{d\bar{x}(\bar{t})}{d\bar{t}}\right) d\bar{t} - \int_{t_1}^{t_2} L\left(t,x(t),\frac{dx(t)}{dt}\right) dt = O(\varepsilon). \qquad (8.14)$$

(b) Alternatively, the fundamental integral is absolutely invariant if and only if

$$L\left(\bar{t},\bar{x}(\bar{t}),\frac{d\bar{x}(\bar{t})}{d\bar{t}}\right)\frac{d\bar{t}}{dt} - L\left(t,x(t),\frac{dx(t)}{dt}\right) = O(\varepsilon). \qquad (8.15a)$$

Definition 8.2 (Divergence-invariance or invariance with nullity). The fundamental integral is divergence-invariant or invariant up to a divergence term, if there exist r functions Φ_s such that

$$L\left(\bar{t},\bar{x}(\bar{t}),\frac{d\bar{x}(\bar{t})}{d\bar{t}}\right)\frac{d\bar{t}}{dt} - L(t,x(t),\dot{x}(t))$$

$$= \varepsilon^s \frac{d\Phi_s}{dt}(t,x(t)) + O(\varepsilon), \text{ summation convention on } s \qquad (8.15b)$$

with the remaining conditions of Definition 8.1 holding true.

This definition is more general than Definition 8.1 in that the left-hand side of (8.15b) is equal to the sum of the exact differentials multiplied by the essential parameters and to first-order terms in ε. Since the addition of the total exact differentials does *not* change the original Euler–Langrange equations associated with L (see Sagan (1969)), we may call this case the *dynamic symmetry condition with nullity*, or simply *the dynamic invariance with nullity*. Alternatively Definition 8.2 is referred to as "invariance up to an exact differential" (See Rund (1966, p. 73)). Then the fundamental invariance identities are given by

$$X_s L + L\frac{d\tau_s}{dt} = \frac{d\Phi_s}{dt} \qquad (8.16a)$$

or

$$\frac{\partial L}{\partial t}\tau_s + \frac{\partial L}{\partial x^i}\xi_s^i + \frac{\partial L}{\partial \dot{x}^i}\left(\frac{d\xi_s^i}{dt} - \dot{x}^i\frac{d\tau_s}{dt}\right) + L\frac{d\tau_s}{dt} = \frac{d\Phi_s}{dt}.$$

$s = 1, \ldots, r$, summation on i. $\qquad (8.16b)$

(See Sato (1981, p. 244, Eq. (17)) for the derivation of (8.16).)

If the fundamental integral is invariant (either absolutely or up to an exact differential) under an r-parameter family (or group) of continuous transformations, the corresponding Lagrangian must satisfy certain conditions involving the Lagrangian, its derivatives and the infinitesimal generators of the continuous transformations. Using the Euler–Lagrange expressions the resulting transformation of these conditions is usually referred to as Noether's theorem. The importance of this theorem lies in the fact that it allows one to construct quantities which are constant along any extremal, that is, a curve which satisfies the Euler–Lagrange equations. Hence, it allows one to obtain relations which may be interpreted as "conservation laws."

We can now present (Sato 1981):

Noether's Invariance Theorem. If the fundamental integral of a problem in the calculus of variations is divergence-invariant under the r-parameter family of transformations, then r distinct quantities Ω_s ($s = 1, \ldots, r$) are constant along any extremal.

In physical and economic applications, those quantities are thus interpreted as the "conservation laws" of the system, where

$$\Omega_s = -H\tau_s + \frac{\partial L}{\partial \dot{x}^i}\xi_s^i - \Phi_s = \text{constant} \quad (s = 1, \ldots, r) \tag{8.17a}$$

where H is the Hamiltonian defined by

$$H = -L + \dot{x}^i \frac{\partial L}{\partial \dot{x}^i}. \tag{8.17b}$$

(See Sato (1981, pp. 242–251) for proof.)

8.5 Income-Wealth Conservation Laws

Using Noether's invariance principle we are now in a position to study the dynamic symmetry conditions in the heterogeneous capital model. Here we require that t and k^i are subjected to the transformations

$$\bar{t} = \phi(t, k, \varepsilon), \quad \varepsilon = (\varepsilon^1, \ldots, \varepsilon^r),$$
$$\bar{k}^i = \psi^i(t, k, \varepsilon) \quad (i = 1, \ldots, n) \tag{8.18a}$$

and, hence, the infinitesimal transformations are given by

$$X_s = \tau_s(t,k)\frac{\partial}{\partial t} + \xi_s^i(t,k)\frac{\partial}{\partial k^i} + \left(\frac{d\xi_s^i}{dt} - \dot{k}^i\frac{d\tau_s}{dt}\right)\frac{\partial}{\partial \dot{k}^i}. \tag{8.18b}$$

We are interested in finding the dynamic symmetry conditions

$$\int_{\bar{t}_1}^{\bar{t}_2} e^{-\rho \bar{t}} U\left[\bar{k}(\bar{t}), \frac{dk(\bar{t})}{dt}\right] d\bar{t} - \int_{t_1}^{t_2} e^{-\rho t} U\left[k(t), \frac{dk(t)}{dt}\right] dt$$
$$= \varepsilon^s \Phi_s(t, k(t)) + O(\varepsilon). \tag{8.19}$$

By applying the infinitesimal transformation (8.18b) on (8.7) and using the fundamental invariance identities (8.16), we obtain

$$e^{-\rho t}\left[-\rho U \tau + \frac{\partial U}{\partial k^i}\xi^i + \frac{\partial U}{\partial \dot{k}^i}\left(\frac{d\xi^i}{dt} - \dot{k}^i\frac{d\tau}{dt}\right) + U\frac{d\tau}{dt}\right] = \frac{d\Phi}{dt}, \tag{8.20a}$$

or

$$\left(U - \dot{k}^i\frac{\partial U}{\partial \dot{k}^i}\right)\frac{d\tau}{dt} = \rho U \tau - \frac{\partial U}{\partial k^i}\xi^i - \frac{\partial U}{\partial \dot{k}^i}\frac{d\xi^i}{dt} + e^{\rho t}\frac{d\Phi}{dt}. \tag{8.20b}$$

Since we assume that we are dealing with a one-parameter transformation group, i.e., $s = 1$, we omit the subscript 1 from τ_1, ξ_1^i etc. but the summation notation is maintained.

From the invariance principle (8.17a) the conservation law is now derived as

$$\Omega = \left(e^{-\rho t}U - e^{-\rho t}\dot{k}^i\frac{\partial U}{\partial \dot{k}^i}\right)\tau + e^{-\rho t}\frac{\partial U}{\partial \dot{k}^i}\xi^i - \Phi = \text{constant}, \tag{8.21a}$$

or

$$\frac{d\Omega}{dt} = -\rho e^{-\rho t}\left(U - \dot{k}^i\frac{\partial U}{\partial \dot{k}^i}\right)\tau + e^{-\rho t}\frac{d}{dt}\left(U - \dot{k}^i\frac{\partial U}{\partial \dot{k}^i}\right)\tau$$
$$+ e^{-\rho t}\left(U - \dot{k}^i\frac{\partial U}{\partial \dot{k}^i}\right)\frac{d\tau}{dt} - \rho e^{-\rho t}\frac{\partial U}{\partial \dot{k}^i}\xi^i$$
$$+ e^{-\rho t}\frac{d}{dt}\left(\frac{\partial U}{\partial \dot{k}^i}\xi^i\right) - \frac{d\Phi}{dt} = 0. \tag{8.21b}$$

Hence we have

$$\left[\frac{d}{dt}\left(U - \dot{k}^i\frac{\partial U}{\partial \dot{k}^i}\right) + \rho \dot{k}^i\frac{\partial U}{\partial \dot{k}^i}\right]\tau = \rho U \tau - \frac{\partial U}{\partial k^i}\xi^i - \frac{\partial U}{\partial \dot{k}^i}\frac{d\xi^i}{dt} - \left(U - \dot{k}^i\frac{\partial U}{\partial \dot{k}^i}\right)\frac{d\tau}{dt}$$
$$+ e^{\rho t}\frac{d\Phi}{dt} + \left[\frac{\partial U}{\partial k^i} + \rho\frac{\partial U}{\partial \dot{k}^i} - \frac{d}{dt}\left(\frac{\partial U}{\partial \dot{k}^i}\right)\right]\xi^i. \tag{8.21c}$$

The term inside the bracket of the last expression of the right-hand side is zero because of the vanishing condition placed on the Euler–Lagrange equations (8.8b). Eliminating $d\Phi/dt$ between (8.20b) and (8.21b) we obtain our first conservation law

$$\frac{d}{dt}\left(U - \dot{k}^i\frac{\partial U}{\partial \dot{k}^i}\right) = -\rho \dot{k}^i\frac{\partial U}{\partial \dot{k}^i}.$$

8.5 Income-Wealth Conservation Laws

It is easy to identify $U - \dot{k}^i \dfrac{\partial U}{\partial \dot{k}^i}$ as income in utility terms—Marshall–Haig–Kuznets' definition, while

$$-\dot{k}^i \frac{\partial U}{\partial \dot{k}^i} \equiv -\sum_{i=1}^{n} \dot{k}^i \frac{\partial U}{\partial \dot{k}^i} \equiv \sum_{i=1}^{n} p^i \dot{k}^i \tag{8.22a}$$

is the utility-value-of-investment. Hence, this conservation law states that along the optimal path

$$\frac{d}{dt}(\text{income at } t) = \rho \times (\text{utility-value-of-investment at } t), \tag{8.22b}$$

$$(\text{rate of change in income at } t) = \rho \times (\text{utility-value-of-investment at } t) \tag{8.22c}$$

For $\rho > 0$, we have along the optimal path

$$\frac{\dfrac{d}{dt}(\text{income at } t)}{(\text{utility-value-of-investment at } t)} = \rho = \text{constant, for all } t. \tag{8.22d}$$

Our first conservation law is equivalent to what Samuelson (1982) calls a *pseudo-net productivity relation*. The *genuine net-productivity* relation for $i = 1$ can be obtained from

$$y(t) = c(t) + \dot{k}(t) = f(k(t)), \tag{8.23a}$$

$$\frac{dy(t)}{dt} = f'(k(t))\dot{k}(t), \tag{8.23b}$$

$$\dot{y} = r(t)\dot{k}(t), \quad \lim_{t \to \infty} r(t) = \rho. \tag{8.23c}$$

Hence, only in the limit, as $t \to \infty$ will the system settle down to stationary equilibrium at market rate equal to the ρ time-preference parameter.

It should be noted that the utility-value-of-net-capital formation is not equivalent to the time derivative of the utility-value-of-capital. The latter usually includes capital gains, or price changes, while the former does not. The ratio of the utility-value-of-income to the utility-value-of-capital-goods is constant in the present model. We shall later discuss this aspect of the invariance conditions in a von Neumann model of economic growth (Sect. 8.8).

Next we can derive the income-wealth conservation law. Let us assume that

$$\tau = 1, \tag{8.24a}$$

$$\xi^i = 0 \quad (i = 1, \ldots, n). \tag{8.24b}$$

We then get, from (8.20a) and (8.8b), along the optimal path

$$\frac{d\Phi}{dt} = -\rho e^{-\rho t} U. \qquad (8.25a)$$

Also from (8.21b) we have

$$\frac{d\Phi}{dt} = -\rho e^{-\rho t}\left(U - \dot{k}^i \frac{\partial U}{\partial \dot{k}^i}\right) + e^{-\rho t}\frac{d}{dt}\left(U - \dot{k}^i \frac{\partial U}{\partial \dot{k}^i}\right)$$

$$= \frac{d}{dt}\left[e^{-\rho t}\left(U - \dot{k}^i \frac{\partial U}{\partial \dot{k}^i}\right)\right]. \qquad (8.25b)$$

Equating (8.25b) with (8.25a) we obtain

$$\frac{d\Phi}{dt} = \frac{d}{dt}\left[e^{-\rho t}\left(U - \dot{k}^i \frac{\partial U}{\partial \dot{k}^i}\right)\right] = -\rho e^{-\rho t} U \quad (0 \le t \le \infty). \qquad (8.25c)$$

Note that the left-hand side of (8.25c) is equal to

$$\frac{d}{dt}\left[e^{-\rho t}\left(U - \dot{k}^i \frac{\partial U}{\partial \dot{k}^i}\right)\right] = -\frac{dH}{dt} \qquad (8.25d)$$

while the right-hand side of (8.25c) is equal to

$$-\rho e^{-\rho t} U = \frac{\partial L}{\partial t}. \qquad (8.25e)$$

Hence (8.25) shows that

$$\frac{d\Phi}{dt} = \frac{\partial L}{\partial t} = -\frac{dH}{dt}. \qquad (8.25f)$$

The null term Φ now turns out to be equal to the integral of the negative value of the Hamiltonian and to the integral of the Lagrangian function. Alternatively, we can say that the absolute value of the rate of change in the Hamiltonian must be equal to the rate of change in the null term for the entire planning period. Integrating (8.25c), we get the null term as

$$\Phi\Big|_t^\infty = e^{-\rho s}\left[U(s) - \dot{k}^i(s)\frac{\partial U(s)}{\partial \dot{k}^i(s)}\right]\Big|_t^\infty = -\rho \int_t^\infty e^{-\rho s} U(s)\,ds \qquad (8.26a)$$

or

$$\Phi\Big|_\infty^t = \rho \int_t^\infty e^{-\rho s} U(s)\,ds. \qquad (8.26b)$$

By the concavity assumption on U and by the transversality condition, we have

$$e^{-\rho s}\left[U(s) - \dot{k}^i(s)\frac{\partial U(s)}{\partial \dot{k}^i(s)}\right] \to 0 \quad \text{as } s \to \infty. \qquad (8.27)$$

8.5 Income-Wealth Conservation Laws

Hence, (8.26a) becomes

$$-e^{-\rho s}\left[U(s) - \dot{k}^i(s)\frac{\partial U(s)}{\partial \dot{k}^i(s)}\right]_{s=t} = -\rho \int_t^\infty e^{-\rho s} U(s)\,ds \qquad (8.28a)$$

or

$$e^{-\rho t}\left[U(t) - \dot{k}^i(t)\frac{\partial U(t)}{\partial \dot{k}^i(t)}\right] = \rho \int_t^\infty e^{-\rho s} U(s)\,ds. \qquad (8.28b)$$

Multiplying both sides of (8.28b) by $e^{\rho t}$, we get the conservation law

$$U(t) - \dot{k}^i(t)\frac{\partial U(t)}{\partial \dot{k}^i(t)} = \rho \int_t^\infty e^{-\rho(s-t)} U(s)\,ds. \qquad (8.29a)$$

The left-hand side of the above is nothing but the utility measure of "income," while the right-hand side is the utility measure of "wealth." Hence, we have

$$\text{income}\,(t) = \rho\;\text{wealth}\,(t) \quad (0 \le t \le \infty). \qquad (8.29b)$$

For $\rho > 0$, we have the income-wealth conservation law (see also Samuelson (1982), Sato (1982), Weitzman (1976) and Kemp and Long (1982)).

$$\text{income}\,(t)/\text{wealth}\,(t) = \rho = \text{constant.} \qquad (8.29c)$$

We can give an alternative interpretation to (8.29b). Since $\int_t^\infty e^{-\rho(s-t)} U(s)\,ds$ is defined as wealth, the integral in the null term in Eq. (8.26b) may be called "discounted wealth," for we have

$$\Phi\Big|_\infty^t = \rho \int_t^\infty e^{-\rho s} U(s)\,ds = \rho e^{-\rho t}\,\text{wealth}\,(t). \qquad (8.30a)$$

This, then, becomes

$$\Phi(t) - \Phi(\infty) = \rho\left[\int_t^0 e^{-\rho s} U(s)\,ds - \int_\infty^0 e^{-\rho s} U(s)\,ds\right]$$

$$= \rho\left[\int_0^\infty e^{-\rho s} U(s)\,ds - \int_0^t e^{-\rho s} U(s)\,ds\right], \qquad (8.30b)$$

$$\Phi\Big|_\infty^\tau = \rho[S^* - S(t)]. \qquad (8.30c)$$

Here $S^* =$ discounted total (maximum) stock of consumption measured in terms of utility and $S(t) =$ discounted stock of consumption also measured in terms of utility up to time t. For short, we shall call S, the stock of consumption. Using (8.26b), (8.28b) and (8.30b), we can express the conservation law as

$$e^{-\rho t}\left[U(t) - \dot{k}^i(t)\frac{\partial U(t)}{\partial \dot{k}^i(t)}\right] + \rho \int_0^t e^{-\rho s}U(s)\,ds = \rho \int_0^\infty e^{-\rho s}U(s)\,ds \quad (8.31a)$$

or

$$\begin{aligned}&\text{discounted income }(t) + \rho \times \text{discounted stock of consumption}\\&= \rho \times \text{maximum discounted stock of consumption}\\&= \text{constant,} \hspace{8cm} (8.31b)\\&\text{discounted income} + \text{discounted stock income}\\&= \text{modified income} = \text{constant.} \hspace{5cm} (8.31c)\end{aligned}$$

This is the alternative formulation of the income-wealth conservation law in terms of the modified income (see Sato (1981)).

8.6 Special Cases

It may be of interest to study special cases of the one capital good model of Ramsey (1928) and of Liviatan and Samuelson (1969). First, the Ramsey model corresponds to the case where $i = 1$ and U takes the form

$$U = U[k,\dot{k}] = U[c(k,\dot{k})] = U[f(k(t)) - \dot{k}(t)] \quad (8.32)$$

where c satisfies

$$U'(c) > 0, \quad U''(c) < 0 \quad (0 < c < \infty), \quad (8.32a)$$

$$U'(0) = \infty \quad (8.32b)$$

and f satisfies

$$f(k) > 0, \quad f'(k) > 0, \quad f''(k) < 0 \quad \text{for } 0 < k < \bar{k} < \infty, \quad (8.33a)$$

$$f(k) < f(\bar{k}) = \bar{c} \quad (0 < k < \bar{k}), \quad (8.33b)$$

$$f(k) \leq f(\bar{k}) \quad (\bar{k} < k) \quad (8.33c)$$

where $\bar{k}$ = golden rule capital and $\bar{c}$ = bliss consumption. Then the income-wealth conservation law (8.29b) reduces to

$$U(t) + \dot{k}(t)U'(t) = \rho \int_t^\infty e^{-\rho(s-t)}U(s)\,ds, \quad (8.34a)$$

$$\begin{aligned}&\text{utility measure of consumption} + \text{utility measure of investment}\\&= \text{utility measure of income}\end{aligned}$$

8.7 Generalized Income/Wealth Conservation Laws

$$= \rho \times \text{utility measure of wealth}. \tag{8.34b}$$

This special case is extensively discussed by Samuelson (1982) and Sato (1982).

Secondly, the Liviatan–Samuelson model corresponds to the case where $i = 1$ and U takes the general form

$$U = U(k,\dot{k}) = U(c) = U(c(k(t),\dot{k}(t))), \tag{8.35a}$$

$$\frac{\partial c}{\partial k} < 0, \quad \frac{\partial^2 c}{\partial k^2} < 0, \tag{8.35b}$$

$$\max c(0,k) \quad (k = \overline{k}), \tag{8.35c}$$

$$\frac{\partial c(0,k)}{\partial k} \lessgtr 0 \quad \text{as} \quad k \lessgtr \overline{k}. \tag{8.35d}$$

Here the conservation law (8.29b) holds for $i = 1$ automatically.

8.7 Generalized Income/Wealth Conservation Laws

We now consider the most general case of utility maximization where the society's purpose is to maximize

$$\int_0^\infty W(t,k(t),\dot{k}(t))\,dt, \quad k(t) = (k^1(t),\ldots,k^n(t)) \tag{8.36}$$

subject to the appropriate initial conditions. More specifically W may be expressed as

$$W(t,k(t),\dot{k}(t)) = e^{-\rho(t)}U(t,k(t),\dot{k}(t)) \tag{8.37}$$

and W satisfies all the requirements of a social welfare function. In this general case the society may have: (1) variable discount rate $\rho(t)$, and (2) taste and technical change $\partial U/\partial t \neq 0$.

Noether's invariance condition for this case is now written as

$$\frac{\partial W}{\partial t}\tau + \frac{\partial W}{\partial k^i}\xi^i + \frac{\partial W}{\partial \dot{k}^i}\left(\frac{d\xi^i}{dt} - \dot{k}^i\frac{d\tau}{dt}\right) + W\frac{d\tau}{dt} = \frac{d\Phi}{dt},$$

$$\Phi = \Phi(t,k). \tag{8.38}$$

Then for the optimal path, we have the conservation law expressed in terms of the time derivative,

$$\frac{d}{dt}\left[\left(W - \dot{k}^i\frac{\partial W}{\partial \dot{k}^i}\right)\tau + \frac{\partial W}{\partial \dot{k}^i}\xi^i - \Phi\right] = 0. \tag{8.39}$$

Using (8.38) and (8.39) we obtain the null term as

$$\frac{d\Phi}{dt} = \frac{d}{dt}\left[\left(W - \dot{k}^i\frac{\partial W}{\partial \dot{k}^i}\right)\tau + \frac{\partial W}{\partial \dot{k}^i}\xi^i\right]$$

$$= \frac{\partial W}{\partial t}\tau + \frac{\partial W}{\partial \dot{k}^i}\xi^i + \frac{\partial W}{\partial \dot{k}^i}\left(\frac{d\xi^i}{dt} - \dot{k}^i\frac{d\tau}{dt}\right) + W\frac{dt}{dt}. \quad (8.40)$$

This is the fundamental equation of the conservation law, which contains many special cases depending upon the forms of τ and ξ^i. Let $\xi^i = 0$ for $i = 1,\ldots,n$. Then integrating (8.40) we have the *generalized income-wealth conservation law*

$$\frac{d}{dt}\left[\left(W - \dot{k}^i\frac{\partial W}{\partial \dot{k}^i}\right)\tau\right] = \frac{\partial W}{\partial t}\tau + \left(W - \dot{k}^i\frac{\partial W}{\partial \dot{k}^i}\right)\frac{d\tau}{dt}, \quad (8.41\text{a})$$

$$\left[\left(W - \dot{k}^i\frac{\partial W}{\partial \dot{k}^i}\right)\tau\right]_{t=T}^{b} = \int_T^b\left[\frac{\partial W}{\partial t}\tau + \left(W - \dot{k}^i\frac{\partial W}{\partial \dot{k}^i}\right)\frac{d\tau}{dt}\right]dt, \quad (8.41\text{b})$$

$$\left[\left(W - \dot{k}^i\frac{\partial W}{\partial \dot{k}^i}\right)\tau\right]_{t=T} = -\int_T^\infty\left[\frac{\partial W}{\partial t}\tau + \left(W - \dot{k}^i\frac{\partial W}{\partial \dot{k}^i}\right)\frac{d\tau}{dt}\right]dt, \quad (8.41\text{c})$$

where we assumed, by the transversality condition, that

$$\left(W - \dot{k}^i\frac{\partial W}{\partial \dot{k}^i}\right)\tau \to 0, \quad \frac{\partial W}{\partial t}\tau + \left(W - \dot{k}^i\frac{\partial W}{\partial \dot{k}^i}\right)\frac{d\tau}{dt} \to 0 \quad \text{as } t \to \infty.$$

The left-hand side of (8.41c) represents *generalized income* with the time transformation τ, while the right-hand side of (8.41c) represents *generalized wealth*. In particular, when

$$\tau = 1 \quad (8.42\text{a})$$

we have

$$\left(W - \dot{k}^i\frac{\partial W}{\partial \dot{k}^i}\right) = \text{utility measure of generalized income} \quad (8.42\text{b})$$

and

$$-\int_t^\infty \frac{\partial W}{\partial s}\,ds = \text{utility measure of generalized wealth.} \quad (8.42\text{c})$$

The economic interpretation of (8.42c) as generalized wealth will become more apparent when we consider a special case of W in (8.37) as

$$W = e^{-\rho(t)}U(k(t),\dot{k}(t)). \quad (8.43\text{a})$$

8.7 Generalized Income/Wealth Conservation Laws

In this case $-\int_t^\infty \frac{\partial W}{\partial s} ds$ is equal to

$$-\int_t^\infty \frac{\partial W}{\partial s} ds = \int_t^\infty \rho'(s) e^{-\rho(s)} U(k(s), \dot{k}(s)) ds. \quad (8.43b)$$

The standard income-wealth conservation law (8.29a) can be derived when $\rho(t)$ takes a special form,

$$\rho(t) = \rho t \quad (8.43c)$$

and

$$-\int_t^\infty \frac{\partial W}{\partial s} ds = \rho \int_t^\infty e^{-\rho(s)} U(k(s), \dot{k}(s)) ds. \quad (8.43d)$$

Another special case of interest occurs when τ and W take the special forms

$$\tau = \frac{1}{\rho'(t)} \quad (8.44a)$$

and

$$W = e^{-\rho(t)} U(k(t), \dot{k}(t)). \quad (8.44b)$$

After some somewhat complicated calculations, we obtain the generalized income-wealth conservation law as

$$\left[U - \dot{k}^i \frac{\partial U}{\partial \dot{k}^i}\right] = \rho_t \int_t^\infty \exp\left(-\int_t^s \rho_p dp\right) \left[U - \dot{k}^i \frac{\partial U}{\partial \dot{k}^i} \frac{d}{ds}\left(\frac{1}{\rho_s}\right)\right] ds, \quad (8.44c)$$

$$\text{income} = \rho_t \times \text{generalized wealth} \quad (8.44d)$$

where

$$\rho_t = \frac{d\rho}{dt} = \rho'(t).$$

The generalized wealth expression now includes capital gains and losses, depending upon whether $-\dot{k}^i \frac{\partial U}{\partial \dot{k}^i} \frac{d}{ds}\left(\frac{1}{\rho_s}\right)$ is positive or negative. This term depends on the supply price of investment, $-\frac{\partial U}{\partial \dot{k}}$, and the *variable* discount rate, $\rho_s(s)$. Needless to say that when $\frac{d}{ds} \rho_s \equiv 0$, i.e., the constant discount rate, (8.44c) reduces to the standard income-wealth conservation law (8.29a). Hence, when ρ = constant, the time transformations $\tau = 1$ and $\tau = 1/\rho$ give the identical results.

Next we consider the effect of taste and technical change in the utility and production functions. The generalized income-wealth conservation law contains the case of the welfare function

$$W = e^{-\rho(t)} U(t, k(t), \dot{k}(t)) \tag{8.45a}$$

where U is subjected to taste and technical change so that

$$\frac{\partial U}{\partial t} \neq 0. \tag{8.45b}$$

The null term in this case is simply equal to

$$\frac{d\Phi}{dt} = e^{-\rho t}\left[-\rho U + \frac{\partial U}{\partial t}\right]. \tag{8.45c}$$

Hence, the conservation law when $\tau = 1$ and $\xi^i = 0$ becomes

$$\left[U - \dot{k}^i \frac{\partial U}{\partial \dot{k}^i}\right] + \int_t^\infty e^{-\rho(s-t)} \frac{\partial U}{\partial s} ds = \rho \int_t^\infty e^{-\rho(s-t)} U(s) ds, \tag{8.45d}$$

income + current worth of taste (technical) change

$= \rho \times$ wealth, \hfill (8.45e)

modified income $= \rho \times$ wealth. \hfill (8.45f)

The value of wealth can be expressed in the same form as in the case when $\partial U/\partial t = 0$, but income must be modified by the amount of taste (technical) change. Note that in deriving (8.45d), we used the trans-versality condition

$$e^{-\rho t}\left[U - \dot{k}^i \frac{\partial U}{\partial \dot{k}^i}\right] \to 0 \quad \text{as } t \to \infty.$$

8.8 Income-Capital (Wealth) Conservation Law in the von Neumann Model

As this problem has already been studied extensively by Samuelson (1970a,b) and Sato (1981), we shall briefly present the results. The von Neumann problem is to maximize

$$\int_0^T \dot{K}_1 dt \quad \text{subject to } F(K_1, \ldots, K_n, \dot{K}_1, \ldots, \dot{K}_n) = 0, \tag{8.46a}$$

8.8 Income-Capital (Wealth) Conservation Law in the von Neumann Model

and subject to the appropriate initial conditions. Here K_i are the ith type of capital, $\dot{K}_i$ are the net capital formation of the ith type of capital $(i = 1,\ldots,n)$ and F is a smooth, neoclassical, concave first-degree-homogeneous transformation function.

The Lagrangian associated with (8.46a) is

$$L(t,\lambda,K_1,\ldots,K_n,\dot{K}_1,\ldots,\dot{K}_n,\lambda)$$
$$= \dot{K}_1 + \lambda F(K_1,\ldots,K_n,\dot{K}_1,\ldots,\dot{K}_n) \qquad (8.46b)$$
$$= \dot{K}_1 + \lambda F(K,\dot{K}) \qquad (8.46c)$$

where

$$K = (K_1,\ldots,K_n).$$

The transformations under consideration are

$$\bar{t} = t + \varepsilon\tau(t,\lambda,K),$$
$$\bar{K}_i = K_i + \varepsilon\xi^i(t,\lambda,K) \quad (i = 1,\ldots,n),$$
$$\bar{\lambda} = \lambda + \varepsilon\omega(t,\lambda,K). \qquad (8.47)$$

The Noether invariance principle requires that

$$\frac{d\Phi}{dt} = F\omega + \frac{d\xi^1}{dt} + \lambda\left(\frac{\partial F}{\partial K_i}\xi^i + \frac{\partial F}{\partial \dot{K}_i}\frac{d\xi^i}{dt} + \dot{K}_i\frac{\partial F}{\partial K_i}\frac{d\tau}{dt}\right). \qquad (8.48)$$

The conservation laws are derived from

$$\Omega = \lambda\left(F - \dot{K}_i\frac{\partial F}{\partial \dot{K}_i}\right)\tau + \xi^1 + \lambda\frac{\partial F}{\partial \dot{K}_i}\xi^i - \Phi = \text{constant}. \qquad (8.49)$$

Let $\tau = 1$, $\omega = 0$, $\xi^i = 0$, and $d\Phi/dt = 0$, i.e., $\Phi = \text{constant} = c$, we then have

$$\Omega = \lambda\left(F - \dot{K}_i\frac{\partial F}{\partial \dot{K}_i}\right) - c = \lambda\dot{K}_i\frac{\partial F}{\partial \dot{K}_i} - c = \text{constant} \qquad (8.50a)$$

where

$$F = K_i\frac{\partial F}{\partial K_i} + \dot{K}_i\frac{\partial F}{\partial \dot{K}_i}$$

by homogeneity. Letting $Y = K_i(\partial F/\partial K_i) = $ national income, the above can be interpreted as

$$\Omega_i = \lambda Y = \text{constant}. \qquad (8.50b)$$

Now let us assume that $\tau = 0$ and $\xi^i = \alpha K_i$ and $\omega = -\alpha\lambda$. Then we have

$$\frac{d\Phi}{dt} = -\alpha\lambda F + \alpha \dot{K}_1 + \alpha\lambda\left(K_i\frac{\partial F}{\partial K_i} + K_i\frac{\partial F}{\partial \dot{K}_i}\right) = \alpha\dot{K}_1. \qquad (8.51a)$$

Hence, we have

$$\Phi = \alpha K_1 + c \quad (c = \text{constant}) \qquad (8.51b)$$

which gives

$$\Omega_2 = \alpha K_1 + \alpha\lambda K_i \frac{\partial F}{\partial \dot{K}_i} - (\alpha K_1 + c)$$

$$= \alpha\lambda K_i \frac{\partial F}{\partial \dot{K}_i} - c = \text{constant} \qquad (8.51c)$$

or

$$\Omega_2 = -\lambda K_i \frac{\partial F}{\partial \dot{K}_i} = \lambda W = \text{constant} \qquad (8.51d)$$

where

$$W = -K_i \frac{\partial F}{\partial \dot{K}_i} = K_i P^i = \text{national wealth}.$$

Using (8.50b) and (8.51d), we have the Samuelson conservation law

$$\frac{\Omega_1}{\Omega_2} = \frac{Y}{W} = \frac{\text{national income}}{\text{national wealth}} = \text{constant}. \qquad (8.52)$$

The conservation law (8.52) is a global law independent of the form of technology. But if we allow for special forms, there may exist different types of conservation law in addition to (8.52). In my earlier work (Sato 1981, p. 289), I posed an open question regarding the existence of any new conservation law for a special separable technology

$$F = Y(K) - I(\dot{K}) = 0, \qquad (8.53a)$$

$$F = K_1^{a_1} K_2^{a_2} \cdots K_n^{a_n} - (\dot{K}_1^2 + \dot{K}_2^2 + \cdots + \dot{K}_n^2)^{1/2} = 0 \qquad (8.53b)$$

with

$$\sum_{i=1}^{n} a_i = 1.$$

8.8 Income-Capital (Wealth) Conservation Law in the von Neumann Model

This form of technology has been used by many economists including Samuelson (1970b), Caton and Shell (1971). Kataoka (1983) has now shown that (8.52) is the only conservation law for this special case. Thus my question has been answered in the negative.

Let us briefly present Kataoka's arguments. To simplify the calculations, we set $i = 1, 2$. Then the invariance principle requires (Sato 1981, p. 289, Eq. (109)) that

$$\frac{\partial \xi^1}{\partial K_1} = \frac{\partial \xi^2}{\partial K_2}, \quad \frac{\partial \xi^1}{\partial K_2} + \frac{\partial \xi^2}{\partial K_1} = 0, \tag{8.54a}$$

$$K_1 K_2 \left(\alpha - \frac{\partial \xi^1}{\partial K_1} \right) + a K_2 \xi^1 + (1-a) K_1 \xi^2 = 0 \tag{8.54b}$$

where $a = a_1$ in (8.53b) and α is the coefficient of the time transformation $\tau = \alpha t + \beta$. Rewriting the first part of (8.54a) as $\dfrac{\partial \xi^1}{\partial K_1} = \dfrac{1}{2} \left(\dfrac{\partial \xi^1}{\partial K_1} + \dfrac{\partial \xi^2}{\partial K_2} \right)$ and substituting it into (8.54b), we have

$$K_1 K_2 \left[\frac{1}{2}\alpha + \frac{1}{2}\alpha - \frac{1}{2}\left(\frac{\partial \xi^1}{\partial K_1} + \frac{\partial \xi^2}{\partial K_2} \right) \right] + a K_2 \xi^1 + (1-a) K_1 \xi^2 = 0. \tag{8.54c}$$

This yields

$$\frac{\alpha}{2} - \frac{1}{2}\frac{\partial \xi^1}{\partial K_1} + a \frac{\xi^1}{K_1} = -\frac{\alpha}{2} + \frac{1}{2}\frac{\partial \xi^2}{\partial K_2} - (1-a)\frac{\xi^2}{K_2}. \tag{8.54d}$$

Assuming $\xi^1 = \xi^1(K_1)$ and $\xi^2 = \xi^2(K_2)$, (8.54d) yields two ordinary differential equations

$$\frac{\alpha}{2} - \frac{1}{2}\frac{\partial \xi^1}{\partial K_1} + a\frac{\xi^1}{K_1} = B = \text{constant},$$

$$-\frac{\alpha}{2} + \frac{1}{2}\frac{\partial \xi^2}{\partial K_2} - (1-a)\frac{\xi^2}{K_2} = B = \text{constant} \tag{8.54e}$$

Among the solutions of (8.54e), the only relevant ones which satisfy (8.54a) and (8.54b) are

$$\alpha = 0, \quad \xi^1 = \gamma K_1, \quad \xi^2 = \gamma K_2 \tag{8.54f}$$

which proves that (8.52) is the only conservation law even for this special technology. Kataoka also shows that even if we specify $\xi^i(K_1, K_2)$ the final solution yields the same result.

8.9 The Total Value Conservation Law of the Firm

It may be of interest to study micro economic conservation laws applicable to industries and firms. To consider a firm's profit maximization, the following long-run profit function (functional) is formulated:

$$J(x) = \int_a^b \Pi(t, x(t), \dot{x}(t)) \, dt \tag{8.55}$$

where $x(t) = (x^1(t), \ldots, x^n(t))$, which equals the vector of functions of quantities and prices, and $\dot{x}(t) = dx/dt$.

For $J(x)$ to be maximized, the necessary condition for the optimal solution is that the Euler–Lagrange equations vanish, thus:

$$E_i = \frac{\partial \Pi}{\partial x^i} - \frac{d}{dt}\left(\frac{\partial \Pi}{\partial \dot{x}^i}\right) = 0 \quad (i = 1, \ldots n). \tag{8.56}$$

Using a system of Lie group transformation and Noether's Invariance Principle, we can derive the following conservation laws for the profit maximizing firm:

$$\left(\Pi - \sum_{i=1}^n \dot{x}^i \frac{\partial \Pi}{\partial \dot{x}^i}\right) \tau(x,t) + \sum_{i=1}^n \frac{\partial \Pi}{\partial \dot{x}^i} \xi^i(x,t) = \Phi(x,t) \tag{8.57}$$

where $\tau(x,t)$ and $\xi(x,t)$ are infinitesimal transformation for t and x respectively and Φ is a null term.

There are several cases where τ and ξ take special values and/or the profit function has a special form. Suppose that there is no x^i transformation, namely $\xi^i \equiv 0$ and that the time transformation is constant, thus, $\tau = \text{constant} = 1$. And if the profit functions has a familiar form such as

$$\Pi = e^{-\rho t} G(x(t), \dot{x}(t)) \tag{8.58}$$

where $\rho =$ the discount rate, then (8.57) can be expressed as

$$G(x(t), \dot{x}(t)) + \sum_{i=1}^n \pi^i \dot{x}^i = \Phi = \rho \int_t^\infty e^{-\rho(s-t)} G(x, \dot{x}) \, ds \tag{8.59}$$

where $\pi^i = e^{\rho t} p^i$, $p^i = -\dfrac{\partial \Pi}{\partial \dot{x}^i} =$ supply price of x^i, and Φ is derived from $-\int_t^\infty \left(\dfrac{\partial \Pi}{\partial s}\right) ds$.

By transforming (8.59), it may be more conveniently expressed as

8.10 Empirical Applications

$$\rho = \frac{G + \sum_{i=1}^{n} \pi^i \dot{x}^i}{\int_t^\infty e^{-\rho(s-t)} G(x,\dot{x}) \, ds}. \tag{8.60}$$

Equation (8.60) says that the current value of profit G and changes in the value of the form, $\sum_{i=1}^{n} \pi^i \dot{x}^i$, divided by the discounted value of the firm, $\int_t^\infty e^{-\rho(s-t)} G(x,\dot{x}) \, ds$, must always be equal to the discount rate ρ. This is the fundamental property of the *total value conservation law of the maximizing firm*.

8.10 Empirical Applications

We will briefly present summaries of the two recent empirical applications of economic conservation laws; the one on macro time series data and the other on micro time series and cross section data (See Sato (2002) and Sato and Fujii (2006). These articles are also included in Sato (2006)).

Macro Conservation Laws

In (Sato 2002; 2006, chap. 8), an attempt is made to test the validity of the simplest optimal growth model of per capita consumption maximization for 12 OECD countries. If these economies are on optimal paths, we may observe the income-wealth conservation law for a given period. The conservation law tested is Eq. (8.29c), i.e.,

$$\frac{\text{income }(t)}{\text{wealth }(t)} = \rho = \text{constant} \quad (t_0 \leq t \leq t_1). \tag{8.29c}$$

The twelve countries included are: USA, Canada, Japan, Great Britain, Australia, Norway, Sweden, Finland, Germany, Greece, Iceland and Italy.

As the first-order approximation, we used GNP data from the national income account and "net national wealth" data or the value of capital goods, $V(t)$, in each country; that is,

$$Y = \text{GNP} \approx \rho \times \text{net national wealth}$$

$$\approx \rho \times \sum_{i=1}^{n} P_i K_i = \rho V(t)$$

where P_i = price of K_i(capital goods). Thus we want to test if the following relation holds:

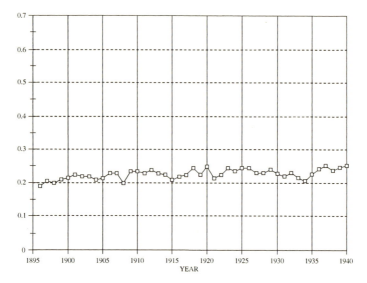

Fig. 8.1 US Income/wealth ratio (prewar)

$$\frac{Y(t)}{V(t)} = \rho. \tag{8.61}$$

The results are remarkably consistent for some countries. For instance, the US economy value of ρ was stable around 0.25 before the World War II (1895–1940) and around 0.3 in the post-World War II (1945–1995). See Figs. 8.1 and 8.2 (Sato 2002, 2006).

This implies that on the average the US economy has been growing on the optimal paths as projected by the model. There were ups and downs both before and after the World War II due to business cycle fluctuations. But unlike other countries, the US economy shows a remarkable consistency operating along the optimal trajectories determined by this simple model of per-capita consumption maximization.

The ratio of income to wealth for the United States has been historically stable, indicating that the income/wealth conservation law may in fact be operating. No observable trend upward or downward occurs for the entire period 1896–1992 (See Fig. 8.3).

For a short period surrounding World War II (1941–1946), the ratios exhibit a pattern of sudden upward shift suggesting that the US economy has experienced a structural change. The post-war ratios were fluctuating approximately about a mean value of 0.3 which is higher than its prewar level, 0.25.

It is shown that the postwar ratios displayed some business-cycle tendencies within their range. For the period immediately after the war and throughout 1950s,

8.10 Empirical Applications

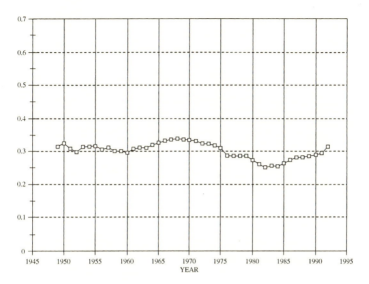

Fig. 8.2 US income/wealth ratio (postwar)

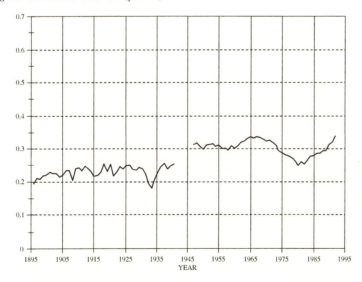

Fig. 8.3 US ratio (GNP/national private wealth)

the US ratios are stable. This is followed in turn by a period with high ratios during the Vietnam War and by a period with low ratios during the Carter era, and so on (See Fig. 8.2).

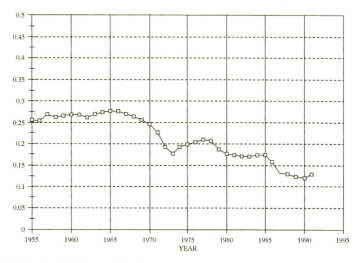

Fig. 8.4 Ratio of GDP/net wealth in Japan

On the other hand, the Japanese economy behaved very differently from the US economy in that ρ is consistently declining and approaches its lowest value during the bubble period of the early 1990s. This suggests that either the discount rate of the Japanese economy may be "variable" or that the Japanese economy may "not" be operating along the trajectories prescribed in the simple model (Fig. 8.4).

For the observed period of 1955 through 1991, the Japanese ratios are comparably lower than the US ratios, with the mean equal to 0.21 (the US ratio is 0.3). This may be due to the fact that the Japanese discount rate is considerably lower than that of the US, and that the Japanese are more long-sighted.

One similarity with the US is a business-cycle-like movement of the Japanese ratios for the 1960s and 1970s. Their rise and fall during these two decades seem to be contemporaneous with the US case. The real divergence in pattern comes in the 1980s, during which the Japanese economy experienced the period of asset price bubbles. In short, the Japanese economy has not grown along the trajectories prescribed by this simple model of optimal growth.

There may be two reasons: first, the assumption of the constant discount rate and second, divergence of the asset price from its equilibrium value. First, as the Japanese economy grew faster than the US economy during the 1980s, the Japanese firms re-evaluated their planning horizon extending to longer period. This means that the discount rate must be constantly declining. Hence, the assumption of a constant discount rate is no longer valid for the Japanese economy. Secondly, because the asset Price P_i may be diverging from its equilibrium price, which means that $\dot{P}_i$ is not zero. Hence the true measure of the wealth–like quantity and the value of capital $V(t)$ in (8.61) may be very different. Most likely $V(t)$ much greater than the wealth-like quantity, especially during the bubble period.

For other OECD countries, there has been a data availability problem. Therefore the study simply focused on one aspect: whether or not the constancy property of the ratio has been met. 10 OECD countries can be roughly grouped into three categories: countries having constant ratios, those with declining ratios, and those with neither characteristic.

The first category consists of Australia, Canada, Norway, and Sweden have constant ratios while Finland, Germany, and the United Kingdom making up the second group have declining ratios. Finally, Iceland and Italy follow neither of the above patterns. For Iceland the ratio is unstable with no trend observable, whereas for Italy the ratio goes up in the beginning and comes down at the end of the period (1955–1990).

It should be remembered that these empirical results are only up to the beginning of the 1990s. But as we need longer time series to test macroeconomic conservation laws, now may be a good time to extend the analysis to the present, the 2010s.

Testing Micro Economic Conservation Laws

There is an attempt to show that at the microeconomic level, economic conservation laws could apply to evaluate corporate performance (Sato and Fujii (2006), also Sato (2006)). The total value conservation law of the firm (Eq. (8.60)) is tested against the Japanese corporate data.

If a firm engages in long-run profit maximizing operations we may be able to observe the outcome from the published corporate financial data and market prices of their shares and securities. The source of the sample firms is listed on the first section of Tokyo Stock Exchange. We used the financial statements collected by Toyo Keizai, a Japanese publisher.

Using the modified version of Eq. (8.60) (see Eq. (6) in Sato and Fujii (2006), and in Chap. 10, Sato (2006)), the discount rate ρ is calculated. To test the constancy of the estimated values of ρ, the regression analysis is employed (Table 8.1).

It is shown that the assumption of a constant discount rate and profit-maximizing behavior of a firm is consistent with observed data for many of the top-performing firms in Japan for the period 1980–2002. Although the results are tentative because of the limited data period and data availability, they suggest that it is promising to extend the notion of conservation laws to the industry level (Table 8.2).

The valuation of a firm is far from simple and easy exercise. A measure related to a conservation law could be used together with traditional standards of performance measurement used in management, accounting and finance theory. Also the integration of optimization theory and uncertainty surrounding corporate decision making may be necessary in order to understand the complicated aspects of corporate behavior.

Table 8.1 Calculated values of the ratio $\hat{\rho}$: manufacturing industries

Industrial category	Number of firms	Mean of $\hat{\rho}$	Standard deviation of $\hat{\rho}$
Construction	124	0.0595	0.1044
Food processing	63	0.0588	0.1060
Chemical	110	0.0522	0.1056
Iron and steel	28	0.0359	0.1247
Machinery	95	0.0494	0.1234
Electric appliances	140	0.0666	0.1402
Automobile and related	65	0.0567	0.0987
Other manufacturing	29	0.0783	0.1368
Manufacturing total	880	0.0566	0.1166

Source: Sato and Fujii (2006)

Table 8.2 Calculated values of the ratio $\hat{\rho}$: non-manufacturing industries

Industrial category	Number of firms	Mean of $\hat{\rho}$	Standard deviation of $\hat{\rho}$
Gas & electricity	17	0.0707	0.0778
Transportation	31	0.0610	0.1014
Wholesale	89	0.0565	0.1033
Retail	47	0.0711	0.1224
Real estate	22	0.0733	0.1381
Services	39	0.0914	0.1378
Non-manufacturing total	290	0.0678	0.1143

Source: Sato and Fujii (2006)

As the theoretical analysis for a "variable" discount rate is given in Sect. 8.7, it may be possible to device a modified method of calculating the discount rate at each moment of time. This task is left as a future research project.

8.11 Summary

In this chapter by using the Noether invariance theorem we have uncovered several "hidden" conservation laws in the model with heterogeneous capital goods. Our first conservation law is a pseudo-net-productivity relation which implies that the rate of change in national income is equal to the discount rate multiplied by the utility-value-of-investment. The second conservation law is an integral version of the first law—the constancy of income-wealth ratio. It is shown that the second law can be interpreted as the law of variance of "modified income."

If we introduce taste change and/or technical change it can be proved that there exist several generalized income-wealth conservation laws. Income and wealth must now include the effects of taste and technical change. Also under a variable discount rate, income-wealth conservation laws contain terms related to capital gains.

The analysis is extended to the von Neumann model of capital accumulation. Here again we confirm the existence of the income capital conservation law. Even if technology is limited to a specialized type, there exist no additional invariances, other than those discovered by Samuelson (1970a) and Sato (1981, 1999).

A micro economic conservation law is presented as the "total value conservation law of the firm." It says that the sum of the current value of profit and changes in the value of investment divided by the discounted value of the firm must be always be equal to the discount rate.

Two empirical applications are summarized: the one on macro data and the other on micro economic data. Twelve OECD countries are selected to test the income/wealth conservation law.

The US economy is shown to exhibit a remarkably consistent and stable macro economic growth with constant discount. This implies that the US economy has been growing on the optimal paths as projected by a simple optimal growth model. On the other hand, the Japanese economy has a declining tendency in the discount rate which has reached the lowest value before the burst of the bubbles in the early 1990s.

The micro economic law of the total value conservation is tested against the Japanese data. It is shown the in general this test can be shown as an alternative measure of corporate performance.

Appendix

Consider the variational integral

$$J(x) = \int_a^b L(t, x(t), \dot{x}(t)) \, dt$$

$$(x(t) = (x^1(t), \ldots, x^n(t)), \quad \dot{x}(t) = (\dot{x}^1(t), \ldots, \dot{x}^n(t))). \tag{8.62}$$

Also consider r-parameter transformations

$$T : \bar{t} = \phi(t, x; \varepsilon), \quad \varepsilon = (\varepsilon^1, \ldots, \varepsilon^n), \quad \bar{x}^i = \psi^i(t, x; \varepsilon) \quad (i = 1, \ldots, n). \tag{8.63}$$

where

$$\phi(t, x; 0) = t,$$
$$\psi^i(t, x; 0) = x^i. \tag{8.64}$$

In addition, it is assumed that T does not change the end points (a, α) and (b, β) where

$$\phi(a,x(a);\varepsilon) = a, \quad \phi(b,x(b);\varepsilon) = b,$$
$$\psi^i(a,x(a);\varepsilon) = \alpha^i, \quad \psi^i(b,x(b);\varepsilon) = \beta^i. \tag{8.65}$$

Let X_s be the infinitesimal transformations for $s = 1,\ldots,r$, then we write X_s as

$$X_s = \tau_s(t,x)\frac{\partial}{\partial t} + \xi_s^i(t,x)\frac{\partial}{\partial x^i} + \eta_s^i(t,x,\dot{x})\frac{\partial}{\partial \dot{x}^i} \tag{8.66}$$

where

$$\tau_s(t,x) = \frac{\partial \phi}{\partial \varepsilon^s}(t,x;0), \quad \xi_s^i(t,x) = \frac{\partial \psi^i}{\partial \varepsilon^s}(t,x;0),$$
$$\eta_s^i(t,x,\dot{x}) = \frac{d\xi_s^i}{dt} - \dot{x}^i\frac{d\tau_s}{dt} \tag{8.67}$$

and (8.65) obeys

$$\tau_s(a,x(a)) = \tau_s(b,x(b)) = 0,$$
$$\xi_s^i(a,x(a)) = \xi_s^i(b,x(b)) = 0. \tag{8.68}$$

If (8.62) is invariant under (8.63), we have

$$\int_a^b X_s(L\,dt) = 0. \tag{8.69}$$

Lemma 8.1. *For any $\tau_s(t,x)$ and $\xi_s^i(t,x)$, we have*

$$N_s = (\xi_s^i - \dot{x}^i\tau_s)E_i + \frac{d\Omega_s}{dt} \tag{8.70}$$

where

$$N_s = \frac{\partial L}{\partial t}\tau_s + \frac{\partial L}{\partial x^i}\xi_s^i + \frac{\partial L}{\partial \dot{x}^i}\left(\frac{d\xi_s^i}{dt} - \dot{x}^i\frac{d\tau_s}{dt}\right) + L\frac{d\tau_s}{dt},$$
$$E_i = \text{Euler–Lagrange equation} = \frac{\partial L}{\partial x^i} - \frac{d}{dt}\left(\frac{\partial L}{\partial \dot{x}^i}\right),$$
$$\frac{d\Omega}{dt} = \frac{d}{dt}\left[\left(L - \dot{x}^i\frac{\partial L}{\partial \dot{x}^i}\right)\tau_s + \frac{\partial L}{\partial \dot{x}^i}\xi_s^i\right].$$

Proof. By differentiating Ω_s with respect to t we have

$$\frac{d\Omega_s}{dt} = \frac{d}{dt}\left[\left(L - \dot{x}^i\frac{\partial L}{\partial \dot{x}^i}\right)\tau_s + \frac{\partial L}{\partial \dot{x}^i}\xi_s^i\right]$$
$$= \frac{\partial L}{\partial t}\tau_s + \frac{\partial L}{\partial \dot{x}^i}\left(\frac{d\xi_s^i}{dt} - \dot{x}^i\frac{d\tau_s}{dt}\right) + L\frac{d\tau_s}{dt}$$

$$+\dot{x}^i\tau_s\left[\frac{\partial L}{\partial x^i} - \frac{d}{dt}\left(\frac{\partial L}{\partial \dot{x}^i}\right)\right] + \frac{d}{dt}\left(\frac{\partial L}{\partial \dot{x}^i}\right)\xi_s^i$$
$$= N_s - (\xi_s^i - \dot{x}^i\tau_s)E_i.$$

□

When (8.62) is optimized, E_i vanishes and (8.70) reduces to

$$\frac{d\Omega_s}{dt} = N_s. \tag{8.71}$$

There are two cases: (1) when $N_s = 0$ and $N_s \neq 0$. The conservation law when $N_s = 0$ is

$$\frac{d\Omega_s}{dt} = 0 \quad \text{or} \quad \Omega_s = \text{constant}. \tag{8.72a}$$

When $N_s \neq 0$ and $d\Phi/dt = N_s$, we have

$$\frac{d(\Omega_s - \Phi_s)}{dt} = 0 \quad \text{or} \quad \Omega_s - \Phi_s = \text{constant}. \tag{8.72b}$$

This is Noether's invariance up to divergence.

References

Bessel-Hagen, E. (1921). Über die Erhaltungssätze der Elektrodynamik. *Mathematische Annalen*, 84, 258–276.

Caton, C., & Shell, K. (1971). An exercise in the theory of heterogeneous capital accumulation. *Review of Economic Studies*, 32, 233–240.

Gelfand, I.M., & Fomin, S.V. (1963). *Calculus of variations* (translated from the Russian by Silverman, R.A.). Englewood Cliffs, NJ: Prentice-Hall.

Kataoka, H. (1983). On the local conservation laws in the von Neumann model. In R. Sato, & M.J. Beckmann (Eds.), *Technology, organization and economic structure: lecture notes in economics and mathematical systems*, vol. 210 (pp. 253–260).

Kemp, M.C., & Long, N.V. (1982). On the evaluation of social income in a dynamic economy. In G.R. Feiwel (Ed.), *Samuelson and neoclassical economics*. Boston: Kluwer-Nijhoff.

Klein, F. (1918). Über die Differentialgesetze für die Erhaltung von Impuls und Energie in der Einsteinschen Gravitationstheorie. *Nachr. Akad. Wiss.* Göttingen, Math-Phys. Kl. II, 171–189.

Lie, S. (1891). In G. Scheffers (Ed.), *Vorlesungen liber Differentialgleichungen, mit bekannten infinitesimalen Transformationen*. Leipzig: Teubner. Reprinted (1967) New York: Chelsea.

Liviatan, N., & Samuelson, P.A. (1969). Notes on turnpikes: stable and unstable. *Journal of Economic Theory*, 1, 454–475.

Logan, J.D. (1977). Invariant variational principles. *Mathematics in science and engineering*, vol. 138. New York: Academic Press.

Lovelock, D., & Rund, H. (1975). *Tensors, differential forms and variational principles*. New York: Wiley.

Moser, J. (1979). Hidden symmetries in dynamical systems. *American Scientists*, 67, 689–695.

Noether, E. (1918). Invariante Variationsprobleme. *Nachr. Akad. Wiss.* Göttingen, Math-Phys. KL II, 235–257. Translated by Tavel, M.A. (1971). Invariant variation problems. *Transport Theory and Statistical Physics, 1,* 186–207.

Nôno, T. (1968). On the symmetry groups of simple materials: applications of the theory of Lie groups. *Journal of Mathematical Analysis and Applications, 24,* 110–135.

Nôno, T., & Mimura, F. (1975/1976/1977/1978). Dynamic symmetries I/III/IV/V. *Bulletin of Fukuoka University of Education, 125/126/127/128.*

Ramsey, F. (1928). A mathematical theory of saving. *Economic Journal, 38,* 543–559.

Rund, H. (1966). *The Hamilton–Jacobi theory in the calculus of variations.* Princeton, NJ: Van Nostrand-Reinhold.

Sagan, H. (1969). *Introduction to the calculus of variations.* New York: McGraw-Hill.

Samuelson, P.A. (1970a). Law of conservation of the capital-output ratio: Proceedings of the National Academy of Sciences. *Applied Mathematical Science, 67,* 1477–1479.

Samuelson, P.A. (1970b). Two conservation laws in theoretical economics. Cambridge, MA: MIT Department of Economics mimeo. Reprint (1990) In R. Sato, & R. Ramchandran (Eds.), *Conservation laws and symmetry: applications to economics and finance* (pp. 57–70). Norwell, MA: Kluwer.

Samuelson, P.A. (1976). Speeding up of time with age in recognition of life as fleeting. In A.M. Tang et al. (Eds.), *Evolution, welfare, and time in economics: essays in honor of Nicholas Georgescu-Roegen.* Lexington, MA: Lexington/Heath Books.

Samuelson, P.A. (1982). *Variations on capital-output conservation laws.* Cambrige, MA: MIT Mimeo.

Sato, R. (1981). *Theory of technical change and economic invariance: application of Lie groups.* New York: Academic Press. Updated edition (1999) Cheltenham: Edward Elgar.

Sato, R. (1982). *Invariant principle and capital-output conservation laws.* Providence, RI: Brown University working paper No. 82-8.

Sato, R. (1985). The invariance principle and income-wealth conservation laws: application of Lie groups and related transformations. *Journal of Econometrics, 30,* 365–389.

Sato, R. (2002). Optimal economic growth: test of income/wealth conservation laws. *Macroeconomic Dynamics, 6,* 548–572.

Sato, R. (2006). *Biased technical change and economic conservation laws.* Springer.

Sato, R., & Fujii, M. (2006). Evaluating corporate performance: empirical tests of a conservation law. *Japan and the World Economy, 18,* 158–168.

Sato, R., Nôno, T., & Mimura, F. (1984). Hidden symmetries: Lie groups and economic conservation laws, essay in honor of Martin Beckmann. In H. Hauptman, W. Krelle, & K.C. Mosler (Eds.), *Operations research and economic theory.* Springer.

Weitzman, M.L. (1976). On the welfare significance of national product in a dynamic economy. *Quarterly Journal of Economics, 90,* 156–162.

Whittaker, E.T. (1937). *A treatise on the analytical dynamics of particles and rigid bodies.* Cambridge: Cambridge University Press, 4th edn. Reprinted (1944), New York: Dover.

Young, E.C. (1978), *Vector and tensor analysis.* New York: Decker.

Chapter 9
Conservation Laws in Continuous and Discrete Models*

In memory of Professor Mineo Ikeda

9.1 Introduction

The study of economic conservation laws is still in its infancy relative to its counterparts in physics and engineering. Yet this is an area where there is great interest and rapid progress is being made. In economics, the conservation law has its roots in the most celebrated article of Frank Ramsey (1928). But it was Paul A. Samuelson (1970a,b) who first explicitly introduced the concept of conservation law to theoretical economics. The recent works by Weitzman (1976); Sato (1981, 1985); Kemp and Long (1982); Samuelson (1971, 1982); Sato, Nôno and Mimura (1984); and Sato and Maeda (1987) provide an indication of the rapid progress being made in this field.

The main purposes of this paper are to subdivide the known universe on continuous dynamic models into five basic types with the help of the Noether theorem (Sato 1981) and to introduce a new method of analyzing discrete economic models. The application of this theorem has enabled researchers to uncover many "hidden" conservation laws in physics and engineering and has also been instrumental for the discovery of some unknown invariances in economic models.

Discrete models have played an important role in economic analysis. In fact, some economists consider discrete models to be more realistic and more suitable for empirical applications than continuous models. In economics, continuous models serve as approximations of discrete models, as economic data is almost always measured in discrete time such as in days, weeks, months and years. The second section of this paper will be devoted to the study of economic conservation laws in discrete-time optimal growth models. As the methodology and results are new, we devoted a relatively large portion of the paper to the analysis of discrete models.

---

*The original version of this chapter was presented at the New York University Japan - U.S. Symposium on "Lie Groups and Related Dynamic Models: Applications to Economics and Finance," May 20, 1987. It was jointly written by R. Sato and S. Maeda while they were at Kyoto University where they were greatly indebted to the late Professor Mineo Ikeda.

It will be shown that there exist several conservation laws including the one very similar to the continuous case. But, the discrete models offer unique invariants and conservatives unknown in the continuous case. There has to be always "adjustment factors" which will modify the standard conservation laws.

9.2 Continuous Models

9.2.1 Review of the Noether Theorem

In the early part of this century, Emmy Noether (1918) discovered the fundamental invariance principle now known as the *Noether Theorem*. Noether not only derived the conservation (law) of total energy from a viewpoint of invariance, but also provided the formal methodology to study the general "invariance" problem of a dynamic system. Influenced by the work of Klein (1918) and Lie (1891) on the transformation properties of differential equations invariant under continuous (Lie) groups, Noether had the ingenious insight of combining the methods of calculus of variations with those of Lie group theory. Since the first application of the Noether invariance principle to particle mechanics by Bessel-Hagen (1921), this area of mathematics has exhibited remarkable development in the last 50 years.

Let us consider a Lagrange function L, which is twice continuously differentiable in each of its $2n+1$ arguments. We have the variational integral

$$J(x) = \int_a^b L(t, x(t), \dot{x}(t)) \, dt, \tag{9.1}$$

where x = the set of all vector functions $x(t) = (x^1(t), \ldots, (x^1(t), \ldots, x^n(t))$, $t \in (a,b)$. Also consider the transformations (often Lie group transformations) given by

$$\bar{t} = \phi(t, x, \varepsilon), \quad \varepsilon = (\varepsilon^1, \ldots, \varepsilon^r),$$
$$\bar{x}^i = \psi(t, x, \varepsilon) \quad (i = 1, \ldots, n) \tag{9.2}$$

where ε = the vector of r real, independent essential parameters. The "infinitesimal" transformations of (9.2) are obtained by expanding the right-hand side of (9.2) in a Taylor series around $\varepsilon = 0$ as

$$\bar{t} = t + \tau_s(t,x)\varepsilon^s + O(\varepsilon),$$
$$\bar{x}^i = x^i + \xi_s^i(t,x)\varepsilon^s + O(\varepsilon) \quad (i = 1, \ldots, n),$$
$$s = 1, \ldots, r, \text{ summation convention in force.} \tag{9.3}$$

Using the customary symbol of the infinitesimal transformations, we write (9.3) as

$$\chi_s = \tau_s(t,x)\frac{\partial}{\partial t} + \xi_s^i(t,x)\frac{\partial}{\partial x^i} + \left(\frac{d\xi_s^i}{dt} - \dot{x}^i\frac{d\tau_s}{dt}\right)\frac{\partial}{\partial \dot{x}^i}. \tag{9.4}$$

9.2 Continuous Models

The fundamental integral (9.1) in invariant under the r-parameter family of transformations (9.2) up to a divergence term, if there exist r functions Φ_s such that

$$L = \left(\bar{t}, \bar{x}(\bar{t}), \frac{d\bar{x}(\bar{t})}{dt}\right)\frac{dt}{dt} - L(t, x(t), \dot{x}(t))$$

$$= \varepsilon^s \frac{d\Phi_s}{dt}(t, x(t)) + O(\varepsilon). \tag{9.5}$$

The *fundamental invariance identities* are given by

$$\chi_s L + L\frac{d\tau_s}{dt} = \frac{d\Phi_s}{dt} \tag{9.6a}$$

or

$$\frac{\partial L}{\partial t}\tau_s + \frac{\partial L}{\partial x^i}\xi_s^i + \frac{\partial L}{\partial \dot{x}^i}\left(\frac{d\xi_s^i}{dt} - \dot{x}^i\frac{d\tau_s}{dt}\right) + L\frac{d\tau_s}{dt} = \frac{d\Phi_s}{dt}. \tag{9.6b}$$

Noether's Theorem on Conservation Laws states that if the fundamental integral (9.1) of a problem in the calculus of variations is invariant up to a divergence term under the r-parameter family of transformations (9.2), then r distinct quantities Ω_s ($s = 1, \ldots, r$) are constant along any extremity and there exist r conservation laws,

$$\Omega_s = -H\tau_s + \frac{\partial L}{\partial \dot{x}^i}\xi_s^i - \Phi_s = \text{constant} \quad (s = 1, \ldots, r) \tag{9.7}$$

where H is the Hamiltonian defined by

$$H = -L + \dot{x}^i \frac{\partial L}{\partial \dot{x}^i}. \tag{9.8}$$

The fundamental invariance identities given by (9.6) serve as the basic equation for determining the existence of the group of transformations under which the integral is invariant. Equation (9.6) is usually written, upon expanding its total derivatives, in the following system of partial differential equations in unknowns rs and τs and ξ_s^is for any given Lagrangian function:

$$\frac{\partial L}{\partial t}\tau_s + \frac{\partial L}{\partial x^i}\xi_s^i + \frac{\partial L}{\partial \dot{x}^i}\left[\frac{d\xi_s^i}{dt} + \frac{d\xi_s^i}{dx^j}\dot{x}^j - \dot{x}^i\left(\frac{\partial \tau_s}{\partial \tau} + \dot{x}^j\frac{\partial \tau_s}{\partial x^j}\right)\right]$$

$$+ L\left(\frac{d\tau_s}{dt} + \frac{d\tau_s}{dx^j}\dot{x}^j\right) = \frac{d\Phi_s}{dt} \quad (s = 1, \ldots, r). \tag{9.9}$$

(See Sato (1981, pp. 242–251) for derivations of the Noether theorem and the invariance identities.)

9.2.2 Model 1: Zero Discount Rate

Frank Ramsey's original model, as well as the von Neumann model of capital accumulation developed by Samuelson (1970a,b), and Liviatan–Samuelson's model of general neoclassical growth (1969) where the time variable t does not enter into the Lagrangian explicitly, are the typical examples belonging to this model. Model 1 can be represented by

$$\max \int_a^b L(x(t), \dot{x}(t)) \, dt \tag{9.10}$$

where L satisfies all the necessary conditions for maximization.

The invariance identities for this problem are:

$$L \frac{d\tau_s}{dt} + \frac{\partial L}{\partial x^i} \xi_s^i + \frac{\partial L}{\partial \dot{x}^i} \left(\frac{d\xi_s^i}{dt} - \dot{x}^i \frac{d\tau_s}{dt} \right) = \frac{d\Phi_s}{dt}. \tag{9.11}$$

One of the solutions to the above give the well-known case of

$$\tau_i = \text{constant} = 1,$$
$$\xi_s^i \equiv 0 \tag{9.12}$$

which immediately leads to the conservation law of the Hamiltonian.

$$H = -L + \dot{x}^i \frac{\partial L}{\partial \dot{x}^i}. \tag{9.13}$$

The Hamiltonian in the Ramsey model is the Ramsey rule for optimal saving. In the Liviatan–Samuelson model it is "a welfare measure of national income" in Kuznets' sense which should remain constant.

In a closed consumptionless system of the von Neumann type, L takes a special form

$$L(t, \lambda(t), K(t); \dot{\lambda}(t), \dot{K}(t)) = \dot{K}_1 + \lambda F(\dot{K}(t), K(t)) \tag{9.14}$$

where $K(t) = $ the vector of n capital goods $(K_1(t), \ldots, K_n(t))$, $F = $ a smooth, neoclassical, concave, first-degree homogeneous transformation function (Samuelson 1970a,b), and $\lambda = $ the multiplier. The Lie group transformations under which (9.14) is invariant are

$$\bar{t} = t + \varepsilon \tau(t, \lambda(t), K(t)),$$
$$\bar{\lambda}(t) = \lambda(t) + \varepsilon w(t, \lambda(t), K(t)),$$
$$\bar{K}_i(t) = K_i(t) + \varepsilon \xi^i(t, \lambda(t), K(t)) \quad (i = 1, \ldots, n). \tag{9.15}$$

9.2 Continuous Models

The invariance equation is

$$\frac{\partial L}{\partial \lambda}w + \frac{\partial L}{\partial K_i}\xi^i + \frac{\partial L}{\partial \dot{K}_i}\left(\frac{d\xi^i}{dt} - \dot{K}_i\frac{d\tau}{dt}\right) + L\frac{d\tau}{dt}$$
$$= \frac{d\Phi}{dt}(t,\lambda,K) \tag{9.16}$$

where

$$L = \dot{K}_1 + \lambda F,$$
$$\frac{\partial L}{\partial K_i} = \lambda \frac{\partial F}{\partial K_i},$$
$$\frac{\partial L}{\partial \dot{K}_1} = 1 + \lambda \frac{\partial F}{\partial \dot{K}_1}$$

and

$$\frac{\partial L}{\partial \dot{K}_j} = \lambda \frac{\partial F}{\partial \dot{K}_j} \quad (j = 2, \ldots, n).$$

Solving the above (see Sato (1981, pp. 279–285)), we get

$$\tau = \gamma,$$
$$\xi^i = \alpha K_i \quad (i = 1, \ldots, n),$$
$$w = -\alpha\lambda,$$
$$\Phi = \alpha K_1 + C \quad (\alpha, \gamma = \text{constant}).$$

Corresponding to the first parameter γ we have the conservation laws,

$$\gamma : \Omega_1 = \lambda\left(F - \frac{\partial F}{\partial \dot{K}_1}\dot{K}_i\right) = \lambda\left(K_1 \frac{\partial F}{\partial K_i}\right) = \lambda Y = \text{constant}$$
$$(i = 1, \ldots, n) \tag{9.17}$$

where Y = national income, and to the second parameter α, we have

$$\alpha : \Omega_2 = -\lambda\left(\frac{\partial F}{\partial \dot{K}_i}K_i\right) = \lambda W = \text{constant} \quad (i = 1, \ldots, n) \tag{9.18}$$

where

$$W = \sum K_i P_i,$$
$$P_i = -\frac{\partial F}{\partial \dot{K}_i} = \text{supply price of } K_i.$$

Dividing Ω_1 by Ω_2,

$$\frac{\Omega_1}{\Omega_2} = \frac{Y}{W} \tag{9.19}$$

we get Samuelson's output-wealth conservation law (Samuelson 1970a,b).

9.2.3 Model 2: Fixed Discount Rate

The typical model of maximization of the discounted present value of welfare is represented by

$$\max \int_0^\infty e^{-\rho t} L(x(t), \dot{x}(t)) \, dt \quad (\rho > 0) \tag{9.20}$$

where L again satisfies all the conditions necessary for maximization. This model is most popular in economics and includes the extension of the Ramsey Model (see Cass (1965); Caton and Shell (1971); Liviatan and Samuelson (1969); Samuelson (1976); Samuelson and Solow (1956) and others), the neo-classical models of investment by Jorgenson (1967) and Lucas (1967) and the endogenous theory of technical change (see Sato and Suzawa (1983) and Sato and Ramachandran (1987)).

The general neo-classical optimal growth model takes the form

$$L(x(t), \dot{x}(t)) = U(c(t)) \tag{9.21}$$

and

$$c(t) = f(k(t), \dot{k}(t)) \tag{9.22}$$

where U = welfare function, c = consumption, k = capital per capita and f = the transformation function.

The general theory of investment takes the form

$$L(x(t), \dot{x}(t)) = pQ(L(t), K(t)) - WL(t) - \phi(\dot{K}(t), K) \tag{9.23}$$

where p = price of output Q, L = labor, K = capital, W = wage rate and ϕ = the adjustment function. The model of endogenous theory of technical change takes a similar form as (9.23); thus,

$$L(x(t), \dot{x}(t)) = p(Q)Q - C(Q, A) - \theta(Q, A, \dot{A}, B, \dot{B})$$
$$- \pi(Q, A, \dot{A}, B, \dot{B}) \tag{9.24}$$

9.2 Continuous Models

where P = price of output Q, C = cost function, A = stock of applied knowledge, B = stock of basic knowledge (or research), θ = R&D expenditure for applied research and π = R&D expenditure for basic research.

One of the most important conservation laws hidden in the neoclassical growth model is the *income-wealth conservation law*, which was discovered by Weitzman (1976). This law was rediscovered by Samuelson (1982); Kemp and Long (1982); and Sato (1982). In Sato (1982), it was presented, for the first time, as a special case of the Noether theorem. We will follow the 1985 version of this approach (Sato 1985).

By applying the infinitesimal transformation (9.3) on (9.20) when (9.20) takes the form (9.21), and by using the fundamental Noether invariance identities (9.6) (Logan 1977), we obtain

$$e^{-\rho t}\left[-\rho U \tau + \frac{\partial U}{\partial k^i}\xi + \frac{\partial U}{\partial \dot{k}^i}\left(\frac{d\xi^i}{dt} - \dot{k}^i\frac{d\tau}{dt}\right) + U\frac{d\tau}{dt}\right] = \frac{d\Phi}{dt}. \quad (9.25)$$

Now assume that

$$\tau = 1,$$
$$\xi^i = 0 \quad (i = 1,\ldots,n).$$

Then we get, from (9.25) and from the Euler equation, along the optimal path,

$$\frac{d\Phi}{dt} = -\rho e^{-\rho t} U. \quad (9.26)$$

Also by differentiating (9.7) with t and setting $\tau = 1$ and $\xi^i = 0$, we have

$$\frac{d\Phi}{dt} = \frac{d}{dt}\left[e^{-\rho t}\left(U - \dot{k}^i\frac{\partial U}{\partial \dot{k}^i}\right)\right]. \quad (9.27)$$

Equating (9.26) and (9.27) and integrating both sides, we get

$$e^{-\rho t}\left[U(t) - \dot{k}(t)\frac{\partial U(t)}{\partial \dot{k}(t)}\right] = \rho \int_t^\infty e^{-\rho s}U(s)\,ds \quad (9.28)$$

(The concavity and transversality conditions are implicitly assumed). By multiplying both sides of (9.28) by $e^{\rho t}$, we can derive the *income-wealth conservation law* as

$$U(t) - \dot{k}(t)\frac{\partial U(t)}{\partial \dot{k}(t)} = \rho \int_t^\infty e^{-\rho(s-t)}U(s)\,ds \quad (9.29)$$

or

$$\text{"Income"} = \rho \times \text{"wealth"}. \quad (9.30)$$

Alternately (9.29) can be rewritten (see Sato (1985, pp. 376–377)) as

$$e^{-\rho t}\left(U(t) - \dot{k}(t)\frac{\partial U(t)}{\partial \dot{k}(t)}\right) + \rho \int_0^t e^{-\rho s} U(s)\,ds = \rho \int_0^\infty e^{-\rho s} U(s)\,ds \quad (9.31)$$

which can be interpreted as

"discounted income" + ρ × discounted stock of consumption

= ρ × maximum discounted stock of consumption

= constant. (9.32)

We will leave it to the reader to come up with an appropriate economic interpretation of the conservation law that is inherent in the models of investment (4.4) and endogenous technical change (4.5).

9.2.4 Model 3: Variable Discount Rate

Samuelson (1982) pondered whether the income-wealth conservation law held when the discount rate varies with time. That is,

$$\text{"Income"} = \rho(t) \times \text{"wealth"}. \quad (9.33)$$

The Lie group approach enabled me to answer this question effectively (Sato 1985). Let the Lagrangian function be

$$L = e^{-\rho(t)} U(k(t), \dot{k}(t)) \quad (9.34)$$

where $d\rho/dt$ is not necessarily constant. When $\rho_0(t) = \rho t$, $\rho_0 =$ constant, this model reduces to Model 2. Again by setting $\xi^i = 0$ and $\tau = 1$, we obtain (see Sato (1985, pp. 379–380))

$$L - \dot{k}^i \frac{\partial L}{\partial \dot{k}^i} = \text{utility measure of generalized income}$$

$$= -\int_t^\infty \frac{\partial L}{\partial t}\,ds = \int_t^\infty \rho'(s) e^{-\rho(s)} U(k(s), \dot{k}(s))\,ds$$

= utility measure of generalized wealth. (9.35)

It is apparent when $\rho'(s) = \rho =$ constant, we obtain Weitzman's standard income-wealth conservation law (9.30).

9.2 Continuous Models

Now let

$$\tau = \frac{1}{\rho'(t)},$$
$$\xi^i = 0. \qquad (9.36)$$

Then (9.35) becomes

$$U - k^i \frac{\partial U}{\partial k^i} = \rho_t \int_t^\infty \left(\exp\left(-\int_t^s \rho_p \, dp\right)\right) \left[U - k^i \frac{\partial U}{\partial k^i} \frac{d}{ds}\left(\frac{1}{\rho_s}\right)\right] ds \qquad (9.37)$$

or

$$\text{"income"} = \rho_t \times \text{"general wealth"} \qquad (9.38)$$

where

$$\rho_t = \frac{d\rho}{dt} = \rho'(t).$$

The generalized wealth now includes capital gains and losses depending upon whether the last term of the integrated is positive or negative. This term depends on the supply price of investment $-\partial U/\partial k$, and the *variable* discount rate.

9.2.5 Model 4: Technical and Taste Change

Let the optimal control problem of the dynamic system be

$$\max \int_0^\infty D(t) L(x(t), \dot{x}(t), t) \, dt. \qquad (9.39)$$

Here L is directly affected by t, which represents taste and/or technical change. Note that there is an additional term $D(t)$. A special case of (9.39) is the usual optimal control problem of welfare maximization when L takes the form

$$D(t)L = D(t)U(c(k(t), \dot{k}(t), t)). \qquad (9.40)$$

It is shown (Sato 1981, pp. 275–278) that if $D(t)$ takes the usual form of $e^{-\rho t}$, then the "factor-augmenting" type of technical progress on k, i.e.,

$$C(k(t), \dot{k}(t), t) = c(k(t), e^{\rho t} \dot{k}(t)) \qquad (9.41)$$

implies the existence of the *conservation law for the current Hamiltonian*. That is,

$$\Omega = -\left(e^{-\rho t} U(c(k, e^{\rho t} k)) - U' \frac{\partial c}{\partial (e^{\rho t} k)} \dot{k}\right) e^{\rho t} = \text{constant}. \qquad (9.42)$$

A more general case of

$$\max \int_0^\infty e^{-\rho t} U(k(t), \dot{k}(t), t)\, dt \qquad (9.43)$$

where taste and technical change are not necessarily of the factor augmenting type, may be analyzed in the same manner as the previous model. The work by Sato, Nôno and Mimura (1984) shows that when $\tau = e^{\rho t}$ and $\xi = b(t) \exp\left[-\int_0^t \frac{U_k}{U_{\dot{k}}} ds\right]$, we have the conservation law:

$$U(t) - \dot{k}(t) \frac{\partial U}{\partial \dot{k}} + \int_t^\infty e^{-\rho(s-t)} \frac{\partial U}{\partial s} ds = \rho \int_t^\infty e^{-\rho(s-t)} U(s)\, ds \qquad (9.44)$$

which may be interpreted as

Income + "Value of Taste (Technical) Change" = $\rho \times$ wealth. $\qquad (9.45)$

There are many "hidden" conservation laws associated with the infinitesimal transformation related to the quantity variable $x(t)$. The reader may refer to Sato, Nôno and Mimura (1984) for a special case when U does not explicitly contain t and

$$\tau = 0, \quad \xi \neq 0. \qquad (9.46)$$

Here we have the *"modified" supply price conservation law*.

$$\Omega = \frac{\text{supply price of investment}}{\Theta'(k)} = \text{constant} \qquad (9.47)$$

where Θ' is determined by $\xi \neq 0$ (see Sato, Nôno and Mimura (1984, p. 40)).

9.2.6 Model 5: "Local" Conservation Laws

Most of the main results in economic dynamics are of *local nature*, we now look for what may be called the *"local" conservation laws* operating in the neighborhood of the stationary point. We assume that existence of the stationary equilibrium point corresponding to $\dot{k} = 0$, i.e., $k = k^*$, $\dot{k} = 0$. We begin with the local Lagrangian near $(0, k(0))$ in the form suggested by Samuelson (1972, p. 113, Eq. (46)),

$$L = e^{-\rho t}\left(-\frac{1}{2}\dot{x}^2 - a x \dot{x} - \frac{1}{2} x^2\right) \qquad (9.48)$$

9.2 Continuous Models

where $x = k(t) - k^*$, $\dot{x} = \dot{k}(t)$. The conservation law derived for the case (see Sato (1981)),

$$\tau = \delta = \text{constant}, \quad \xi = \frac{\rho\delta}{2}x \qquad (9.49)$$

is

$$\Omega = \frac{e^{-\rho t}}{2}[(\dot{x}^2 - x^2) - \rho x(\dot{x} + ax)], \quad \delta = 1$$

$$= H - \frac{\rho x}{2}\frac{\partial L}{\partial \dot{x}} = \text{constant.} \qquad (9.50)$$

The value of the modified Hamiltonian (or income) remains constant, where the modification factor is equal to ρ *multiplied by the value of capital.* This is the local version of the income-wealth conservation law discussed in the earlier sections.

9.2.7 Total Value Conservation Law of the Firm

The models discussed up to this point may be applied to microeconomics. The theory of economic conservation laws may be used to test whether corporations are maximizing long-run profits. Then, the income-wealth conservation law in macroeconomics can be reinterpreted as the total value conservation law of the firm (Sato 2004; Sato and Fujii 2005).

To consider a firm's profit-maximization, the following profit function is formulated,

$$J(x) = \int_a^b \Pi(t, x(t), \dot{x}(t))\,dt$$

where $x(t) = (x^1(t), \ldots, x^n(t)) = $ the vector of quantities and prices, and $\dot{x}(t) = \dfrac{dx(t)}{dt}$.

If the profit function has a familiar form such as,

$$\Pi = e^{-\rho t}G(x(t), \dot{x}(t))$$

where ρ is the discount rate (fixed), then the conservation law can be expressed as

$$G(x(t), \dot{x}(t)) + \sum \pi^i x^i = \rho \int_t^\infty e^{-\rho(s-t)}G(x, \dot{x})\,ds. \qquad (9.51)$$

$$\rho = \frac{G + \sum \pi^i x^i}{\int_t^\infty e^{-\rho(s-t)}G(x, \dot{x})\,ds}. \qquad (9.52)$$

This is the micro version of the income-wealth conservation law. Equation (9.52) says that the sum of the current value of profit, G, and changes in the value of the firm, $\sum \pi^i \dot{x}^i$, divided by the discounted value of the firm, $\int_t^\infty e^{-\rho(s-t)} G(x,\dot{x})\,ds$, must always be equal to the discount rate. Alternatively Eq. (9.51) states that the discounted total value of the firm multiplied by the discount rate must always be equal to the sum of each year's profit and investment. This is the meaning of the total value conservation law operating for any profit maximizing firm.

9.3 Discrete Models (2012 Version) by Shigeru Maeda

9.3.1 Introduction

In applied mathematics and engineering, attention has also been paid to the analysis of discrete mechanics to determine whether or not continuous Hamiltonian and Lagrangian formalisms will apply and also whether or not the Noether theorem can be extended to the study of discrete mechanics (Maeda 1982).

A few remarks are in order. First, in the study of discrete mechanics, the Noether theorem is not of great use because no infinitesimal change of time can be admitted (see Maeda (1982)), and because no energy-like integral can be derived from this approach. It is still an open problem except for a few limited cases whether or not an individual discrete system conserves the energy-like integral. Hence, another method must be devised which will enable us to proceed. Secondly, as long as we focus our attention on the local aspects of the discrete dynamic system, we need not rely on the Noether-like theorem. Section 9.3.2 presents a mathematical methodology to attack this problem. While no method is universally applicable, this method has proved to be very powerful, provided that one looks only for "local" conservation laws. We begin with a general description of the discrete-time growth model.

9.3.2 Model 6: Discrete Growth Models

We first present a general form of discrete-time N-sector growth models. Let t denote a discrete time variable $t = 0, 1, 2, \ldots$, and let $q = (q^1, q^2, \ldots, q^N)$ be a set of N capital goods measured in terms of unit of labor input. The symbol q_t means the value of q at the tth period. Given a well-defined social welfare (utility) index function, the society's objective is to maximize the sum of discounted utility over the infinite time horizon from $t = 0$ to $t = +\infty$. For simplicity we assume that no technical change is explicitly considered so that the welfare function does not contain t explicitly.

9.3 Discrete Models (2012 Version) by Shigeru Maeda

We begin by recalling a simple Ramsey model where the transformation function between consumption and capital accumulation is linear. Let f and U represent a neoclassical production function and a utility function respectively. Then, the society's welfare in the discrete model is represented by

$$U_t = U(q_t, q_{t+1}) = U(f(q_t) + q_t - (1+n)q_{t+1}) \tag{9.53}$$

where n is the growth rate of labor (Samuelson 1967). The society maximizes the discounted sum of welfare "functional"

$$\sum_{t=0}^{\infty}(1+\delta)^{-t}U_t = \sum_{t=0}^{\infty}\lambda^{-t}U_t \quad (\lambda = 1+\delta) \tag{9.54}$$

where $\delta \geq 0$ is a fixed time discount rate. As is usual, it is assumed that f and U satisfy $f > 0$, $f' > 0$, $f'' < 0$, $U' > 0$, $U'' < 0$. Also, it is implicitly assumed that q, a set of capital goods, takes a non-negative value satisfying certain inequality conditions. The optimal growth path generated by the maximization of (9.54) is assumed to have an equilibrium solution q^*, which enables one to look for conservation laws operating near the equilibrium point. By adopting a new variable $q_t - q^*$, rather than q itself, one can look for "local" conservation laws operating near the equilibrium point q^*. By approximating the original utility function up to the second order, one can study the dynamic behavior with the approximated Lagrangian function which is quadratic homogeneous in $q_t - q^*$. As long as we deal with a local area, no inequality condition on q_t is necessary. As there is no need to confine the analysis to the Ramsey-type model, we write a general discrete version of the Samuelson–Solow model and define the society's objective welfare "functional" as

$$\max \sum_{t=0}^{\infty} \lambda^{-t} L(q_t, q_{t+1}) \quad (\lambda = 1+\delta) \tag{9.55}$$

where L denotes a social welfare function of C^2 class satisfying the appropriate conditions. Assume also that the variable (q_t, q_{t+1}) is contained in an admissible convex set and the equilibrium point q^* is admitted in the domain. The function L is assumed to be strictly concave and its Hessian matrix at the equilibrium point is negative definite. Let v_t denote the forward difference of q_t, i.e., $v_t = q_{t+1} - q_t$. For notational convenience, we let q_t stand for $q_t - q^*$ and v_t stand for $q_{t+1} - q_t$. Also, in order to formulate the system in terms of discrete Lagrangian mechanics, we consider L as a function of (q_t, v_t). By approximating the Lagrangian near the equilibrium point up to the second order, the problem of maximizing the society's welfare function is reduced to

$$\max \sum_{t=0}^{\infty} \lambda^{-t} L(q_t, v_t), \quad L_t = \frac{v'B_0 v}{2} + v'C_0 q + \frac{q'D_0 q}{2} \tag{9.56}$$

where B_0 and D_0 are symmetric, and B_0 and $B_0 - C_0$ are nonsingular matrices. The elements of B_0, C_0 and D_0 are the cross-derivatives of the original function in (9.55) evaluated at (q^*, q^*) as

$$b_{ij} = \frac{\partial^2 L}{\partial q^i_{t+1} \partial q^j_{t+1}}(q^*, q^*),$$

$$c_{ij} = b_{ij} + \frac{\partial^2 L}{\partial q^i_{t+1} \partial q^j_t}(q^*, q^*),$$

$$d_{ij} = c_{ij} + \frac{\partial^2 L}{\partial q^j_{t+1} \partial q^i_t}(q^*, q^*) + \frac{\partial^2 L}{\partial q^i_t \partial q^j_t}(q^*, q^*). \tag{9.57}$$

The next task is to make the discounted social welfare function $\lambda^{-t} L$ *independent of t*. We introduce a new variable Q in place of q as

$$Q_t = \lambda^{-t/2} q_t \tag{9.58}$$

and also V_t, the forward difference of Q_t as

$$V_t = Q_{t+1} - Q_t = \lambda^{-t/2} [\lambda^{-1/2} v_t + (\lambda^{-1/2} - 1) q_t] \tag{9.59}$$

Then the welfare function becomes quadratic homogeneous in Q and V:

$$\lambda^{-t} L = \tilde{L} = \frac{V'BV}{2} + V'CQ + \frac{Q'DQ}{2} \tag{9.60}$$

where

$$B = \lambda B_0,$$
$$C = (\lambda - \lambda^{1/2}) B_0 + \lambda^{1/2} C_0,$$
$$D = (\lambda^{1/2} - 1)^2 B_0 + (\lambda^{1/2} - 1)(C_0 + C'_0) + D_0. \tag{9.61}$$

The discrete Euler equation (Euler difference equation) for maximization is transformed to a Hamiltonian system by the Legendre transformation (Maeda 1980). If we introduce the implicit prices P or "momentums," conjugate to V (not v), as

$$P_{t+1} = \frac{\partial \tilde{L}_t}{\partial V} = BV_t + CQ_t \tag{9.62}$$

then, the Euler difference equation may be written as a linear system in (Q, P).

We are now in a position to study the dynamic behavior of the model near the equilibrium point. After some tedious calculations, we obtain the linearized equation in the Hamiltonian formalism as

9.3 Discrete Models (2012 Version) by Shigeru Maeda

$$x_{t+1} = Ax_t \tag{9.63a}$$

where

$$A = \begin{bmatrix} -(B-C')^{-1} & I \\ -B(B-C')^{-1} & C \end{bmatrix} \begin{bmatrix} C-D & -I \\ I & 0 \end{bmatrix} \tag{9.63b}$$

and

$$x' = (Q^1, \ldots, Q^n, P_1, \ldots, P_n). \tag{9.63c}$$

According to the theory of discrete dynamics (Maeda 1980, 1982), the transition matrix A is a symplectic matrix; that is, it satisfies

$$A'JA = J \quad \text{where} \quad J = \begin{bmatrix} 0 & I \\ -I & 0 \end{bmatrix}. \tag{9.64}$$

In order to derive conservation laws associated with the linear dynamic system given by (9.63), we must construct first integrals of the form

$$f_S(x) = \frac{x'Sx}{2}, \quad S' = S \tag{9.65}$$

such that it satisfies the condition

$$f_S(x_{t+1}) = f_S(x_t) \quad \text{for all } t. \tag{9.66}$$

In what follows, we digress to show how such integrals can be obtained.

9.3.3 Quadratic Conservatives: A Mathematical Digression[1]

The problem of optimizing the functional;

$$\max \sum_{t=0}^{T} L(q_t, q_{t+1}, t) = L(q_t, v_t, t) \tag{9.67}$$

through the discrete variational principle will yield the system of Euler difference equations:

$$\frac{\partial L_t}{\partial v_t^i} - \frac{\partial L_{t-1}}{\partial v_t^i} - \frac{\partial L_t}{\partial q_t^i} = 0 \tag{9.68}$$

---

[1] This section is largely due to Maeda (1988).

where $v_t^i = q_{t+1}^i - q_t^i$ is the forward difference of the coordinates. Like the continuous case there are two formalisms: the Lagrangian and Hamiltonian formalisms. Any system in one formalism can be expressed in the other formalism under the appropriate conditions. Suppose that a Lagrangian function satisfies

$$\det\left(\frac{\partial^2 L}{\partial v^i \partial v^j}\right) \neq 0, \quad \det\left(\frac{\partial^2 L}{\partial v^i \partial v^j} - \frac{\partial^2 L}{\partial v^i \partial q^j}\right) \neq 0.$$

Then by putting

$$p_{i,t+1} = \frac{\partial L_t}{\partial v_t^i} \tag{9.69a}$$

and

$$H(q_t, p_{t+1}) = p_{i,t+1} v_t^i - L(q_t, v_t)$$

(The summation convention in force.) (9.69b)

Equation (9.68) can be transformed to

$$q_{t+1}^i - q_t^i = \frac{\partial H}{\partial p_{i,t}}, \quad p_{i,t+1} - p_{i,t} = -\frac{\partial H}{\partial q_t^i}. \tag{9.70}$$

By a "discrete system" is meant a system described by ordinary difference equations of the first order. Equation (9.70) is a discrete system generated from the optimization. In general the discrete system is expressed as $x_{t+1} = \phi(x_t)$. A point sequence $\{x_t\}$ subject to the discrete system is called a solution, and a real smooth function is called a first integral (F.I.) if its value remains constant along any solution. The discrete system (9.70) inherits two important properties intrinsic to any Hamiltonian system (Abraham and Marsden 1978):

1. If f and g are F.I.'s, so is $\{f, g\}$, where $\{.\}$ denotes the Poisson bracket;
2. If h is an F.I., then X_h is a symmetry operator where X_h is the Hamiltonian operator with the Hamiltonian h.

Here, a symmetry operator of a discrete system is defined to be an infinitesimal operator such that its flow commutes with the mapping corresponding to the discrete system. It is shown that a set of all F.I.'s and all symmetry operators form Lie algebras respectively, and that the mapping $f \to -X_f$ gives a Lie algebra homomorphism (Maeda 1980).

A discrete linear Hamiltonian system is called symplectic, as it preserves the standard symplectic structure $\Omega = dp_i \wedge dq^i$ (Sato 1981). The discrete system corresponding to a linear symplectic mapping is expressed in the normal form as

$$x_{t+1} = A \cdot x_t \tag{9.71}$$

where $x' = (q^1, q^2, \ldots, q^n, p_1, p_2, \ldots, p_n)$.

9.3 Discrete Models (2012 Version) by Shigeru Maeda

Let G and g denote the $2N$-dimensional symplectic group $Sp(N,R)$ and its Lie algebra, respectively:

$$G = \{ A \in M(2N, \mathbf{R}) \mid A'JA = J \}$$

$$g = \{ X \in M(2N, \mathbf{R}) \mid X'J + JX = 0 \}$$

where $J = \begin{bmatrix} 0 & -I \\ I & 0 \end{bmatrix}$ and dash denotes matrix transpose. Our problem is to establish a systematic approach to finding the quadratic form

$$f_S(x) = \frac{x'Sx}{2}, \quad S' = S \tag{9.72}$$

conserved along any solution of the linear recurrence on $\mathbf{R}^N$

$$x_{t+1} = Ax_t \tag{9.73a}$$

where A is an arbitrary element of G. The whole of conservatives given by (9.72) forms a Lie algebra with respect to the Poisson bracket (Maeda 1980).

Linear space Ξ. We introduce a linear space Ξ of all matrices commuting with A, and it is proved that one of its subspaces is Lie algebra isomorphic to the whole of quadratic conservatives given by (9.72).

Now, (9.72) is conserved along any solution of (9.73a), if and only if A and JS commute. Then, the whole of quadratic conservatives is identified with the following linear space of all coefficient matrices:

$$\Omega = \{ S \in M(2N, \mathbf{R}) \mid [A, JS] = 0, S' = S \} \tag{9.73b}$$

where $[A, B] = AB - BA$. Ω forms a Lie algebra with respect to the bracket

$$<S, T> = SJT - TJS \tag{9.73c}$$

which is a representation of the Poisson bracket on Ω. Apart from looking into Ω directly, we introduce a linear space Ξ of all matrices that commute with A:

$$\Xi = \{ L \in M(2N, \mathbf{R}) \mid [A, L] = 0 \}.$$

We define two linear mappings $\eta : \Xi \to \Xi$ and $\sigma : \Xi \to \Omega$ by

$$\eta(L) = JL'J, \quad \sigma(L) = \frac{J(L + \eta(L))}{2} = \frac{JL + (JL)'}{2}.$$

Lemma 9.1. $\eta^2 = id., \eta(\Xi) = \Xi.$

Proof. Let $L \in \Xi$. Then, it follows from direct calculation that $\eta^2(L) = L$ and $[\eta(A), \eta(L)] = \eta([A,L]) = 0$. Since A is symplectic, we have $\eta(A) = -A^{-1}$ and accordingly $[A, \eta(L)] = 0$, which means $\eta(\Xi) \subset \Xi$. This together with $\eta^2 = id$. leads to $\eta(\Xi) = \Xi$. □

The lemma shows that η is an involution map on Ξ. Then, η has two eigenvalues ± 1 and Ξ is a direct sum of the two eigenspaces. That is, $\Xi = \Theta \dotplus \Phi$, where

$$\Theta = \{\, L \in \Xi \mid \eta(L) = L \,\}, \quad \Phi = \{\, L \in \Xi \mid \eta(L) = -L \,\}.$$

The projector P from Ξ onto Θ is given by

$$P(L) = \frac{L + \eta(L)}{2}.$$

The condition $\eta(L) = L$ is equivalent to $L'J + JL = 0$ so that Θ, which is an intersection of g and Ξ, is a subalgebra of $sp(N, \mathbf{R})$. Then P produces an element of g from any matrix commuting with A. It is to be stressed that A is an element of a Lie group and $P(L)$ is an element of a Lie algebra.

Now, Ξ is connected with Ω in the following manner:

Lemma 9.2. $\sigma(\Xi) = \Omega, \sigma^{-1}(0) = \Phi$.

Proof. We choose an arbitrary L. By definition, $\sigma(L)$ is symmetric. Moreover, since $J\sigma(L) = -(L + \eta(L))/2$, it belongs to Ξ and commutes with A. Thus $\sigma(L) \in \Omega$. Conversely, for any $S \in \Omega$, we put $L = -JS$. Then, it is easily proved that $L \in \Xi$ and $\sigma(L) = S$. The second assertion is obvious from the definitions of σ and Φ. □

Since $\Xi = \Theta \dotplus \Phi$, Lemma 9.2 shows that Ω is linearly isomorphic to Θ. Furthermore, it holds after slight calculation that

$$\sigma([L,M]) = <\sigma(L), \sigma(M)>$$

where $<,>$ is given by (9.73b), and L and M belong to Θ. Combining this and Lemma 9.2, we have

Lemma 9.3. Θ *is Lie algebra isomorphic to* Ω.

The linear mapping σ restricted on Θ gives a momentum mapping $\hat{J}$ in symmetry reduction theory of classical mechanics (Abraham and Marsden 1978). Furthermore, we note that

$$\sigma(P(L)) = \sigma(L)$$

holds for any $L \in \Xi$.

Now, we have found that each quadratic first integral is closely related to a symmetric matrix which commutes with A and belongs to $sp(N, \mathbf{R})$. It is already known that all of such coefficient matrices can be constructed in terms of some kinds

9.3 Discrete Models (2012 Version) by Shigeru Maeda

of eigenvectors and generalized eigenvectors of A (See Appendix). The construction procedure is of great use for the purpose of studying the structure of symmetry algebra, whereas it is difficult to see how the derived F.I. is connected with the Lagrangian L, since the matrix A does not appear in an explicit manner. This may lead to the difficulty of finding economical meaning of the conservative. Then, in what follows, we intend to seek for first integrals constructed directly from A, which may not necessarily cover the whole of quadratic first integrals.

A subspace Ξ_1 of Ξ. Considering the fact that an arbitrary polynomial in A commutes with A, we introduce a linear space

$$\Xi_1 = \{I, A^{\pm 1}, A^{\pm 2}, \ldots\}.$$

Ξ_1 is a subspace of Ξ. We denote by ϕ_A and f_A the minimal polynomial and the eigenpolynomial of A, respectively. When ϕ_A equal to f_A, any matrix that commutes with A is expressed as a polynomial in A, so that Ξ_1 coincides with Ξ, and almost any element in G has this property.

Now, we put

$$\Theta_1 = \Xi_1 \cap \Theta, \quad \Phi_1 = \Xi_1 \cap \Phi, \quad \Omega_1 = \sigma(\Xi_1) = \sigma(\Theta_1).$$

Our interest centers in $\dim \Omega_1 (= \dim \Theta_1)$, which is the number of linearly independent conservatives (9.68) obtained from polynomials in A.

Lemma 9.4. *Let $d = \dim \Omega$ and $k = \deg \phi_A$, and one of the following three cases holds good:*

1. *If $k = 2s + 1$, then $d = s$.*
2. *If $k = 2s$ and $\phi_A(0) = 1$, then $d = s$.*
3. *If $k = 2s$ and $\phi_A(0) = -1$, then $d = s - 1$.*

Here, s is an integer.

Proof. We note that k is equal to $\dim \Xi_1$. For any integer i, we put

$$B_i = A^i - A^{-i} \tag{9.74}$$

and $C_i = A^i + A^{-i}$. Then, it holds that $B_i \in \Theta_1$ and $C_i \in \Phi_1$. When k is an odd number $2s + 1$, $\{B_1, \ldots, B_s, C_0, \ldots, C_s\}$ forms a basis of Ξ_1, and we have $k = s$. Next, when k is equal to $2s$, the $2s - 1$ matrices $\{B_1, \ldots, B_{s-1}, C_0, \ldots, C_{s-1}\}$ are linearly independent and further either B_s or C_s is linearly independent of these. Now, since A is symplectic, its minimal polynomial ϕ_A satisfies $\phi_A(A) = \phi_A(A^{-1}) = 0$. Then, ϕ_A must take one of the following forms:

(a) $(x^{2s} + 1) + a_1(x^{2s-1} + x) + \cdots + a_{s-1}(x^{s+1} + x^{s-1}) + a_s x^s$
(b) $(x^{2s} - 1) + a_1(x^{2s-1} - x) + \cdots + a_{s-1}(x^{s+1} - x^{s-1})$

When $\phi_A(0) = 1$ and (a) holds, B_s becomes linearly independent. When $\phi_A(0) = -1$ and (b) holds, C_s does. □

Next, we propose a simple scheme to construct a basis of Ω_1. If we do not know dim Θ_1 in advance, this scheme naturally produces a maximum number of linearlly independent elements.

Lemma 9.5. *Suppose that* $\{\sigma(A), \sigma(A^2), \ldots, \sigma(A^d)\}$ *are linearly independent and* $\sigma(A^d)$ *is linearly dependent on these d matrices. Then, the former d matrices form a basis of* Ω_1.

Proof. Since A^i belongs to G, we have $\sigma(A^i) = JB_i/2$, where B_i is given by (9.74). As is seen in the proof of Lemma 9.4, when dim $\Theta_1 = d$, the set $\{B_1, \ldots, B_d\}$ forms a basis of Θ_1, and the converse is true. Since $(1/2)J\cdot : \Theta_1 \to \Omega_1$ gives a linear isomorphism, the assertion is verified. □

Again, we remark that for almost every element A of G, its minimal polynomial ϕ_A coincides with the eigenpolynomial f_A. In this case, any matrix commuting with A is expressed as a polynomial in A so that Ω_1 is Ω itself.

Lemma 9.6. *Suppose that for an element A of G, its minimal polynomial coincides with the eigenpolynomial. Then,* $\{\sigma(A), \ldots, \sigma(A^N)\}$ *forms a basis of* Ω.

Proof. Under the supposition, it holds that dim $\Omega_1 = 2N$ and $\phi_A(0) = f_A(0) = \det(A) = 1$. Then, we have the conclusion from Lemma 9.4. □

We can obtain all quadratic conservatives for $A \in \Omega$ in the case of this lemma. Furthermore, all polynomials in A commute with one another, the following lemma is obvious.

Lemma 9.7. *Under the same condition as in Lemma 9.6, the linear discrete system (9.71) is completely integrable (Maeda 1987).*

In the remaining part of this subsection, a few remarks are made. First, due to the relation $\sigma(A^i) = JB_i$, $\sigma(A^i) = 0$ is equivalent to $A^{2i} = I$. In particular, $\sigma(A)$ vanishes, if and only if every discrete orbit of (9.71) is at most two periodic, that is, each component of q can take at most two distinct values as time passes. In this unreal case alone, the above approach can yield no quadratic F.I.'s. Such an unreal system will be disregarded, and accordingly, each system to be treated admits the first integral corresponding to $\sigma(A)$.

Secondly, by use of the relation $(A + A^{-1})B_i = B_{i+1} + B_{i-1}$ and the fact of $A \in G$, the following recurrence holds good:

$$\sigma(A^{i+1}) = (A' - JAJ)\sigma(A^i) - \sigma(A^{i-1})$$

which might serve the purpose of calculating $\sigma(A^i)$ step by step.

9.3 Discrete Models (2012 Version) by Shigeru Maeda

We have seen that the generic linear Hamiltonian system admits as many quadratic F.I.'s as the number of sectors. If the matrix A has distinct Jordan blocks with an identical eigenvalue, another kind of F.I.'s are admitted. We close this section by illustrating a simple example.

Example 9.1. Consider a linear Hamiltonian system with one degree of freedom.

$$q_{t+1} = aq_t + bp_t, \quad P_{t+1} = cq_t + dp_t$$

where a, b, c and d are real constants subject to $ad - bc = 1$. In this case A equals to $\begin{bmatrix} a & b \\ c & d \end{bmatrix}$, and we have $\sigma(A) = \begin{bmatrix} c & (d-a)/2 \\ (d-a)/2 & -b \end{bmatrix}$. Then, under the condition $A^2 \neq I$, the corresponding F.I. is given by

$$\frac{1}{2}\{cq^2 + (d-a)qp - bp^2\}.$$

9.3.4 Economic Conservation Laws

Let us recall the linear Hamiltonian system (9.63). Our aim is to derive $f_{\sigma(A)}$ and to represent it in terms of the original variables (q, v), which is the conservation law in the system.

The matrix A in (9.63b) belongs to $Sp(N, \mathbf{R})$. Therefore, we can apply Lemma 9.6 to the system to obtain quadratic F.I.'s in terms of (Q, P) by calculating the coefficient matrices $\sigma(A^j)$ $(j = 1, 2, \ldots)$. The F.I.'s thus obtained will be rewritten as function of (q_t, v_t) through the coordinate transformation given by (9.58), (9.59) and (9.61). Combining (9.58), (9.59) and (9.62), we obtain the transformation relating $(Q.P)$ with (q, v) as

$$\begin{bmatrix} Q \\ P \end{bmatrix} = \lambda^{-t/2} \cdot T \begin{bmatrix} q \\ v \end{bmatrix} \qquad (9.75a)$$

where

$$T = \begin{bmatrix} I & 0 \\ (C-D) + (\lambda^{-1/2} - 1)(B - C') & \lambda^{-1/2}(B - C') \end{bmatrix} \qquad (9.75b)$$

or

$$\begin{bmatrix} Q_t \\ P_t \end{bmatrix} = \lambda^{-t/2} \cdot \tilde{T} \begin{bmatrix} q_t \\ \lambda^{-1/2} q_{t+1} \end{bmatrix} \qquad (9.76a)$$

where

$$\tilde{T} = \begin{bmatrix} I & 0 \\ (C-D)-(B-C') & B-C' \end{bmatrix}. \quad (9.76b)$$

Then, calculate $T'JAT$ and express its elements in terms of B_0, C_0 and D_0, to obtain

$$T'JAT = \lambda^{-1/2} \begin{bmatrix} \lambda C_0 - C_0' + D_0 & \lambda B_0 - C_0' + D_0 \\ -B_0 + C_0 & -B_0 + C_0 \end{bmatrix} \quad (9.77)$$

where $J = \begin{bmatrix} 0 & I \\ -I & 0 \end{bmatrix}$ as defined by Eq. (9.64). Recall that $\sigma(A) = \dfrac{JA + (JA)'}{2}$ and then we have

$$T'\sigma(A)T = \frac{T'JAT + (T'JAT)'}{2}. \quad (9.78)$$

By setting $\lambda f_{\sigma(A)} = I_1$, we obtain the following quadratic polynomial I_1, which is the conservation law in the system:

$$I_1 = \lambda^{-1} \left[\frac{v'(-B_0+C_0)v}{2} + \frac{v'\{(\lambda-1)B_0+D_0\}q}{2} \right.$$
$$\left. + \frac{q'\{(\lambda-1)C_0+D_0\}q}{2} \right]. \quad (9.79)$$

This conservation law can be expressed in a simple form using the original Lagrangian (9.56) as

$$I_1 = \lambda^{-1} \left[-\left(v'\frac{\partial L}{\partial v} - L\right) + \frac{1}{2}v'\frac{\partial L}{\partial q} + \frac{\lambda-1}{2}q'\frac{\partial L}{\partial v} \right]. \quad (9.80)$$

Thus, we have the following theorem.

Theorem 9.1. *Every discrete-time optimal growth model given by (9.55) admits a local conservation law (9.80).*

Alternatively using (q_t, q_{t+1}) and the transformation $\tilde{T}$, we can derive another form of the conservation law from

$$\tilde{T}'JA\tilde{T} = \begin{bmatrix} -(B-C) & 2B-C+D-C' \\ 0 & -(B-C) \end{bmatrix} \quad (9.81)$$

Due to the definition of B, C and D, each component of minor matrices in the above is given by

$$-(B-C)_{ij} = \lambda^{1/2}\alpha_{ij}, \quad (2B-C+D-C')_{ij} = \beta_{ij}$$

9.3 Discrete Models (2012 Version) by Shigeru Maeda

where α_{ij} and β_{ij} are calculated from

$$\alpha_{ij} = \frac{\partial^2 L}{\partial q^i_{t+1} \partial q^j_t}(q^*, q^*),$$

$$\beta_{ij} = \lambda \frac{\partial^2 L}{\partial q^i_{t+1} \partial q^j_{t+1}}(q^*, q^*) + \frac{\partial^2 L}{\partial q^i_t \partial q^j_t}(q^*, q^*).$$

Moreover, since $\sigma(A)$ is the symmetrization of JA, $y'\sigma(A)y = y'JAy$ holds for any $2N$-tripled column vector y. Then, from (9.76) and (9.81), we obtain the conservation law in terms of (q_t, q_{t+1}) as

$$\tilde{I}_1 = \lambda^{-1} \{\lambda \alpha_{ij} q^i_t q^j_t + \beta_{ij} q^i_t q^j_{t+1} + \alpha_{ij} q^i_{t+1} q^j_{t+1}\}.$$

(The summation convention in force.) \hfill (9.82)

The economic meaning of (9.80) is very similar to the conservation law for the continuous-time model (Sato 1981, p. 264). It is to be noted, however, that the term $\frac{1}{2} v' \frac{\partial L}{\partial q}$ is additional. This term

$$\sum \frac{(\text{capital accumulation}) \times \text{marginal utility of consumption}}{2}$$

= sum of the values of investment measured in terms of welfare

is considered as a correction term against the finiteness of the time period. It should also be noted that when $\lambda = 1$ (no discount rate), the conservation law is reduced to

$$I_0 = -\left(v'\frac{\partial L}{\partial v} - L\right) + \frac{1}{2} v' \frac{\partial L}{\partial q} \qquad (9.83)$$

which is expressed in terms of q_t and q_{t+1} as

$$I_0 = -\frac{1}{2}(q_{t+1} - q_t)'\left(\frac{\partial}{\partial q_{t+1}} - \partial q_t\right) L_t - L_t. \qquad (9.84)$$

When $\lambda \neq 1$ (more specifically $\lambda > 1$), the third term in (9.80) measures the modifying factor due to the discount rate, very similar to the continuous case (Sato 1981, p. 264).

Finally, let us work out in detail the conservation law associated with the discrete Ramsey model defined by (9.53). The model is a one-sector model and is assured to have one linearly independent quadratic F.I. (or the conservation law).

In this case, the coefficients α and β in (9.82) are given by

$$\alpha = \frac{\partial^2 L}{\partial q_{t+1} \partial q_t}(q^*, q^*) = -(1+n)U''(c^*)(1+f'(q^*)),$$

$$\beta = \lambda \frac{\partial^2 L}{\partial q_{t+1}^2}(q^*, q^*) + \frac{\partial^2 L}{\partial q_t^2}(q^*, q^*)$$

$$= \{\lambda(1+n)^2 + (1+f'(q^*))^2\}U''(c^*) + f''(q^*)U'(c^*)$$

where $c^* = f(q^*) - nq^*$. The Euler difference equation is reduced to

$$\alpha q_{t+1} + \beta q_t + \lambda \alpha q_{t-1} = 0.$$

The linearized discrete canonical equations are given by

$$\begin{bmatrix} q_{t+1} \\ p_{t+1} \end{bmatrix} = \begin{bmatrix} \dfrac{\xi - \eta}{\xi} - \dfrac{\eta^2 - \xi\zeta}{\xi(\xi-\eta)} & \dfrac{\lambda t}{\xi - \eta} \\ -\lambda t \times \dfrac{\eta^2 - \xi\zeta}{\xi - \eta} & \dfrac{\xi}{\xi - \eta} \end{bmatrix} \begin{bmatrix} q_t \\ p_t \end{bmatrix}$$

where

$$\xi = \frac{\partial^2 L_t}{\partial q_{t+1}^2}(q^*, q^*),$$

$$\eta = \frac{\partial^2 L_t}{\partial q_{t+1}^2}(q^*, q^*) + \frac{\partial^2 L_t}{\partial q_{t+1} \partial q_t}(q^*, q^*),$$

$$\zeta = \frac{\partial^2 L_t}{\partial q_{t+1}^2}(q^*, q^*) + 2\frac{\partial^2 L_t}{\partial q_{t+1} \partial q_t}(q^*, q^*) + \frac{\partial^2 L_t}{\partial q_t^2}(q^*, q^*).$$

The expressions ξ, η and ζ are related with α and β by

$$\alpha = \eta - \xi, \quad \beta = (1+\lambda)\xi - 2\eta + \zeta.$$

The characteristic roots associated with the canonical equations can be derived from

$$\alpha x^2 - (2\alpha - \zeta)x + \alpha = 0.$$

The reader can show that under the usual assumptions on f and v, the two roots are positive with one root greater than unity and the other root less than unity—the saddle point property.[2]

The conservation law is now given by

$$I_1(q_t, q_{t+1}) = \frac{1}{2\lambda}(\alpha q_{t+1}^2 + \beta q_{t+1} q_t + \lambda \alpha q_t^2).$$

One can easily check the validity of this conservation law from the Euler difference equation. Since $S' \times \lambda^{-1} \times M \times S = \lambda^{-(t-1)} M$, we have

$$I_1(q_t, q_{t+1}) = I_1(q_{t-1}, q_t)$$

where

$$S = \begin{bmatrix} -\beta/\alpha & \lambda \\ 1 & 0 \end{bmatrix}, \quad M = \begin{bmatrix} \alpha & \beta/2 \\ \beta/2 & \lambda\alpha \end{bmatrix}.$$

We close this section by adding a few remarks on discrete systems. First, the discrete Noether theorem is not as powerful as in the continuous case. Second, the method presented here is not almighty either. It is a powerful and systematic method as long as one deals with linear systems. Finally, through the transformations (9.58) and (9.59), the system is reduced to the one independent of t explicitly. This was possible because the term involving t is multiplicative in the Lagrangian. If a technical change factor is introduced in the system in a general manner, then there may be no transformations which reduce the system to the desirable form.

9.4 Summary

The purpose of this chapter is first to show how powerful the Noether theorem and Lie groups are in discovering both hidden and unhidden symmetries and conservation laws in continuous dynamic systems. Second, the discrete time optimization case requires a new methodology especially useful in linear systems. The resulting conclusions for the discrete systems are much more complicated than the continuous case. The main results of this chapter are summarized in the following Table 9.1.

---

[2] The reader can also check the saddle point property directly from the Euler difference equation using $1 + f(q^*) = \lambda(1+n)$.

Table 9.1 Summary of conservation laws table

	Lagrangian	Infinitesimal transformation	Conservation laws	Examples
Model I	$L = L(x(t), \dot{x}(t))$	$\tau = 1$ $\xi = 0$	$H =$ Wealth measure of national income $=$ constant	Original Ramsey model
	$L = \dot{K}_1$ $+ \lambda F(K, \dot{K})$	$\tau = \gamma =$ constant $\xi^i = \alpha K_i$ $w = -\alpha\lambda$ $\Phi = \alpha K_1 + C$ $\alpha, C =$ constant	$\lambda Y =$ constant $\lambda W =$ constant i.e., $\frac{Y}{W} = \frac{\text{output}}{\text{wealth}}$ $=$ constant	von Neumann–Samuelson model
Model II	$e^{-\rho t}L(x(t), \dot{x}(t))$ $(\rho > 0)$	$\tau = 1$ $\xi = 0$ $\Phi \neq 0$ $\frac{d\Phi}{dt} = -\rho e^{-\rho t}L$	Income-wealth conservation law $=$ Discounted income $+ \rho \times$ discounted stock of consumption $= \rho \times$ max discounted stock of consumption $=$ constant	Neoclassical growth model (Weitzman) Neoclassical theory of investment Endogenous theory of technical change Total conservation laws of the firm
Model III	$e^{-\rho t}L(x, \dot{x})$	$\tau = \frac{1}{\rho'(t)}$ $\xi^i = 0$	Income $= p'(t) \times$ "generalized" wealth	Variable discount rate (Samuelson, Sato)
Model IV	$e^{-\rho t}L(x, \dot{x}, t)$ $= e^{-\rho t}L(x, e^{\rho t}\dot{x})$	$\tau = e^{\rho t}$ $\xi = 0$ $=$ constant	Current Hamiltonian	"Factor-Aug. technical change on K" (Sato)

(continued)

Table 9.1 (continued)

	Lagrangian	Infinitesimal transformation	Conservation laws	Examples
	General Case $e^{-\rho t}L(x,\dot{x},t)$	$\tau = e^{\rho t}$ $\xi = b(t) \times$ $\exp \int_0^t \left(-\frac{L_x}{L_{\dot{x}}}\right) ds$	Income + "Value of Taste (technical) change" $= \rho \times$ wealth	General Technical and taste change (Sato, Nôno & Mimura)
		$\tau = 1$ $\xi \neq 0$	Modified Supply price of investment	same as above
Model V	$e^{-\rho t}Q$ $Q =$ Quadratic in x and $\dot{x}$	$\tau = \delta =$ constant $\xi = \frac{\rho \delta}{2}\xi$ $=$ constant	Modified Hamiltonian: income $+ \rho \times$ value of capital	Near the steady-state (Sato)
Model VI	$\sum \lambda^{-t}L_t$ $L_t =$ Quadratic in $x(t) = q(t) - q^*$ and $(x+1) - x(t)$ $= v(t)$ $\lambda = 1 + \delta$		Modified Hamiltonian (1) Discrete model modification and (2) Discount factor modification $\lambda^{-1}\left[\left(-v'\frac{\partial L}{\partial v} -L\right) + \frac{1}{2}v'\frac{\partial L}{\partial q} + \frac{(\lambda-1)}{2}q'\frac{\partial L}{\partial v}\right]$ $=$ constant	Discrete dynamic system (Local approximation) (Sato–Maeda)

Appendix (2012 Version) by Shigeru Maeda: Construction of All Quadratic First Integrals by Use of Eigenvectors and Generalized Eigenvectors

Brief Preliminaries

In this appendix, we propose a procedure to construct all quadratic first integrals of a linear symplectic mapping (9.71). A quadratic first integral is of the form

$$f_S(x) = \frac{1}{2}x'Sx, \quad S' = S$$

and the symbol Ω is used to mean the whole of coefficient matrices of F.I.'s as in (9.73b). The following is a restatement of a condition for S to belong to Ω.

Proposition 9.1. $f_S(x)$ is a quadratic invariant of (9.71), if and only if

$$A'SA = S \quad or \quad (A')^{-1}SA^{-1} = S. \tag{9.85}$$

Hereafter, we assume that ± 1 are not eigenvalues of A, that is, (9.71) does not admit at most 2-periodic solutions. Furthermore, we assume that matrices and vectors are complex-valued for the time being, the field of scalars being C, and the symbols L and $<,>$ mean C^{2N} and a symplectic inner product $<x,y> = x'Jy$ on L.

Proposition 9.2. Let $\xi_1, \xi_2, \ldots, \xi_u$ be linearly independent vectors. Then, the u^2 matrices defined by $(J\xi_i)(J\xi_j)'$ are linearly independent, and further, it holds that $(A')^{-1}\{(J\xi_i)(J\xi_j)'\}A^{-1} = \{J(A\xi_i)\}\{J(A\xi_j)\}'$.

Proof. Choose a vector η subject to $(J\xi_j)'\eta \neq 0$ and $(J\xi_k)'\eta = 0$ ($^\forall k \neq j$). Put $\sum c_{ij}(J\xi_i)(J\xi_j)' = 0$ and multiply η from the right, and it follows that $\sum_i ((J\xi_j)'\eta) \cdot c_{ij}J\xi_i = 0$. Since $J\xi_i$ are linearly independent, we have $c_{ij} = 0$. The second assertion is obvious from to $A'JA = J$. □

Quadratic Invariant

Let $\{\xi_1, \xi_2, \ldots, \xi_u\}$ and $\{\eta_1, \eta_2, \ldots, \eta_v\}$ be generalized eigenvectors of A which form two distinct Jordan blocks with eigenvalues a and b, respectively. That is,

$$A\xi_1 = a\xi_1, \quad A\xi_i = a\xi_i + \xi_{i-1} \quad (2 \leq i \leq u),$$

$$A\eta_1 = b\eta_1, \quad A\eta_i = b\eta_j + \eta_{j-1} \quad (2 \leq j \leq v).$$

For every vector ζ, $\xi_u \neq (A - aI)\zeta$ and $\eta_v \neq (A - bI)\zeta$.

We define uv matrices M_{ij} and introduce a linear combination S of them:

$$M_{ij} = (J\xi_i)(J\eta_j)' \quad (1 \leq i \leq u, 1 \leq j \leq v), \quad S = \sum_{1 \leq i \leq u, 1 \leq j \leq v} c_{ij}M_{ij} \tag{9.86}$$

where c_{ij} are complex constants. Our first schedule is to obtain a condition for S to satisfy (9.85) by disregarding a restriction that S is both real and symmetric.

Owing to Proposition 9.2, $(A^{-1})'SA^{-1}$ is equal to S, if and only if all of the following equations hold good.

$$(1 - ab)c_{uv} = 0,$$

$$(1 - ab)c_{iv} = bc_{i+1,v} \quad (1 \leq i \leq u-1),$$

$$(1 - ab)c_{uj} = bc_{u,j+1} \quad (1 \leq j \leq v-1),$$

$$(1 - ab)c_{ij} = ac_{i,j+1} + bc_{i+1,j} + c_{i+1,j+1} \quad (1 \leq i \leq u-1, 1 \leq j \leq v-1).$$

By m is denoted $\min(u, v)$. When $ab \neq 1$, it is easy to prove that all of c_{ij} vanish. When $ab = 1$, c_{ij} vanish for $i + j > m + 1$ and the remaining coefficients are subject to $ac_{i,j+1} + bc_{i+1,j} + c_{i+1,j+1} = 0$. Concerning the latter ones, we put

Appendix

$$c_{ij} = \left(-\frac{a}{b}\right)^{i-1} f_{(m+1)-(i+j)}(i) \quad (2 \le i+j \le m+1).$$

Then, the equations among the remaining c_{ij} are transformed equivalently to

$$\begin{cases} f_0(i) = \text{arb. const.}, \quad f_k(1) = \text{arb. const.} \quad (0 \le k \le m-1) \\ f_{k+1}(i) = f_{k+1}(1) - \dfrac{1}{b}(f_k(2) + f_k(3) + \cdots + f_k(i)). \\ \quad (1 \le k \le m-2, 2 \le i \le m+1-k) \end{cases} \quad (9.87)$$

Thus, we have the following proposition.

Proposition 9.3. *With respect to matrices which are linear combinations of M_{ij} and satisfy (9.85), the followings hold good.*

(a) When $ab \ne 1$, there exist no non-zero matrix.

(b) When $ab = 1$, there are m linearly independent matrices S_k subject to

$$S_k = f_{k-1}(1)M_{1,m+1-k} + (-a^2)f_{k-1}(2)M_{2,m-k}$$
$$+ \cdots + (-a^2)^{m-k} f_{k-1}(m+1-k)M_{m+1-k,1} \quad (1 \le k \le m) \quad (9.88)$$

where $f_k(i)$ are constants defined by (9.87).

According to Proposition 9.2, an arbitrary matrix S is expressed as a linear combination of $(J\xi_i)(J\xi_j)'$, where $\{\xi_1, \xi_2, \ldots\}$ denotes a whole of eigenvectors and generalized ones and is a basis of L. By use of Propositions 9.2 and 9.3, we have the following immediately.

Proposition 9.4. *A matrix S satisfies (9.85), if and only if S is expressed as a linear combination of matrices S_k which are constructed from all combinations of generalized eigenvectors with eigenvalues a and $1/a$ in a manner as in (9.88).*

Now, we are in a position to study quadratic invariants. Since the coefficient matrix of a quadratic invariant is real and symmetric, two conditions $S' = S$ and $\overline{S} = S$ must be satisfied besides (9.85). Define S_k under the condition $f_{k-1}(1) \ne 0$ $(k = 1, \ldots, m)$. Then, according to Proposition 9.2, $S'_k \ne S_k$ holds and $S_k + \overline{S}_k$ are linearly independent. Furthermore, put, for each S_k,

$$U_k = \frac{1}{4}(S_k + \overline{S}_k + S'_k + \overline{S}'_k),$$

$$V_k = \frac{\sqrt{-1}}{4}(S_k - \overline{S}_k + S'_k - \overline{S}'_k) \quad (1 \le k \le m) \quad (9.89)$$

and the matrices U_k and V_k belong to Ω, since $A'S'A = S'$ and $A'\overline{S}A = \overline{S}$ follow from $A'SA = S$ automatically. Due to Proposition 9.4, every element of Ω is expressed as a linear combination of U_k and V_k with real constants, though they are not necessarily linearly independent.

It is well known that if a is an eigenvalue of a real symplectic matrix, so are $1/a$, $\bar{a}$, and $1/\bar{a}$ (Arnold 1989). The above matrices U_k and V_k are constructed from the generalized eigenvectors selected from the four generalized eigenspaces, in other words, they depend on a quartette of $\tilde{W}_a$, $\tilde{W}_{1/a}$, $\tilde{W}_{\bar{a}}$, and $\tilde{W}_{1/\bar{a}}$. Hereafter, we adopt a convention that a means an eigenvalue subject to

$$|a| \geq 1, \quad 0 \leq \arg(a) \leq \pi. \tag{9.90}$$

Owing to this convention, only one eigenvalue is selected among the four. Next, suppose that $\tilde{W}_a$ is a direct sum of u subspaces B_i corresponding to respective Jordan blocks. We choose a set of generalized eigenvectors as follows.

$$B_i = \text{span}\{\xi_1^{(i)}, \ldots, \xi_{j(i)}^{(i)}\} \quad (i = 1, \ldots, u) \quad \text{s.t.}$$

$$A\xi_j^{(i)} = a\xi_j^{(i)} + (1 - \delta_{j1})\xi_{j-1}^{(i)}$$

$$(j = 1, \ldots, j(i), j(1) \geq j(2) \geq \cdots \geq j(u)) \tag{9.91}$$

where $\dim \tilde{W}_a = j(1) + \cdots + j(u)$. In this case, there exists a unique basis $\{\eta_j^{(\beta)}\}$ of $\tilde{W}_{1/a}$ which satisfy $<\xi_i^{(\alpha)}, \eta_j^{(\beta)}> = \delta_{ij}\delta_{\alpha\beta}$, and $\tilde{W}_{1/a}$ is a direct sum of the following u subspaces (See the proof in the final part).

$$C_i = \text{span}\{(A - I/a)^{j(i)-1}\eta_1^{(i)}, (A - I/a)^{j(i)-2}\eta_1^{(i)}, \ldots, \eta_1^{(i)}\} \quad (i = 1, \ldots, u).$$

Here, $(A - I/a)^{j(i)-1}\eta_1^{(i)}$ is an eigenvector. As is easily seen, B_i and C_j are skew-orthogonal to each other when $i \neq j$. With respect to the remaining two generalized eigenspaces, we may define subspaces $\bar{B}_i$ and $\bar{C}_j$ similarly.

Now, under the condition that ± 1 are not eigenvalues, there are three cases with respect to reduction of eigenvalues, that is,

(a) Case of $a \in R$ and $|a| > 1$; $\bar{a} = a$.
(b) Case of $|a| = 1$ and $0 < \arg(a) < \pi$; $a = 1/\bar{a}$.
(c) Case of $a \notin R$ and $|a| > 1$;   Four eigenvalues.

Case of (a). Since all generalized eigenvectors can be selected as real-valued, V_k in (9.89) vanishes. Then, according to Proposition 9.3, we obtain $j(1) + 3j(2) + \cdots + (2u-1)j(u)$ linearly independent quadratic invariants from combinations of B_i and C_j.

Case of (b). In this case, B_i equals to $\bar{C}_i$. Then, from combinations of B_i and C_j, only U_k are obtained, whereas neither U_k nor V_k vanish when $i \neq j$. Then, we have $j(1) + 5j(2) + \cdots + (4u-3)j(u)$ linearly independent invariants related to an eigenvalue a.

Case of (c). For all eigenvalues of B_i and C_j, both U_k and V_k are obtained. Then, $2j(1) + 6j(2) + \cdots + (4u-2)j(u)$ linearly independent quadratic invariants are obtained.

Appendix

For an eigenvalue a, we put

$$\text{num}(a) = \begin{cases} j(1) + 3j(2) + \cdots + (2u-1)j(u) & \text{(Case (a))} \\ j(1) + 5j(2) + \cdots + (4u-3)j(u) & \text{(Case (b))}. \\ 2j(1) + 6j(2) + \cdots + (4u-2)j(u) & \text{(Case (c))} \end{cases} \quad (9.92)$$

Proposition 9.5. *The discrete system (9.71) admits $\Sigma' \text{num}(a)$ linearly independent quadratic invariants, where Σ' means summation over eigenvalues subject to (9.90).*

Let us pay attention to the fact that if V_k does not vanish, its rank equals to 4, and if U_k does not vanish, its rank equals to 4 or 2. Furthermore, because of Proposition 9.4, rank U_k is 2, if and only if there exist non-zero vectors ξ and η such that $A\xi = a\xi$ and $A\eta = (1/a)\eta$, where a is real, or complex with the absolute value one. In the former case, the signature of U_k is (1.1), and in the latter case U_k is (semi) positive-definite. This leads to the following.

Proposition 9.6. *The discrete system (9.71) leaves a 2-dimensional plane Γ invariant, and every solution on Γ lies on an elliptic curve, if and only if (9.71) admits a quadratic invariant $f_S(x)$ such that S is (semi) positive-definite and is of rank 2. In the case, Γ is characterized as $J \cdot Im(S)$.*

Remarks on Symmetry Generated by Quadratic Invariants

According to Maeda (1980), the whole of quadratic invariants is closed with respect to the Poisson bracket (Arnold 1989), and forms a Lie algebra Θ. The Poisson bracket is represented on Ω as follows.

$$\{S, T\} = SJT - TJS.$$

Return to M_{ij} defined by (9.86), and put $M_1 = (J\xi_1)(J\eta_1)'$ and $M_2 = (J\xi_2)(J\eta_2)'$. Then, we have

$$\{M_1, M_2\} = <\eta_1, \xi_2>(J\xi_1)(J\eta_2)' - <\eta_2, \xi_1>(J\xi_2)(J\eta_1)'.$$

As is seen in the proof in the final part, $\{M_1, M_2\}$ vanishes, if $\{\xi_1, \eta_1\}$ and $\{\xi_2, \eta_2\}$ belong to different quartettes of the four generalized eigenspaces mentioned above. Therefore, U_k and V_k in §3 forms a closed subalgebra and Θ is a direct sum of those subalgebras. In a word, the symmetry group generated by quadratic invariants is determined only by the structure of respective generalized eigenspaces.

Finally, we give proofs of two facts referred to without verification in the appendix.

Proof of skew-orthogonality of $\tilde{W}_a$ and $\tilde{W}_b$ ($ab \neq 1$).

Let $\{\xi_1, \xi_2, \ldots, \xi_u\}$ and $\{\eta_1, \eta_2, \ldots, \eta_v\}$ be generalized eigenvectors of A which form two distinct Jordan blocks subject to (9.91). Then, since A is symplectic, it holds that

$$<\xi_i, \eta_j> = ab <\xi_i, \eta_j> + a(1-\delta_{j1})<\xi_i, \eta_{j-1}> + b(1-\delta_{i1})<\xi_{i-1}, \eta_j>$$
$$+ (1-\delta_{j1})(1-\delta_{i1})<\xi_{i-1}, \eta_{j-1}>.$$

When $ab \neq 1$, we find that every $<\xi_i, \eta_j>$ vanishes, starting from $<\xi_1, \eta_1> = 0$. Then, by considering all combinations of Jordan blocks, $\tilde{W}_a$ proves to be skew-orthogonal to $\tilde{W}_b$. In particular, when $a \neq \pm 1$, $\tilde{W}_a$ is skew-orthogonal to itself, that is, null. □

Proof of commutation relation between $\tilde{W}_a$ and $\tilde{W}_{1/a}$ ($a \neq 1$).

Suppose that $\tilde{W}_a$ is a direct sum of u Jordan blocks $K_1, \ldots, K_u$, and K_i is spanned by a set of generalized eigenvectors $\{\xi_1^{(i)}, \xi_2^{(i)}, \ldots, \xi_{j(i)}^{(i)}\}$ subject to $A\xi_j^{(i)} = a\xi_j^{(i)} + (1 - \delta_{j1})\xi_{j-1}^{(i)}$. Then, the followings hold good.

(1) There is a unique basis $\{\eta_1^{(1)}, \ldots, \eta_{j(1)}^{(1)}, \ldots, \eta_1^{(u)}, \ldots, \eta_{j(u)}^{(u)}\}$ of $\tilde{W}_{1/a}$ such that $<\xi_i^\alpha, \eta_j^\beta> = \delta_{ij}\delta_{\alpha\beta}$.

(2) For any i subject to $1 \leq i \leq u$, it holds that $(A - I/a)^k \eta_1^{(i)} \neq 0$ ($0 \leq k \leq j(i) - 1$) and $(A - I/a)^{j(i)} \eta_1^{(i)} = 0$. In other words, $\{(A - I/a)^k \eta_1^{(i)}\}_{k = j(i)-1, \ldots, 0}$ constructs a Jordan block in $\tilde{W}_{1/a}$.

(3) $(A - I/a)^k \eta_1^{(i)}$ ($0 \leq k \leq j(i) - 1$) is expressed as a linear combination of $\eta_{j(i)}^{(i)}, \ldots, \eta_{k+1}^{(i)}$.

First, we intend to verify the following proposition. When L is a direct sum of three subspaces: $L = L_1 \dot{+} L_2 \dot{+} L_3$ such that L_1 and L_2 are null, and L_3 is skew-orthogonal to L_1 and L_2, then it holds that

(a) $\dim L_1 = \dim L_2$.
(b) For an arbitrary basis $\{\xi_i\}$ of L_1 there is a unique basis $\{\eta_i\}$ of L_2 subject to $<\xi_i, \eta_j> = \delta_{ij}$.

It is to be noted that for any non-zero vector $\xi \in L_1$ there is a vector η subject to $<\xi, \eta> = 1$ because of nondegeneracy, and η can be chosen as a vector in L_2 by supposition. By using the fact, induction with respect to k can prove that there are vectors $\xi_1, \ldots, \xi_k \in L_1$ and $\eta_1, \ldots, \eta_k \in L_2$ subject to $<\xi_i, \eta_j> = \delta_{ij}$ as far as $k \leq \dim L_1$. Exchanging roles of L_1 and L_2, we have (a) and have shown that there are bases of L_1 and L_2 subject to $<\xi_i, \eta_j> = \delta_{ij}$. Next, fix the bases mentioned above, and choose an arbitrary basis $\{\xi_i^c\}$ of L_1 such that $\xi_i^c = \sum_j a_{ji} \xi_j$. Then, $\eta_i^c = \sum_j b_{ji} \eta_j$ satisfies $<\xi_i^c, \eta_j^c> = \delta_{ij}$, if and only if $\sum_k a_{kj} b_{ki} = \delta_{ij}$. This proves (b).

If we put $L_1 = \tilde{W}_a$ and $L_2 = \tilde{W}_{1/a}$, and let L_3 be a direct sum of the remaining generalized eigenspaces, the assumption is satisfied and Assertion (1) is verified.

Assertion (1) means that there is a symplectic matrix X such that $X^{-1}AX$ is block-diagonal, and a half of its blocks are Jordan ones. For each Jordan block G, another block $(G')^{-1}$ exists, for $X^{-1}AX$ is also symplectic. That is, with respect to the vectors listed in (1), it holds that

$$A(\xi_1^{(i)},\ldots,\xi_{j(i)}^{(i)}) = (\xi_1^{(i)},\ldots,\xi_{j(i)}^{(i)}) \begin{bmatrix} a & 1 & 0 & \cdot & \cdots \\ 0 & a & 1 & 0 & \cdots \\ 0 & 0 & a & 1 & \cdots \\ \cdot & \cdot & \cdot & \cdot & \cdots \end{bmatrix},$$

$$A(\eta_1^{(i)},\ldots,\eta_{j(i)}^{(i)}) = (\eta_1^{(i)},\ldots,\eta_{j(i)}^{(i)}) \begin{bmatrix} 1/a & 0 & 0 & 0 & \cdots \\ -1/a^2 & 1/a & 0 & 0 & \cdots \\ 1/a^3 & -1/a^2 & 1/a & 0 & \cdots \\ \cdot & \cdot & \cdot & \cdot & \cdots \end{bmatrix}.$$

This proves (2) and (3).

References

Abraham, R., & Marsden, J.E. (1978). *Foundations of mechanics*, 2nd edn. Benjamin.
Arnold, V.I. (1989). *Mathematical methods of classical mechanics*, 2nd edn. (trans: K. Vogtmann & A. Weinstein). New York: Springer.
Bessel-Hagen, E. (1921). Über die erhaltungssatze der Elektrodynamik. *Mathematische Annalen*, 84, 258–276.
Cass, D. (1965). Optimal growth in the aggregate model of capital accumulation, *Review of Economic Studies*, 32, 233–240.
Caton, C., & Shell, K. (1971). An exercise in the theory of heterogeneous capital accumulation. *Review of Economic Studies*, 38, 13–22.
Jorgenson, D.W. (1967). Theory of investment behavior. In R. Ferber (Ed.) *Determinants of investment behavior*. New York: NBER.
Kemp, M.C., & Long, N.V. (1982). On the evaluation of social income in a dynamic economy. In G.R. Feiwel (Ed.) *Samuelson and neoclassical economics*. Boston: Kluwer-Nijhoff.
Klein, F. (1918). Über die differentialgesetze fur die Erhaltung von impuls und energie in der Einsteinschen gravitationstheorie. *Nachr. Akad. Wiss, Göttingen, Math-Phys, Kl, 11*, 171–189.
Lie, S. (1891). In G. Scheffers (Ed.), *Vorlesungen über Differentialgleichungen, mit bekannten infinitesimalen Transformationen*. Leipzig: Teubner. Reprinted 1967, New York: Chelsea Publishing.
Liviatan, N., & Samuelson, P.A. (1969). Notes on turnpikes: Stable and unstable. *Journal of Economic Theory*, 1454–1475.
Logan, J.D. (1977). Invariant variational principles. *Mathematics in science and engineering*, vol. 138. New York: Academic Press.
Lucas, R.E. (1967). Optimal investment policy and the flexible accelerator. *International Economic Review* (February 8).
Maeda, S. (1980). Canonical structure and symmetries for discrete systems. *Math. Japon*, 25, 405–420.
Maeda, S. (1982). Lagrangian formulation of discrete systems and concept of difference space. *Math. Japon*, 27, 336–345.

Maeda, S. (1987). Completely integrable symplectic mapping. *Proc. Japan Academy, 63A*, 198–200.
Maeda, S. (1988). Quadratic conservatives of linear symplectic Systems. *Proc. Japan Academy, 64A*, 45–48.
Noether, E. (1918). Invariante variantionsprobleme. *Nachr. Akad. Wiss. Göttingen, Math-Phys, KI, II*, 235–257. Translated by Tavel, M.A. (1971). Invariant variation problems. *Transport Theory and Statistical Physics, 1*, 186–207.
Ramsey, F. (1928). A mathematical theory of saving. *Economic Journal, 38*, 543–559.
Samuelson, P.A. (1967). A turnpike refutation of the golden rule in a welfare-maximizing many-year plan. In Shell, K. (Ed.) *Essays on the theory of optimal economic growth*. MIT. Press.
Samuelson, P.A. (1970a). Law of conservation of the capital-output ratio, Proceedings of the National Academy of Sciences. *Applied Mathematical Science, 67*, 1477–1479.
Samuelson, P.A. (1970b). Two conservation laws in theoretical economics. Cambridge, MA: M.I.T., Department of Economics mimeo (July).
Samuelson, P.A. (1972). The general saddlepoint property of optimalcontrol motions. *Journal of Economic Theory, 5*, 102–120.
Samuelson, P.A. (1976). Speeding up of time with age in recognition of life as fleeting. In A.M. Tang et al. (Eds.) *Evolution, welfare and time in economics: essays in honor of Nichols Georgescu-Roegen*. Lexington, MA: Lexington-Heath Books.
Samuelson, P.A. (1982). *Variations on capital/output conservation laws*. Cambridge, MA: M.I.T., Department of Economics mimeo (January).
Samuelson, P.A., & Solow, R.M. (1956). A complete capital model involving heterogeneous capital goods. *Quarterly Journal of Economics, 70*(4), 537–562.
Sato, R. (1981). *Theory of technical change and economic invariance: application of Lie groups*. New York: Academic Press.
Sato, R. (1982). *Invariant principle and capital/output conservation laws*. Providence, Rhode Island: Brown University working paper No. 82–8.
Sato, R. (1985). The invariance principle and income-wealth conservation laws: Application of Lie groups and related transformations. *Journal of Econometrics, 3*, 365–389.
Sato, R. (2004). Economic conservation laws as indices of corporate performance. *Japan and the World Economy, 16*(3), 247–267.
Sato, R., & Fujii, M. (2005). Evaluating corporate performance: empirical tests of a conservation law. *Japan and the World Economy, 18*(2), 158–168.
Sato, R., & Maeda, S. (1987). Local conservation laws of the discrete optimal growth model. Kyoto University, Mimeo.
Sato, R., Nôno, T., & Mimura, F. (1984). Hidden symmetries: Lie groups and economic conservation laws, essay in honor of Martin Beckmann. In: H. Hauptman, W. Krelle, & K.C. Mosler (Eds.), *Operations research and economic theory* (pp. 35–54). Springer.
Sato, R., & Ramachandran, R. (1987). Factor price variation and the Hicksian hypothesis: A micro economic approach. *Oxford Economic Papers, 39*, 343–356.
Weitzman, M.L. (1976). On the welfare significance of national product in a dynamic economy. *Quarterly Journal of Economics, 90*, 156–162.

Chapter 10
Quantity or Quality: The Impact of Labour Saving Innovation on US and Japanese Growth Rates, 1960–2004*

10.1 Introduction

Japan's economic growth after the World War II was miraculous. Hundreds of economic studies have been done to analyse the high performance of the economy. Recently, however, attention has turned to worrisome expectations for the future. Will Japan's population decline put an end to the country's macroeconomic growth?

The USA also experienced a high growth rate after the Second World War. President Kennedy's policies in the 1960s supported economic growth through innovation. The high growth was also backed by capital accumulation and population growth. However, recent rapid population growth coming from the influx of immigrants to the USA has been followed by much ambivalence toward population growth; many worry about problems that may come from lack of assimilation and overpopulation.

There is no economic or popular consensus on whether population growth is good or bad for long-run economic growth. This chapter compares and contrasts the economies of Japan and the USA after the 1960s using traditional or basic growth models. The elements of the analysis are GDP, capital, labour and total factor productivity (TFP). This last element is comparable to the index of Hicks-neutral economic progress, which explains the total efficiency of capital and labour.

The novel contribution of this chapter, accruing from those of Sato and Ramachandran (1987) and Sato (1970), is that we analyse not only how the TFP has increased or decreased, but also analyse separately the efficiency of capital and the efficiency of labour. The result of this analysis will allow us to make a policy proposal that in order to raise TFP growth, we have to consider how and how much the efficiency of either or both of capital and labour must be increased. Merely knowing the TFP is generally considered sufficient for economic analysis. However, our comparison of the two countries will show that because each country's

---

*This chapter is a revised version of Sato and Morita (2009).

composition of TFP is fundamentally different, knowing only total efficiency does not suffice.

In order to analyse the efficiency of capital and labour, we need to know the production function or the elasticity of (factor) substitution, which is the summary index of production function. In general terms, elasticity of substitution is a technology index. As Sato and Beckmann (1968) and Rose (1968) discovered, elasticity of substitution plays a critical role in the analysis of the efficiency of each input factor. Our growth analysis uses the concept of the elasticity of substitution and applies the concept to the data of the two countries.

In this chapter we contrast the difference in the economic structures of Japan and the USA by comparing the rates of factor augmenting technical progress. Our investigation reveals that whether or not capital and labour are efficiently used has a strong impact on economic growth.

Following the theoretical explanation in Sect. 10.2, we conduct in Sect. 10.3 the estimations of the growth rates of biased technical change using both countries' macro data from 1960 to 2004. The data are then divided into two periods—Period I (1960–1989) and Period II (1990–2004)—because the analysis of Period II is particularly useful in highlighting the characteristics of each economy. Period II for Japan includes the "lost decade," the period of long lasting stagnation after the burst of the asset price bubble,[1] while the same period of time for the USA is often described as the "new economy," whose rapid growth was driven by newly developed industries such as IT and biotechnology.

In Sect. 10.3.1, we determine that we can apply the model of factor augmenting (biased) technical change to the Japanese and US economies. We find this by testing to confirm that the production functions in both countries are not Cobb–Douglas and the technical progress in both countries is not Hicks-neutral. In Sect. 10.3.2, we estimate the production functions with biased technical change. During the estimation process, we compare the 44 years' performance of each economy. The simulation results using the estimated production functions are shown in the next subsection. In Sect. 10.3.4, we figure out how the roles of biased technical change differed in the two economies. The estimation results explain how Japan's high growth was sustained by the efficiency of labour. Section 10.3.5 shows that Japan responded to external shocks such as oil crises more flexibly than did the USA. Then, in Sect. 10.3.6, we present another way to contrast the two countries by applying the stability condition theoretically explained in Sect. 10.2.3. We found that although US economic growth may have been at the steady state, the growth in Japan has not yet neared the steady state.

It transpired that broadly defined innovation has been and will be the engine of growth for the Japanese economy. Japan does not have to be pessimistic about the declining birth rate because value added labour can compensate for the decline.

---

[1] Many scholars and economists have attempted to analyse Japan's lost decade using TFP. Recognized contributions include an industry level research of TFP by Fukao and Kwon (2006) and a TFP analysis focusing on information technology by Jorgenson and Motohashi (2005).

10.1.1 Recent Studies

Several recent studies have focused on biased technical progress.[2] As for the theoretical investigation, Acemoglu (2002, 2003) proposes a microfoundation for biased factor augmenting technological progress. Acemoglu develops a simple framework to analyse the forces that shape the biases of technical change. Two major forces affect equilibrium bias: the price effect and the market size effect. The elasticity of substitution between different factors regulates how powerful these effects are. Acemoglu's approach assumes an aggregate output produced from two types of goods—labour intensive and capital intensive. In this chapter, we make no distinction, but assume a single homogeneous good in the economy.

Klump, McAdam and Willman (2007) present a careful estimation of CES production functions for the US economy in the presence of biased technical progress. Their paper is related to the earlier studies by Klump and Preissler (2000), Yuhn (1991) and Sato (1970). Klump et al. (2007) work with the hypothesis of conventional constant growth rates as well as with a form that nests exponential, logarithmic and hyperbolic growth as special cases. Using the US data from 1953–1998, they find that the elasticity of substitution is significantly below unity and that technical progress shows an asymmetrical pattern where the growth of labour augmenting technical progress is exponential while that of capital is hyperbolic or logarithmic.

It may be of interest to mention two points regarding the present work. First, this chapter will also show that the elasticity of substitution is below unity for the relevant period. Second, the method of estimating the growth rates of biased technical change does not a priori assume exponential, hyperbolic, or any other form. This is done by estimating each year's growth rates and the average values are calculated from each year's values.[3]

10.2 A Model of Biased (Labour Saving) Technical Change

Consider an aggregative economy where at each year t, one output $(Y(t))$ is produced by two factor inputs, capital $(K(t))$ and labour $(L(t))$, under the neo-classical constant returns to scale technology. Production of $Y(t)$ depends also on the general technical change $(T(t))$. Then the production function takes the form

$$Y(t) = F[K(t), L(t), T(t)] \qquad (10.1)$$

where F satisfies the usual regularity conditions.

---

[2] The authors are grateful to the referee for suggesting comparison of the present study with recent existing literature on this subject.

[3] See Eqs. (10.6) and (10.7) and Table 10.8 for the estimation of each year's growth rates.

For the purpose of empirical analysis, it is convenient to study a special case of Eq. (10.1), where technical change is of the factor augmenting type (or Sato–Beckman–Rose neutral type).[4] Thus, Eq. (10.1) takes the form

$$Y(t) = F[A(t)K(t), B(t)L(t)] = F[\overline{K}(t), \overline{L}(t)] \qquad (10.2)$$

where $A(t)$ and $B(t)$ are efficiencies of capital and labour, respectively; and $\overline{K}(t) = A(t)K(t)$ and $\overline{L}(t) = B(t)L(t)$, or the effective capital and the effective labour. Notice that $T(t)$ in Eq. (10.1) is divided up into $A(t)$ and $B(t)$ in Eq. (10.2). Thus when $A(t) \equiv B(t) \equiv T(t)$, Eq. (10.2) is reduced to the case of Hicks-neutral technical change, while when $A(t) \equiv 1 \neq B(t) \equiv T(t)$ it is reduced to the Harrod-neutral type and when $A(t) \equiv T(t) \neq B(t) \equiv 1$ it is reduced to the Solow–Ranis–Fei type. Because Eq. (10.1) is a linear homogeneous production function, under the Hicks-neutral case Eq. (10.2) can be rewritten as,

$$Y(t) = T(t)F[K(t), L(t)] \qquad (10.3)$$

under the Harrod-neutral case as

$$Y(t) = F[K(t), T(t)L(t)] = F[K(t), \overline{L}(t)], \quad T(t) = B(t) \qquad (10.4)$$

and under the Solow–Ranis–Fei-neutral case as

$$Y(t) = F[T(t)K(t), L(t)] = F[\overline{K}(t), L(t)], \quad T(t) = A(t). \qquad (10.5)$$

10.2.1 Importance of the Elasticity of Factor Substitution

There are three reasons that the elasticity of substitution $\sigma(t)$ plays a crucial role in the analysis of the factor augmenting type of technical progress.

The first reason comes from the underlying invariance or neutrality theorem.[5] The factor augmenting (biased) type of technical change, Eq. (10.2), is theoretically justified by an invariant condition. That is to say, Eq. (10.2) is a result of derivation of the production function under the invariant condition that "inventions are neutral in the sense that the elasticity of substitution $\sigma(t)$ remains unchanged (or invariant) before and after inventions as long as the relative income shares of factor inputs, $\alpha(t)$ for capital and $\beta(t) = 1 - \alpha(t)$ for labour, are unaffected or vice versa" (Sato and Beckmann 1968, p. 139).

---

[4]See Sato and Beckmann (1968) and Rose (1968) for the conditions for the factor augmenting technical change.

[5]See Sato and Beckmann (1968) for the invariant conditions for various types of production functions.

10.2 A Model of Biased (Labour Saving) Technical Change

This is a direct contrast to the Hicks-neutral case where the invariance condition does not depend on the elasticity of the substitution concept. The Hicks-neutral case is the result of the invariance (or neutrality) condition that "inventions are neutral in the sense that the relative income shares are not affected before and after inventions as long as the capital-labour ratio remains constant" (Sato and Beckmann 1968, p. 135).

The second reason why the elasticity of substitution $\sigma(t)$ plays a crucial role in the analysis of the factor augmenting type of technical progress is that once $\sigma(t)$ is known, one can derive (or integrate) the underlying production function F.

If one attempts to estimate $A(t)$ and $B(t)$ using empirical data, one will confront the situation where the elasticity of factor substitution $\sigma(t)$ must be predetermined. This is because the efficiencies of capital and labour, $A(t)$ and $B(t)$, are estimable only from the equations

$$\frac{\dot{A}(t)}{A(t)} = \frac{\sigma \frac{\dot{r}(t)}{r(t)} - \left(\frac{\dot{Y}(t)}{Y(t)} - \frac{\dot{K}(t)}{K(t)}\right)}{\sigma(t) - 1} \tag{10.6}$$

and

$$\frac{\dot{B}(t)}{B(t)} = \frac{\sigma \frac{\dot{w}(t)}{w(t)} - \left(\frac{\dot{Y}(t)}{Y(t)} - \frac{\dot{L}(t)}{L(t)}\right)}{\sigma(t) - 1} \tag{10.7}$$

where dot = Newton's time derivative, $r(t)$ = return to capital and $w(t)$ = wage rate of labour.[6]

Where $\sigma(t)$ is known, the elasticity of substitution $\sigma(t)$ can be looked at as a second-order (non-linear) differential equation whose solution is the production function. The relationship between $\sigma(t)$ and F is shown by the solution,

$$y = A(t)f(C(t)x)$$

$$= A(t)\exp \int^{C(t)x} G(\mu)\partial \log \mu \quad (10.35, \text{ in Appendix I})$$

where $y = Y/K$ and $x = 1/k = L/K$, $\mu = C(t)v$, so that we obtain[7]

$$Y(t) = F[A(t)K(t), B(t)L(t)] = F[\overline{K}(t), \overline{L}(t)]. \tag{10.8}$$

---

[6]These equations are derived in Sato (1970).

[7]In Appendix I, we show the process to obtain Eq. (10.8), which originated with Sato and Beckmann (1968).

Thus, once $\sigma(t)$ is known, one can derive $F[A(t)K(t), B(t)L(t)]$ using Eqs. (10.6)–(10.8) simultaneously. In Sect. 10.3, we do this using the US and Japanese data.

The third reason why the elasticity of substitution $\sigma(t)$ plays a crucial role is that technical change can be classified as biased (or non-neutral) in the sense of Hicks (at the constant $K(t)/L(t)$) using the relative shares of capital and labour, $\dot{A}/A$, $\dot{B}/B$ and $\sigma(t)$.

As Sato (1970) shows, if we define the marginal rate of substitution ω as $\omega = r/w$ and $k = K/L$, we get

$$\frac{\dot{\omega}}{\omega} = \frac{\dot{r}}{r} - \frac{\dot{w}}{w} = \left(\frac{\dot{A}}{A} - \frac{\dot{B}}{B}\right)\left(1 - \frac{1}{\sigma}\right) - \frac{1}{\sigma}\frac{\dot{k}}{k}. \tag{10.9}$$

Using Eq. (10.9), one can classify various cases as modeled in Hicks (1932). He defines "labour saving" inventions as those whose initial effects are to increase the ratio of the marginal product of capital to that of labour (at the constant capital-labour ratio). Such inventions increase the marginal product of capital more than they increase the marginal product of labour, thus raising the relative share of capital and reducing the relative share of labour. We classify technical change into several cases, as summarized below.

1 Labour saving:
   (a) When the elasticity of substitution is less than unity, $\sigma(t) < 1$ and the efficiency of labour increases faster than that of capital, i.e. $\dot{B}/B > \dot{A}/A$ at the constant capital-labour ratio, technical change is labour saving.
   (b) When $\sigma(t)$ is greater than unity, $\sigma(t) > 1$ and $\dot{A}/A > \dot{B}/B$ at the constant capital-labour ratio, technical change is labour saving.
2 Capital saving:
   When $\sigma(t) < 1, \dot{A}/A > \dot{B}/B$ or $\sigma(t) > 1$ and $\dot{B}/B > \dot{A}/A$ at $K(t)/L(t) =$ constant, technical change is capital saving.
3 Hicks-neutral:
   When $\dot{A}/A \equiv \dot{B}/B$ under $K(t)/L(t) =$ constant, technical change is Hicks-neutral, regardless of whether $\sigma(t)$ is greater than (or less than) unity.
4 When $\sigma(t) = 1$, or the Cobb–Douglas case, any factor augmenting type will appear as the Hicks-neutral case. That is to say, one cannot differentiate $A(t)$ and $B(t)$.

We will present in Sect. 10.3 that both the Japanese and US economies' technical progress since 1960 can be categorized into labour saving technical progress.

10.2.2 Why Do We Need Biased Technical Change?

Theoretical Inequality Versus Empirical Identity

For the factor augmenting type of production function, Eq. (10.2), the growth rate of Y may be expressed as

$$\frac{\dot{Y}(t)}{Y(t)} = \frac{\partial F(t)}{\partial \overline{K}(t)} \frac{\overline{K}(t)}{Y(t)} \left(\frac{\dot{\overline{K}}(t)}{\overline{K}(t)}\right) + \frac{\partial F(t)}{\partial \overline{L}(t)} \frac{\overline{L}(t)}{Y(t)} \left(\frac{\dot{\overline{L}}(t)}{\overline{L}(t)}\right)$$

$$= \frac{\partial F(t)}{\partial K(t)} \frac{K(t)}{Y(t)} \left(\frac{\dot{A}(t)}{A(t)} + \frac{\dot{K}(t)}{K(t)}\right) + \frac{\partial F(t)}{\partial L(t)} \frac{L(t)}{Y(t)} \left(\frac{\dot{B}(t)}{B(t)} + \frac{\dot{L}(t)}{L(t)}\right) \quad (10.10)$$

where

$$\frac{\partial F(t)}{\partial K(t)} \frac{K(t)}{Y(t)} = \text{the relative income share of capital} = \alpha(\overline{k}(t)),$$

$$\frac{\partial F(t)}{\partial L(t)} \frac{L(t)}{Y(t)} = \text{the relative income share of labor} = \beta(\overline{k}(t)),$$

$$\alpha(\overline{k}(t)) + \beta(\overline{k}(t)) = 1 \quad \text{and} \quad \overline{k}(t) = \frac{\overline{K}(t)}{\overline{L}(t)} = \frac{A(t)K(t)}{B(t)L(t)}.$$

To highlight the difference between the Hicks-neutral case and the general factor augmenting (biased) case, we may denote the relative shares of capital and labour as $\alpha^B(\overline{k}(t))$ and $\beta^B(\overline{k}(t))$ for the general factor augmenting type and $\alpha^N(k(t))$ and $\beta^N(k(t))$ for the Hicks-neutral case. Using these definitions, Eq. (10.10) may be written as

$$\frac{\dot{Y}(t)}{Y(t)} = \alpha^B(\overline{k}(t))\frac{\dot{A}(t)}{A(t)} + \beta^B(\overline{k}(t))\frac{\dot{B}(t)}{B(t)} + \alpha^B(\overline{k}(t))\frac{\dot{K}(t)}{K(t)}$$

$$+ \beta^B(\overline{k}(t))\frac{\dot{L}(t)}{L(t)} \quad (10.10')$$

for the factor augmenting type and

$$\frac{\dot{Y}(t)}{Y(t)} = \frac{\dot{T}(t)}{T(t)} + \alpha^N(k(t))\frac{\dot{K}(t)}{K(t)} + \beta^N(k(t))\frac{\dot{L}(t)}{L(t)} \quad (10.10'')$$

for the Hicks-neutral case, where $A(t) \equiv B(t) \equiv T(t)$ and $Y(t) = T(t)F[K(t), L(t)]$.
For any given value of $\dot{Y}(t)/Y(t)$ we have

$$\alpha^B(\overline{k}(t))\frac{\dot{A}(t)}{A(t)} + \beta^B(\overline{k}(t))\frac{\dot{B}(t)}{B(t)}$$

$$= \frac{\dot{Y}(t)}{Y(t)} - \left(\alpha^B(\overline{k}(t))\frac{\dot{K}(t)}{K(t)} + \beta^B(\overline{k}(t))\frac{\dot{L}(t)}{L(t)}\right) \quad (10.11)$$

and

$$\frac{\dot{T}(t)}{T(t)} = \frac{\dot{Y}(t)}{Y(t)} - \left(\alpha^N(k(t))\frac{\dot{K}(t)}{K(t)} + \beta^N(k(t))\frac{\dot{L}(t)}{L(t)}\right). \quad (10.12)$$

Unless $A(t) \equiv B(t) \equiv T(t)$, we have $\alpha^B(\bar{k}(t)) \neq \alpha^N(k(t))$ and $\beta^B(\bar{k}(t)) \neq \beta^N(k(t))$. Hence we have "theoretical inequality" between Eq. (10.11) and (10.12).

Equations (10.11) and (10.12) are also linked by an important statistical (or empirical) identity. We have no a priori knowledge about the existence and magnitudes of $A(t)$ and $B(t)$. This means that we have no a priori knowledge about whether or not capital's income share (also labour's income share) is affected by $A(t)$ and $B(t)$. In other words, we cannot identify a priori whether the observed share of capital α is α^N or α^B and whether that of β is β^N or β^B.

In working with the empirical estimation of $\dot{T}(t)/T(t)$ using the Solow–Kendrick method (Eq. (10.12)), one may be, in effect, estimating Eq. (10.11). Thus Eqs. (10.11) and (10.12) may coincide with each other. Hence, the estimated value of $\dot{T}(t)/T(t)$, $\dot{T}(t)/T(t)|_{\text{estimated}}$ by Eq. (10.11) must be identical with the estimated value of the weighted sum of $\dot{A}(t)/A(t)$ and $\dot{B}(t)/B(t)$, weights given by the relative income shares, which are affected by $A(t)$ and $B(t)$, or by $\bar{k}(t) = A(t)K(t)/B(t)L(t)$. Hence,

$$\frac{\dot{T}(t)}{T(t)}\bigg|_{\text{estimated}} \equiv \alpha^B(\bar{k}(t))\frac{\dot{A}(t)}{A(t)} + \beta^B(\bar{k}(t))\frac{\dot{B}(t)}{B(t)}. \quad (10.13)$$

We shall call Eq. (10.13) the "empirical identity". This states that the percentage change of the estimated Hicks-neutral technical change factor or TFP is always equal to the weighted sum of the percentage changes of the biased technical change factors, where the weights are given by their observed relative income shares.

More Than Total Productivity

One might argue that as long as we know $\dot{T}(t)/T(t)$ we do not have to be bothered with the relative efficiencies of capital and labour, $\dot{A}/A$ and $\dot{B}/B$. Nevertheless, the relative efficiencies are exactly the point. There may be an infinitely large number of different combinations between $\dot{A}/A$ and $\dot{B}/B$ that satisfy Eq. (10.12). For example, $\dot{A}/A$ can and may be negative, while $\dot{B}/B$ may be positive and large, so that $\dot{T}(t)/T(t)$ can still be positive. (See Sect. 10.3.4 for the Japanese estimate.)

A negative $\dot{A}/A$ value has a profound implication in terms of R&D or innovation policy. This is the reason why we need the analysis of biased technical change. Estimating only TFP does not give the full story behind the country's economic performance and productivity growth.

10.2.3 Equilibrium Growth and Stability Under Biased Technical Change

It is well known that a growing economy with constant returns to scale technology and exogenous technical progress may have a stable balanced growth path only when exogenous technical progress is at least asymptotically Harrod-neutral (pure labour augmenting technical progress). In this chapter, it will be shown that an economy with endogenous biased technical change will have a stable balanced growth path under a general factor augmenting type of technical change, i.e. under positive growth rates of technical change for both capital and labour.

In this subsection, succeeding the theoretical framework of Sato (2006), we present the equilibrium growth rate and stability condition for the economy with endogenous biased technical change.

Let $Y(t) = F[K(t), L(t)]$ be the production function before technical change. To distinguish the production function after the factor augmenting type of technical change from the production function before the technical change, we may denote the function as $\overline{Y}(t)$ so that

$$\overline{Y}(t) = F[\overline{K}(t), \overline{L}(t)] \tag{10.2'}$$

where $\overline{K}(t) = A(t)K(t)$, $\overline{L}(t) = B(t)L(t)$ and $\overline{Y}(t)$ is output after technical change. This equation can be viewed as the production function after K has been transformed to $\overline{K}$ and L to $\overline{L}$.

Let the efficiency improvement of labour depend on the amount of expenditure devoted to education and training. Then, the growth rate of the effective labour is given by

$$\frac{\dot{\overline{L}}}{\overline{L}} = \frac{\frac{d}{dt}(BL)}{BL} = \frac{\dot{B}}{B} + \frac{\dot{L}}{L} = s_B \frac{\overline{Y}}{\overline{L}} + n \tag{10.14}$$

where S_B is a fraction of output devoted to education and training.

Also, assume $\overline{K}$ is endogenously determined by

$$\frac{\dot{\overline{K}}}{\overline{K}} = \frac{\frac{d}{dt}(AK)}{AK} = \frac{\dot{A}}{A} + \frac{\dot{K}}{K} = s_A \frac{\overline{Y}}{\overline{K}} + s_K \frac{\overline{Y}}{\overline{K}} = s \frac{\overline{Y}}{\overline{K}} = s\overline{y} \tag{10.15}$$

where $\overline{y} = \overline{Y}/AK$, s_A is a fraction of output (or income) $\overline{Y}$ devoted to increase the efficiency of capital, s_K is a fraction of output devoted to increase physical capital, $s = s_A + s_K$ is a fraction of output used to create additional effective capital and $1 > s > 0$.

Using the capital-labour ratio in efficiency units,

$$\bar{k}(t) = \frac{\overline{K}(t)}{\overline{L}(t)} = \frac{A(t)K(t)}{B(t)L(t)} \tag{10.16}$$

we may write

$$\frac{\dot{\bar{k}}}{\bar{k}} = \frac{\dot{\overline{K}}}{\overline{K}} - \frac{\dot{\overline{L}}}{\overline{L}} = \frac{s\overline{Y}}{\overline{K}} - \frac{s_B \overline{Y}}{\overline{L}} - n = sF\left(1, \frac{1}{\bar{k}}\right) - s_B F(\bar{k}, 1) - n$$

$$= sf(\bar{k}) - s_B g(\bar{k}) - n \tag{10.17}$$

where $1 > s + s_B > 0$.

The stability condition is satisfied if

$$\frac{d\left(\frac{\dot{\bar{k}}}{\bar{k}}\right)}{d\bar{k}} = s\frac{df}{d\bar{k}} - s_B \frac{dg}{d\bar{k}} < 0. \tag{10.18}$$

The first term $s \cdot df/d\bar{k}$ is negative. The second term is always positive because $dg/d\bar{k}$ is the marginal product of effective capital. Hence Eq. (10.18) is automatically satisfied. The growing economy is dynamically stable under the endogenous factor augmenting type of technical progress.[8]

To apply the balanced growth condition to the data, we rearrange Eq. (10.11) as

$$\frac{\dot{Y}}{Y} = \alpha\left(\frac{\dot{A}}{A} + \frac{\dot{K}}{K}\right) + \beta\left(\frac{\dot{B}}{B} + \frac{\dot{L}}{L}\right) = \alpha\frac{\dot{\overline{K}}}{\overline{K}} + \beta\frac{\dot{\overline{L}}}{\overline{L}}. \tag{10.19}$$

At steady state $\bar{k} = \bar{k}^*$, $(\dot{\overline{K}}/\overline{K})^* = (\dot{\overline{L}}/\overline{L})^*$ holds. Because $\alpha + \beta = 1$, if we put $(\dot{\overline{K}}/\overline{K})^* = (\dot{\overline{L}}/\overline{L})^* = G^*$, Eq. (10.19) becomes

$$\left(\frac{\dot{Y}}{Y}\right)^* = \alpha\left(\frac{\dot{\overline{K}}}{\overline{K}}\right)^* + \beta\left(\frac{\dot{\overline{L}}}{\overline{L}}\right)^* = \alpha G^* + \beta G^* = G^*$$

such that

$$\left(\frac{\dot{Y}}{Y}\right)^* = \left(\frac{\dot{\overline{K}}}{\overline{K}}\right)^* + \left(\frac{\dot{\overline{L}}}{\overline{L}}\right)^* = G^* \tag{10.20}$$

is the condition for the stable growth. In Sect. 10.3.6, we examine the economies of Japan and the USA to see whether they satisfy this condition.

---

[8] We thank the referee for clarifying the differences between exogenous and endogenous types of technical change.

10.3 Applications to the US and Japanese Data

10.3.1 Tests of Non-unity of σ

Before we conduct the estimation of biased technical progress, we must ensure that the production functions are not Cobb–Douglas. If the function is Cobb–Douglas, there is no way to separate A and B. Also, we have to determine whether technical progress is Hicks-neutral. If it is so, A should always be equal to B, which means we have no need to estimate the biased technical growth.

To determine whether the production functions are Cobb–Douglas, we use Test 1, the average elasticity of substitution method and then we apply Test 2, the Hicks-neutrality test to examine the fitness of the data of both countries.

Test 1: Average Elasticity of Substitution Method

This is a test introduced by Sato (1970, pp. 192–193) to identify whether the production function of each country is a Cobb–Douglas type. Define $z = Y/L$, $x = L/K$ and $R(z/w)$ to be equal to the ratio of $\dot{z}/z$ to $\dot{w}/w$, then from Eq. (10.7), we get

$$R\left(\frac{z}{w}\right) = \frac{\sigma}{1 + (\sigma - 1)\dfrac{\dot{B}/B}{\dot{z}/z}}. \qquad (10.21)$$

Also, define $R(y/r)$ as the ratio of $\dot{y}/y$ to r/r and $R(x/\omega)$ as the ratio of $\dot{x}/x$ to $\dot{\omega}/\omega$. Then,

$$R\left(\frac{y}{r}\right) = \frac{\sigma}{1 + (\sigma - 1)\dfrac{\dot{A}/A}{\dot{y}/y}} \qquad (10.22)$$

and

$$R\left(\frac{x}{\omega}\right) = \frac{\sigma}{1 + (\sigma - 1)\dfrac{\dot{A}/A - \dot{B}/B}{\dot{x}/x}}. \qquad (10.23)$$

If $\sigma = 1$, then $R(z/w)$, $R(y/r)$ and $R(x/\omega)$ should be, on average, the same and equal to unity, regardless of whether or not A and B are the same. That is,

$$\overline{R}\left(\frac{z}{w}\right) = \overline{R}\left(\frac{y}{r}\right) = \overline{R}\left(\frac{x}{\omega}\right) = 1 \qquad (10.24)$$

where the upper bar indicates the average value of R's. Therefore, Eq. (10.24) may be used as a test of the Cobb–Douglas function.

The average values calculated are presented in Table 10.1.

Table 10.1 Average elasticity of substitution method results

	Japan	USA
$\bar{R}(z/w)$	1.0366 (0.9358)	0.7178 (1.6730)
$\bar{R}(y/r)$	0.6831 (0.8642)	0.5133 (1.4028)
$\bar{R}(x/\omega)$	0.6445 (0.9227)	0.4687 (2.4109)

SD is in parenthesis. In the US case, extreme 4 data are excluded from $R(z/w)$, 1 and 2 data are excluded from $R(y/r)$ and $R(x/\omega)$ respectively.

In both countries' cases, the three variables are very different from one another and Eq. (10.24) does not hold. Therefore, we can conclude σ is not unity, which means that the production functions of both countries are not Cobb–Douglas.

Test 2: Test of Hicks-Neutrality

Next we determine whether the technical progress is Hicks-neutral. When technical progress is biased, the following fundamental equations hold,[9]

$$\frac{\dot{w}}{w} = \frac{\dot{B}}{B} - \frac{\alpha}{\sigma}\left(\frac{\dot{B}}{B} - \frac{\dot{A}}{A} - \frac{\dot{k}}{k}\right) \quad (10.25)$$

and

$$\frac{\dot{r}}{r} = \frac{\dot{A}}{A} + \frac{\beta}{\sigma}\left(\frac{\dot{B}}{B} - \frac{\dot{A}}{A} - \frac{\dot{k}}{k}\right) \quad (10.26)$$

where $k = 1/x = K/L$.

When technical progress is Hicks-neutral, equations must satisfy the following two equations,

$$\frac{\dot{w}}{w} = \frac{\dot{T}}{T} + \frac{\alpha}{\sigma}\frac{\dot{k}}{k} \quad (10.25')$$

and

$$\frac{\dot{r}}{r} = \frac{\dot{T}}{T} - \frac{\beta}{\sigma}\frac{\dot{k}}{k} \quad (10.26')$$

where $\dot{T}/T = \dot{A}/A = \dot{B}/B$. If the technical progress is Hicks-neutral, the two regressional estimates of $\dot{T}/T$ from Eqs. (10.25′) and (10.26′), should be equal. Results are in Table 10.2.

In both countries' cases, the coefficients of determinations are very low, except for Japan's $\dot{w}/w$; $\dot{T}/T$ obtained from the two equations for each country are very

---

[9]See Sato (1970, p. 183) for the discussion on these fundamental relations.

10.3 Applications to the US and Japanese Data

Table 10.2 The Hicks-neutrality test results

	Japan		USA	
Average $\dot{T}/T$	2.13%		1.07%	
a	0.2934		0.3133	
B	0.7066		0.6867	
Regression Results Eq. (10.25′)	$\dfrac{\dot{w}}{w} = -0.0086 + 0.7938\dfrac{\dot{k}}{k}$ $\phantom{\dfrac{\dot{w}}{w} =}(-2.74)(20.95)$		$\dfrac{\dot{w}}{w} = 0.0139 + 0.0969\dfrac{\dot{k}}{k}$ $\phantom{\dfrac{\dot{w}}{w} =}(5.03)(0.93)$	
	Adj $R^2 = 0.9106$		Adj $R^2 = -0.0030$	
	Estimated $\dot{\bar{T}}/T$	-0.86%	Estimated $\dot{\bar{T}}/T$	1.39%
	Estimated σ	0.3696	Estimated σ	3.2332
Regression Results Eq. (10.26′)	$\dfrac{\dot{r}}{w} = 0.0019 + 0.4653\dfrac{\dot{k}}{k}$ $\phantom{\dfrac{\dot{r}}{w} =}(0.13)(-2.61)$		$\dfrac{\dot{r}}{w} = 0.0217 + 1.1326\dfrac{\dot{k}}{k}$ $\phantom{\dfrac{\dot{r}}{w} =}(3.39)(-4.69)$	
	Adj $R^2 = 0.1188$		Adj $R^2 = 0.3277$	
	Estimated $\dot{\bar{T}}/T$	0.19%	Estimated $\dot{\bar{T}}/T$	2.17%
	Estimated σ	1.5170	Estimated σ	0.6064

Average $\dot{T}/T$ in the first row are calculated from Eq. (10.28) in the next subsection.

different. Thus, these results suggest that technical progress is non-neutral. We are now ready to estimate production functions with biased technical change.

10.3.2 Estimates of Production Functions

We take four steps in the estimation of the production functions with biased technical change for Japan and the USA. We should note here that there are always inevitable limitations in the application of the theory. In our case, all the theoretical equations are time continuous, while actual data are discrete (in our case, annual). Thus, we should approximate the derivatives by the difference. To do so, for a year t, we substitute the growth rate $\dot{Y}(t)/Y(t)$ for $\Delta Y(t)/Y(t) = (Y(t+1) - Y(t))/Y(t)$. In the remainder of this chapter, we continue to use the derivatives even in the application, for the sake of simplicity.

Step 1: Estimation of Hicks-Neutral Technical Progress

As discussed in Sect. 10.2, we need to know the elasticity of substitution, $\sigma(t)$, in advance of estimating the growth rate of biased technical progress $\dot{A}/A$ and $\dot{B}/B$. For the purpose of finding out the elasticity, we first derive Solow–Kendrick TFP for each country.

The production function with Hicks-neutral technical progress should take the form of Eq. (10.3). As we have observed, with the share of capital $\alpha(t) = r(t)K(t)/Y(t)$ and that of labour $\beta(t) = w(t)L(t)/Y(t)$, the growth rate of Y is expressed as

Table 10.3 Average relative share of input factors

		Japan (%)			USA (%)		
		1960–2004	1960–1989	1990–2004	**1960–2004**	1960–1989	1990–2004
Average relative share of capital α		**29.34**	31.60	24.82	**31.33**	30.80	32.39
Average relative share of capital β		**70.66**	68.40	75.17	**68.67**	69.20	67.61
Total		**100**	100	100	**100**	100	100

Averages for the whole periods are in *bold*

Table 10.4 Growth rate of Hicks-neutral technical change and other factors

		Japan (%)			USA (%)		
		1960–2004	1960–1989	1990–2004	**1960–2004**	1960–1989	1990–2004
Growth rate of output	$\dot{Y}/Y$	**4.65**	6.35	−1.03	**3.08**	3.05	3.13
Growth rate of Hicks neutral technical change	$\dot{T}/T$	**2.13**	2.91	−0.45	**1.07**	0.90	1.43
Growth rate of capital	$\dot{K}/K$	**7.32**	9.25	−3.18	**3.31**	3.58	2.72
Growth rate of labour	$\dot{L}/L$	**0.28**	0.56	−0.31	**1.39**	1.49	1.19
Growth rate of output per labour	$\dot{z}/z$	**4.35**	5.76	−1.34	**1.66**	1.54	1.92

Averages for the whole periods are in *bold*

$$\frac{\dot{Y}(t)}{Y(t)} = \frac{\dot{T}(t)}{T(t)} + \alpha(t)\frac{\dot{K}(t)}{K(t)} + \beta(t)\frac{\dot{L}(t)}{L(t)}. \qquad (10.27)$$

If we further define $z = Y/L$, $k = K/L$, so that $\dot{z}/z = \dot{Y}/Y - \dot{L}/L$, $\dot{k}/k = \dot{K}/K - \dot{L}/L$, then, by rearranging Eq. (10.27), we get

$$\frac{\dot{T}(t)}{T(t)} = \frac{\dot{z}(t)}{z(t)} - \alpha(t)\frac{\dot{k}(t)}{k(t)}. \qquad (10.28)$$

With the data divided by time periods into Period I (1960–1989) and Period II (1990–2004), the period averages of observed relative share of factor inputs used in Eq. (10.28) are shown in Table 10.3. The period averages of estimated $\dot{T}(t)/T(t)$ are shown in Table 10.4, together with other variables. The period averages for the period $t = [0, S]$ are calculated as $\left(\frac{\dot{T}}{T}\right)_{AVG} = \frac{1}{S}\sum_{t=0}^{S}\frac{\dot{T}(t)}{T(t)}$.

Given these results, we take a bird's eye view to compare the performance over 44 years of the economies of Japan and the USA. From 1960 to 2004, the average annual growth rate $\dot{Y}/Y$ for Japan was 4.65%, while that for the USA was 3.08%. In

10.3 Applications to the US and Japanese Data

Table 10.5 Relative contributions to economic growth by technical change and factor inputs

	Japan (%)			USA (%)		
	1960–2004	1960–1989	1990–2004	**1960–2004**	1960–1989	1990–2004
$(\dot{T}/T)/(\dot{Y}/Y)$	**45.76**	45.87	44.30	**34.80**	29.58	45.69
$(\alpha(\dot{K}/K))/(\dot{Y}/Y)$	**46.14**	46.05	76.90	**33.65**	36.11	28.15
$(\beta(\dot{L}/L))/(\dot{Y}/Y)$	**4.30**	6.03	−22.60	**31.09**	33.73	25.71
Statistical adjustment	**3.80**	2.05	1.41	**0.46**	0.58	0.45
Total	**100**	100	100	**100**	100	100

To apply actual data to the theory, we have to approximate differentiation by difference. Thus the weighted sum of the increase of each factor is not equal to the growth rate. We show the discrepancy as "Statistical adjustment."
Averages for the whole periods are in *bold*

the same period, labour increased only 0.28% per annum in Japan, while it increased 1.39% in the USA.

The Japanese economy grew much faster with a much lower growth rate of labour. From Table 10.5, we can learn that in Japan the relative contribution of labour $(\beta \cdot (\dot{L}/L))/(\dot{Y}/Y)$ was just 4.30% of total GDP growth. Although it turned negative in Period II, this downturn may have been caused not by population decline but by the lack of effective demand. In lieu of labour contribution, the increase of capital $\dot{K}/K$ and technical progress $\dot{T}/T$ supported high economic growth. Capital contributed as much as 46.14% to the GDP growth and technical progress contributed nearly as much (45.76%). Actually, Japan's capital increase (annually 7.32%) was more than twice that of the USA (annually 3.31%). The rate of Hicks-neutral technical change was 2.13% per annum, also nearly double that of the USA (1.07%). We found that the engines of Japanese economic growth were booming capital investment and properly combined technical progress of capital and labour.

These results indicate that the source of Japan's economic growth was quality improvement—rather than quantity increase—of population and labour force. In contrast, the source of economic growth for the USA was quantity increase—rather than quality improvement—of population and labour force. The growth rate of output per unit of labour $\dot{z}/z$ was only four-tenths that of Japan (Table 10.4). The US economic growth was sustained by technical progress and the increase of the labour force.

We should note that in the USA, the relative contributions to economic growth of technical progress, capital increase and labour increase are balanced. The contribution rates are 34.8%, 33.65% and 31.09%, respectively (Table 10.5). Discussion on this balanced growth appears in Sect. 10.3.6. In a country blessed with abundant land and natural resources, population increase played a major role in US economic growth. Population increase made economic expansion possible without much improvement in the efficiency of factors.

Step 2: Deriving Average Elasticity of Substitution σ^N

Next, we estimate average elasticity of substitution under the assumption of Hicks-neutral technical progress, σ^N.

Table 10.6 Growth rate of biased technical exchange

		Japan (%)			USA (%)		
		1960–2004	1960–1989	1990–2004	**1960–2004**	1960–1989	1990–2004
Growth rate of Hicks-neutral technical change (%)	$\dot{T}/T$	**2.13**	2.91	0.45	**1.07**	0.90	1.43
Estimated elasticity of substitution	σ_{AVG}^N	**0.57**	0.63	0.50	**0.46**	0.51	0.38
Growth rate of capital efficiency (%)	$\dot{A}/A$	**−1.61**	−1.63	−1.36	**−1.41**	−0.59	0.08
Growth rate of labour efficiency (%)	$\dot{B}/B$	**3.86**	5.11	1.01	**1.74**	1.56	1.97

Averages for the whole periods are in *bold*

For a year t, σ^N is estimated using

$$\sigma^N(t) = \frac{d\left(\frac{K(t)}{L(t)}\right)/\left(\frac{K(t)}{L(t)}\right)}{d\left(\frac{w(t)}{r(t)}\right)/\left(\frac{w(t)}{r(t)}\right)} = \frac{\frac{\dot{K}(t)}{K(t)} - \frac{\dot{L}(t)}{L(t)}}{\frac{\dot{w}(t)}{w(t)} - \frac{\dot{r}(t)}{r(t)}}.$$

The average elasticity of substitution for the period $[0, S]$ is calculated as

$$\sigma_{AVG}^N = \frac{1}{S}\sum_{t=0}^{S}\sigma^N(t). \tag{10.29}$$

Some of the σ_t^N s give extraordinarily high or negative values. Since σ in developed countries are known to range $0 < \sigma < 1$, we excluded negatives and those over one from the summation in Eq. (10.29).

The estimated σ^N for Japan from 1960 to 2004 is 0.57. In Period I only it is 0.63 and in Period II only it is 0.50. For the USA, the average elasticity of substitution for these periods is 0.46, 0.51 and 0.38, respectively (Table 10.6). The results are also appear later in Sect. 10.3.3.

Step 3: Estimation of CES Functions with Hicks-Neutral Technical Change

Since we discovered that production functions in both countries are not the Cobb–Douglas type and there are no trends of σ correlating with the values k or time t, we assume the constant elasticity of substitution (CES) production function and identify how σ^N fits the actual data. Before we directly estimate the production function with factor augmenting (biased) technical change, we estimate the function with Hicks-neutral technical change in order to make a comparison.

10.3 Applications to the US and Japanese Data

With Hicks-neutral technical change, the function should take the form of

$$Y^N(t) = T(t)[\alpha K(t)^{-\rho^N} + \beta L(t)^{-\rho^N}]^{-1/\rho^N} \tag{10.30}$$

where $\sigma^N = 1/(1+\rho^N)$. $T(t)$ is assumed to grow at a constant rate during a period, which is given as the average of each $\dot{T}(t)/T(t)$ estimated in Eq. (10.28). We also assume Cobb–Douglas α and β are constant throughout the period and we apply period averages of observed α and β.

Step 4: Estimation of CES Functions with Factor Augmenting Technical Change

We are now ready to estimate the CES function with factor augmenting (biased) technical change. We substitute the estimates of elasticity σ^N into Eqs. (10.6) and (10.7) to derive $\dot{A}/A$ and $\dot{B}/B$. Theoretically, the elasticity of substitution of factor augmenting technical change has to be stated as Eq. (10.31) because when technical progress is non-neutral, the value of the elasticity itself is influenced by the efficiencies of capital and labour.[10] We thus have the following equation,

$$\sigma^B = \frac{d\left(\frac{AK}{BL}\right)\Big/\frac{AK}{BL}}{d\left(\frac{\partial F/\partial BL}{\partial F/\partial AK}\right)\Big/\frac{\partial F/\partial BL}{\partial F/\partial AK}}. \tag{10.31}$$

In view of the fact that we cannot observe σ^B directly, we use σ^N instead. As presented in Appendix III, in the simulation of $Y^B(t)$, variational changes of σ around σ^N do not give significant deviation to their results. Thus, σ^N qualifies to be the proxy of σ^B.

Then, the CES function takes the form of

$$Y^B(t) = [\alpha(A(t)K(t))^{-\rho^N} + \beta(B(t)L(t))^{-\rho^N}]^{-1/\rho^N}. \tag{10.32}$$

Estimated $Y^B(t)$ summarizes our model. It represents both the form of the production function and the biasedness of technical change.

In this way, we will obtain two series, Y^N and Y^B.

10.3.3 Simulation Results

Equipped with average σ^N, $\dot{A}/A$ and $\dot{B}/B$ (Table 10.6), we estimated Y^N and Y^B. CES production functions with Hicks-neutral technical change Y^N are plotted with thick grey lines in Figs. 10.1 and 10.2. As our tests have suggested, the technical

---

[10] See Sato (1970) for detailed discussion on the elasticity of substitution under factor augmenting technical change.

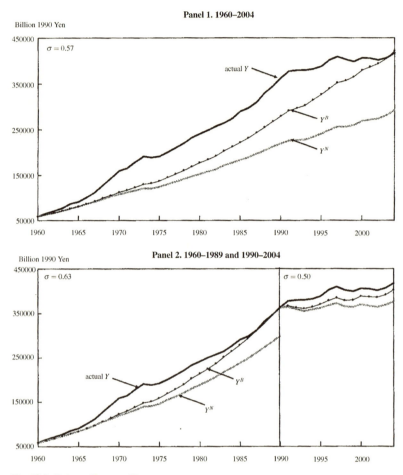

Fig. 10.1 Estimated output of Japan

progress in both countries may not be Hicks-neutral. Hence, Y^N deviates far from actual Y. Hicks-neutral technical change assumes the rate of the efficiency of capital and labour changing at equal rates, which is not true for Japan and the USA.

As for the estimated CES production functions with biased technical change Y^B, shown by thin lines with markers in Figs. 10.1 and 10.2, they all fit much better than do Y^N. This supports our view that the economies of Japan and the USA both experienced biased technical growth. Also, it suggests that estimation of TFP is not enough to diagnose the economic performance and to prescribe any policy for either of these countries.

10.3 Applications to the US and Japanese Data

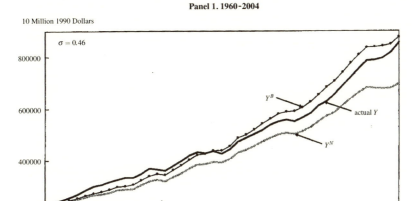

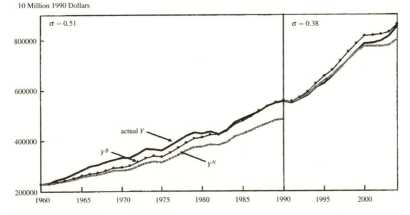

Fig. 10.2 Estimated output of the USA

10.3.4 Biased Technical Change of Japan and the USA

As our neutrality tests and simulation results suggested, the estimation with neutral technical change lacks the ability to explain the actual economic growth. Conversely, the factor augmenting (biased) technical change explains further the characteristics of each economy. Once we know the growth rate of efficiency of each factor ($\dot{A}/A$ and $\dot{B}/B$), we are able to more adequately tailor policies to raise the total efficiency ($\dot{T}/T$).

Table 10.7 Relative contributions to Hicks-neutral technical change by biased technical change

	Japan (%)			USA (%)		
	1960–2004	1960–1989	1990–2004	**1960–2004**	1960–1989	1990–2004
$\alpha(\dot{A}/A)/(\dot{T}/T)$	−22.18	−17.67	−74.09	−11.96	−20.18	1.86
$\beta(\dot{B}/B)/(\dot{T}/T)$	**128.14**	119.97	167.09	**111.44**	119.80	92.95
Statistical adjustment	**−5.95**	−2.30	7.00	**0.52**	0.38	5.19
Total	**100**	100	100	**100**	100	100

Averages for the whole periods are in *bold*

Tables 10.6 and 10.7 summarize the average growth of efficiency of factors. Both countries' σ is less than one and $\dot{A}/A$ is smaller than $\dot{B}/B$ in all periods. According to the definition in Sect. 10.2.1, both countries experienced labour saving technical progress.

In Japan, labour saving technical progress helped the economic growth despite labour itself declining. Japan's labour saving technical progress offset the low labour increase. The growth rate of labour efficiency $\dot{B}/B$ in Japan for 44 years was annually 3.86%, a figure more than double that of the USA (1.74%). This labour efficiency sustained Japan's high growth. The Japanese economy developed without depending too much on its population growth.

Another fact revealed in the analysis on biased technical change is that Japan experienced overinvestment. As implied in the economic conservation law,[11] overly rapid capital accumulation lowers the efficiency of capital. This mainly happened in Period I, when the growth rate of capital was as high as 9.25%. As we will argue in Sect. 10.3.6, the income-capital ratio in Japan was much higher than it needed to be to ensure Japan's stable growth.

Now we focus on Period II (1990–2004), which includes the Japan's lost decade and the USAs' new economy. As is well known, the growth rate of the USA surpassed that of Japan in Period II. In Japan, the growth rate of GDP, labour and labour efficiency all declined in Period II compared with the rates in Period I. The growth rate of labour efficiency slowed to 1.01% from 5.11% in Period I. This 4.1% point decline was much larger than that of labour (a decline of 0.87 points, to −0.31% from 0.56%).

Capital efficiency continuously decreased during 1960–2004, although in Period II it showed a scant 0.27 point improvement to −1.36% from −1.63%. This fact indicates that Japan's lost decade suffered from overinvestment and the consecutive accumulation of bad loans. To raise total productivity, Japan needs to turn the capital efficiency toward the positive, as was done in the USA and it needs to raise labour efficiency to a greater extent.

In the USA, capital efficiency turned moderately positive in Period II to 0.08% from −0.59%. Capital efficiency growth is very close to zero, so we can assume Harrod-neutral growth for the US economy.

---

[11] The income-capital conservation law is summarized in Sato (1985).

10.3 Applications to the US and Japanese Data

The idea of biased technical change itself is not new, but not many applications have been done so far. Our findings revealed that analysing only TFP or Hicks-neutral technical change is not sufficient as a basis for evaluating the economic performance of Japan and the USA.

10.3.5 Contrast in Response to Oil Crises

In this subsection, we contrast the economic response of the two countries toward external shocks, i.e. the two oil crises in 1973 and 1979. If it were not for deflationary pressures in Japan and the USA, the recent hike in oil price would have caused another crisis. Looking ahead, due to complex international relationships around the Middle Eastern countries and policy changes in oil producing South American countries, the worldwide crude oil supply could face shortages at any time. It is worth examining the response toward past price shocks.

The two oil crises affected both countries. We assume the time lags of the shocks were the same for both countries and compare the total data (with the oil crisis periods included) to the data with those years excluded (the years during lagged shocks are chosen as 1974–1975 and 1980–1982.) By this comparison, we can see how the two countries responded to the shocks in different ways. Table 10.8 lists the technical progress in each year with the averages for all years and for those excluding 1974–1975 and 1980–1982. Table 10.9 shows the average growth rates of other factors, also excluding those periods.

The Japanese response toward oil crises was superior to that of the USA. Especially in 1974 and 1975, Japan's growth rates of capital efficiency were very positive, which means that Japan overcame the price pressures by substituting capital for energy. Energy saving measures were developed quickly enough in Japan, an energy scarce country. This did not happen in the USA, an energy abundant country, where both factor efficiencies declined after the crises. Needless to say, if the efficiency of factors had not dropped because of the crises, both economies would have grown faster.

Table 10.8 Technical progress with and without oil crises

	Japan (%)			USA (%)		
σ_{AVG}^N	0.57			0.46		
Rates of technical change	$\dot{A}/A$	$\dot{B}/B$	$\dot{T}/T$	$\dot{A}/A$	$\dot{B}/B$	$\dot{T}/T$
Average	−1.61	3.86	2.13	−0.41	1.74	1.07
Average excluding 1974–1975, 1980–1982	−1.97	4.39	2.34	0.10	1.94	1.36
1961	−4.80	14.24	7.07	−0.91	3.18	1.90
1962	−0.16	5.89	3.81	1.29	4.20	3.29
1963	−0.75	4.75	3.02	0.89	2.60	2.06
1964	−1.31	12.22	7.45	1.32	4.09	3.21
1965	0.82	1.77	1.62	0.48	3.54	2.56

(continued)

Table 10.8 (continued)

σ_{AVG}^N	Japan (%) 0.57			USA (%) 0.46		
Rates of technical change	$\dot{A}/A$	$\dot{B}/B$	$\dot{T}/T$	$\dot{A}/A$	$\dot{B}/B$	$\dot{T}/T$
1966	−3.06	9.32	5.11	1.46	4.03	3.22
1967	−7.19	13.13	5.99	−0.44	1.27	0.74
1968	−6.42	15.32	7.28	1.20	1.79	1.64
1969	−2.26	13.44	7.49	1.91	−1.51	−0.41
1970	−5.21	12.19	5.33	−5.10	4.79	1.75
1971	−2.33	0.80	−0.12	−0.56	−1.49	−1.17
1972	−2.78	8.01	4.19	0.98	1.05	1.03
1973	0.99	4.40	3.29	2.37	1.49	1.76
1974*	5.44	−6.00	−1.43	−3.23	−2.15	−2.48
1975*	3.65	−1.53	0.31	−8.57	3.90	0.11
1976	−0.14	1.46	1.16	0.87	1.91	1.60
1977	1.70	2.05	2.02	0.08	1.62	1.16
1978	−6.75	5.84	2.29	0.46	1.52	1.19
1979	−7.82	6.33	2.29	−1.12	−0.23	−0.51
1980*	−5.50	4.01	1.26	−3.22	−0.46	−1.33
1981*	3.59	0.15	1.25	−3.21	1.28	−0.11
1982*	−1.35	2.08	1.02	−3.74	−1.62	−2.29
1983	0.62	−0.82	−0.29	−3.01	3.80	1.75
1984	−1.74	4.30	2.50	1.97	1.80	1.85
1985	−9.77	7.88	2.90	−0.54	1.94	1.14
1986	−2.76	2.01	0.52	−0.22	0.78	0.46
1987	−0.57	2.37	1.54	1.08	−0.02	0.33
1988	−0.99	6.48	4.14	1.54	1.89	1.78
1989	0.96	2.44	1.98	−1.48	1.43	0.51
1990	0.76	2.74	2.36	0.13	0.42	0.34
1991	2.74	2.15	2.28	−2.63	0.41	−0.57
1992	−2.04	1.69	0.82	0.16	2.04	1.46
1993	2.24	−0.73	0.19	−0.34	1.35	0.82
1994	1.48	−0.93	−0.27	−1.19	3.57	2.09
1995	0.94	0.02	0.27	0.04	0.19	0.14
1996	−4.28	3.81	1.82	−1.34	4.06	2.27
1997	−0.13	0.86	0.62	0.85	2.21	1.75
1998	−1.18	−0.18	−0.41	4.15	0.09	1.49
1999	−0.45	−1.03	−0.88	2.18	1.43	1.69
2000	0.95	0.17	0.36	3.31	1.01	1.81
2001	2.25	−0.35	0.30	−2.14	1.63	0.41
2002	−3.28	0.73	−0.19	−1.58	2.78	1.38
2003	−1.24	1.14	0.60	−1.36	4.45	2.57
2004	−13.71	5.30	0.86	−0.80	4.45	2.73

The $\dot{A}/A$ and $\dot{B}/B$ presented here are calculated from the σ^N for each country. We have also calculated the $\dot{A}/A$ and $\dot{B}/B$ from various values of σ. Interested readers may get the results upon request.

Years affected by the oil crises are noted with *asterisks*

10.3 Applications to the US and Japanese Data

Table 10.9 Average growth rates with and without oil crises

		Japan (%)		USA (%)	
		1960–2004	1960–2004 excluding OC	1960–2004	1960–2004 excluding OC
Growth rate of output	$\dot{Y}/Y$	4.65	**4.98**	3.08	**3.56**
Growth rate of Hicks-neutral technical change	$\dot{T}/T$	2.13	**2.34**	1.07	**1.36**
Growth rate of capital	$\dot{K}/K$	7.32	**7.35**	3.31	**3.25**
Growth rate of labour	$\dot{L}/L$	0.28	**0.40**	1.39	**1.67**
Growth rate of output per labour	$\dot{z}/z$	4.35	**4.56**	1.66	**1.86**
Growth rate of capital efficiency	$\dot{A}/A$	−1.61	**−1.97**	−0.41	**0.10**
Growth rate of labour efficiency	$\dot{B}/B$	3.86	**4.39**	1.74	**1.94**

In the columns in *bold*, the years excluded are 1974–1975 and 1980–1982.

10.3.6 Economic Performance Revisited

In this subsection, we test the equilibrium condition derived in Sect. 10.2.3 to determine each economy's performance.

For simplicity, we take three average growth rates, that of Period I (1960–1989), Period II (1990–2004) and the whole period (1960–2004), denoted by $i = 1, 2$ and W, respectively.

From Eqs. (10.15) and (10.19), we can derive following two equations.

$$\begin{cases} \left(\dfrac{\dot{Y}}{\overline{\overline{Y}}}\right)_i = \alpha_i s_i \overline{y}_i + \beta_i \left(\dfrac{\dot{L}}{\overline{\overline{L}}}\right)_i \\ \left(\dfrac{\dot{K}}{\overline{\overline{K}}}\right)_i = s_i \overline{y}_i \end{cases} \quad \begin{cases} i = W : & 1960\text{–}2004 \\ i = 1 : & 1960\text{–}1989 \\ i = 2 : & 1990\text{–}2004 \end{cases}$$

In each period, there exists steady-state growth rate G_i^* that satisfies Eq. (10.20) and optimal output per effective capital $\overline{y}_i^* = (\overline{Y}/\overline{K})_i^* = (\overline{Y}/AK)_i^*$ for each s_i.

In Japan, $\overline{y}_i$ is much higher than $\overline{y}_i^*$. Japanese capital stock has grown very fast, but it was not utilized to increase the economy's total income (GDP). For the entire period (Fig. 10.3, Panel 1), $\overline{y}_W = 0.92$ and $\overline{y}_W^* = 0.63$. In Period I (Fig. 10.3, Panel 2), $\overline{y}_1 = 0.93$ and $\overline{y}_1^* = 0.69$. Especially before the first oil crisis in 1973, an extremely high rate of investment supported the country's miraculous economic growth. In Period II (Fig. 10.3, Panel 3), $\overline{y}_2 = 0.60$ and $\overline{y}_2^* = 0.23$. Japanese economic growth was still lower than the growth rate of effective capital and had not reached its steady state. We can find here that there was overinvestment that kept the return on investment very low.

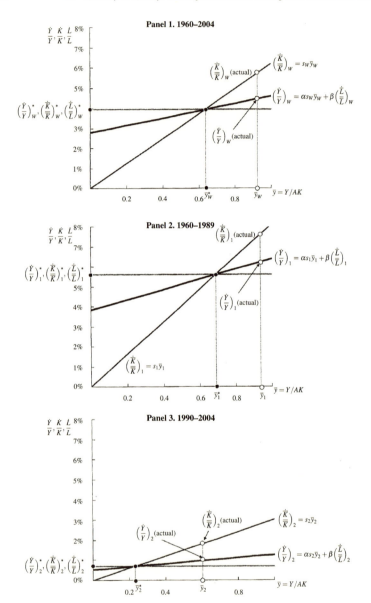

Fig. 10.3 Output-effective capital ratio (Japan)

10.3 Applications to the US and Japanese Data

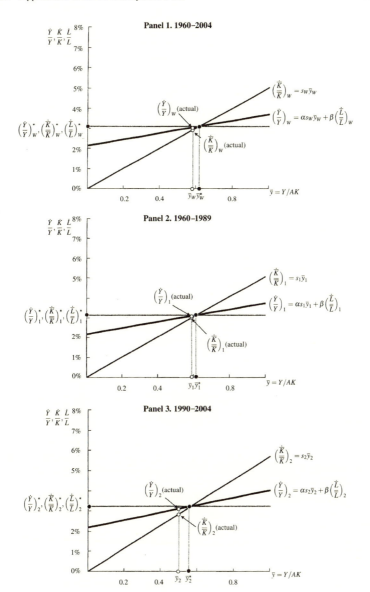

Fig. 10.4 Output-effective capital ratio (USA)

As for the USA, $\bar{y}_i$ is very close to $\bar{y}_i^*$ in every panel and the actual output in period i was just below the optimal output. For the entire period (Fig. 10.4, Panel 1), $\bar{y}_W = 0.58$ and $\bar{y}_W^* = 0.62$. In Period I (Fig. 10.4, Panel 2), $\bar{y}_1 = 0.59$ and $\bar{y}_1^* = 0.62$ and in Period II (Fig. 10.4, Panel 3), $\bar{y}_2 = 0.49$ and $\bar{y}_2^* = 0.56$. The growth rates of effective capital and effective labour were balanced with the economic growth rate of GDP.

Figures 10.3 and 10.4 indicate that the USA might already be at a steady-state growth rate, but Japan is not.

10.4 Conclusion

Population decline in Japan is becoming a major concern. The declining birth rate together with the increase of people reaching retirement age will surely reduce the size of the workforce. The Ministry of Health, Labour and Welfare estimated that the labour force would peak at 67.7 million in 2005 and decline to 63 million in 2025 (Cabinet Office, Government of Japan 2004), which would mark an approximate 0.36% annual decline. The Japanese government believes that the expected demographic change will undermine the fundamentals of Japan's economy and society. Anticipating such a national crisis, the Basic Law on Measures for the Society with a Declining Birthrate was legislated (Japanese Ministry of Health 2003).

As for the USA, the population has been steadily increasing. After recording 100 million in 1915, it doubled to 200 million in 1967. The year 1967 was during the prosperous Johnson presidency and people welcomed the number. Thirty-nine more years added another 100 million; the population amounted to 300 million in October 2006. Now, however, the mood regarding the growing population is not congratulatory. One reason is the foreseen environmental problems congestion might provoke. Another reason is the immigration issue—diverse views exist on the rising number of immigrants. The proportion of immigrants to the total population was just 4% in 1967, but it had increased to 12% by 2004. About half of the newly added 100 million members of the population were Hispanic, an ethnic group that makes up a larger proportion of the US population than do African Americans. The US Census Bureau estimates that the Hispanic population will reach 20% of total US population by 2030 (US Census Bureau 2004, Table 1a). Many worry about problems that may come from lack of assimilation.

In this chapter we contrasted the economic structures of Japan and the USA by comparing the rates of factor augmenting technical progress. Our investigation revealed that efficient utilization of capital and labour will affect economic growth.

Comparing the 44 years' performance of each economy, we found that the Japanese economy grew much more strongly with much lower labour growth. The high economic growth was supported by the increase of capital and technical progress. We found that the engines of Japanese economic growth were booming capital investment and the properly combined technical progress of capital efficiency and labour efficiency.

10.4 Conclusion

Concisely stated, the source of Japan's economic growth was quality improvement—rather than quantity increase—of population and labour force. In contrast, for the USA, what supported its economic growth was quantity increase—rather than quality improvement—of population and labour force. The growth rate of GDP per unit of labour was only 38% of that of Japan. Economic growth in the USA was sustained by technical progress and the growth of the labour force. In a country blessed with abundant land and natural resources, population increase played a major role in US economic growth. Population increase made economic expansion possible without much improvement in the efficiency of factors.

Several policy recommendations can be drawn from our findings. Value added labour can compensate for the decline in the workforce in Japan. Investment in education and training would improve the efficiency of labour; however, Japan needs to improve the performance of its education system. Also, the Japanese government should be well prepared for the aging of the population in two ways. First, it should be prepared to drastically reform Japan's social security system because the present system was designed with the premise that the country's population would continuously grow. Social security reform is a matter of great urgency. Second, Japan must consider the possibility that the time may have come to accept immigration of lower skilled workers who would help to care for the elderly. An increase in immigration may have a detrimental social effect, but may alleviate the impact of the expected population decline.

As far as the macroeconomy is concerned, labour decline itself has not been a cause of problems in Japan. More important was the fact that the burst of the bubble economy eroded firms' capacity to promote technical progress. Technical progress here does not necessarily mean either development of information technology or introduction of brand new, innovative technology.[12] In our context, technical progress includes all ingenuity that can be used to improve the efficiency of capital and labour.

Broadly defined, innovation has been and will be the engine of the development and growth of the Japanese economy. Thus, Japan does not have to be overly pessimistic about the declining birth rate. Innovation can be brought about by policies that encourage people's motivations and expectations.

Acknowledgements The authors wish to acknowledge helpful criticism by the anonymous referee, Kazuo Mino, Masao Fukuoka and Masako Murakami. We also thank Donna Amoroso and Patricia Decker for editorial assistance.

---

[12] Basu and Fernald (2002) show that the aggregate Solow residual (TFP) qualifies to be an index of welfare change as long as the economic profits are small.

Appendix I: Theoretical Justification of Production Function with Biased Technical Change

Sato and Beckmann (1968) precisely provide the theoretical justification of this production function. They set the general production function as $Y = F[K,L]$, which is homogeneous of degree one, then under the condition that factor shares are invariant as long as a remains constant, i.e. σ is a function of β only, they deduce the general production function which incorporates the above invariance condition.

Define $k = K/L$, $x = 1/k = L/K$, $y = Y/K$, then $y = f(x)$ and $Y = Kf(x)$. In this case, marginal productivities are $F_K = \partial Y/\partial K = y - xy_x$ and $F_L = \partial Y/\partial L = y_x$. The income share of labour is expressed as $\beta = xy_x/y$. Now we define marginal rate of substitution r/w as ω. Then,

$$MRS = \omega = \frac{r}{w} = \frac{F_K}{F_L} = \frac{y - xy_x}{y_x}.$$

In this case σ is

$$\sigma = \frac{d\left(\frac{L}{K}\right)/\frac{L}{K}}{d\left(\frac{F_K}{F_L}\right)/\frac{F_K}{F_L}} = \frac{dx/x}{d\omega/\omega}$$

and inverse of σ can be expressed as

$$\frac{1}{\sigma} = \frac{d\log\omega}{d\log x}. \tag{10.33}$$

Since σ must be a function of β, we define the function ϕ as $(1/\sigma) = \phi(\beta)$. Therefore,

$$\frac{1}{\sigma} = \frac{\partial \log \omega}{\partial \log x} = \frac{\partial \log\left(\frac{y - xy_x}{y_x}\right)}{\partial \log x} = \phi\left(\frac{xy_x}{y}\right) = \phi(\beta),$$

$$\phi(\beta) = x\frac{\partial \log(x(\beta^{-1} - 1))}{\partial x}. \tag{10.34}$$

Solving and integrating Eq. (10.34) makes

$$\frac{\partial x}{x} = \frac{\partial \beta}{(1 - \phi(\beta))(1 - \beta)\beta},$$

$$\log x + \log C(t) = g(\beta) = \int \frac{\partial \beta}{(1 - \phi(\beta))(1 - \beta)\beta}.$$

Appendix I: Theoretical Justification of Production Function...

$$C(t)x = e^{g(\beta)} = \exp\left\{\int \frac{\partial \beta}{(1-\phi(\beta))(1-\beta)\beta}\right\}. \quad (10.35)$$

Here, $\log C(t)$ is the arbitrary constant arising from integrating $\partial x/x$, which measures the technical progress factor.

From Eq. (10.35), we can derive β as a function of $C(t)x$ as $\beta = xy_x/y = G(C(t)x)$. Arrange and integrate the above, so

$$\frac{x}{y} \cdot \frac{\partial y}{\partial x} = G(C(t)x),$$

$$\frac{\partial y}{y} = \frac{G(C(t)x)}{x} \partial x,$$

$$\int \frac{\partial y}{y} = \int \frac{G(C(t)x)}{x} \partial x,$$

$$\log y - \log A(t) = \log \int \frac{G(C(t)x)}{x} \partial x,$$

$$y = A(t) \exp \int^x \frac{G(C(t)v)}{C(t)v} C(t) \partial v$$

where $A(t)$ is the arbitrary constant arising from integrating $\partial y/y$, which satisfies $C(t) = B(t)/A(t)$.

Substituting $C(t)v = \mu$, the above can be simplified as

$$y = A(t) \exp \int^{C(t)x} G(\mu) \partial \log \mu \quad (10.36)$$

where the integration is carried out at constant t,

$$y = A(t) f(C(t)x). \quad (10.37)$$

From Eq. (10.37), we can derive the production function with the factor augmenting type of technical progress,

$$\frac{Y}{K} = A(t) f\left(\frac{B(t)}{A(t)} \cdot \frac{L}{K}\right) = A(t) \cdot F\left[1, \frac{B(t)}{A(t)} \cdot \frac{L}{K}\right],$$

$$Y = F[A(t)K, B(t)L].$$

In the economy in which σ is constant as long as β is constant, we are able to estimate A and B.

Appendix II

Data

To complete the historical data, we take data of 1960–1990 from Sato, Ramachandran and Kim (1999), which is derived from OECD statistics. After 1991, we adjusted the data for the relevant variables using different sources listed below.

Japan
Y: Real gross domestic products excluding government consumption
    (OECD 2007b)
K: Real private capital stock (Cabinet Office, Government of Japan 2007a)
L: Labour force (OECD 2007a)
    multiplied by hours worked per worker
    (Cabinet Office, Government of Japan 2007b)
w: Real compensation of employees (OECD 2007b)
    divided by labour force (L)

USA
Y: Real gross domestic products of private sector
    (US Department of Commerce 2007b)
K: Real private fixed assets (US Department of Commerce 2007a)
L: Total hours worked, private (US Department of Commerce 2007b)
w: Real compensation of employees (OECD 2007b)
    divided by labour force (L)

Appendix III

Simulation Results for Different Values of σ

Because no methods exist for identifying the exact value of σ under the biased technical change (Impossibility Theorem, see Sato (1970)), we experimented with conducting simulation with different values of σ in the neighbourhood of the value corresponding to the assumed case of Hicks-neutral type σ^N (Y^N).

As shown in Figs. 10.5 and 10.6, the results are encouraging in the sense that the variations of σ do not significantly affect the simulation path. We only show the figures for the overall period due to limited space, but those for Periods I and II also indicate that the variations of σ were significantly small.

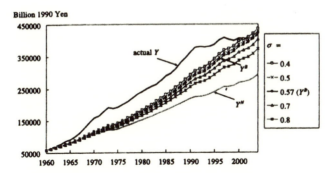

Fig. 10.5 Simulation path using the σ around σ^N (Japan, 1960–2004)

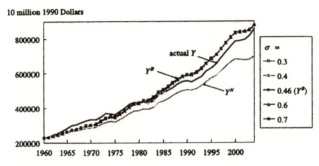

Fig. 10.6 Simulation path using the σ around σ^N (USA, 1960–2004)

References

Acemoglu, D. (2002). Directed technical change. *Review of Economic Studies, 69,* 781–809.
Acemoglu, D. (2003). Labor- and capital-augmenting technical change. *Journal of European Economic Association, 1*(1), 1–37.
Basu, S., & Fernald, J.G. (2002). Aggregate productivity and aggregate technology. *European Economic Review, 46,* 963–991.
Cabinet Office, Government of Japan. (2004). Shousika shakai hakusho (White paper on declining birth rate society), p. 77.
Cabinet Office, Government of Japan. (2007a). Annual report on gross capital stock of private enterprises, systems of national accounts. http://www.esri.cao.go.jp/jp/sna/toukei.html. Accessed Feb 2007.
Cabinet Office, Government of Japan. (2007b). Systems of national accounts. http://www.esri.cao.go.jp/jp/sna/toukei.html. Accessed Feb 2007.
Fukao, K., & Kwon, H.U. (2006). Why did Japan's TFP growth slow down in the lost decade? An empirical analysis based on firm-level data of manufacturing firms. *The Japanese Economic Review, 57*(2), 195–228.
Hicks, J.R. (1932, Second edition in 1963). *The theory of wages.* London: Macmillan.

Japanese Ministry of Health. (2003). Labour and welfare, basic law: measures for the society with a declining birthrate, Law no. 133 (30 July 2003).

Jorgenson, D.W., & Motohashi, K. (2005). Information technology and the Japanese economy, NBER Working Paper, No. 11801.

Klump, R., McAdam, P., & Willman, A. (2007). Factor substitution and factor augmenting technical progress in the US: A normalized supply-side system approach. *Review of Economics and Statistics, 89*(1), 183–192.

Klump, R., & Preissler, H. (2000). CES production functions and economic growth. *Scandinavian Journal of Economics, 102*(1), 41–56.

Rose, H. (1968). The condition for factor-augmenting technical change. *The Economic Journal, 78*(312), 966–971.

OECD. (2007a). Labor force survey, main economic indicators. http://new.sourceoecd.org/vl=1563494/cL=22/nw=l/rpsv/home.htm. Accessed Feb 2007.

OECD. (2007b). OECD national accounts database. http://new.sourceoecd.org/vl=1563494/cL=22/nw=1/rpsv/home.htm. Accessed Feb 2007.

Sato, R. (1970). The estimation of biased technical progress and the production function. *International Economic Review, 11*, 179–208. Reprinted in R. Sato (1996). *Growth theory and technical change, the selected essays of Ryuzo Sato, economists of the twentieth century series, vol. 1* (pp. 144–173). Cheltenham; Brookfield: Edward Elgar.

Sato, R. (1985). The invariance principle and income-wealth conservation laws. *Journal of Econometrics, 30*, 365–389. Reprinted in R. Sato (1999). *Production, stability and dynamic symmetry, the selected essays of Ryuzo Sato, economists of twentieth century series, vol. 2* (pp. 223–247). Cheltenham; Northampton, MA: Edward Elgar.

Sato, R. (2006). The stability of the Solow-Swan model with biased technical change. In *Biased technical change and economic conservation laws* (pp. 25–30). New York: Springer.

Sato, R., & Beckmann, M.J. (1968). Neutral inventions and production functions. *The Review of Economic Studies, 35*(1), 57–66. Reprinted in R. Sato (1996). *Growth theory and technical change, the selected essays of Ryuzo Sato, economists of the twentieth century series, vol. 1* (pp. 133–143). Cheltenham; Brookfield: Edward Elgar.

Sato, R., & Morita, T. (2009). Quantity or quality: the impact of labour saving innovation on US and Japanese growth rates, 1960–2004. *The Japanese Economic Review, 60*(4), 407–434.

Sato, R., & Ramachandran, R. (1987). Factor price variation and the Hicksian hypothesis: A microeconomic model. *Oxford Economic Papers, 39*, 343–356. Reprinted in R. Sato (1996). *Growth theory and technical change, the selected essays of Ryuzo Sato, economists of the twentieth century series, vol. 1* (pp. 199–211). Cheltenham; Brookfield: Edward Elgar.

Sato, R., Ramachandran, R., & Kim, Y. (1999). Estimation of biased technical progress. In R. Sato (Ed.), *Global competition and integration* (pp. 127–170). Boston; Dordrecht; London: Kluwer Academic. Reprinted in R. Sato (2006). *Biased technical change and economic conservation laws* (pp. 63–93). New York: Springer.

US Census Bureau. (2004). US interim projections by age, sex, race, and hispanic origin. http://www.census.gov/ipc/www/usinterimproj/. Accessed Feb 2007.

US Department of Commerce. (2007a). Fixed asset tables, bureau of economic analysis. http://www.bea.gOv/national/FA2004/SelectTable.asp. Accessed Feb 2007.

US Department of Commerce. (2007b). National income and product accounts tables, bureau of economic analysis. http://www.bea.gov/national/nipaweb/Index.asp. Accessed Feb 2007.

Yuhn, K. (1991). Economic growth, technical change biases, and the elasticity of substitution: a test of the de la grandville hypothesis. *Review of Economics and Statistics, 73*(2), 340–346.

Chapter 11
A Survey on Recent Developments

11.1 Introduction

The recent book by Vincent Martinet (2012) on *Economic Theory and Sustainable Development: What Can We Preserve for Future*, illustrates how far we came and how much we have achieved in the theory of growth and economic invariance. This book is about ecological economics but utilizes group theory and Noether's invariance principle to derive meaningful theoretical propositions.

Conservation laws and invariance theories in growth theory provide the fundamental framework in applications to ecological economics of sustainable development. This book (Martinet 2012, p. 106) refers to the original derivation of "Samuelson's Law of Conservation of the Capital-Output Ratio" with the aid of Lie group transformations by Sato (1981, 1999). It also refers to the original edition of this volume (Sato and Ramachandran 1998), which describes "how symmetry and invariance properties have contributed to a large class of discoveries (Martinet 2012, p. 106)." The research paper by de León and de Diego (1998) also refers to our work on conservation laws and symmetry in economic growth models (Sato and Ramachandran 1990).

We will present a brief survey on recent developments in the area of conservation laws and their applications. It is, by no means, comprehensive, but will provide a snap picture of how this new area of theoretical economics is branching out.

11.2 Extensions of the Income-Wealth Conservation Law

The original version of the income-wealth conservation law, which is independently derived by Weitzman and Sato (See Samuelson 2004, p. 244), states that the ratio of income to wealth both in the utility measure must be equal to the constant discount rate. This simple law has been extended to cover many cases such as Case I where the discount rate is variable, Case II where technical and taste change is introduced, and Case III where the original differential equation model is replaced by a discrete-time difference equation model (See Summary Table in Sato and Maeda 1990; revised and extended to Chap. 9 of this volume).

Consider, as an example, Case II where technical and/or taste change of exogenous type, 't' is introduced:

$$\max \int_0^\infty e^{-\rho t} U[k(t), \dot{k}(t), t] \, dt \tag{11.1}$$

where U = utility function, ρ = discount rate (fixed), $k(t)$ is a vector of capital goods, and $\dot{k}(t)$, its time derivative, and t = index of exogenous technical and taste change.

With the aid of infinitesimal transformations for time, $\tau = e^{-\rho t}$ and for k, $\xi = b(t) \exp[-\int_0^t (U_k) ds]$, we can show

$$U(t) - \dot{k}\frac{\partial U}{\partial \dot{k}} + \int_t^\infty e^{-\rho(s-t)} \frac{\partial U}{\partial s} ds$$

$$= \rho \int_t^\infty e^{-\rho(s-t)} U(s) \, ds \tag{11.2}$$

(See Sato, Nôno and Mimura 1984, also Eq. (9.44) in Chap. 9 of this book.)

The above can be interpreted as

Income (measured in utility) + "Value of Technical (or Taste) Change"

$$= \rho \times \text{Wealth}. \tag{11.3}$$

This result is independently confirmed by Mino (2004, Eq. 14) with the aid of the Hamilton-Jacobi-Bellman approach.

Consider also the case where the discount rate is time dependent (Case I). Let the maximization problem be

$$\max \int_0^\infty e^{-\rho(t)} U(k(t), \dot{k}(t)) \, dt \tag{11.4}$$

where $\frac{d\rho}{dt} = \rho'(t) = \rho_t(t)$ is not necessarily constant. By setting $\xi = 0$ and $\tau = \frac{1}{\rho'(t)}$, we can obtain

$$U - k\frac{\partial U}{\partial k} = \rho'(t) \int_t^\infty \left\{ e^{-\int_t^s \rho_p dp} [U - \dot{k}\frac{\partial U}{\partial \dot{k}} \frac{d}{ds}(\frac{1}{\rho_s})] \right\} ds \tag{11.5}$$

11.3 Externalities and Policy Interventions

We can give an interpretation to the right hand side as "generalized wealth with capital gains and losses" (See Sato 1981, 1999; Eq. (9.38) Chap. 9 of this book).

Also as a special case of Case II, we have the "factor-augmenting type" of technical change with respect to k. Then the maximization problem becomes:

$$\max \int_0^\infty e^{-\rho t} U[c\left(k, e^{\delta t}\dot{k}\right)] \qquad (11.6)$$

The conservation law, when $\rho = \delta$, is:

$$\Omega = -\left(e^{-\rho t} U\left[c\left(k, e^{\delta t}\dot{k}\right)\right] - U'\frac{\partial c}{\partial(e^{\delta t}\dot{k})}\dot{k}\right) e^{\rho t} = \text{const.} \qquad (11.7)$$

This is the constancy of the *current Hamiltonian* (See Sato 1981, 1999).

11.3 Externalities and Policy Interventions

The Weitzman-Sato result of the simple "Income-Wealth" ratio conservation law is derived for the command economy where the planner formulates the dynamic optimization problem. Kazuo Mino (2004) extends the analysis to a market economy where these exist distortions. There are many factors which makes the market economy diverge from the command economy. Mino takes up two types of market distortions: Marshallian externalities and policy interventions.

In dealing with externalities the model is designed to include a competitive economy in which capital stocks generates external effects. If the production technology of an individual firm is affected by external effects generated by the aggregate capital in the economy at large, the private technology depends on the social level of capital denoted by $\bar{k}$. This implies that the maximum level of utility is

$$v = v(\dot{k}, k, \bar{k}) \qquad (11.8)$$

The optimal dynamic path for the competitive economy is the path derived from the solution of the following:

$$\max \int_0^\infty e^{-\rho t} v(\dot{k}(t), k(t), \bar{k}(t)) dt \qquad (11.9)$$

Here Mino makes a drastic assumption that "the number of agents" in the competitive economy "is normalized to one." This implies that

$$\bar{k}(t) = k(t) \tag{11.10}$$

Using this Hamilton-Jacobi-Bellman equation, the following modified conservation law is derived:

$$\rho \int_t^\infty e^{-\rho(s-t)} U(s) ds = Y(t) + \int_t^\infty e^{-\rho(s-t)} \frac{\partial v(s)}{\partial \bar{k}} z(s) ds \tag{11.11}$$

where $Y(t) = U(t) + pz(t)$, p is the price of investment and $v(s) = v(z(s), k(s), \bar{k}(s))$, $\bar{k}(s) = k(s)$ and $\dot{k}(s) = z(s)$. The second term in the right hand side of Eq. (11.11) shows the "capital gain" due to the presence of externalities.

We now turn our attention to Mino's second distortion, i.e. the economy where the government distorts the market equilibrium.

Suppose that the government's polices affects consumption and production decisions of the private agents. Let $g(t)$ be the vector of policy variables. Then the maximum utility under policy intervention is given by

$$v(t) = v(z(t), k(t), g(t)), \; z(t) = \dot{k}(t) \tag{11.12}$$

If the government selects the sequence of the policy variables without considering the private sector's behavior and if the private agents perfectly anticipate the sequence of $g(t)$, then the model reduces to the case of exogenous technical change which has already been discussed.

On the other hand if the policy maker adopts a feedback rule that relates $g(t)$ to the current level of $z(t) = \dot{k}(t)$, and $k(t)$, then the model reduces to the case where external effects of capital distort the original conservation law.

Mino then turns his attention to the situation where the government and the private agents engage in game-theoretical interactions. More specifically a Stackelberg differential game is introduced. First he takes up the case where the government adopts an open-loop policy under which each policy variable depends on time alone. It is shown that the original conservation law at $t = 0$ has to be modified by the term dependent on the private and social prices of capital at $t = 0$. (See Mino 2004, p. 322, Proposition 2.)

In view of the fact that the open loop policy is generally time inconsistent, a Markov feedback rule is introduced. Then the conservation law may be written as

$$Y(t) = \rho \int_t^\infty e^{-\rho(s-t)} U(s) ds + [q(t) - p(t)] z(t), \; z(t) = \dot{k}(t) \tag{11.13}$$

where $p(t)$ = private price of capital at time t, and
$q(t)$ = social price of capital at time t.

In discussing Mino's paper, Geir B. Asheim (2004) refers to some earlier contributions including the book by Aronsson, Johansson and Löfgren (1997), and a series of articles by Aronsson, Johanson and Löfgren, as well as the contribution by Vellinga and Withagen (1996). He also points out that the issue of conservation laws is closely related to the sustainability problem. We will discuss this in a later section.

11.4 Stochastic Income and Wealth Conservation Law

Weitzman's recent works (Weitzman 2003, 2004) seek to extend the Income-Wealth Conservation Law in stochastic environments. In the deterministic case any policy function $I(k(t))$ generates a corresponding time trajectory $k(t)$, which satisfies the differential equation

$$\frac{dk(t)}{dt} = I(k(t))$$

or (11.14)

$$dk(t) = I(k(t))\,dt$$

By introducing genuine uncertainty by

$$dk(t) = I(k(t))\,dt + \sigma(k(t))\,dz(t) \tag{11.15}$$

where $z(t)$ is a driftless Wiener process.

Let us compare the dynamic optimization problem with and without $z(t)$, i.e. compare Eq. (11.14) with Eq. (11.15). Using Comin's illustration (Comin 2004), Weitzman's original problem of dynamic optimization without $z(t)$ (Weitzman 1976), i.e., no uncertainly, may be formulated as follows:

$$V(k) = \max_I G(k,I)\Delta t + \frac{1}{1-\rho\Delta t}V(k+I) \tag{11.16}$$

where $V(k)$ = the state evaluation function equal to "wealth," $G(k,I)$ = the profit flow during a small interval of Δt, I = investment, k = capital, and ρ = the discount rate.

Let $I^*(k)$ denote the level of investment that solves the maximization problem, when the current stock of capital is k. By using the Bellman equation and $\Delta t \to 0$, we get

$$\rho V(k) = Y(k) \tag{11.17}$$

where $Y(k) = G(k, I^*(k)) + P(k)I^*(k)$, $P(k) = $ price of capital $= \frac{dV(k)}{dk} = V'(k) = -\frac{\partial G}{\partial I^*}$. $V(k)$ and $Y(k)$ are wealth and income measured in utility units respectively.

We now turn to the case where these exist uncertainty, i.e. Eq. (11.15). Applying Ito's lemma to the Bellman equation, we obtain (See Weitzman 2004. p. 297).

$$\rho V(k(0)) = EY(\lambda) + \left(\frac{1}{2} - \lambda\right) V''(k(0)) \sigma^2(k(0)). \qquad (11.18)$$

where $0 \leq \lambda \leq 1$ defines the weighted-average accounting price of capital, accumulated throughout the time interval $[0, h]$. If $\lambda = \frac{1}{2}$, which means that the price of capital is computed at the middle of the time interval, then expected income is the return on expected wealth, i.e.

$$\rho V(k(0)) = EY(\frac{1}{2}) \qquad (11.19)$$

This is the Income-Wealth Conservation Law Under Uncertainty.

Comin presents a further extension by introducing stochastic productivity growth embodied in new capital:

$$dk = AI\, dt \qquad (11.20)$$

where A is the level of embodied productivity expressed by

$$dA = A\alpha dt + A\sigma dz \qquad (11.21)$$

He presents an extension of the stochastic income-wealth conservation law which now includes the growth factor in investment opportunities.

11.5 Warning

The reader might wonder how the Noether invariance theorem is related to the extensions by Weitzman, Mino, Comin, Asheim and others. They have shown that as long as the income-wealth conservation laws are concerned, the Hamilton-Jacobi-Bellman equation will give the same results as the cases derived by the Noether invariance theorem.

For instance, the result in Sato (1981, 1999) using the Noether theorem for technical exchange, Eq. (11.3) is the same as Mino's equation (Mino 2004, Eq. (11.14)) which is derived by the Hamilton-Jacobi-Bellman equation.

But there is a definite advantage in using the Noether theorem, because of the fact that the Noether approach will enable us to uncover "hidden" conservation laws. (See Sato et al. 1984.) As long as one is looking for only the income-wealth laws or its variations, introducing infinitesimal transformations may be an extra work that may be avoided.

It is shown that using the Noether invariance theorem, the von Neumann model has the only one conservation law, the income-capital conservation law originally found by Samuelson (Sato (1981, 1999) Chap. 7, VI).

11.6 Conservation Laws and Helmholtz Conditions

Mimura and Nôno (1990) applied the Helmholtz conditions to derive conservation laws in the neo-classical growth models. This is an alternative approach in deriving conservation laws, alternative to the Noether invariance approach. Thus, the Helmholtz conditions may enable one to uncover hidden conservation laws of the non-Noether type.

The basic idea is to solve the inverse problem for Lagrangian dynamics and to uncover the constants of motion (conservation laws). The problem is to determine whether a given system of ordinary differential equations can arise as the Euler-Lagrange equations for some other Lagrange function.

Jesse Douglas (1941) provided necessary and sufficient conditions for the problem to have a solution: these conditions are known as the "Helmholtz conditions."

Given a system of differential equations,

$$G_i(\ddot{x},\dot{x},x,t) = 0$$

$$i = 1,\cdots,n$$

$$x = (x_1,\cdots,x_n), \ \dot{x} = (\dot{x}_1,\cdots,\dot{x}_n), \text{ and } \ddot{x} = (\ddot{x}_1,\cdots,\ddot{x}_n), \quad (11.22)$$

the problem is to identify these equations with the Euler-Lagrange equations for some Lagrangian function, $L(\dot{x},x,t)$:

$$[L]_i = \frac{d}{dt}\left(\frac{\partial L}{\partial \dot{x}_i}\right) - \frac{\partial L}{\partial x_i} = 0. \quad (11.23)$$

The Helmholtz conditions are as follows:

$$\frac{\partial G_i}{\partial \ddot{x}_j} = \frac{\partial G_j}{\partial \ddot{x}_i}, \quad (11.24a)$$

$$\frac{\partial G_i}{\partial \dot{x}_j} + \frac{\partial G_j}{\partial \dot{x}_i} = \frac{d}{dt}\left(\frac{\partial G_i}{\partial \ddot{x}_j} + \frac{\partial G_j}{\partial \ddot{x}_i}\right) \quad (11.24b)$$

$$\frac{\partial G_i}{\partial x_j} - \frac{\partial G_j}{\partial x_i} = \frac{1}{2}\frac{d}{dt}\left(\frac{\partial G_i}{\partial \dot{x}_j} - \frac{\partial G_j}{\partial \dot{x}_i}\right). \tag{11.24c}$$

From the equivalent Euler-Lagrange equations $[L]_i = 0$ and $[\mathcal{L}]_i = 0$, with the Lagrangians L and $\mathcal{L}$, they are related as

$$[\mathcal{L}]_i = C_i^j(\dot{x},x,t)[L]_j = 0 \tag{11.25}$$

from which one can derive conservation laws: i.e.

$$tr\left(C_i^j\right)^k = \text{constant for integer } k. \tag{11.26}$$

For the case $n = 1$, Mimura and Nôno derived conservation laws including those which cannot be obtained from the Noether symmetries. They showed

$$[\mathcal{L}] = C(\dot{x},x,t)[L] = 0 \tag{11.27}$$

and C is a constant of the motion, the conservation law of the original optimization problem associated with $[L] = 0$.

They proceeded to investigate neo-classical growth model originally studies by Sato (1981, 1999), and compared their results with Sato's. The conservation laws discovered by Sato and by Mimura–Nôno are distinguished by Greek letters Ω and Ξ, respectively.

1. The Ramsey model:

$$L = e^{-\rho t} U(c)$$
$$c = g(x) - \dot{x} \tag{11.28}$$

(a) $\rho = 0$: no discount rate.

$$\Omega = \Xi = U(c) + \dot{x}U'(c) = \text{const.} \tag{11.29}$$

i.e., "utility measure of income is constant." Thus, there is no new conservation law!

(b) $\rho > 0$: positive discount rate.

$$\Omega = -\dot{x} + \rho x = c = \text{const.} \tag{11.30}$$

$$\Xi = e^{-\rho t}\dot{x} = \text{const.} \tag{11.31}$$

Equation (11.30), when $c = 0$ can be written as

11.6 Conservation Laws and Helmholtz Conditions

$$\rho x = \dot{x} \text{ or } \frac{\dot{x}}{x} = \rho \tag{11.30'}$$

which implies that capital must be growing at the rate ρ. (Note that the special result of this case comes from the assumption that consumption depends on a linear technology $c = \rho x + \beta - \dot{x}$.) Superficially the Mimura–Nôno result Eq. (11.31) seems different from Eq. (11.30), but it is the same, because Eq. (11.31) says that $\frac{\dot{x}}{e^{\rho t}} = c$ implies that x is growing at the rate of $\rho\%$.

Therefore, Ω and Ξ are not independent. The original Sato result is the only conservation law under this linear consumption technology. (Of course the income-wealth conservation law holds for any technology as it is derived from the Noether invariance theorem when the Null term is not zero.)

2. The Liviatan-Samuelson model
   Here we assume

$$L = e^{-\rho t} U(c), \; c = f(\dot{x}, x) \tag{11.32}$$

$$\frac{\partial^2 f}{\partial \dot{x}^2} < 0.$$

For their special type of $f(\dot{x}, x)$, Mimura and Nôno derived two new conservation laws

$$\Xi = \rho \int e^{q(x)} dx - e^{q(x)} \dot{x} = \text{constant}. \tag{11.33}$$

$$\Xi = e^{-\rho t + q(x)} \dot{x} = \text{constant}. \tag{11.34}$$

where $q(x) = \int e^{h(x)} dx$, $h(x)$ is determined by the integrating factor $g(x)$ (See Mimura and Nôno 1990, p. 125). Compared with the Ramsey model, the variable x must be growing at the rate given by the discount rate and by the amount $q(x)$.

3. Quadratic utility Function
   Given,

$$L = e^{-\rho t} U(c), \; U(c) = -\frac{1}{2} \dot{x}^2 - ax\dot{x} - \frac{1}{2} x^2$$

$$-1 < a < 1 \tag{11.35}$$

Mimura and Nôno found another conservation law which superficially books different from Sato's. It turns out the Mimura–Nôno's law Ξ is not independent from the two independent laws already discoursed by Sato (1981, 1999, p. 268).

Thus,

$$\Xi = \Omega_1^{r+\rho} \Omega_2^{r-\rho} \tag{11.36}$$

Ω_1 and Ω_2 are two independent laws originally derived by Sato (1981, 1999) where $r =$ the characteristic root of the system.

11.7 Comparisons: Three Approaches

Mimura and Nôno's use of the Helmholtz conditions is certainly a new endeavor and enabled them to derive a new class of conservation laws of the Non-Noether type. However, as far as their application to the neo-classical growth models is concerned, they did not show a break-through.

We have shown that there are basically three methodologies to the analysis of invariance conditions. The simplest is the Hamilton-Jacobi-Bellman maximum principle, the Noether invariance theorem and the Helmholtz conditions.

As long as one is interested in the income-wealth conservation law or its variations, the Hamilton- Jacobi- Bellman maximum principle will provide an adequate tool. The Helmholtz conditions require painstaking mathematical calculations which one may want to avoid. Finally, the Noether theorem is just a compromise between the first and the third, because it offers systematic investigations into both income-wealth types and other hidden conservation laws which may be beyond the scope of the Hamilton-Jacobi-Bellman approach.

11.8 Hartwick Rule and Conservation Laws

In a series of influential paper, stating Solow (1974), Hartwick (1977) and Dixit et al. (1980), the investment rules for intergenerational equity have been proposed. Hartwick (1977) investigates the specific utility path: society invests all rents from exhaustible resources in reproducible capital goods–known as Hartwick's rule. This rule keeps the total value of net investment, equal to zero and is shown to be sufficient for a constant utility path.

Economic conservation laws provide constancy and invariance along an optimal path. In the paper by Sato and Kim 2002, we examined whether Hartwick's rule can be derived from one of the conservation laws, and further more whether it can be extended to obtain a more general rule.

It is shown that, in fact, Hartwick's rule is a special case when the Hamiltonian of the optimal model is identically equal to zero. Since in general, the Hamiltonian need not be equal to zero (zero being a special case of constant numbers) we can obtain more general investment policy rules.

11.8 Hartwick Rule and Conservation Laws

Let $Y(t)$ be output at time t, then it is divided by consumption $C(t)$, investment spending on physical capital $I(t) = \dot{K}(t)$, and extraction cost of natural resources $aR(t)$, where $a > 0$ is the extraction cost. Thus we have

$$Y(t) = C(t) + \dot{K}(t) + aR(t). \tag{11.37}$$

Assuming the constant-return-to-scale production function

$$Y(t) = f(K(t), R(t)) \tag{11.38}$$

the society's problem is to find the largest constant consumption subject to Eq. (11.37), or equivalently to find the feasible pattern of resource use and investment that minimizes the cumulative use of resources over infinite time. Thus, the stated problem is to minimize,

$$\int_0^\infty R(t)$$

subject to

$$\dot{K}(t) = f(K(t), R(t)) - C(t)$$

and

$$\dot{X} = -R(t) \tag{11.39}$$

where $\dot{X}$ is derived from

$$X(t) = S - \int_0^t R(s)\,ds$$

S = total stock of exhaustibe resources.

The Lagrangian function for this case is

$$\mathscr{L} = R(t) + q_1[\dot{K}(t) - f(K(t), R(t)) + C(t) + aR(t)] + q_2[\dot{X}(t) + R(t)] \tag{11.40}$$

where q_1 and q_2 are the implicit prices associated with $\dot{K}$ and $\dot{X}$. Since Eq. (11.40) does not contain time t explicitly, the conservation law for this system is the constancy of the Hamiltonian function:

$$H = \mathscr{L} - \dot{K}\frac{\partial \mathscr{L}}{\partial \dot{K}} - \dot{X}\frac{\partial \mathscr{L}}{\partial \dot{X}} = -A(=\text{const.}) \tag{11.41}$$

which will yield

$$\dot{K}(t) = (f_R - a)(R(t) + \frac{A}{1+q_2}). \quad (11.42)$$

If A is zero, we get Hartwick's rule

$$\dot{K}(t) = (f_R - a)R(t). \quad (11.43)$$

This requires that keeping investment equal to the rents from exhaustible resources, yields a path of maximum constant consumption. Obviously A need not be equal to zero, and thus Eq. (11.42) gives a more general rule. Note that the initial and terminal conditions must be taken into account, if A is not zero.

Sato and Kim (2002) extended the analysis to the optimal capital accumulation model under the Benthamite utility function. Thus

$$\max \int_0^\infty e^{-\rho t} U(C(t)) dt$$

subject to :

$$\dot{K}(t) = f(K(t), R(t)) - C(t) - aR(t)$$

and

$$\dot{X} = -R(t). \quad (11.44)$$

Using the income-wealth conservation law discussed earlier, the new rule is shown as (Sato and Kim 2002),

$$\dot{K}(t) = (f_R - a)R(t) + \frac{(\frac{d}{dt})f_K \cdot K(t)}{f_K} \quad (11.45)$$

Unlike Hartwick's rule, consumption is no longer constant. It will increase as long as $f_k > \rho$ and decrease when $f_k < \rho$ and remains constant when $f_k = \rho$. Optimal consumption is constant for all t if and only if $\rho = 0$.

Mimura, Fujiwara and Nôno (1999) extended the basic model to include the case where the stock of exhaustible resources is changing and the consumption is increasing exponentially. (The assumption of an exponential growth of consumption is not realistic.) If we set the model such as

11.8 Hartwick Rule and Conservation Laws

$$\max \int_0^\infty e^{-\rho t} U(C(t))\, dt$$

subject to :

$$\dot{K}(t) = f(K(t), R(t)) - C(t) - aR(t)$$

and

$$\dot{X} = \dot{S}(t) - R(t) \quad (11.46)$$

where $\dot{S}(t)$ is a known function of time, t, the solution will give us a more realistic picture, such as, the stock of the resources is not fixed, but most likely increasing. The big oil companies are constantly exploring to find more oil resources even deep in the oceans. The assumption of $\dot{S}(t) \neq 0$, may be interpreted as cases which represent constantly expanding new frontiers.

In his recent paper, Hartwick (2004) attempted to expand his earlier work on resource economics by employing the concept and methodology in classical mechanics. The central question examined by Hartwick is the relationship between capital resource economics and classical mechanics. These two disciplines are intimately related in a natural and unforced way. The reason for this is that the phase space of resource economics and the phase space of classical mechanics have the same geometry (Russell 2004).

Hartwick uses the Solow-Phelps model as a template. Consider the aggregate model: $F(K(t)) =$ output, $K(t) =$ capital, $C(t) =$ consumption, and the current capital decay, $\delta K(t)$, must be covered by $\dot{K}(t) = F(K(t)) - C(t)$, such that $\dot{K} = \delta K$. This is the sustainability constraint. We must find the equilibrium capital K^* such that current consumption, $F(K(t)) - \dot{K}(t)$, is maximum. Hartwick then compares this model with that of classical mechanics. The energy cost per period of restorations for inputs is balanced by energy inflows per period from the respective inputs. In the terminology of economics, incomes from inputs in units of energy must balance with expenditures on inputs restorations in units of energy. He can show that these are a variety of movements of economic variables similar to those in classical mechanics.

Martinet's book (Martinet 2012) is a comprehensive treatise on the relationship between conservation laws and sustainability. The reader is urged to study this outstanding research work.

11.9 Factor-Augmenting Technical Changes as the Magnification Type of Lie Group Transformations: Justification for Biased Technical Change

Both theoretical and empirical economists have often used the factor–augmenting type of technical change as a simple but realistic way to incorporate innovative activities of economic agents. Many micro economists dealing with a firm's innovative activities adopt the factor-augmenting type of technical change with the CES production function and they show that innovation can be labor–saving or capital– saving depending upon the degree of bias and the elasticity of substitution. They then proceed to estimate the degree of biased technical change.

Macro theorists confront with the dilemma when they deal with the stability of growth equilibrium with technical change. If one uses a general class of neo–classical production function, the type of technical change consistent with the stable growth equilibrium must be limited to the labor–augmenting type. But empirical macro economists always insist that technical change is not limited to the labor–augmenting type, and show that the assumption of the general factor–augmenting or the total factor productivity is more acceptable. Under total factor productivity assumption the system cannot achieve stable growth.

In the recent work (Sato 2006), it is shown that macro economists, either theoretical or empirical, no longer have to face with this dilemma. By introducing appropriate investment functions, both theoretical and empirical economists can solve the stability issue with the empirical conflict, which justifies the factor-augmenting type of technical change. In other words, the growth equilibrium is stable under the assumption of a general neo–classical production function together with the general class of factor–augmenting type of technical change. We no longer have to limit ourselves to the Cobb–Douglas production function, nor to the labor–augmenting type.

We begin with the Lie group justification of the factor-augmenting type of technical change. Let the technical progress functions for capital K and Labor L be represented by the factor–augmenting type:

$$\bar{K}(t) = A(t)K(t) = e^{\alpha t}K(t) \qquad (11.47\text{a})$$

$$\bar{L}(t) = B(t)L(t) = e^{\beta t}L(t) \qquad (11.47\text{b})$$

where $\bar{K}(t)$ and $\bar{L}(t)$ are capital and labor after technical change takes place, with the annual rates of α % for K and β % for L respectively.

It should be immediately noticed that Eq. (11.47a,b) is nothing but the magnification type of Lie group transformations. Let Eq. (11.47a,b) be expressed by its infinitesimal transformation (Sato 1981, 1999, p. 48),

11.9 Factor-Augmenting Technical Changes...

$$U = \alpha K \frac{\partial}{\partial K} + \beta L \frac{\partial}{\partial L} \quad (11.48)$$

Then the holothetic technology F under Eq. (11.44) can be derived by

$$UF = \alpha K \frac{\partial F}{\partial K} + \beta L \frac{\partial F}{\partial L} = \emptyset(F) \neq 0 \quad (11.49)$$

The solution to the above partial differential equation is to obtain the holothetic technology F under Eq. (11.48);

$$Y = F\left[K^{\gamma/\alpha} Q(L^\alpha/K^\beta)\right] = F\left[L^{\gamma/\beta} P\left(K^\beta/L^\alpha\right)\right] \quad (11.50)$$

This is the general class of "almost homothetic" type of production functions. This class of production is holothetic under the factor-augmenting type.

If, in dealing with macro economic analysis, we use the class of neo-classical production function with constant returns to scale,

$$\lambda Y = F[\lambda K, \lambda L] \quad (11.51)$$

then Eq. (11.51) is not holothetic under Eqs. (11.47a,b) or (11.48), except for the case of the Cobb-Douglas production function. Therefore, under the general neoclassical production function with constant returns to scale, Eq. (11.51), we can use the factor-augmenting type to separate the true bias, i.e., capital-saving from labor-saving.

Incidentally, the Cobb-Douglas function is a special example of the holothetic technology under both homothetic and almost homothetic types. Therefore it is not possible to separate the degree of capital-saving from that of labor-saving under Eqs. (11.50) and (11.51). Under the Cobb-Douglas function any combination of the two types (capital-saving and labor-saving) will appear simply as the total factor productivity index, or as the so-called Hicks neutral type.

It should be noted that when $\alpha = \beta$ (uniform magnification group), we get Hicks neutral while $\alpha = 0$ and $\beta \neq 0$, we have Harrod neutral or labor-saving and $\alpha \neq 0$ and $\beta = 0$, Solow neutral (capital-saving) respectively.

As in Sato (2006), we now want to show growth stability under the Solow-Swan neo–classical model with biased technical change. Let the aggregate production function (Eq. 11.51) with biased technical change of the factor-augmenting type (Eq. 11.47a,b) be given by

$$\bar{Y}(t) = F[A(t)K(t), B(t)L(t)] = F[\bar{K}(t), \bar{L}(t)] \quad (11.52)$$

It is assumed that both $A(t)$ and $B(t)$ are to be endogenously determined. Let us assume that both $A(t)$ and $K(t)$ are thought to be dependent on $Y(t)$. A certain percentage of income will be allocated to both capital investment and to technological development. A nation will make appropriate investments to improve the quantity and quality of its physical capital. This means

$$\dot{K}(t) = \frac{d}{dt}(A(t)K(t)) = s\bar{Y}(t)$$
$$= (s_1 + s_2)\bar{Y}(t) \tag{11.53}$$

Hence

$$\frac{\dot{K}(t)}{\bar{K}(t)} = \frac{\frac{d(A(t)K(t))}{dt}}{A(t)K(t)} = \frac{\dot{A}(t)}{A(t)} + \frac{\dot{K}(t)}{K(t)} = \frac{s\bar{Y}(t)}{\bar{K}(t)} = s_1 \frac{\bar{Y}(t)}{\bar{K}(t)} + s_2 \frac{\bar{Y}(t)}{\bar{K}(t)} \tag{11.54}$$

The efficiency of capital $\frac{\dot{A}(t)}{A(t)}$ rises with the finance of s_1 % of income $\bar{Y}$, while physical capital rises by $\frac{\dot{K}(t)}{K(t)}$ with the finance of s_2 % of income $\bar{Y}$.

The efficiency of labor can also be increased in the same way by financing on education and training with s_3 % of income $\bar{Y}(t)$, i.e.

$$\frac{\dot{B}(t)}{B} = s_3 \frac{\bar{Y}(t)}{L(t)} \tag{11.55}$$

Finally we assume that labor is growing at the rate of n % per year.

The growth stability is defined as the constancy of $\bar{K}(t) = \frac{\bar{K}(t)}{L(t)}$. Then it is shown (Sato 2006, p. 29) that

$$\frac{\dot{\bar{k}}}{\bar{k}} = \frac{\dot{\bar{K}}}{\bar{K}} - \frac{\dot{L}}{L} = (s_1 + s_2)\frac{\bar{Y}}{\bar{K}} - s_3 \frac{\bar{Y}}{L} - n$$
$$= (s_1 + s_2)f\left(\frac{1}{\bar{k}}\right) - s_3 g(\bar{k}) - n \tag{11.56}$$

where $F\left(1, \frac{1}{\bar{k}}\right) = f\left(\frac{1}{\bar{k}}\right)$ and $F(\bar{k}, 1) = g(\bar{k})$.

The stability of the growth equilibrium is satisfied if

$$\frac{d\left(\frac{\dot{\bar{k}}}{\bar{k}}\right)}{d\bar{k}} = (s_1 + s_2)\frac{df}{d\bar{k}} - s_3 \frac{dg}{d\bar{k}} < 0$$
$$0 < (s_1 + s_2 + s_3) < 1 \tag{11.57}$$

The above condition is always satisfied as shown in Sato (2006, p. 28). Here we have a more general model of economic growth with biased technical change.

These are several papers extending the idea of endogenous biased technical change by introducing optimal allocation of resources among, capital accumulation, increases in capital efficiency and labor efficiency. In other words, the percentages of output spent on K, A and B, s_1, s_2 and s_3, are endogenously determined by maximizing long run welfare of the nation. We will simply mention three papers, i.e. Sato (1996), Sato, Ramachandran and Lian (1999) and Sato and Ramachandran (2000).

In the history of how the factor-augmenting technical change came to be recognized as the convenient form, we want to refer to the two papers, the one by Sato and Beckmann (1968) and the other by Rose (1968). The two papers independently derived the form of the factor-augmenting technical change as the solution to the "neutrality condition" of technical change.

The original Hicks neutrality was derived from the condition that "technical change is neutral when the relative income shares of capital and labor remain unaffected before and after technical change as long as the capital-labor ratio remains unchanged." The mathematical formulation to satisfy the above condition is that the technical change factor is multiplicative to the production function. (This corresponds to the case where $\alpha = \beta$ in our Lie group formulation (Eq. 11.47a,b).)

The factor-augmenting type is derived by the generalized neutrality condition that "technical change is neutral when the relative income shares of capital and labor are unaffected by technical change as long as the elasticity of substitution remains unchanged" (Sato and Beckmann 1968, case XIV). The mathematical solution to the above neutrality condition gives the combination of the production function and the type of technical change exactly identical with Eq. (11.52).

The neutrality condition is further extended to the "group-neutrality" condition, or in short "G-neutral" by Professor Nôno and others (See Nôno 1971, also see Sato 1981, 1999, Chap. 4). From the mathematical point of view most of economic variables such as the income shares, the elasticity of substitution and others are expressed as differential equations. Thus, it is possible to derive the invariance conditions of the differential equations under the Lie group transformations. In fact, most of the known forms of technical change in economics must come from special cases of "G-neutral" technical change.

11.10 Empirical Estimation of Biased Technical Change and Aggregate Production in Function

It is almost impossible to refer to all of the research works in the empirical analysis of technical change. We will simply suggest the reader to consult with "References" in Chap.10 of this book, one of the latest works in this area.

Going back to Sato (1970), it was first suggested that the invariance of the income shares of capital and labor does not necessarily imply that the underlying production function is the Cobb-Douglas type. It may rather suggest that technical change is factor-augmenting and the elasticity of substitution is not unity, most likely less than unity.

The paper (Sato 1970), using the Kendricks' US data, estimated both the efficiencies of capital and labor and the elasticity of substitution. It was concluded that the efficiency of labor $B(t)$ grows much faster than that of capital $A(t)$. The elasticity of substitution is in the neighborhood of 0.6, less than unity (Cobb-Douglas case). Hence technical change is "labor-saving."

The recent paper by Sato and Morita (2009) (included in this volume as Chap. 10) applied the model in a more sophisticated way to the US and Japanese economies, 1960–2004. It is suggested that the total productivity index $\frac{\dot{T}(t)}{T(t)}$ will not give the true picture of what is happing in the economy. First, the total productivity index is always equal to the weighted sum of the percentage changes of $A(t)$ and $B(t)$, i.e.

$$\frac{\dot{T}(t)}{T(t)} = \text{capital's share} \times \frac{\dot{A}(t)}{A(t)} + \text{labor's share} \times \frac{\dot{B}(t)}{B(t)} \qquad (11.58)$$

Even if $\frac{\dot{T}(t)}{T(t)}$ is positive, this does not imply that $\frac{\dot{A}(t)}{A(t)}$ and $\frac{\dot{B}(t)}{B(t)}$ are always positive. In fact, Japan's efficiency factor of capital, $\frac{\dot{A}}{A}$ is negative throughout the entire period (−1.61 %), but the total productivity index $\frac{\dot{T}}{T}$ is positive (2.13 %). This implies that the efficiency of labor, $\frac{\dot{B}}{B}$, is positive and large (3.86 %). In other words, Japan's growth is largely due to the efficiency increase in labor.

A recent paper by Noda and Kyo (2011) is a further extension of the paper by Sato and Morita (2009). They proposed a new approach to time-series analysis by constructing Bayesian linear models. Parameter estimations of the CES production function with the labor–augmenting type of technical change for Taiwan and South Korea are calculated using the maximum likelihood method and Bayesian model averaging approach.

11.11 More Abstract Applications of Group Theory to Economics and Finance

Pioneer works in abstract allocations of group theory are first carried out by Russell (1990) and Boyd (1990). The purpose of Russell's paper is to provide a differential geometric framework for the analysis of individual choice under uncertainly. Boyd's paper also presents a geometric approach to dynamic economic problems that integrates the solution procedure with the economics of the problem.

Russel states that many choice problems of interest in economics have the following structure. An individual is presented with a set of risky prospects which can be viewed as a family of univariate random variables with density function $f(x, \theta)$ where θ is an n dimensional label or parameter which varies smoothly across the family.

Differential geometry enters the picture because, given some mild regularity conditions, a family of density functions $f(x, \theta)$ can be given the structure of a smooth dimensional manifold, i.e. an object which locally looks like dimensional Euclidean space.

11.11 More Abstract Applications of Group Theory to Economics and Finance

Russel then presents the elements of differential geometry and applies the model to the theory of portfolio and asset pricing and to the issue of diversification and generalized preferences.

Boyd shows that a form of Markov decision model provides a natural setting for investigation of symmetries in stochastic dynamic models. After discussing stochastic preliminaries of the Markov decision model he applies it to general portfolio problems and to Merton's portfolio choice model. He also takes up optimal stochastic growth and equilibration models.

We will briefly mention two recent developments in more abstract applications of group theory to economics. The first is by Chiappori and Ekeland on exterior differential calculus (Chiappori and Ekeland 2004) and the second, by Godfrey Cadogan on group representation for risk and uncertainty (Cadogan 2012a–c).

In his comments on Chiappori and Ekeland, Kamiya (2004) states that "this is an interesting paper that attempts to understand how exterior differential calculus is applied to the characterization of aggregate demand." Chiappori and Ekeland gives two specific examples of how the tools have very natural applications in consumer theory (see also Sato 1981, 1999, Chaps. 4 and 9). The first is maximization under linear constraint. The second is aggregate demand.

Kamiya is not completely happy with exterior differential calculus because he says that "although this paper (by Chiappori and Ekeland) presents a general approach to the problem, these still exists some gap between exterior differential calculus approach and Sonnenschein, Mantel and Debreu's results on decomposition." Sonnenschein (1973), Mantel (1974) and Debreu (1974) showed that market excess demand functions are arbitrary as long as they satisfy continuity, Walras' law and homogeneity of degree zero. Nevertheless we can say that the application of exterior differential calculus is a significant step and is very stimulating for future research in group theory.

Cadogan has three papers on group theory in economics (Cadogan 2012a–c). First he employs Lie group constructs on Markowitz–Tversky–Kahneman topology and extends behavioral economics to group theory. The second paper extends decision making under risk and uncertainty to group theory via representations of the algebraic structure of the psychological space for prospect theory. In the third paper Cadogan uses asset pricing models to study the algebraic structure and invariant properties of a group of assets, and a group of options isomorphic with it.

In his third paper he applies "the model to foundations of asset pricing that include the tangent space of indifference curves on the efficient frontier in risk–return space," and shows that Samuelson–Merton's bucket shop assumption will be satisfied in price–quantity space. On the asset supply side, he uses Tobin's asset pricing model for fundamental valuation of assets to include speculation and liquidity constraints. This is certainly a fresh application of group theory in the field of economics and finance.

References

Aronsson, T., Johansson, P. O., & Löfgren, K. G. (1997). *Welfare measurement, sustainability and green national accounting.* Boston: Edward Elgar.

Asheim, G. B. (2004). Perspectives on Weitzman's stationary equivalent, discussion of Kazuo Mino's 'Weitzman's rule with market distortions'. *Japan and the World Economy, 16*(3), 331–335.

Boyd, G. H., III. (1990). Symmetry, dynamic equilibria, and the value function. In R. Sato & R. Ramachandran (Eds.), *Conservation laws and symmetry: applications to economics and finance* (pp. 225–259). Boston: Kluwer.

Cadogan, G. (2012a). Representation theory for risk on Markowitz-Tversky-Kahneman topology. Research paper, *Information technology in finance*, Institute for Innovation and Technology Management, Ryerson University, Toronto.

Cadogan, G. (2012b). Group representations for decision making under risk and uncertainty. Working paper, *Information technology in finance*, Institute for Innovation and Technology Management, Ryerson University, Toronto.

Cadogan, G. (2012c). Group representation for asset pricing models. Work-in-progress, *Information technology in finance*, Institute for Innovation and Technology Management, Ryerson University, Toronto.

Chiappori, P. -A., & Ekeland, I. (2004). Applying exterior differential calculus to economics: a presentation and some new results. *Japan and the World Economy, 16*(3), 363–385.

Comin, D. (2004). Discussion of M. Weitzman's stochastic income and wealth. *Japan and the World Economy, 16*(3), 303–305.

de León, M., & de Diego, D. F. (1998). Conservation laws and symmetry in economic growth models: a geometrical approach. *Extracta Mathematical, 13*(3), 335–348.

Debreu, G. (1974). Excess demand functions. *Journal of Mathematical Economics, 1*, 15–21.

Dixit, A., Hammond, P., & Hoel, M. (1980). On Hartwick's rule for regular maximum path of capital accumulation and resource depletion. *Review of Economic Studies, 47*, 551–556.

Douglas, J. (1941). Solutions of the inverse problem of the calculus of variations. *Transactions of American Mathematical Society, 50*, 71–128.

Hartwick, J. M. (1977). Intergenerational equity and the investing of rents from exhaustible resources. *American Economic Review, 66*, 992–974.

Hartwick, J. M. (2004). Sustaining periodic motion and maintaining capital in classical mechanics. *Japan and the World Economy, 16*(3), 337–358.

Kamiya, K. (2004). Applying exterior differential calculus to economics: a presentation and some new results: a comment. *Japan and the World Economy, 16*(3), 387–389.

Mantel, R. (1974). On the characterization of excess demand. *Journal of Economic Theory, 7*, 348–353.

Martinet, V. (2012). *Economic theory and sustainable development: what can we preserve for future generations?* New York: Routledge.

Mimura, F., Fujiwara, F., & Nôno, T. (1999). New derivation of conservation laws for optimal control problem and its application to economic growth models. In R. Sato, R. Ramachandran, & K. Mino (Eds.), *Global competition and integration.* Boston: Kluwer.

Mimura, F., & Nôno, T. (1990). Conservation laws derived via the application of helmholtz conditions. In R. Sato, & R. Ramachandran (Eds), *Conservation laws and symmetry: applications to economics and finance* (pp. 107–134). Boston: Kluwer.

Mino, K. (2004). Weitzman's rule with market distortions. *Japan and the World Economy, 16*(3), 307–329.

Noda, H., & Kyo, K. (2011). Bayesian estimation of the CES production function with labor- and capital-augmenting technical change. Discussion paper 2011 – EO 1, Yamagata University, FLSS Discussion Paper Series.

Nôno, T. (1971). A classification of neutral technical change: an application of lie theory. *Bulletin of Fukuoka University of Education, 20*, 47–62.

References

Rose, H. (1968). The conditions for factor-augmenting technical change. *Economic Journal, 78*(312), 966–971.

Russell, T. (1990). Choice as geometry. In R. Sato & R. Ramachandran (Eds.), *Conservation laws and symmetry: applications to economics and finance* (pp.175–224). Boston: Kluwer.

Russell, T. (2004). Investing capital rentals to sustain periodic motion in classical mechanics by John Hartwick. *Japan and the World Economy, 16*(3), 359–362.

Samuelson, P. (2004). Conservation laws in economics. *Japan and the World Economy, 16*(3), 243–246.

Sato, R. (1970). The estimation of biased technical progress and the production function. *International Economic Review, 11*, 179–208. Reprinted in R. Sato (1996). *Growth theory and technical change: the selected essays of Ryuzo Sato economists of the twentieth century series*, vol.1. (pp. 144–173). Cheltenham: Edward Elgar.

Sato, R. (1981). *Theory of technical change and economic invariance: application of Lie groups*. New York: Academic Press. Updated edition (1999) Cheltenham: Edward Elgar.

Sato, R. (1999). *Production, stability and dynamic symmetry: the selected essays of Ryuzo Sato*, Vol. 2. *Economists of the twentieth century series*. Cheltenham: Edward Elgar.

Sato, R. (2006). *Biased technical change and economic conservation laws*. Heidelberg: Springer.

Sato, R., & Beckmann, M.J. (1968). Neutral inventions and production functions. *The Review of Economic Studies, 35*(1). Reprinted in R. Sato (1996). *Growth, theory and technical change: the selected essays of Ryuzo Sato*, Vol. 1. Boston: Edward Elgar.

Sato, R., & Kim, Y. (2002). Hartwick's rule and economic conservation laws. *Journal of Economic Dynamics and Control, 26*, 437–449.

Sato, R., & Maeda, S. (1990). Conservation laws in continuous and discrete models. In R. Sato & R. Ramachandran (Eds.), *Conservation laws and symmetry* (pp.135–174). Boston: Kluwer.

Sato, R., & Morita, T. (2009). Quantity or quality: the impact of labour saving innovation on US and Japanese growth rates, 1960–2004. *The Japanese Economic Review, 60*(4), 407–434.

Sato, R., Nôno, T., & Mimura, F. (1984). Hidden symmetries in Lie groups and economic conservation laws. In H. Houptmann, W. Krelle, & K. C. Mosler (Eds.), *Operations research and economic theory*. Heidelberg: Springer.

Sato, R., & Ramachandran, R. (Eds.). (1990). *Conservation laws and symmetry: applications to economics and finance*. Boston: Kluwer.

Sato, R., & Ramachandran, R. (1998). *Symmetry and economic invariance*: an introduction. Boston: Kluwer.

Sato, R., & Ramachandran, R. (2000). Optimal growth with endogenous technical change: Hicksian bias in a macro model. *Japanese Economic Review, 51*(2), 193–206.

Sato, R., Ramachandran, R., & Lian, C. (1999). Model of optimal economic growth with endogenous bias. *Macroeconomic Dynamics, 3*. Reprinted in R. Sato (2006). *Biased technical change and economic conservation laws*. Springer, Heidelberg.

Solow, R. (1974). Intergenerational equity and exhaustable resources. *Review of Economic Studies*, Symposium, 29–46.

Sonnenschein, H. (1973). Do Walras' identity and continuity characterize a class of community excess demand functions? *Journal of Economic Theory, 6*, 345–354.

Vellinga, N., & Withagen, C. (1996). On the concept of green national income. *Oxford Economic Papers, 48*, 499–514.

Weitzman, M. (1976). On the welfare significance of national product in a dynamic economy. *Quarterly Journal of Economics, 90*, 156–162.

Weitzman, M. (2003). *Income, wealth and the maximum principle*. Cambridge: Harvard University Press.

Weitzman, M. L. (2004). Stochastic income and wealth. *Japan and the World Economy, 16*(3), 277–301.

Chapter 12
Appendix to Part II. Symmetry: An Overview of Geometric Methods in Economics

12.1 Introduction

Symmetry is the study of mapping of a state space into itself that leaves a geometric object, generally a set of subspaces defined by an equivalence relation, invariant. Thus, in economics, we can examine whether there exists a transformation to which the indifference curves, subspaces defined by a preference relation, are invariant. However to appreciate the relevance of such a question, it is necessary to have an understanding of the basic principles of geometric spaces. The idea that the quantitative variables of a science are describable by geometric objects and that the laws governing these variables are expressible as geometric relation between the objects, can be traced back to Felix Klein's inaugural address at the Erlanger University in 1872.[1]

Every science identifies, as its field of study, a subset of properties of a given set of objects. In consumer theory, the objects are human beings and the properties are their preferences and purchasing power. In human biology, the properties studied may be the genetic characteristics of the individuals. A demographer has the same objects though he would be interested in their age distribution and sex composition. A mathematician, in contrast, examines the cardinality of the sets, whether the elements are human beings or pebbles.

Further, the level of abstraction in the definition of an object in a science can vary between its theories; particularly relevant for the study of geometry is the changes in the conception of space. Felix Klein lived at a time when the universality of Euclidean geometry was being questioned. The necessity for a reformulation of geometry to incorporate the new developments was obvious. Klein, influenced by the French mathematician Camille Jordan, used groups to classify geometries. Consider elementary Euclidean geometry that we all studied in school; it considers

---

[1] Misner, Thorne and Wheeler (1973, p. 48). For a description of the Erlanger Program, see Yaglom (1988) and Klein (1972, pp. 917–921).

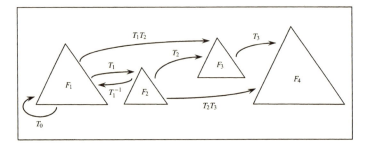

Fig. 12.1 Similarity mapping of triangles

two types of "equalities" between figures (Yaglom 1988, pp. 111–124). We know that two figures are *congruent* (equal in one sense) if there exists an isometry (mapping that preserves distances between points) from one figure to another. But in another sense of equality, figures are equal if they are *similar* (mapping that preserves ratio between segments). Many theorems in school geometry require only similarity and we can think of a geometry which strictly identifies similar objects.

Notice that a similarity mapping or transformation satisfies the following relations:

1. *Identity*: There is a transformation, T_0, that sends a figure to itself (see Fig. 12.1).
2. *Inverse*: If there is a transformation, T_1, which sends F_1 to F_2, then there is an inverse transformation T_1^{-1} which sends F_2 to F_1.
3. *Closure*: If there is a transformation, T_1 from F_1 to F_2 and another, T_2, from F_2 to F_3 then the set of transformations contains the "product" transformation $T_1 T_2$ from F_1 to F_3.
4. *Associativity*: The product of two transformations with a third equals the product of the first with the other two (taken in the same order); $(T_1 T_2) T_3 = T_1 (T_2 T_3)$.

A set of transformations that satisfy the above conditions form a *group* of transformations.

We can now introduce the concept of distance and define equality in the sense of congruence. The set of congruence transformations form a group as it satisfies the four relations stated above. A geometry based on congruence will be different from the one based on similarity transformations: every congruent transformation is a similarity transformation but the converse is not true.

This is the crux of the idea that Klein exploited to classify geometries. As generally stated, the Erlanger Program defined geometry as the study of the properties of figures invariant to a given group of transformations.[2] Klein's perspective shed light on the theory of relativity in physics. Newtonian physics postulated an

---

[2]Like all grand visions, the Erlanger Program had its limitations. See the references in footnote 1, above.

12.1 Introduction

absolute space in which all physical bodies are embedded. But its laws of motion cannot distinguish between a coordinate system which was at rest relative to the absolute space and one which was moving at a uniform velocity; in other words, if we sat in an airplane which was flying at a constant speed, then we would not observe anything *within the plane* to distinguish it from one at rest. The laws of Newtonian mechanics are invariant to a Galilean transformation (corresponding here to a relative motion of coordinate systems at constant velocity).

In contrast, consider electromagnetic waves which travel through space with a constant velocity c. If the earth was travelling with a velocity v, in the same direction as a ray of light, then the speed of light as measured on earth should read $c - v$ (just as a plane overtaking yours should appear to be travelling slower than its speed relative to the earth). The famous Michelson–Morley experiment disproved this hypothesis when it showed that the measured speed of light was the same in all directions. The special theory of relativity explained the experimental result by replacing the Euclidean assumptions with a space-time continuum and Lorentz transformation. Newtonian mechanics became a special case for systems that move with velocities substantially below that of light.

The justification for rejecting Galilean transformations (for a wider class of transformations) was that it had consequences which could not be verified experimentally. While Klein originally looked upon the group of transformations as a taxonomic tool, Einstein and philosophers of science like Reichenbach (1960) integrated it into the methodological foundations of physics.[3]

In consumer economics, the problem of utility measurement was widely discussed. In the intellectual ferment of the 1930s, marginal utility was dethroned from the preeminent position it had held in consumer theory. Instead of assuming that we know the consumer's utility surface, the new theory assumed that we know only his indifference curves or level sets. Hicks (1946, p. 17) noted that this approach had wide methodological significance as the indifference curves conveyed less information than utility surfaces. Though each set of indifference curves could be thought of as the contour lines of a utility surface, the numbers were arbitrary as long as they preserved the order and so the utility surface could be replaced by a monotonic transformation of itself.

Starting from a given scale of preferences, attention was confined to the properties of the utility function which were invariant to the monotonic transformation. All theorems with observable consequences like the equilibrium and stability conditions could be derived from these properties. Alchain (1953) emphasized sets of transformations in a lucid presentation of the meaning of utility measurement. He noted that measurement in the broadest sense was the assignment of numbers to entities. He distinguished between the purposes of measurement, the process of assigning numerical values to entities and the degree of arbitrariness of such assignments.

---

[3] See Friedman (1983) for a recent and somewhat critical review of the interaction between relativity physics and positivist philosophy.

Alchian noted the differences between transformations unique up to an addictive or multiplicative constant, general linear transformations, and monotone transformations. In neo-classical theory, differences in the utility levels of various bundles of goods had to be ranked and the numerical assignments had to be unique up to linear transformations. In the ordinal approach, only the basket of goods needed be ordered and utility had to be unique up to monotonic transformations only. Contemporaneous with the revolution in demand theory, criticisms of interpersonal comparisons of utility resulted in the use of the Pareto-principle rather than sum-ranking in welfare economics. The ordinal approach which assumed less information about individual's preferences, became standard in economics. In these discussions, the non-uniqueness in the assignment was emphasized but the idea that the set of transformations form a group was not utilized. The ordinal utility can be identified with the symmetry group of the transformations that leaves the equivalence classes of the preference relation, invariant.

At first sight it would look that mechanics concerned itself with the transformation of coordinate axes while economists were concerned with the transformation of (utility) surfaces. Coordinates were assigned to a point when it was associated with an ordered n-tuple of real numbers $(x^1,\ldots,x^n)$ with distinct points associated with distinct n-tuples. As Reichenbach (1960, p. 90) noted, it was not inherent in the nature of reality that space should be described by coordinates; it was a subjective assignment whose empirical implications had to be examined. Further, all coordinate transformation could be treated as groups of manifold transformation (Friedman 1983, p. 56). The distinction is more apparent than real.

Consider the effects of technical progress on surfaces defined by a linear homogeneous production function with Hicks-neutral technical progress. The production function can be written as $Y = A(t)f(K,L) = F_t(K,L)$ or $Y = f[A(t)K,A(t)L]$. In the first formulation, the input space is not affected by technical progress but the production surface shifts over time. In the second, the input axes based on efficiency units are transformed by technical progress but the surfaces represented by the functional relation $f(\ )$ is not affected, These considerations suggest that technical progress can be viewed as a transformation of the production surface in a given input space or as a transformation of the input space.

As early as 1920s, Clapham (1922) objected to the separation of changes in the efficiency resulting from differences in size from that arising from inventions. The debate with Pigou (1922) that ensued was widely studied in economics. Thirty-five years later, Solow (1957) published his famous article attributing 87.5% of the increase in per capita productivity in the United States between 1909 and 1949, to technical changes defined as shifts in production function. Since then innumerable articles and books have sought to explain productivity increases. In one such attempt, Stigler (1961) used US and British data to allocate a sizable portion of productivity growth to returns to scale. Stigler used cross-section data across the countries to get around the conceptual problems of confining such analysis to one economy. Solow (1961, p. 67), in his comments, pointed out that Stigler's approach would not solve the econometric problems and argued that separating economies of scale from technical change "is an econometric puzzle worthy of everybody's talents."

12.1 Introduction

Most econometric studies use Hicks-neutral technical progress. Sato and Ramachandran (1974) examined a production process moving along an expansion path, in input space, at a given rate. Using a technique developed by Zellner and Revankar (1969), we derived a differential equation relating growth in output and in inputs under two alternate assumptions about the production process: first, linear homogeneous production function with Hicks-neutral technical progress, and second, a homothetic production function. We showed that there was a one-to-one mapping from one differential equation to the other. The informational implication was that, from the analysis of data alone, we could not distinguish between the two models. The paper did not explicitly use group-theoretic methods and could not be extended to other forms of technical progress. That step was taken in Sato (1975, 1981) when he used Lie groups to examine all known forms of technical progress functions and derive the corresponding form of scale effects.

The Norwegian mathematician and collaborator of Felix Klein, Sophus Lie, took up the notion of continuous transformation implicit in concepts like the Galilean and Lorentz groups and applied it to the classification, not of geometries, but of differential equations. He showed that the plethora of special methods used in solving differential equations hid the connection between various types of solvable equations, namely the invariance of the integrals to certain types of transformations. He also showed that the invariance could be established without first solving the equation; this in turn, help in determining whether an equation had a solution.

Interest in Lie groups of differential equations waxed and waned in the twentieth century. By 1930s, as Yaglom (1988, pp. 107–108) points out, this aspect of Lie's work no longer elicited much enthusiasm.[4] With the development of computers, solvability in quadratures lost its previous importance. But by 1970s, physicists and later mathematicians rediscovered that Lie's theory not only characterized solvability but also symmetry and there came about a resurgence of interest in his theory. We shall outline this theory in the next section and then proceed to use symmetry to analyze the productivity problem and also derive the conservation laws for two economic models.

Group theory cannot pull rabbits out of a hat. It is a useful tool to identify the informational implications of various assumptions and encourage the development of theories that correspond to the parsimonious information that is available. The concern of Pigou (1922, p. 451) that Clapham's proposal cannot be adopted without injury to the *corpus* of economics is understandable. Returning to Sato and Ramachandran (1974) formulation, microeconomics considerations suggest that a competitive firm under increasing returns should not be expanding at a given rate but must seek to increase it indefinitely. One is left with the option of modifying the theory without waiting for an econometric millennium or expeditiously improving our empirical methods. Sixty-five years of debate since the Clapham–Pigou controversy has failed to produce a conclusive development in either direction.

---

[4]Lie algebra and the topological implications of Lie's work were actively researched during this period.

In economics as in many other sciences, geometric methods are used to characterize quantitative variables by geometric objects. But this method also brings out the fact that geometric objects are independent of the coordination adopted; the latter introduces implicitly or explicitly additional assumptions. As noted above, the implications of numerical assignments or coordination were recognized by economists in a number of contexts and solutions specific to each one of them were adopted. But, unlike in physical sciences, there was no comprehensive consideration of the implications of the invariance of geometric objects to groups of transformations.

12.2 Toolbox

Every discipline has its own terminology and analytical tools. In this section, we outline the mathematical structure needed to understand the geometric approach to symmetry. We begin by taking a fresh look at some concepts which are widely used in economics and finance and then proceed to add new concepts.

12.2.1 Mapping

A *map*, *mapping* or *function*, $f : X \to Y$, from a set X to a set Y, is a rule which associates an element $y \in Y$ with each element $x \in X$; to indicate which element of Y is associated with one in X, we can write $f : x \to y$. The set of elements of Y to which the elements of X are mapped is the *image* of X, $\text{im} f = \{f(x) \in Y | x \in X\}$. If $\text{im} f = Y$, then f is *into* map or *surjection*.

However, it is not necessary that a unique element $x \in X$ to be associated with any element $y \in Y$. The symbol $f^{-1}(Y)$ represents the set of elements included in X that are mapped into Y by f, the *preimage* of Y. If $f^{-1}(y)$, the preimage of any element y, consists of a single element, then the map $f : X \to Y$ is called *one-to-one* or an *injection*. The symbol $f^{-1}( )$ is a map only if f is an injection.

If the map is both an injection and a surjection, then it is a *bijection*. Further, if $f : X \to Y$ and $g : Y \to Z$, then $g \bullet f : X \to Z$. By convention, the right-hand most mapping is done first and then the one to the left; the same principle can be applied to the composition of more than two maps. If $z \in Z$ is the element to which $x \in X$ is mapped by $g \bullet f$, then we can write $g \bullet f : x \to z$. For a bijective function f, $f^{-1} \bullet f$ maps an element of x into itself; it is the identity map.

Notice that we have not said anything about the nature of the elements of sets X, Y, or Z. The readers are, of course, familiar with functions between sets whose elements are real numbers. Even if the elements of X and Y are not numbers, we may associate an ordered n-tuple of real numbers with each element. Thus, in Euclidean geometry, the elements of space are associated with a 3-tuple of ordered real numbers; in special theory of relativity, space-time is represented by a 4-tuple. This is the process of coordination referred to in Sect. 12.1.

We may think of a map from X to Y either as an abstract map from the elements of X to the elements of Y or from the coordinates of $x \in X$ to the coordinates of $y \in Y$: the first is a coordinate free definition while the second is not.

12.2.2 Charts and Manifolds

Every point on the surface of the globe, except the North and South Poles and the Greenwich meridian can be represented by two numbers, the longitude and latitude, that can be taken to be the coordinates of the point. Hence parts of the globe are "locally" like the $\mathbf{R}^2$ plane as one recognizes by looking at the pages of an atlas. The poles are excluded as every longitudinal curve passes through the poles and the meridian because it is both the 0 degree and 360 degree East; in either case the uniqueness condition is infringed. Theoretically one can take two other points on the globe, call them East and West poles, and map every point other than the two new poles and a new meridian (but including the North and South Poles and the Greenwich meridian) using a new system of "longitudes and latitudes." The two systems will together give a one-to-one mapping of every point of the globe to $\mathbf{R}^2$. A stereographic map is more efficient in that it maps the whole surface of the globe, except a pole, into $\mathbf{R}^2$.

A pair consisting of an open neighborhood of $x \in X$ and an injective map to an open subset of $\mathbf{R}^n$ is called a *chart*. The set X is a *manifold* if each element belong to a chart.[5] The set of charts that cover a manifold is appropriately called an *atlas*. Note that at least two charts are needed to cover the surface of earth.

A point on the manifold may belong to two charts. Thus in the two systems of longitude and latitude proposed earlier, every point on the globe other than the four poles and the two meridians, belong to both sets. Let f be the function that maps a point to its first set of coordinates $(x^1,\ldots,x^n)$ and g the function that maps it to the second set of coordinates $(y^1,\ldots,y^n)$. On a point where the charts overlap, one can use the principle of composition of maps to obtain a functional relation between one set of coordinates and another. Thus $g \bullet f^{-1}$ defines y^i $(i = 1,\ldots,n)$ as a function of $(x^1,\ldots,x^n)$; this is called coordinate transformation. A set of charts of a manifold such that $g \bullet f^{-1}$ is C^k for every point where it is defined, is a C^k manifold. If $k \geq 1$, then the manifold is a differentiable manifold (Fig. 12.2).

If a metric is defined on a manifold, then the open sets can be expressed in terms of the standard ε-δ definition. But metric is an additional structure and manifolds can be defined without it. Misner et al. (1973, p. 8) has an interesting example. Households with telephone can be identified by the telephone numbers which also

---

[5] An n-dimensional topological manifold M^n is a Hausdorff topological space with a countable basis for the topology, which is locally homeomorphic to R^n. A differentiable manifold is a topological manifold with a differential structure. See Bröcker and Jänich (1973, pp. 1–4).

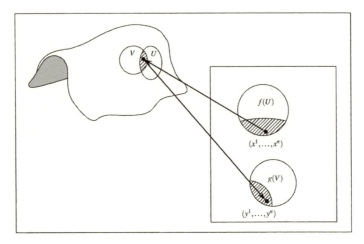

Fig. 12.2 Differential manifolds and coordinate maps

identify the locality where the households are located. But one cannot determine from telephone numbers, how many meters away any two of them are.

Three points should be noted. First, surface of earth can be visualized without latitudes and longitudes; coordinates are not essential to the reality of the geometric objects. Second, we instinctively think of the earth's surface as part of a three dimensional space; the existence of such a space is not an integral part of the definition of the manifold given earlier. *An idealized ant crawling on the earth can visualize the surface without seeing the third dimension.* Third, the centrality of the concept of manifolds is brought out by the abstract definition of Lie groups as a differential manifold with group properties.[6]

12.2.3 Curves and Functions

A demand curve can be thought of as a continuous line, each point of which corresponds to one value of the quantity demanded. This idea can be generalized. A *curve* is a differential mapping from an open interval of a real line to a manifold M. If the points on the open interval are represented by the real number λ, then the

---

[6] A Lie group is a group X which is also a manifold with C^∞ structure such that $(x, x') \to xx'$ and $x \to x^{-1}$ are C^∞ functions (Spivak 1979, p. 501). Just as there are function spaces, there are manifolds of transformation. They should be differentiated from manifolds of the underlying space. The reader is referred to Dubrovin, Fomenko and Novikov (1984, 1985) and Spivak (1979) for a formal definition of the other concepts discussed in this section.

12.2 Toolbox

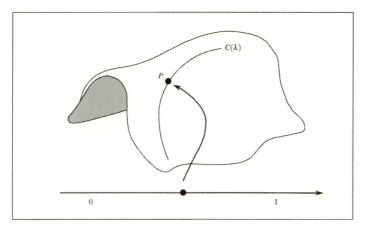

Fig. 12.3 Parametrization of curves on a manifold

curve is *parameterized* by λ and each point of the curve $C(\lambda)$ is an image point of λ. If the differential manifold is coordinated, then the coordinates are differential functions of λ. Again notice that this definition is independent of a metric so that distance along the curve is not defined (Fig. 12.3).

A function is a rule for assigning real numbers to the points of a manifold M. If the differential manifold has coordinates, then the function, expressed in terms of the coordinates, takes the familiar form

$$y = f(x^1, \ldots, x^n). \tag{12.1}$$

The value of this function along a curve $C(\lambda)$ is given by

$$y = f(x^1(\lambda), \ldots, x^n(\lambda)) \equiv g(\lambda). \tag{12.2}$$

12.2.4 Vectors and Tangents

In economics we speak of the surfaces generated by utility or production functions. It is easy to visualize a plane tangent to the surface at a point (Fig. 12.4). From P, the point of tangency, we can draw a vector on the tangent plane. For any vector PQ on the tangent plane, it is possible to draw a curve, lying on the surface, that has PQ as a tangent at P. Reversing the idea of a vector as a directed line ("arrow"), we can think of every vector as a tangent to some curve.

The last approach is very useful in making generalizations essential to differential geometric approach. The intuitive approach of drawing vectors in a tangential plane

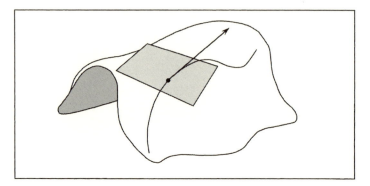

Fig. 12.4 Tangent planes and tangent vectors

as in Fig. 12.4 assumes that the manifold is in a space of higher dimension. As already noted, the existence of a higher dimensional space is not intrinsic to the definition of the manifold. What we need is a definition of a vector which depends only on one point ("local") and not two ("bilocal"); after all, our ant does not know the existence of any point outside the earth's surface. The idea of thinking about a vector as a tangent to some curve on the manifold provides exactly the needed local concept.

Suppose we want to define a tangent vector to the curve $C(\lambda)$ at the point given by $\lambda = 0$. Now define a differentiable function $g : M \to R$ on the manifold; this function has a value at each point of the curve. Let us assume, for the moment, that the manifold is coordinated. Then we can differentiate the function $g(\lambda)$ (see Eq. (12.2)) to get

$$\frac{dg}{d\lambda} = \sum_i \frac{dx^i(\lambda)}{d\lambda} \frac{\partial f}{\partial x^i}. \tag{12.3}$$

Now we abstract the operator $d/d\lambda$ from the function g and the coordinates and call it the *directional derivative* (direction being that of the curve $C(\lambda)$), which applied to any arbitrary differentiable function g satisfies Eq. (12.3).[7]

---

[7]A reader who is not familiar with the approach would enjoy the aside in Misner et al. (1973, p. 227):

"Tangent vectors equal directional derivative operator? Preposterous! A vector started out as a happy, irresponsible trip from $\mathbb{P}_0$ to $\mathbb{Q}_0$. It ended up with the social responsibility to tell how something changes at $\mathbb{P}_0$. At what point did the vector get saddled with the unexpected load? And did it really change its character all that much, as it seems to have done?"

The answer to the last question is no; otherwise this whole exercise is meaningless.

A technical note: many curves may be tangent to each other at P and the tangent vector is defined in terms of the equivalence classes of curves.

12.2 Toolbox

The directional derivatives like $d/d\lambda$ form a vector space which provides some intuition why they can be identified with vectors. Consider two curves through P, $C(\lambda)$ and $C'(\mu)$. As before, defining a function g, form the expression

$$a\frac{dg}{d\lambda} + b\frac{dg}{d\mu}.$$

We can now draw another curve through P with parameter θ such that

$$\frac{dg}{d\theta} = a\frac{dg}{d\lambda} + b\frac{dg}{d\mu}$$

showing that the operator $d/d\lambda$ satisfies the vector addition law

$$\frac{d}{d\theta} = a\frac{d}{d\lambda} + b\frac{d}{d\mu}. \tag{12.4}$$

To examine the relationship from another angle, assume that the space is coordinated. Then $\partial g/\partial x^i$ gives the partial derivative of the function in the direction of the coordinate axis e_i. This is true for all functions and we can write $\partial/\partial x^i$ as a directional derivative. The set of n such directional derivatives form the basis of the tangent space TM_P at the point P and we can write

$$\frac{\partial}{\partial \lambda} = \sum v^i \frac{\partial}{\partial x^i} \tag{12.5}$$

where $v^i = dx^i(\lambda)/d\lambda$ refers to a particular curve. This is similar to the expression for any vector in terms of basis vectors, $v = \sum v^i e_i$. Hence we consider $\partial/\partial x^i$ ($i = 1,\ldots,n$) as the basis vectors of the tangent space.

Having drawn the tangent space at P, we can draw tangent spaces at all other points on the manifold. The collection of these tangent spaces forms the *tangent space to the manifold*. Vector operations are defined on TM_P or TM_Q (where P and Q are two points on the manifold) but a vector on TM_P cannot be added to one on TM_Q.[8] The logic of defining a tangent space as the collection of tangent spaces at individual points is the following. The tangents at P and Q to a curve PQ on the manifold lie on TM_P and TM_Q respectively. Hence the tangent space TM is the "space" in which the tangents to a curve lie.

Another approach to defining vectors is by the rule of their transformation when coordinate bases change (Dubrovin et al. 1984, pp. 146–147). The components of a tangent vector to a curve $C(\lambda)$ in the coordinate system $(x^1,\ldots,x^n)$ has the components $(dx^1/d\lambda,\ldots,dx^n/d\lambda)$. Suppose we now use a new coordinate system $(z^1,\ldots,z^n)$; let $x^i = x^i(z^1(\lambda),\ldots,z^n(\lambda))$ express the old in terms of the new coordinates. Then by chain rule of differentiation,

---

[8] A clear discussion of these niceties, using a special manifold E^n, is in Edelen (1985, pp. 26–27).

$$\frac{dx^i}{d\lambda} = \sum_j \frac{\partial x^i}{\partial z^j} \frac{dz^j}{d\lambda}. \tag{12.6}$$

In the next subsection, we can contrast this rule of transformation with that of 1-form.

12.2.5 1-Forms

Even if the formulation of the last subsection may look unusual, vector analysis is widely used in economics and finance. Differential forms are not so familiar but they are among the most useful concepts in differential geometry.

The simplest type of a differential form is the 1-form. It can be defined as an operator or a "machine" which outputs a number when a vector is input into it. We represent 1-form by Greek letters. Inserting vector v into a 1-form produces an output $< a, v >$ or $a(v)$. In addition to being a real valued function, 1-forms are linear machines so that

$$< \alpha, au + bv >= a < \alpha, u > + b < \alpha, v > . \tag{12.7}$$

Also we can add 1-forms

$$< \alpha + \beta, v >=< \alpha, v > + < \beta, v > .$$

The 1-forms constitute a vector space TM_P^* which is the *dual* of the tangent space TM_P at P of the manifold.

A familiar example of 1-form is the gradient, though the gradient is presented in elementary calculus as a vector. The relation between the gradient df and the directional derivative $d/d\lambda$ is brought out by the equation (Misner, Throne and Wheeler 1975, pp. 59–60)

$$< df, \frac{d}{d\lambda} >= df\left(\frac{d}{d\lambda}\right) = \frac{df}{d\lambda}. \tag{12.8}$$

df is, therefore, a machine for calculating the change in f along any desired vector v. This can be represented by an isoquant diagram where v represents a direction along the input space, df then calculates the number of isoquants pierced by v. In elementary calculus, a particular vector corresponding to the direction that maximizes the increase of the output per unit length of the vector is called the gradient; it is the direction of steepest ascent. Schutz (1980, p. 54) points out the limitation of this definition; it depends on the concept of length which is yet undefined. The definition of 1-form as a linear operator is not associated with any metric (Fig. 12.5).

12.2 Toolbox

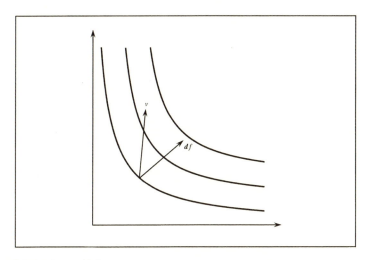

Fig. 12.5 Gradient and 1-form

The linear space TM_P^* has the same dimension as the tangent space. Once a basis $(e_1, \ldots, e_n)$ is chosen for the tangent space, the dual basis is given by the 1-forms e^i or ω^i $(i = 1, \ldots, n)$. Here ω^i is the 1-form that operates on v to produce the ith component of the vector.

$$<\omega^i, v> = \omega^i(v) = v^i.$$

Given any coordinate basis $(x^1, \ldots, x^n)$, a natural base for the tangent space is $(\partial/\partial x^1, \ldots, \partial/\partial x^n)$. The base for dual base is $(dx^1, \ldots, dx^n)$ as

$$<dx^i, \frac{\partial}{\partial x^j}> = \frac{dx^i}{dx^j} = \begin{cases} 1 & (i = j) \\ 0 & (i \neq j) \end{cases}. \tag{12.9}$$

The components of 1-form df denoted as $f_{,i}$ is given by

$$df = \sum_i f_{,i} dx^i \tag{12.10}$$

where

$$f_{,i} = <df, \frac{d}{dx^i}> = \frac{\partial f}{\partial x^i}. \quad \text{(see Eq. (12.8))}$$

Hence

$$df = \sum_i \frac{\partial f}{\partial x^i} dx^i$$

where df is the rigorous form of the differential of elementary calculus.

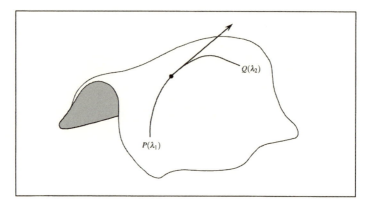

Fig. 12.6 Tangent vector and length of a curve

Consider finally the change of coordinates from $(x^1,\ldots,x^n)$ to $(z^1,\ldots,z^n)$. Then

$$\frac{\partial f}{\partial z^j} = \sum_i \frac{\partial x^i}{\partial z^j} \frac{\partial f}{\partial x^i}. \tag{12.11}$$

Compare (12.11) with (12.6). Relative to $\partial x^i/\partial z^j$, the expression involving the new coordinates z^k ($k = 1,\ldots,n$), appear on the left hand side of Eq. (12.11) and on the right hand side of (12.6). In this sense, vectors and 1-forms transform in opposite ways.

12.2.6 Tensors

Vectors and 1-forms are special cases of tensors. A *Tensor* is defined as a "linear machine" which accepts vectors and 1-forms as inputs and produces a scalar as output.[9]

A familiar example is the metric tensor or the distance function which we have assiduously avoided until now. In Fig. 12.6, consider the length of the curve $C(\lambda)$ from P to Q. In terms of orthogonal axes, the tangent vector is $(dx^1/d\lambda, dx^2/d\lambda)$. To obtain the length of the curve, we take the square root scalar product of the tangent vector with itself and integrate from $P(\lambda_1)$ to $Q(\lambda_2)$ to obtain

$$\int_{\lambda_1}^{\lambda_2} \sqrt{\left(\frac{dx^1}{d\lambda}\right)^2 + \left(\frac{dx^2}{d\lambda}\right)^2}\, d\lambda.$$

---

[9]Misner et al. (1973, pp. 74–76) and Schutz (1980, p. 57).

12.2 Toolbox

But this form, called the Euclidean metric, is very special as can be seen when the distance function is expressed in polar coordinates (r, θ). Then

$$x^1 = r\cos\theta,$$
$$x^2 = r\sin\theta,$$
$$\frac{dx^1}{d\lambda} = \cos\theta\left(\frac{dr}{d\lambda}\right) - r\sin\theta\left(\frac{d\theta}{d\lambda}\right),$$
$$\frac{dx^2}{d\lambda} = \sin\theta\left(\frac{dr}{d\lambda}\right) + r\cos\theta\left(\frac{d\theta}{d\lambda}\right).$$

Substituting in the expression for length, we obtain

$$\int_{\lambda_1}^{\lambda_2} \sqrt{\left(\frac{dr}{d\lambda}\right)^2 + r^2\left(\frac{d\theta}{d\lambda}\right)^2}\, d\lambda.$$

Instead of unity as the coefficients of the squares under the root sign, we have now 1 and r^2. Further generalizing, the Riemannian metric is defined in terms of a positive definite matrix (g_{ij}) and coordinates $(z^1, \ldots, z^n)$ as

$$l = \int_{\lambda_1}^{\lambda_2} \sqrt{\sum_{i,j} g_{ij}(\lambda) \frac{dz^i}{d\lambda}\frac{dz^j}{d\lambda}}\, d\lambda. \tag{12.12}$$

The matrix (g_{ij}) for the Euclidean and polar coordinates are

$$\begin{bmatrix} 1 & 0 \\ 0 & 1 \end{bmatrix} \quad \text{and} \quad \begin{bmatrix} 1 & 0 \\ 0 & r^2 \end{bmatrix}.$$

If we think of the process as inputting the same vector twice and obtaining a scalar, then the Riemannian metric is a $\begin{bmatrix} 0 \\ 2 \end{bmatrix}$ tensor. The upper index indicates that no 1-form is accepted by the linear machine. In general, $\begin{bmatrix} 0 \\ 2 \end{bmatrix}$ tensors can accept two separate vectors and generate a number as in the taking of scalar product of two vectors.

In the last subsection, we defined a 1-form as a machine which accepts a vector and generates a number. If we define vectors as strictly column vectors, then in terms of vector multiplication, a "row vector" accepts a column vector and generates a scalar; hence the row vector can be visualized as a 1-form. Taking the argument one step further, consider a $n \times n$ matrix. By post-multiplying by a column vector and pre-multiplying by a row vector, this matrix generates a number. Hence the matrix can be considered to be $\begin{bmatrix} 1 \\ 1 \end{bmatrix}$ tensor (Schutz 1980, p. 58).

This leads us to tensor products. The product of a $\begin{bmatrix} 0 \\ 1 \end{bmatrix}$ tensor and a $\begin{bmatrix} 1 \\ 0 \end{bmatrix}$ tensor can be thought of as a linear machine that accepts one vector and one 1-form to generate a scalar. If e_i $(i = 1,\ldots,n)$ be the basis of vector space and e^j $(j = 1,\ldots,n)$ that of 1-forms then the basis elements of the tensor product are written as $e_i \otimes e^j$. Here i and j takes all the n values independently leading to n^2 basis elements for the tensor. These elements could be written as n^2-tuple with one entry equal to one and all others equal to zero, just as we use an n-tuple to represent a vector (Dubrovin et al. 1984, p. 154). The notation given above is useful and universally adopted.

In general, if $(e_1,\ldots,e_n)$ are the basis of vectors and $(e^1,\ldots,e^n)$ that of 1-forms, then the $\begin{bmatrix} p \\ q \end{bmatrix}$ tensor can be written as

$$\mathsf{T} = \sum_{i,j} \mathsf{T}^{i_1\cdots i_p}_{j_1\cdots j_q} e_{i_1} \otimes \cdots \otimes e_{i_p} e^{j_1} \otimes \cdots \otimes e^{j_q} \qquad (12.13)$$

where $\mathsf{T}^{i_1\cdots i_p}_{j_1\cdots j_q}$ form a set of numbers for each point in space and are obtained by inputting the basis vectors and 1-forms into the linear machine. The i's and j's take all n values independently leading to n^{p+q} bases. The tensor products of $\begin{bmatrix} p \\ q \end{bmatrix}$ and $\begin{bmatrix} r \\ s \end{bmatrix}$ tensors is a $\begin{bmatrix} p+r \\ q+s \end{bmatrix}$ tensor.

The 1-forms are special cases of differential forms; differential forms, in turn, can be thought of as skew-symmetric tensors of type $\begin{bmatrix} 0 \\ k \end{bmatrix}$ where $k < n$. A tensor is skew-symmetric if $T_\sigma(i_1,\ldots,i_k) = \text{sign}\,\sigma T_{i_1,\ldots,i_k}$ where σ is a permutation of indices and has a sign $+1$ or -1 according as σ is even or odd (Dubrovin et al. 1984, pp. 163–164). In the case of a two-form

$$\sum_{i,j} T_{ij} e^i \otimes e^j = \sum_{i \leq j} T_{ij} e^i \otimes e^j + \sum_{i \geq j} T_{ij} e^i \otimes e^j$$

$$= \sum_{i<j} T_{ij}(e^i \otimes e^j - e^j \otimes e^i).$$

The last inequality arises from the properties of skew symmetry, $T_{ij} = -T_{ji}$ and $T_{ii} = -T_{ii} = 0$. Now we define a wedge product as

$$e^i \wedge e^j = e^i \otimes e^j - e^j \otimes e^i \qquad (12.14)$$

and a $\begin{bmatrix} 0 \\ 2 \end{bmatrix}$ skew symmetric tensor can be written as

$$\sum_{i<j} T_{ij} e^i \wedge e^j = \sum_{i,j} T_{ij} e^i \otimes e^j.$$

Consider the number of independent bases $e^i \wedge e^j$. We already know that there are n^2 expressions, $e^i \wedge e^j$. But the coefficients of $e^i \wedge e^i$, T_{ii}, are zero and the remaining $n^2 - n$ expressions can be bracketed into $1/2(n^2 - n)$ as in Eq. (12.14). In general a $\begin{bmatrix} 0 \\ k \end{bmatrix}$ skew symmetric tensor in an n space has $n!/(n-k)!k!$ bases expressed as wedge products of k basis elements.

12.2.7 Vector Field, Connections and Covariant Derivatives

We have already considered the construction of TM_P, the tangent space at a point. By definition, the tangent space at a point contains many vectors; in fact, it is the set of vectors tangent to the manifold at P. A *field* of vectors X is an assignment of one tangent vector to each point of the manifold. The tangent vector was written as $\sum v^i(\partial/\partial x^i)$ in a local coordinate chart. If f is a differentiable function and if $\sum v^i(P)(\partial f/\partial x^i)$ is a differentiable function for all f, then X is called a *vector field* (Millman and Parker 1977, p. 216). In short, it is an assignment of vectors to the points of the manifold that is "smooth" in some sense.

Consider vectors at different points of the manifold. In Euclidean geometry, there is an intrinsic notion of parallelism; if two vectors are at different points in this page, we can ascertain whether they are parallel or not. In contrast, consider two vectors tangential to the earth's surface (considered as a two dimensional manifold). Let one vector be in the tangent space at New York and the other in the tangent space at Chicago. For us who see the surface in a three dimensional Euclidean space, the question whether the vectors are parallel has an answer. But if one is confined to look at the manifold only, like our imaginary ant, then no answer is possible without further structure.

One approach is to make our ant carry the vector from Chicago to New York so that they can be compared in the same tangent space. But the poor ant may turn the vector around as it drags it along and the comparison between the transported vector and the one in New York becomes arbitrary. To avoid this, we must give the ant a rule which prevents it from turning the vector around or a rule to transport the vector parallel to itself. The rule is the additional structure needed to determine parallelism and is called the *affine connection*. A differential manifold may admit many connections but they cannot be totally arbitrary. A connection must satisfy certain linearity and derivative-of-product rule (Fig. 12.7).

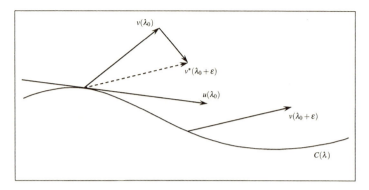

Fig. 12.7 Affine connection and parallel transportation of vectors

Consider a curve $C(\lambda)$ on a differential manifold with a connection and let $U = \partial/\partial\lambda$ (the tangent vector to $C(\lambda)$ at λ is $u(\lambda)$). Let V be a vector field defined on the curve with $v(\lambda_0)$ the vector at λ_0 and $v(\lambda_0+\varepsilon)$ the vector at $\lambda_0+\varepsilon$. Let $v^*(\lambda_0+\varepsilon)$ be $v(\lambda_0+\varepsilon)$ parallel transported to λ_0. Then the covariant derivative can be defined as

$$\nabla_U V = \frac{v^*(\lambda_0+\varepsilon) - v(\lambda_0)}{\varepsilon}. \tag{12.15}$$

If (U, f) be a proper coordinate chart at P, then the covariant derivative can be expressed using Christoffel symbol Γ^k_{ij}, a scalar. First consider the covariant derivative of basis vectors.

$$\nabla_{\partial_j} \partial_i = \sum_k \Gamma^k_{ij} \frac{\partial}{\partial x^k} \tag{12.16}$$

where $U = \partial/\partial x^j = \partial_j$ and $V = \partial_i$.

The expression can be extended to the covariant derivative of any tensor field since tensors are all expressible as linear combination of basis tensors and they (vectors and 1-form) are derivable from the vector basis.[10]

---

[10] An alternate definition of the Christoffel symbol is based on differentiation of an arbitrary tensor. Consider for simplicity, the vector field T^i on a space of coordinates $(x^1, \ldots, x^n)$. Then the quantities $T^i_s = \partial T^i/\partial x^s$ transforms like the components of a $\begin{bmatrix} 1 \\ 1 \end{bmatrix}$ tensor for all linear coordinate changes $x^i = \sum_j a^i_j z^j$. Hence

$$\overline{T}^j_{;1} = \frac{\partial T^j}{\partial z^1} = \sum_{i,p} T^i_{;p} \frac{\partial x^p}{\partial z^1} \frac{\partial z^j}{\partial x^i}$$

12.2 Toolbox

Given any connection, we can define a geodesic as the curve which parallel transports its tangents.[11] This is the closest thing, on the manifold, to a straight line which we intuitively associate with the shortest path between two points. But we have not used the metric! If a distance is defined on the manifold, it will define its own set of shortest curves, the metric geodesic. A connection is compatible with metric if the two geodesics coincide; the condition is that the covariant derivative of the metric tensor is identically zero.

12.2.8 Groups in Differential Equations

We already mentioned the abstract definition of Lie groups in footnote 6. One of Lie's main results is that it is possible to assign to every Lie group a much simpler algebraic object, the Lie algebra. The converse question, whether a Lie group can be associated with a Lie algebra is of great importance and is discussed in Spivak (1979). We will restrict ourselves to the application of Lie groups to differential equations and, to simplify matters, confine to the case of two variables and one parameter.[12]

A set of transformations

$$x' = \phi(x,y,t), \quad y' = \psi(x,y,t) \qquad (12.17)$$

is said to form a parameter group if the results of successive transformations is an element of the group.[13] In terms of the definition of a group given in Sect. 12.1, group property requires:

---

where $\overline{T}^j$ is the component in $(z^1, \ldots, z^n)$. But if the coordinate transformation is nonlinear, then

$$T^j_{;1} = \frac{\partial T^j}{\partial z^1} + \sum_s \Gamma^j_{s1} T^s$$

where

$$\Gamma^j_{s1} = -\sum_{i,m} \frac{\partial x^i}{\partial z^s} \frac{\partial x^m}{\partial z^1} \frac{\partial^2 z^j}{\partial x^i \partial x^m}, \text{ the Christoffel symbol;}$$

note that Γ^j_{s1} vanishes when the transformation is linear. For a detailed treatment of this approach, see Dubrovin et al. (1984, pp. 271–295).

[11] Another approach is to begin with the geodesic ("line of free fall") and define parallel transport and covariant derivative. See Misner et al. (1973, pp. 248–249).

[12] In this subsection, we basically follow the excellent discussion of one parameter group by Cohen (1931). For a compact summary of r-parameter group, see Sato (1981).

[13] Transformations form a manifold and the two definitions of Lie groups are consistent. See Dubrovin et al. (1984, pp. 120–136; 1985, pp. 10–15).

1. There exists a t'' depending on t and t' such that
$$\phi(x',y',t') = \phi(x,y,t''), \quad \psi(x',y',t') = \psi(x,y,t'').$$

2. There exists a t_0 such that
$$x = \phi(x,y,t_0), \quad y = \psi(x,y,t_0).$$

3. There exists a t_{-1} such that
$$x = \phi(x',y',t_{-1}), \quad y = \psi(x',y',t_{-1}).$$

We assume that ϕ and ψ are real valued analytic functions.[14] We have already mentioned in Sect. 12.1 that Lie's theory permits us to determine the invariance of an integral of a differential equation without knowing the integral. This is a consequence of the fact that continuous groups of functions, ϕ and ψ are completely determined by the values of its partial derivatives at t_0. Without loss of generality, we can take $t_0 = 0$.

Define an *infinitesimal operator*

$$U = \left(\frac{\partial \phi}{\partial t}\right)_0 \frac{\partial}{\partial x} + \left(\frac{\partial \psi}{\partial t}\right)_0 \frac{\partial}{\partial y} = \xi \frac{\partial}{\partial x} + \eta \frac{\partial}{\partial y} \tag{12.18}$$

where $\xi = \left(\frac{\partial \phi}{\partial t}\right)_0$ and $\eta = \left(\frac{\partial \psi}{\partial t}\right)_0$. Note also that $\xi = Ux$ and $\eta = Uy$.

The effect of a finite transformation in parameter from $t_0 = 0$ to t can be derived as follows. Expanding by Maclaurin's series,

$$x' = \phi(x,y,t) = x + t\left(\frac{\partial \phi}{\partial t}\right)_0 + \frac{t^2}{2!}\left(\frac{\partial^2 \phi}{\partial t^2}\right)_0 + \cdots.$$

Now $\phi(x,y,0) = x$, $\psi(x,y,0) = y$ and $(\partial \phi/\partial t)_0 = Ux$ so that

$$\left(\frac{\partial^2 \phi}{\partial t^2}\right)_0 = \left[\frac{\partial}{\partial t}\frac{\partial \phi}{\partial t}\right]_0 = \left[\frac{\partial}{\partial x}\left(\frac{\partial \phi}{\partial t}\right)\frac{\partial \phi}{\partial t} + \frac{\partial}{\partial y}\left(\frac{\partial \phi}{\partial t}\right)\frac{\partial \psi}{\partial t}\right]_0$$

$$= \left[U\left(\frac{\partial \phi}{\partial t}\right)\right]_0 = UUx = U^2 x$$

---

[14] We assume that
$$\begin{vmatrix} \frac{\partial \phi}{\partial x} & \frac{\partial \phi}{\partial y} \\ \frac{\partial \psi}{\partial x} & \frac{\partial \psi}{\partial y} \end{vmatrix} \neq 0.$$

A technical requirement is that the parameters must satisfy group composition properties; here t is a real number and the condition is satisfied.

and so on. Similarly

$$\psi(x,y,t) = y + tUy + \frac{t^2}{2!}U^2y + \cdots.$$

This shows that the value of function $f(x,y)$ at (x',y') is determined by Ux and Uy.

So far we derived the infinitesimal transformation knowing the group functions ϕ and ψ. The converse problem is to determine these functions from the infinitesimal generators. Given the infinitesimal transformation

$$\delta x = Ux \cdot \delta t = \xi \cdot \delta t, \quad \delta y = \eta \cdot \delta t, \quad (12.19)$$

the point (x,y) is carried to a neighboring point $(x + \xi \delta t, y + \eta \delta t)$. The repetition of this process a number of times is equivalent to moving along the integral curve of the system of differential equations[15]

$$\frac{dx'}{\xi(x',y')} = \frac{dy'}{\eta(x',y')} = \frac{dt}{1}. \quad (12.20)$$

The first two give an integral of the form

$$u(x',y') = \text{constant}$$

and from the second pair, we can find a solution

$$v(x',y') - t = \text{constant}.$$

From these simultaneous equations, the value of x' and y' can be determined and shown to satisfy the group properties.

The infinitesimal transformations can be used to define invariances of a function, of a set of curves and of an equation, to the group of transformations. A function $f(x,y)$ is *invariant* under the group of transformations of x and y if $f(x,y) = f(x',y')$. Expanding by Taylor's series and using infinitesimal transformations, this can be written as

$$f(x',y') = f(x,y) = f(x,y) - t \cdot Uf + \frac{t^2}{2!}U^2f + \cdots$$

so that the necessary and sufficient condition for invariance is that $Uf \equiv 0$. Notice that the condition involves only the infinitesimal transformations.

A family of curves $C(x,y) = $ constant, is invariant if $C(x',y') = $ constant generates the same set of curves. This is satisfied if for each value of t, a curve of $C(x,y) = $ constant, is mapped by the transformation (12.17) to another curve. If the family of curves, $C(x,y) = $ constant, is considered to be the level sets of a function (e.g.,

---

[15] For a simple but modern treatment of the system of equations, see Zachmanoglou and Thoe (1986). A diagrammatic treatment of the case of technical progress is given in Sect. 12.3 below.

indifference curves are level sets of a utility function), then the transformation leaves the level sets invariant, making it a symmetry of the system.

The condition for the invariance of a set of curves is that the transformation maps each curve to another curve in the same set

$$C(x',y') = h\{C(x',y')\}.$$

Expanding by Taylor series,

$$C(x',y') = C(x,y) + t \cdot UC + \frac{t^2}{2!}U^2C + \cdots.$$

The necessary and sufficient condition for the invariance of the family of curves is that UC should be a function of C alone (i.e., not of the coordinates of the individual points).

$$U(C) = G(C). \qquad (12.21)$$

Finally an equation $F(x,y) = 0$ is invariant if $F(x',y') = 0$ whenever $F(x,y) = 0$. A necessary and sufficient condition is that $UF = 0$.

A transformation (12.17) carries with it the transformation of $p = dy/dx$, as

$$\frac{dy'}{dx'} = p' = \frac{\frac{\partial \psi}{\partial x}dx + \frac{\partial \psi}{\partial y}dy}{\frac{\partial \phi}{\partial x}dx + \frac{\partial \phi}{\partial y}dy} = \frac{\frac{\partial \psi}{\partial x} + \frac{\partial \psi}{\partial y}p}{\frac{\partial \phi}{\partial x} + \frac{\partial \phi}{\partial y}p}.$$

We now have the once extended transformation

$$x' = \phi(x,y,t), \quad y' = \psi(x,y,t), \quad p' = \chi(x,y,p,t). \qquad (12.22)$$

The differential equation

$$L(x,y,p) = 0 \qquad (12.23)$$

is invariant under the transformation (12.17) (i.e., one integral curve is mapped to another) if and only if it is invariant under (12.22). The condition for this is (compare it with the condition for the algebraic equation $F(x,y) = 0$ above)

$$U'L \equiv \xi \frac{\partial L}{\partial x} + \eta \frac{\partial L}{\partial y} + \eta' \frac{\partial L}{\partial p} = 0$$

where

$$\eta' = \frac{\partial \eta}{\partial x} + \left(\frac{\partial \eta}{\partial y} - \frac{\partial \xi}{\partial x}\right)p - \frac{\partial \xi}{\partial y}p^2.$$

Consider a curve $F(x,y) = 0$. If (x,y) is a point on the curve, p is the slope of the tangent to the curve. The transformation (12.17) takes (x,y) to (x',y'), $F(x,y)$

12.2 Toolbox

to $F(x',y')$ and p to p'. But p' depends only on x, y, and p; so any curve tangent to $F(x,y) = 0$ at (x,y) will be transformed into a curve tangent to $F'(x',y') = 0$ at (x',y'). The extended transformation tells us not only how indifference curves are transformed but how their slopes are transformed by (12.17).[16]

12.2.9 Calculus of Variation and the Hamiltonian Formulation

Earlier we defined a curve as a mapping from an open interval of a real line to a manifold. In this subsection we consider the choice of curves that maximize an integral. First we derive the Euler equations for the simplest case where the system has one degree of freedom[17]; taking the parameter to be t, we want to choose a curve $x(t)$, $t = a$ to $t = b$, that maximize the integral $\int F(t,x,\dot{x})\,dt$ where $\dot{x} = \dfrac{dx}{dt}$.

A well-known example is the choice of consumption expenditure that maximizes inter-temporal utility. Then we will state its extension to systems with n degrees of freedom and, reformulate the problem using the Hamiltonian.

Divide the interval, $t = a = t^0$ to $t = b = t^{n+1}$, into $(n+1)$ equal parts of length Δt, $(t^0, t^1), \ldots, (t^n, t^{n+1})$. The purpose is to approximate the integral by a sum; the process is similar to that used in elementary calculus to approximate the area under a curve. Additional complications arise from the fact that $F(\ )$ is not a function of t alone but also of x and t. We first approximate $x(t)$ by a polynomial line with vertices $(t^0, x^0), (t^1, x^1), \ldots, (t^{n+1}, x^{n+1})$. The slope of the line with vertices (t^i, x^i) and (t^{i+1}, x^{i+1}) is $(x^{i+1} - x^i)/\Delta t$. We use this expression to approximate $\dot{x}(t^i)$. Substituting we can approximate the integral by the sum

$$J'(t^0, t^{n+1}) = \sum_{i=0}^{n+1} F\left(t^i, x^i, \frac{x^{i+1} - x^i}{\Delta t}\right) \Delta t.$$

The curve maximizes the sum if marginally changing x at t^i (see Fig. 12.8) leads to no variation in the sum. We examine the variation of the sum by partially differentiating it with respect to x^i.

$$\frac{\partial J'}{\partial x_i} = F_x(\ )\Delta t + F_{\dot{x}}\left(t^{i-1}, x^{i-1}, \frac{x^i - x^{i-1}}{\Delta t}\right)$$

$$- F_{\dot{x}}\left(t^i, x^i, \frac{x^{i+1} - x^i}{\Delta t}\right).$$

---

[16] The extended transformation is a special case of contact transformations.

[17] Gelfand and Fomin (1963) provides an excellent introduction to the Euler equations and the Hamiltonian formulation.

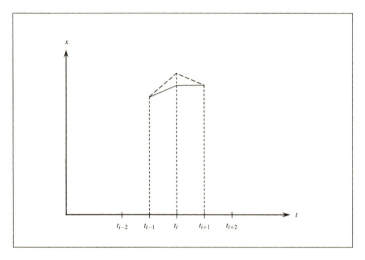

Fig. 12.8 Change in integral of a curve from a local shift

Dividing both sides by Δt,

$$\frac{\partial J'}{\partial x_i \Delta t} = F_x(\ ) + \frac{F_{\dot{x}}(t^{i-1},\ldots) - F_{\dot{x}}(t^i,\ldots)}{\Delta t}.$$

As $\Delta t \to 0$, this expression converges to the limit called the variational derivative of $J(t)$, given by

$$\frac{\delta J}{\delta x} = F_x(t,x,\mathring{x}) - \frac{\partial}{\partial t} F_{\dot{x}}(t,x,\mathring{x}).$$

The integral reaches an extremal if this variational derivative is zero and thus we derive the second order differential equation known as Euler equation

$$F_x - \frac{d}{dt} F_{\dot{x}} = 0.$$

If the system has n degrees of freedom so that $x(t) = (x^1(t),\ldots,x^n(t))$, then we have n Euler equations

$$F_{x_i} - \frac{d}{dt} F_{\dot{x}_i} = 0. \qquad (12.24)$$

The n second order partial differential equations can be reduced to a system of $2n$ first order partial differential equations by defining a set of $2n+1$ canonical variables $t, x^1, \ldots, x^n, p^1, \ldots, p^n$ related to the earlier set of variables by the equations

12.2 Toolbox

$$t = t, \quad x^i = x^i, \quad p^i = F_{\dot{x}^i}.$$

In economic models, p^i is interpreted as shadow prices. Now write a new function called the Hamiltonian

$$H = -F + \sum_i \dot{x}^i p^i. \tag{12.25}$$

We shall now seek to express the Euler equations in terms of "canonical variables." Computationally the most convenient approach (Gelfand and Fomin 1963, p. 69) is to take the partial derivatives of the function H

$$dH = -dF + \sum p^i d\dot{x}^i + \sum \dot{x}^i dp^i$$
$$= -\frac{\partial F}{\partial t} dt - \sum \frac{\partial F}{\partial x^i} dx^i - \sum \frac{\partial F}{\partial \dot{x}^i} d\dot{x}^i + \sum p^i d\dot{x}^i + \sum \dot{x}^i dp^i$$
$$= -\frac{\partial F}{\partial t} dt - \sum \frac{\partial F}{\partial x^i} dx^i + \sum \dot{x}^i dp^i.$$

Partial differentials of H can now be shown to be given by the coefficients of the differentials on the right-hand side

$$\frac{\partial H}{\partial t} = -\frac{\partial F}{\partial t}, \quad \frac{\partial H}{\partial x^i} = -\frac{\partial F}{\partial x^i}, \quad \frac{\partial H}{\partial p^i} = \dot{x}^i. \tag{12.26}$$

The Euler equation can now be written as

$$\frac{dx^i}{dt} = \frac{\partial H}{\partial p^i}, \quad \frac{dp^i}{dt} = -\frac{\partial H}{\partial x^i} \quad (i = 1, \ldots, n).$$

12.2.10 Conservation Laws and Noether Theorems

In dynamic models, we want to study the motion of the system over time. One approach, "the vectorial method," seeks to study the forces acting on the system when it is at a point and determine the direction of motion there. The integration of the resulting differential equation, subject to the appropriate boundary value conditions, gives the locus of motion. In an alternate approach, "analytical mechanics," we seek to characterize the entire trajectory as that which minimizes an action integral.

The idea that the dynamics of a natural phenomenon can be explained by the minimization of some action integral and that it reflects the simplicity inherent in the system has a long tradition. Yourgrau and Mandelstram (1979, p. 4) traces it back to a passage in Aristotle. Hero of Alexandria established a genuinely scientific minimum principle when he showed that the path of light reflected by a mirror takes the shortest possible path to the observer's eyes. The law is a direct antecedent of Fermat's principle of least time. Maupertius proclaimed it to be a universal law in the spirit of Platonic–Pythagorian cosmology and so made it a controversial proposition. It was left to the English physicist, Sir William R. Hamilton, to put analytical dynamics on a solid mathematical foundation.

We shall now show how an infinitesimal transformation of a $(n+1)$ space, $(t,x^1,\ldots,x^n)$ affects the action integral of a dynamic system and how the assumptions of the invariance of an integral leads to conservation laws. Logan (1977), Lovelock and Rund (1975) and Sato (1981) give detailed and rigorous mathematical analysis of the invariance identities. Here we will avoid purely technical details; after stating the Noether theorem, we shall provide an intuitive explanation of the special case when t does not appear explicitly in the Hamiltonian H in Eq. (12.25).

Unlike in Sect. 12.2.7, we will consider transformations that depend on r essential parameters, $\varepsilon = (\varepsilon^1,\ldots,\varepsilon^r)$. The number of conservation laws depends on the number of parameters and arbitrarily setting it equal to one affects the analysis substantially. Let the transformation be given by the equations

$$\bar{t} = \phi(t,x,\varepsilon),$$
$$\bar{x}^k = \psi^k(t,x,\varepsilon) \quad (k=1,\ldots,n, \ x=(x^1,\ldots,x^n)). \tag{12.27}$$

The identity transformations are given by $\varepsilon = 0$. Expanding the right-hand side of (12.26) by Taylor series about $\varepsilon = 0$, we get

$$\bar{t} = t + \sum_s \tau_s(t,x)\varepsilon^s + O(\varepsilon),$$
$$\bar{x}^k = x^k + \sum_s \xi_s^k(t,x)\varepsilon^s + O(\varepsilon) \quad (s=1,\ldots,r).$$

The principal linear parts, τ_s and ξ_s^k are the infinitesimal generators of the transformation (12.26) and is given by

$$\tau_s(t,x) = \frac{\partial \phi}{\partial \varepsilon^s}(t,x,0) \quad \text{and} \quad \xi_s^k(t,x) = \frac{\partial \psi^k}{\partial \varepsilon^s}. \tag{12.28}$$

Consider any curve $x(t)$, $t=a$ to $t=b$, in the original configuration space $(t,x^1,\ldots,x^n)$. The transformation of the space to $(\bar{t},\bar{x}^1,\ldots,\bar{x}^n)$ maps $x(t)$ to $\bar{x}(\bar{t})$. The integrand referred to as Lagrangian, $L(t,x(t),\dot{x}(t))$ is similarly transformed to $L(\bar{t},\bar{x}(\bar{t}),(d\bar{x}(\bar{t})/d\bar{t}))$. Finally, the action integral

$$J(x) = \int_a^b L(t,x(t),\dot{x}(t))\,dt \tag{12.29}$$

12.2 Toolbox

is transformed to

$$J(x) = \int_{\bar{a}}^{\bar{b}} L\left(\bar{t}, \bar{x}(\bar{t}), \frac{d\bar{x}(\bar{t})}{d\bar{t}}\right) d\bar{t}.$$

We will now state the Noether theorem, skipping the derivation. Define

$$E_k = \frac{\partial L}{\partial x^k} - \frac{d}{dt}\frac{\partial L}{\partial \dot{x}^k} \quad (k = 1, \ldots, n). \tag{12.30}$$

E_k is the left hand side of the Euler equation (12.24); Noether identities state that if the integral is invariant to the transformation, then there are linear combinations of E_k that can be expressed as exact differentials, $d\Omega_s/dt$ of a function Ω_s, where

$$\Omega_s = \left(L - \sum_k \dot{x}^k \frac{\partial L}{\partial \dot{x}^k}\right) \tau_s + \frac{\partial L}{\partial \dot{x}^k} \xi_s - \Phi_s$$

$$= -H\tau_s + \sum_k \frac{\partial L}{\partial \dot{x}^k} \xi_s^k - \Phi_s \quad (k = 1, \ldots, n, \ s = 1, \ldots, r). \tag{12.31}$$

If $\Phi_s \equiv 0$, then the fundamental integral (12.29) is absolutely invariant; if Φ_s has to be determined in the process of solving the system, then the integral is said to be *divergence invariant*.

But along an extremal, E_k is equal to zero and so $(d/dt)\Omega_s = 0$ implying that Ω_s is a constant. This leads to the Noether theorem.

Noether Theorem: *If the action integral of a problem is invariant under the r-parameter family of transformation, then r distinct quantities Ω_s ($s = 1, \ldots, r$), are constant along any extremal.*

In other words, Ω_s are the constants we were looking for or Ω_s = constant are the conservation laws. An intuitive understanding of the result can be obtained by considering the special case where the objective is to maximize the integral

$$J(x) = \int_a^b L(x^1, \ldots, x^n, \dot{x}^1, \ldots, \dot{x}^n) dt$$

where L does not depend on t explicitly. In this case, the corresponding Hamiltonian (Eq. (12.25)) is not an explicit function of t. It is clear that L and the integral remains invariant if we replace t with a new variable $t + \varepsilon$ for an arbitrary ε. In fact, given a curve $x(t)$, the transformed curve is given $x(t^* - \varepsilon) = x^*(t^*)$ with the appropriate limits of integration. So

$$J(x^*) = \int_{a+\varepsilon}^{b+\varepsilon} L(x^{1^*}, \ldots, x^{n^*}, \dot{x}^{1^*}, \ldots, \dot{x}^{n^*}) dt^*$$

$$= \int_{a+\varepsilon}^{b+\varepsilon} L(x^1(t^* - \varepsilon), \ldots, \dot{x}^n(t^* - \varepsilon)) d(t^* - \varepsilon)$$

$$= \int_a^b L(x^1(t),\ldots,\overset{\scriptscriptstyle(n)}{x}(t))\,dt$$
$$= J(x).$$

The transformation can be written as $t^* = t + \varepsilon$, $x^{s^*} = x^s$ ($s = 1,\ldots,n$). The corresponding infinitesimal transformation is $\tau = 1$ and $\xi^s = 0$. In this case, Eq. (12.31) can be written as

$$\Omega_s = -H \cdot 1 + \frac{\partial L}{\partial x_s} \cdot 0 = -H = \text{a constant.} \tag{12.32}$$

When t does not appear explicitly in $L(\ )$ or H, then the Hamiltonian itself is conserved. This special case is of great importance in economics.

12.3 Holotheticity: Symmetry of the Isoquant Map

Isoquants or level sets of a production function establish a relation between the quantities of inputs and that of output. In Sect. 12.1, we pointed out that technical progress can be viewed either as a shift in production itself or as an increase in inputs measured in efficiency units. If technical progress is Hicks-neutral, then the input vector OP_1 in Fig. 12.9 acts as if it is OP'_1. The example leads to two questions: What way can this concept of technical progress be generalized? What are the common restrictions on the functions needed to make them meaningful?

If $\overline{K}$ and $\overline{L}$ are inputs in efficiency units, then it can be expressed in natural units as,

$$\overline{K} = A(t)K = \lambda_1(t)K, \quad \overline{L} = A(t)L = \lambda_2(t)L \tag{12.33}$$

where $\lambda_1 = \lambda_2 = A(t)$. The standard case of factor augmenting biased technical progress is

$$\overline{K} = \lambda_1(t)K, \quad \overline{L} = \lambda_2(t)L.$$

We can relax the assumption that λ_i depends only on t. The next generalization is to make it a function of K/L also; the rate of technical progress differs from a ray to another. A further generalization is to make it a function of K and L. We can classify these cases as

12.3 Holotheticity: Symmetry of the Isoquant Map

Case 1	Case 2
$\lambda_1 = \lambda_2$	$\lambda_1 \neq \lambda_2$
$\lambda_1(t) = \lambda_2(t)$	$\lambda_1(t) \neq \lambda_2(t)$
$\lambda_2(t, K/L) = \lambda_2(t, K/L)$	$\lambda_1(t, K/L) \neq \lambda_2(t, K/L)$
$\lambda_1(t, K, L) = \lambda_2(t, K, L)$	$\lambda_2(t, K, L) \neq \lambda_2(t, K, L)$

(12.34)

The common restriction needed is that the impact of technical progress in period $t^2 - t^0$ should equal the sum of changes in period $t^1 - t^0$ and $t^2 - t^1$. If this restriction is not met, we cannot unambiguously speak of the efficiency at time t^2 relative to time t^0. Similarly we want the $\lambda_i(,0) = 1$. Finally we want to say that if the inputs have higher efficiency at time t^1 relative to time t^0, the reverse is true at time t^0 relative to time t^1. These elementary considerations suggest that the scalar functions λ_i must satisfy group properties.

Consider the case where

$$\lambda_1(t) = \lambda_2(t) = e^{\alpha t}.$$

For this case, the infinitesimal operator is

$$U = \alpha K \frac{\partial}{\partial L} + \alpha L \frac{\partial}{\partial L} \tag{12.35}$$

since $(dK/dt)_0 = \alpha K = UK$ and $(dL/dt)_0 = \alpha L = UL$. Expanding the technical progress function using Taylor series

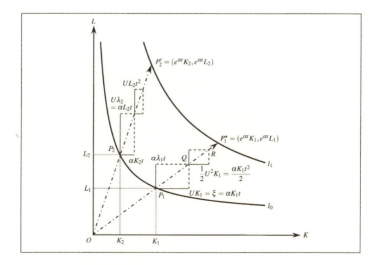

Fig. 12.9 Hicks neutral technical change and isoquant diagram

$$K' = K + UK \cdot t + U^2 K \frac{t^2}{2!} + \cdots, \tag{12.36}$$

$$L' = L + \alpha L \cdot t + U^2 L \frac{t^2}{2!} + \cdots. \tag{12.37}$$

We can interpret this process economically as follows. A firm which employs an input vector (K_1, L_1) produces an output $F(K_1, L_1)$ initially. Over a period of time t, the factors increase in efficiency, so that they now have the productive capacity of the vector $(e^{\alpha t} K_1, e^{\alpha t} L_1)$. We can figuratively speak of a *virtual expansion path* in the input space as given by the infinite series (12.36).

Now consider the process starting from another input combination (K_2, L_2) on the same isoquant. Technical progress will transform it to $(e^{\alpha t} K_2, e^{\alpha t} L_2)$. If the production function is holothetic to the technical progress or is symmetry of the isoquant map, then P_1' and P_2' must lie on the same isoquant.

Starting from a linear homogeneous production function, we can enquire whether there is a transformation of the production surface that maps one isoquant to the other the same way as the technical progress function did. If it does, the economies of scale corresponding to the transformed production function have the same effect on productivity as the technical progress itself. The possible transformation can be obtained by solving (see Eq. (12.21))

$$Uf = \xi \frac{\partial f}{\partial K} + \eta \frac{\partial f}{\partial L} = G(f). \tag{12.38}$$

The solution of (12.38) can be derived from the corresponding system of ordinary differential equation

$$\frac{dK}{\xi} = \frac{dL}{\eta} = \frac{df}{G(f)}. \tag{12.39}$$

Substituting $\xi = \alpha K$ and $\eta = \alpha L$ for the Hicks-neutral case, it can be shown that the function holothetic to Hicks-neutral technical progress is the homothetic function (Sato 1981, pp. 30–34). This was the conclusion derived in Sato and Ramachandran (1974) but the new method is not confined to Hicks neutral case.

In the case of biased technical progress with $\lambda_1(t) = e^{\alpha t}$ and $\lambda_2(t) = e^{\beta t}$, the infinitesimal generators are $\xi = \alpha K$ and $\eta = \beta L$. Substituting in (12.39), the holothetic production function is seen to be

$$Y = F(K^{1/\alpha} Q(L^{\alpha}/K^{\beta})). \tag{12.40}$$

The almost homogeneous production function proposed by Lau (1978) and the almost homothetic function of Sato (1977) are special cases of (12.40). Sato (1981) examines many other technical progress functions and their corresponding holothetic production functions.

12.4 Examples of Conservation Laws in Economics

Consider a Solow–Swan type economy with an aggregate production function

$$Y = F(K,L). \tag{12.41}$$

Labor grows at an exogenous rate $\dot{L}/L = n$. Then per capita output, per capita capital and per capita consumption are given by

$$y = \frac{Y}{L}, \quad k = \frac{K}{L} \quad \text{and} \quad c = \frac{C}{L}.$$

Further

$$\frac{\dot{k}}{k} = \frac{\dot{K}}{K} - \frac{\dot{L}}{L} = \frac{Y-C}{K} - n = \frac{Y}{K} - \frac{C}{K} - n.$$

Hence $\dot{k} = y - c - nk$ or $c = c(k,\dot{k}) = y - nk - \dot{k}$.

The objective of the society is to maximize utility from consumption over time. In a classical paper, Ramsey (1928) considered a special case of this model with $n = 0$ and L normalized to 1. Ramsey suggested that the appropriate criteria for the economy is to maximize

$$J(C) = \int_0^\infty (B - U(C)) \, dt$$

$$\text{subject to } c = \frac{C}{1} = F(K) - \dot{K} \tag{12.42}$$

where B is the upper bound of $U(\ )$ is called the bliss point. The problem can be reformulated using the Hamiltonian (Note that a minimization problem can be converted into maximization problem by multiplying by -1)

$$H = -(B - U(C)) + p(t)\dot{K}$$
$$= -(B - U(C)) + p(t)(F(K) - C). \tag{12.43}$$

The control variable, C, is selected so as to maximize H (see Burmeister & Dobell (1970) for a discussion of the details of control theory and the Ramsey problem).

$$\frac{\partial H}{\partial C} = U'(C) - p(t) = 0,$$
$$U'(C) = p(t).$$

Substituting in the Hamiltonian which is not explicitly a function of t

$$-(B - U(C)) + U'(C)K = \text{constant by (12.32)},$$

$$\dot{K} = \frac{B - U(C) + \text{constant}}{U'(C)}. \tag{12.44}$$

An economic interpretation of this rule can be obtained by considering the loss in present utility due to a contemporaneous increase in capital formation with the added consumption flow that the resulting capital formation would generate. This approach was proposed by Keynes. If capital formation is increased at time t by h for a period Δt, then the loss in utility due to reduced consumption is approximately $hU'(C)\Delta t$. The increased output at any point of time is $hF'(K)\Delta t$ and the present value of this flow is

$$\int_0^\infty h\Delta t F'(K) U'(C) \, dt.$$

Hence, equating the extra cost to extra benefit,

$$\int_0^\infty h\Delta t F'(K) U'(C) \, dt = hU'(C) \, dt.$$

Differentiating with respect to t

$$-F'(K)U'(C) = \dot{U}'(C).$$

This is nothing but the Euler equation of a variational problem stated earlier, $\text{Max} J(C)$ with $C = F(K) - \dot{K}$. Since the integrand does not contain t explicitly, it was shown that the first integral of the Euler equation is

$$B - U = KU'(C) + \text{constant}$$

which takes us back to the Ramsey rule.

While Ramsey's model has one sector and an objective function that seeks to maximize the intertemporal utility from consumption, von Neumann model has n sectors but no consumption.[18] Hence the rate of increase of the stock of any good equals its output. The vector of capital goods at time t is $K_t = (K_t^i)$ and is used to produce the vector of net capital formation which equals output. The transformation function relating K_t to $\dot{K}_t$ is

$$F(K_t, \dot{K}_t) = 0.$$

---

[18]See Chap. 2 of this volume for Samuelson's classic paper on conservation law for the von Neumann model.

12.4 Examples of Conservation Laws in Economics

We assume that F is homogeneous of degree one, concave and smoothly differentiable. The process is considered to have begun at time $t = 0$ with capital vector K_0 and terminates at time T. If the terminal vector $K'_t = (K_t^2, \ldots, K_t^n)$ is given, then the objective is to maximize K_t^1 subject to K_0 and K_t.

The variational problem in continuous time can be written as

$$\max \int_0^\infty K_t^1 \, dt$$

subject to $\quad F(K_t, \dot{K}_t) = 0 \quad$ and the boundary conditions. $\quad$ (12.45)

Since the integral does not contain t, explicitly, the Hamiltonian is constant.

$$H = L_t - \sum_j \dot{K}_t^j \frac{\partial L_t}{\partial \dot{K}_t^j}$$

$$= K_t^1 + \lambda_t F - \sum_j \dot{K}_t^j \frac{\partial (\dot{K}_t - \lambda_t F)}{\partial \dot{K}_t^j}$$

$$= -\lambda_t \sum_j \dot{K}_t^j \frac{\partial F}{\partial \dot{K}_t^j}.$$

Samuelson (1970), in deriving the first explicit statement of a conservation law, shows that $H = -\lambda_t Y_t$. It follows that

$$\lambda_t Y_t = \text{constant.} \quad (12.46)$$

Samuelson also derived another conservation law involving wealth but no general principle like the constancy of the Hamiltonian for the first law, was evident. Sato (1981) showed that a second law can be derived, after lengthy manipulations from the principle of divergence-invariance

$$\lambda_t W_t = \text{constant.} \quad (12.47)$$

Taking the ratios of the two conservation laws to eliminate λ_t, the unobservable shadow price, we obtain a constancy of capital-output ratio

$$\frac{W_t}{Y_t} = \text{constant.} \quad (12.48)$$

Chapters 8 and 9 of this volume deal with conservation laws for different economic models.

The insight of symmetry analysis is in the recognition that conservation laws are not *ad hoc* derivations of the constancy of a scalar function. It is intimately connected with the structure of the model. The Ramsey conservation law and the first conservation law arise from a transformation of the time axis through a shift in the origin. In other words, time in economic models has no distinguished origin. The second conservation law has infinitesimal generators that are constant multiples of the inputs; it is a transformation of the units of inputs.

12.5 Conclusion

The differential geometric approach provides a unified methodological framework for invariance, symmetry and conservation laws. Its strength lies in examining the informational implications of the assumptions behind economic models. Do we have any information about production functions over and above that is in the isoquant map? If not, how are we to distinguish between transformations that map the isoquants isomorphically? Conservation laws, on the other hand, arise from the transformations which leave the dynamics of a model invariant.

This volume seeks to explore varied applications of these techniques.

Reader's Guide

A reader who randomly picks a book on differential geometry or Lie groups in a library is in for a surprise. Mathematical textbooks adopt either the abstract or the computational approach. The former expects considerable "mathematical maturity" while the latter will look like a riot in indices. Application-oriented books will be full of examples from physical sciences. The following annotated list is intended to assist one with a background in economics or finance to get started; it is a subjective choice and not a ranking of available books.

1. Dubrovin, B.A., Fomenko, A.T. & Novikov, S.P. (1984, 1985). *Modern geometry—methods and applications*. New York: Springer.
   Part 1: The geometry of surfaces, transformation groups and fields.
   Part 2: The geometry and topology of manifolds.

   Another addition to the lucid textbooks that Russian mathematicians specialize in writing. The first volume has a chapter on calculus of variations. Because of leisurely presentation, manifolds appear only in the second volume.

2. Spivak, M. (1979). *A comprehensive introduction to differential geometry*. Wilmington, Delaware: Publish or Perish. (Volume 1, 2nd ed.)

   The great American differential geometry book provides an intelligible and authoritative account. The first chapter is devoted to manifolds and Chap. 10 to Lie groups.

3. Schutz, B. (1980). *Geometric methods in mathematical physics*. Cambridge: Cambridge University Press.

Do not be misled by the title. Four of six chapters require no knowledge of physics and contain short and clear explanations of concepts that should be intelligible to one who followed this chapter.

4. Edelen, D.G.B. (1985). *Applied exterior calculus.* New York: John Wiley & Sons.

A detailed discussion of differential forms. Part 1 discusses differential forms, Part 2 its applications in mathematics including calculus of variations, and Part 3 applications to physics.

5. Cohen, A. (1931). *An introduction to the Lie theory of one parameter groups.* New York: G.E. Stechert.

An elementary book on Lie groups of differential equations that has no match.

6. Yaglom, I.M. (1988). *Felix Klein and Sophus Lie: Evolution of the idea of symmetry in the nineteenth century.* Boston: Birkhäuser.

The subtitle is more descriptive of the book. An information-packed but occasionally rambling account of the mathematical tradition from Galois to Klein.

7. Chalmers, A.F. (1982). *What is this thing called science?* St. Lucia: University of Queensland Press. (2nd ed.)

A short, readable introduction to the many issues in the philosophy of science.

References

Alchain, A. (1953). The meaning of utility measurement. *American Economic Review, 42,* 26–50.
Bröcker, T., & Jänich, K. (1982). *Introduction to differential topology.* Cambridge: Cambridge University Press.
Burmeister, E., & Dobell, A.R. (1970). *Mathematical theories of economic growth.* London: Macmillan.
Chalmers, A.F. (1982). *What is this thing called science?* (2nd ed.). St. Lucia: University of Queensland Press.
Clapham, J.H. (1922). Of empty economic boxes. *Economic Journal, 32,* 305–314.
Cohen, A. (1931). *Introduction to the Lie theory of one parameter groups.* New York: G.E. Stechert & Co.
Dubrovin, B.A., Fomenko, A.T., & Novikov, S.P. (1984, 1985). *Modern geometry — methods and applications* (Part 1: The geometry of surfaces, transformation groups, and fields. Part 2: The geometry and topology of manifolds). New York: Springer.
Edelen, D.G.B. (1985). *Applied differential calculus.* New York: Wiley.
Friedman, M. (1983). *Foundations of space-time theories.* Princeton, NJ: Princeton University Press.
Gelfand, I.M., & Fomin, S.V. (1963). *Calculus of variations.* Englewood Cliffs, NJ: Prentice-Hall.
Hicks, J.H. (1946). *Value and capital* (2nd ed.). London: Oxford University Press.
Klein, M. (1972). *Mathematical thoughts from ancient to modern times.* New York: Oxford University Press.
Lau, L.J. (1978). Application of profit functions. In M. Fuss, & D. McFadden (Eds.), *Production economics: A dual approach to theory and applications* (vol. 1). Amsterdam: North-Holland.

Logan, J.D. (1977). *Invariant variational principles*. New York: Academic Press.
Lovelock, D., & Rund, H. (1975). *Tensors, differential forms and variational principles*. New York: Wiley.
Millman, R.S., & Parker, G.D. (1977). *Elements of differential geometry*. Englewood Cliffs, NJ: Prentice-Hall.
Misner, C., Thorne, K.S., & Wheeler, J.A. (1973). *Gravitation*. San Francisco: W.H. Freeman and Company.
Pigou, A.C. (1922). Empty economic boxes: A reply. *Economic Journal, 32*, 458–465.
Ramsey, F.P. (1928). A mathematical theory of saving. *Economic Journal, 38*, 543–559.
Reichenbach, H. (1960). *The theory of relativity and a priori knowledge*. Berkeley, California: University of Berkeley Press.
Samuelson, P.A. (1970). Law of conservation of the capital-output ratio. *Proceedings of the National Academy of Science, Applied Mathematical Section, 67*, 1477–1479.
Sato, R. (1975). The impact of technical change on the holotheticity of production functions. Working paper presented at the World Congress of Econometric Society, Toronto.
Sato, R. (1977). Homothetic and nonhomothetic functions. *American Economic Review, 67*, 559–569.
Sato, R. (1981). *Theory of technical change and economic invariance: application of Lie groups*. New York: Academic Press.
Sato, R., & Ramachandran, R. (1974). *Models of endogenous technical progress, scale effect and duality of production function*. Providence, Rhode Island: Brown University, Department of Economics discussion paper.
Schutz, B. (1980). *Geometric methods of mathematical physics*. Cambridge: Cambridge University Press.
Solow, R.M. (1957). Technical change and aggregate production function. *Review of Economics and Statistics, 39*, 312–320.
Solow, R.M. (1961). Comment, In *Output, input, and productivity measurement* (vol. 25, Studies in income and wealth). Princeton, NJ: Princeton University Press.
Spivak, M. (1979). *A comprehensive introduction to differential geometry* (vol. 1). Wilmington, Delaware: Publish or Perish.
Stigler, G.J. (1961). Economic problems in measuring changes in productivity. In *Output, input, and productivity measurement* (vol. 25, Studies in income and wealth). Princeton, NJ: Princeton University Press.
Yaglom, I.M. (1988). *Felix Klein and Sophus Lie: Evolution of the idea of symmetry in the nineteenth century*. Boston: Birkhauser.
Yourgrau, W., & Mandelstram, S. (1979). *Variational principles in dynamics and quantum theory*. New York: Dover.
Zellner, A., & Revankar, N.S. (1969). Generalized production functions. *Review of Economic Studies, 36*, 241–250.
Zachmanoglou, E.C., & Thoe, D.W. (1976). *Introduction to partial differential equations with applications*. New York: Dover.

Biographies

Ryuzo Sato

Ryuzo Sato is C.V. Starr Professor Emeritus of Economics at the Stern School of Business, New York University. He was director of the Center for Japan–U.S. Business and Economic Studies at the Stern School. Prior to becoming a Stern faculty member, he was a professor of economics at Brown University. Professor Sato also taught at Harvard University, The University of Tokyo, Kyoto University, and Bonn University. He was the founding chief editor of *Japan and the World Economy*, an international theory and policy journal.

For more than 40 years, Professor Sato has divided his time between Japan and the US, and he conducts research, gives lectures, and writes on the subject of Japan–US relations.

Recent work includes *Biased Technical Change and Economic Conservation Laws* (Springer, 2006), *Growth Theory and Technical Change: The Selected Essays of Ryuzo Sato*, vol. 1 (Edward Elgar, 1996), *Production, Stability and Dynamic Symmetry: The Selected Essays of Ryuzo Sato*, vol. 2 (Edward Elgar, 1999), and *Theory of Technical Change and Economic Invariance: Application of Lie Groups* (Academic Press, 1981; reprint, new version, Edward Elgar, 1999). Professor Sato also writes columns regularly for several Japanese newspapers.

Professor Sato, who was a Fulbright Scholar, received his B.A. in economics and his Dr. Economics from Hitotsubashi University in Tokyo, and his Ph.D. in economics from Johns Hopkins University. His principal areas of research interest are mathematical economics and economic growth.

Rama V. Ramachandran

Rama V. Ramachandran received his master's degree from Madras University, India, and his Ph.D. from Brown University in the USA. He was a faculty member of the Department of Economics of Southern Methodist University and the Department of Economics of the Stern School of Business, New York University. He was associate director of the Center for Japan–U.S. Business and Economics at the Stern School. His research interests were in microeconomics and growth theory. After retirement, he has focused on economic pedagogy and authored an innovative introduction to microeconomics, *Opportunities and Choices: Understanding Our Economic Decisions* (http://www.visualeconomicanalysis.info/index.html).

Index

A
Abraham, R., 158, 160
Additive preferences, Houthakker, 62
Additivity, 59–62
Alchian, A., 234

B
Bessel-Hagan, E., 113
Biased technical progress, virtual expansion path for, 27
Boxes, economic, empty, 13–16
Bracket, Lie, holotheticity and, 37–40
Burmeister, E., 261

C
Capital goods models, 115–116
Caton, C., 131, 148
Circular reversal test, 77, 79
Clapham, J., 12, 15, 234–235
Classification, of mathematical structure, 4–7
Cobb–Douglas utility function, Marshallian, inverse, demand curves, 67
Commensurability invariance test, 78
Condition, integrability, Lie bracket, 51
Conservation law(s)
 in continuous and discrete models, 143–175
 dynamics, 87–105, 218
 economic, 163–167
 hidden, 114–116, 138, 143, 149, 152, 167, 214–215, 218
 income-wealth, 113–140, 149–150, 153–154, 168, 211, 213–214, 217–218, 220
 invariance and, 10–12
 in von Neumann model, 101–104, 128–131
 wealth, 113–141, 149–150, 153–154, 168, 209–226
Consumer theory, duality in, 55–58
Continuous models
 local conservation laws, 152–153
 Noether theorem, 143–154, 255–257
 technical and taste change, 151–152
 variable discount rate, 150–151
 zero discount rate, 146–148
Cost functions, 12, 58, 69–72
 implicit self-duality of, 69–72

D
Demand, 4, 12, 14, 16, 43–53, 56–58, 62–69, 71, 72, 191, 227, 234, 238
Demand curves, inverse, Marshallian, for Cobb–Douglas utility function, 67
Demand functions, self-dual empirical
 estimation of, 68
 method of deriving, 66–68
Demand theory
 equations, in groups, 56, 62, 64
 forms, 62
 self-duality in, 62–66
Differential equations, system of, integral curve, virtual expansion path, 32
Dimensional Invariance Axiom, 76
Directly additive preferences, Houthakker, 62
Direct utility functions, indirect, 56–58, 62, 63, 81
Discrete models
 vs. continuous, 143–175
 quadratic conservatives, 157–162
Divisia index, 74, 82–85

Dobell, A., 261
Duality, 12
  in consumer theory, 55–58
Dual quantity index, 81
Dubrovin, B., 238, 241, 246, 249, 264
Dynamics, conservation laws, 87–105, 215, 255

E

Econometric applications, 12, 119
Economic applications, Lie groups, 12
Economic boxes, empty, 13–16
Economic conservation laws, 163–167
Economics of scale, holotheticity and, 13–28
Elasticity, scale, homotheticity and, 16–18, 21
Empirical estimation, self-dual demand functions, 68
Empty economic boxes, 13–16
Estimation, empirical, self-dual demand functions, 68
Expansion path, virtual integral curve, system of differential equations, 32
Extended transformation, marginal rate of transformation, 34–37

F

Factor reversal test, 78–79, 82
Fleetwood, W., 80
Fomenko, A., 238, 264
Fomin, S., 88, 90, 111, 253, 255
For technical progress, biased, 24–25, 27–29, 33–34, 37, 41, 70, 179, 187–189, 258, 260
Friedman, M., 7, 233–234
Functions, utility, strongly separable, 61, 62

G

Gelfand, I., 88, 90, 111, 251, 253, 255
Generators, infinitesimal, tangent vectors, 31
Geometric methods, overview, 231–265
Geometric representation, virtual expansion path, 26
Group theory
  mathematical structure, classification, 4–7
  overview
    Erlanger Program, 5–6
    Klein, Felix, 5–6, 231
    in new physics, 6–7
    non-Euclidean space, 6–7
Group transformation
  translation of point, 23
  translation of point as, 8, 23

H

Hamilton, W., 7, 87, 113
Hamiltonian formulation, 7, 94–98, 100, 105, 253–255
Hamiltonian formulation, control theory and, 94–98
Hicks, J., 10, 19–22, 43, 59, 62, 182, 233
Hicks neutrality, holotheticity and, 25–27
Hicks neutral technical progress homotheticity, correspondence between, 19–22
Hicks neutral technical progress homotheticity, correspondence between isoquant mapping, homothetic production function, 22
Holotheticity
  Hicks neutrality and, 25–27
  technical progress, taxonomy of, 24–25
Holotheticity (holothetic technology)
  interpretation of, using operators, 39
  Lie bracket and, 37–40
  problem reformulation, 13–22
  technical progress and economics of scale: concept of, 13–28
Holotheticity, Lie bracket and, 37–40
Holothetic production functions, technical substitution, marginal rate of, 29–41
Homogeneity invariance axiom, 76
Homogeneity-of-degree-minus-one test, 76
Homotheticity
  Hicks neutral technical progress, correspondence between, 19–22
  scale elasticity and, 16–19
Homothetic production function, mapping of isoquants, Hicks neutral technical progress, 22
Houthakker, directly additive preferences, 62

I

Identity axiom, 76
Income-capital conservation law, 128–131, 139, 196, 215
Income, national, income-wealth ratios, measurement, 104–105
Income-wealth conservation law, 113–141, 149–150, 153–154, 209–211, 213–214, 217–218, 220
Income-wealth ratios, national income and, measurement, 104–105
Index numbers, theory of
  circular reversal test, 77, 79
  commensurability invariance test, 78
  dimensional invariance axiom, 76
  Divisia index, 74, 82–85

Index

dual quantity index, 81
economic, 12, 79–85
factor reversal test, 78, 82
Fleetwood, William, 80
homogeneity invariance axiom, 76
homogeneity-of-degree-minus-one test, 76
identity axiom, 76
mean value test, 76
monotonicity axiom, 75
price index, 74–78, 80–82
proportionality test, 76
quantity index, 74, 77, 78, 80–82, 84
statistical approach, 73–74
test approach, 74–79
time reversal test, 77
Indifference curve
  in plane, 50
  separable utility, 60
Indirect utility functions, 56–58, 62, 63, 81
Infinitesimal generators
  Lie groups, 8–10, 12
  tangent vectors, 31
Integrability condition, Lie bracket, 51
Integrability conditions, 47–53
Integral curve, system of differential equations, virtual expansion path, 32
Interpretation of holotheticity, using operators, 39
Invariance
  conservative laws and, 10–12, 209, 264
  symmetry and, 10–12, 264
Invariance principle
  literature summary, 113–114
  model, 115–116
  Noether's theorem, 116–119
Inverse, Marshallian, demand curves, for Cobb–Douglas utility function, 67
Isoquants, mapping of, homothetic production function, Hicks neutral technical progress, 22
Isoquant, tangent vectors, expansion path, 38

J
Jorgenson, D., 148, 178

K
Kataoka, H., 114, 131
Kemp, M., 104, 114, 115, 123, 143, 149
Klein, F., 5–6, 113, 144, 231-233, 235, 265

L
Legendre transformation, 94–96, 156
Lie bracket
  holotheticity and, 37–41
  integrability condition, 51
Lie groups
  economic applications of, 12
  infinitesimal generators, 8–10, 12
  invariance and, 8–12
Liviatan, N., 124, 148
Long, N., 104, 114, 115, 123, 143, 149
Lucas, R., 148

M
Maeda, S., 113, 143, 154–167, 169–175, 210
Mapping of isoquants, homothetic production function, Hicks neutral technical progress, 22
Maps, 5, 236–238, 252, 256, 260
Marginal rate, transformation, extended transformation and, 34–37
Marsden, J., 158, 160
Marshallian, inverse, demand curves, for Cobb–Douglas utility function, 67
Mathematical structure, classification, 4–7
Mean value test, 76
Microeconomics, 48, 153, 235, 268
Mimura, F., 113–115, 143, 152, 169, 210, 215–218, 220
Misner, C., 231, 237, 240, 242, 244, 249
Models, continuous and discrete, 143–175
Monotonicity axiom, 75

N
National income, income-wealth ratios, measurement, 104–105
Neo-classical growth model, steady state, golden rule, 95
Neoclassical theory, 168
Neutral technical progress, Hicks, holotheticity, correspondence between, 19–22
Noether theorem(s), 84, 98–101, 104, 105, 113, 143-145, 149, 154, 167, 214, 218, 255-258
  implications of, 98–101
Nôno, T., 113–115, 143, 152, 169, 210, 215–218, 220, 225
Novikov, S., 238, 264

P

Parameter group of transformations, orbits, field of tangent vectors, 9
Pareto-principle, 234
Path, of virtual expansion, geometric representation of, 26
Pigou, A., 12, 15, 234, 235
Plane, one, indifference curve in, 50
Point, translation of, as group transformation, 8, 23
Preference ordering, self-dual, 62–65, 81
Price index, 59, 74–78, 80–82
Production functions, holothetic, technical substitution, marginal rate of, 29–41
Production, implicit self-duality of, 69–72
Progress functions, technical, types of, holotheticity, 30–34
Progress, technical
   holotheticity and, 25–27, 30–34, 39
   taxonomy of, holotheticity, 24–25
Proportionality test, 76

Q

Quantity index, 59, 74, 77–79, 81, 82, 84

R

Ramachandran, R.V., 19, 27, 148, 177, 206, 209, 225, 235, 260
Ramsey, F., 12, 88, 90–94, 98, 99, 105, 114–115, 124, 143, 146, 148, 155, 165, 168, 216–217, 261, 262–263
Ramsey–Keynes rule, 92
Ramsey rule, variational problem, 88–92
Reformulation of problem, holotheticity, 13–22
Reichenbach, H., 233, 234
Revankar, N., 235

S

Samuelson, P.A., 3, 4, 12, 43, 62, 63, 73, 74, 77, 80, 81, 83, 84, 91–93, 103, 105, 106, 113–115, 117, 121, 123–125, 128, 130, 131, 139, 143, 146, 148–150, 152, 154, 168, 209, 215, 263
Sato, R., 4, 12, 13, 19, 27, 30, 31, 33–36, 40, 44, 45, 49, 51, 52, 62–64, 68–70, 72, 74, 77, 81, 83, 84, 106, 107, 113–116, 118, 119, 123–126, 128, 130, 133, 134, 137–139, 143, 145, 147–153, 158, 165, 168, 169, 177–183, 185, 187, 188, 193, 196, 204, 206, 209, 211, 214–218, 220, 222, 227, 235, 249, 256, 260, 263
Scale contours, 17
Scale, economics of, holotheticity and, 13–28
Scale economics, significance of, 18–19
Scale elasticity, homotheticity and, 16–18
Schutz, B., 242, 244, 245, 264
Self-dual demand functions
   empirical estimation of
      clothing, 68
      food, 68
      fuel, 68
      housing, 68
      light, 68
   method of deriving, 66–68
Self-dual functions, weakly, 65–66
Self-duality, 12, 55–72, 78, 81
   demand, implicit, 71
   in demand theory, 62–66
   production, implicit, 69–72
Self-dual preference ordering, 62–65
Separability
   weak, 59–61
Separable utility functions, 62
Separable utility, indifference curve, 60
Shell, K., 129, 146
Solow, R., 18, 19, 84, 92, 93, 97, 103, 203, 218, 234
Statistical approach, 73–74
Steady state
   golden rule, neo-classical growth model, 95
   golden rules, 93–94
Stigler, G., 19, 234
Substitution, technical, marginal rate of, holothetic production functions and, 29–41
Symmetry, invariance and, conservative laws, overview of, 10–12, 264

T

Tangent vectors
   infinitesimal generators as, 31
   to isoquant, expansion path, 38
   parameter group of transformations, orbits, 9
Taxonomy, technical progress, holotheticity, 24–25
Technical progress
   biased, virtual expansion path for, 27
   holotheticity and, 13–28, 30–34
   significance of, homotheticity and, 18–19
   taxonomy of, holotheticity, 24–25

Technical progress functions, types of, holotheticity, 30–34
Technical substitution, marginal rate of, holothetic production functions and, 29–41
Tensors, 244–249
Thoe, D., 251
Thorne, K., 231
Time Reversal Test, 77
Tools (and mathematical structure)
  charts and manifolds, 237, 238
  conservation laws, 255–258
  covariant derivatives, 247–249
  curves and functions, 238, 239
  differential equations, 249–253
  Hamiltonian formulation, 253–255
  mapping, 236, 237
  Noether theorems, 255–258
  1-forms, 242–244
  tensors, 244–247
  variation, calculus of, 253–255
  vector field, 247–249
  vectors and tangents, 239–242
Transformation
  extended, marginal rate of transformation, 34–37
  group
    translation of point, 23
    translation of point as, 8, 23
  marginal rate of, extended transformation and, 34–37
Transformation group, overview, 9, 22–25, 44, 120, 264
Transformations, parameter group of, orbits, field of tangent vectors, 9
Translation, of point, as group transformation, 8, 23

U

Utility, 4, 12, 43–53, 55–58, 69, 80, 90–93, 97, 98, 100, 104, 105, 114, 115, 121, 123, 125, 126, 150, 154, 165, 209, 212, 214, 216, 218, 233, 234, 239, 253, 261, 262
  separable, indifference curve, 60
Utility functions
  direct, 56–58, 62, 81
  strongly separable, 61, 62

V

Variational derivative, geometric interpretation of, 89
Variational problem, Ramsey rule, 88–92
Vectors, tangent, to isoquant, expansion path, 38
Virtual expansion path
  for biased technical progress, 27, 33
  geometric representation of, 26
  integral curve, system of differential equations, 32
von Neumann model
  conservation laws in, 101, 128–131
  diagrammatic representation of, 101, 102

W

Weakly self-dual functions, 65–66
Weak separability, 59–61
Wealth Conservation Laws, 125–131, 213, 214
Weitzman, M., 114, 115, 123, 143, 149, 150, 168, 209, 213, 214
Wheeler, J., 231, 242

Y

Yaglom, I., 231, 232, 235, 265

Z

Zachmanoglou, E., 251
Zellner, A., 17, 18, 35, 235

RYUZO SATO
Biographical and Bibliographical Data

佐藤 隆三

ニューヨーク大学名誉教授
(C.V. Starr Professor Emeritus of Economics (C.V.スター財団冠講座経済学部名誉教授))

学歴
・秋田県湯沢市生まれ（1931年）
・秋田県立湯沢高校卒業（1950年）
・一橋大学経済学部卒業（1954年）
・フルブライト大学院留学生として渡米（1957年）
・ジョンズ・ホプキンス大学大学院卒業（Ph.D.取得）（1962年）
・一橋大学より経済学博士号取得（1969年）
・*Who's Who in Economics*（1700年以降の著名経済学者名鑑）1983年の初版以来世界著名経済学者の一人として名前が掲載されている。

主たる勤務先
・ニューヨーク大学 C.V.スター財団冠講座経済学部教授（1985〜2005年）
・同大学日米経営・経済研究センター所長（1985〜2005年）
・東京大学大学院経済学研究科客員教授（2003〜2004年，2006〜2008年）
・ブラウン大学経済学部教授（1965〜1985年）
・ハーバード大学ケネディ行政大学院兼任教授（1983〜2002年）
・京都大学工学部招聘教授（1978〜1979年）
・一橋大学経済研究所客員教授（1975〜1976年）
・独ボン大学経済学部客員教授（1974〜1975年）
・英ケンブリッジ大学招聘教授（1970〜1971年）

その他
・全米経済研究所（NBER）研究理事（1982～1990年）
・米国グーゲンハイム財団研究フェロー（1975～1976年）
・米国フォード財団研究フェロー（1970年～1971年）

・ワシントン大学（シアトル）、ハワイ大学、デトロイト大学、ICU（国際キリスト教大学）、日本大学、IUJ（国際大学）、松下政経塾などで教鞭または研究活動に従事した。

主たる編集活動
・*Springer Series, Advances in Japanese Business and Economics*, Editor in Chief（2013～現在）
・*Japan and the World Economy: International Journal of Theory and Policy*, Editor（1987～2005年）
・*Journal of Economic Literature*（American Economic Association）, Associate Editor（1975～1980年）
・*Lecture Notes in Economics and Mathmatical Systems,*（Springer）, Associate Editor（1975～2005年）
・読売新聞客員調査研究員（1990～2000年）
・静岡新聞社客員論説委員（1988～現在）
・その他：1980年代の初めより、プライベート・ワークショップ（佐藤ワークショップ）を主宰している。

主要著書および論文リスト（2016年12月現在）

1. 主要著書

佐藤隆三著作集（*The Selected Works of Ryuzo Sato*，日本評論社，2016年）
　第1巻，文化・社会の日米比較
　第2巻，米国から見た日本経済
　第3巻，日本企業と大学の実態
　第4巻，経済成長の理論
　第5巻，技術変化と経済不変性の理論：リー群論の応用
　第6巻，*The Selected Scientific Papers of Ryuzo Sato on Production, Technical Change and Dynamics*
　第7巻，*Symmetry and Economic Invariance*

Symmetry and Economic Invariance, Second Enhanced edition, with R. V. Ramachandran, Advances in Japanese Business and Economics Series Volume one, 2014年，佐藤隆三著作集第7巻に収録

『メジャー級アメリカ経済学に挑んで：学究生活50年の軌跡』，日本評論社，2011年，佐藤隆三著作集第3巻に収録

Biased Technical Change and Economic Conservation Laws, Springer Science, 2006.

New Strategies for Aimless Japan, Forbes Japan, 2001.（『戦略なき日本：再生の知恵』），(株) ぎょうせい，佐藤隆三著作集第2巻に収録

Production, Stability and Dynamic Symmetry: The Selected Essays of Ryuzo Sato, Volume Two (Economists of the Twentieth Centuiy Series), Edward Elgar Publishing, 1999.

Theory of Technical Change and Economic Invariance: Application of Lie Groups, Academic Press, 1981. Reprint with amendments, Edward Elgar Publishing, 1999. 日本語訳（『技術変化と経済不変性の理論——リー群論の応用』）濃野隆之監訳，三野和雄・筒井俊一訳，勁草書房，1984年，佐藤隆三著作集第5巻に収録

Global Competition and Integration, Ryuzo Sato, Rama V. Ramachandran and Kazuo Mino (eds.), (Research Monographs in Japan-U.S. Business and Economics), Kluwer Academic Publishers, 1999.

Symmetry and Economic Invariance: An Introduction（with Rama V. Ramachandran），(Research Monographs in Japan-U. S. Business and Economics) Kluwer Academic Publishers, 1998.

Growth Theory and Technical Change: The Selected Essays of Ryuzo Sato, Volume One (Economists of the Twentieth Century Series), Edward Elgar Publishers, 1996.

Reconstruction of the Japanese Economy, (『日本経済再建論』), NHK Publishing, 1996.

Issues: Japan-U.S. Center Distinguished Lecture Series, Vol.1, Ryuzo Sato (ed.), New York University Press, 1996.

Health Care Systems in Japan and the United States: A Simulation Study and Policy Analysis (with Elias Grivoyannis, Barbara Byrne and Chengping Lian), (Research Monographs in Japan-U.S. Business and Economics) Kluwer Academic Publishers, 1997.

Organization, Performance and Equity: Perspectives in the Japanese Economy, Ryuzo Sato, Hajime Hori and Rama V. Ramachandran (eds.), (Research Monographs in Japan-U.S. Business and Economics), Kluwer Academic Publishers, 1996.

Japan, Europe, and International Financial Markets: Analytical and Empirical Perspectives, Ryuzo Sato, Richard M. Levich and Rama V. Ramachandran (eds.) Cambridge University Press, 1994.

Challenge to YEN DAKA Problems, (『円高亡国論』 講談社), Kodansha, 1995. 佐藤隆三著作集第2巻に収録

The Chrysanthemum and the Eagle: The Future of U.S.-Japan Relations, New York University Press, 1994.

Global You-ism, Japan Productivity Center, 1993. (『グローバル・ユーイズム——21世紀を変える日米関係』)

New Age of U.S.-Japan Relations, (『日米新時代への決断——グローバル・ユーイズムで発想の大転換を』) Yomiuri Shimbun Publishing House, 1991.

The Chrysanthemum and the Eagle: The Future of U.S-Japan Relations, (in Japanese) Kodansha, 1990. (Awarded the First Yomiuri Rondansho Prize in March 1991. English Translation, New York University Press, 1994). 『菊と鷲』第1回読売論壇賞受賞 (1990年), 佐藤隆三著作集第2巻に収録

U.S. Demands and Japanese Excuses, (『アメリカの言い分 日本の言い訳』), Nihon Keizai Shinbun, 1991.

A New American Dream: Bush's Presidency and U.S.-Japan Relations, (『アメリカ

の新しい夢』), Yomiuri Shimbun Publishing House, 1990.

U.S.-Japan Relations in the Post-Reagan Era, Ryuzo Sato (ed.), HBJ Publishing, 1990.

Conservation Laws and Symmetry, Ryuzo Sato and Rama V. Ramachandran (eds.), Kluwer Academic Publishers, 1990.

Developments in Japanese Economics, Ryuzo Sato and Takashi Negishi (eds.), Academic Press, 1989.

Beyond Trade Friction: Japan-U.S. Relations, R. Sato and Julianne Nelson (eds.), Cambridge University Press, March 1989.

Unkept Promises, Unclear Consequences: U.S. Economic Policy and The Japanese Response, Ryuzo Sato and John A. Rizzo (eds.), Cambridge University Press, 1988.

Lessons from U.S.A.-Mature Country, Nihon Keizai Shimbun, 1988. (『アメリカ 豊かなる没落──ボストンからのエッセイ』)

Economics of Mergers and Acquisitions, (『M&A の経済学』) T.B.S. Britannica, 1987. 佐藤隆三著作集第3巻に収録

"Plus-Sum" Solution to Economic Conflict, (『プラスサム社会の経済学──どうすれば日本の繁栄は続くのか』) PHP Publishing House, 1987.

Trade Friction and Economic Policy: Problems and Prospects for Japan and the United States, Ryuzo Sato and Paul Wachtel (eds.), Cambridge University Press, 1987.

Challenges from America, PHP Matsushita Publishing Co., 1985.

Economics of Technological Change, (『技術の経済学──戦略としてのテクノロジーゲーム』) PHP Matsushita Publishing Co., 1985. 佐藤隆三著作集第3巻に収録

Economic Policy and Development: New Perspective, Toshio Shishido and Ryuzo Sato (eds.), Auburn House Publishers, 1985.

Entrepreneurship in the U.S. and Japan, (『現代のベンチャー精神──福沢諭吉の実学にみる』) Kodansha Co., 1984. 佐藤隆三著作集第1巻に収録

Technology, Organization and Economic Structure, Essays in Honor of Isamu Yamada, Ryuzo Sato and Martin J. Beckmann (eds.), Springer-Verlag, 1983.

Invariance Principle and Structure of Technology, (with Takayuki Nôno),

Springer-Verlag, 1983.

Research and Productivity: Endogenous Technical Change, (with Gilbert Suzawa), Auburn House Publishers, 1983.

Trade Friction, Saburo Okita and Ryuzo Sato (eds.),(『貿易フリクション――世界は経済戦争に入るか』）Yuhikaku Co., 1983.

"Me" Society vs."We" Society: USA vs. Japan,（『Me 社会と We 社会――アメリカ主義・日本主義・資本主義』）Nihon Keizai Shimbun, 1983. 佐藤隆三著作集第1巻に収録

"Me" Decade – Economic and Sociological Study of the American Society, (『ミー時代のアメリカ――「私」優先社会の危機』) Nihon Keizai Shimbun, 1982. 佐藤隆三著作集第1巻に収録

Dual Upbringing in USA and Japan,（『日米ダブル教育体験記――太平洋を通学したわが家の子供たち』）Diamond Publishing, 1981. 佐藤隆三著作集第1巻に収録

Resource Allocation and Division of Space, Ryuzo Sato and Takashi Fujii (eds.), Springer-Verlag, 1977.

Theory of Economic Growth,（『経済成長の理論』日経図書文化賞受賞）Keiso Syobo, 1968. 佐藤隆三著作集第4巻に収録

2. 主要論文 ＊印の論文は佐藤隆三著作集第6巻に収録

"貨幣を含む一般化された需要理論における可積分・定符号条件の検証の不可能性" ポール・サミュエルソン＋佐藤隆三（森田玉雪訳）根岸隆＋三野和雄編著「市場・動学・経済システム：佐藤隆三教授記念論文集」第6章, pp.71〜90, 日本評論社, 2011年

"Quantity or Quality: The Impact of Labour Saving Innovation on US And Japanese Growth Rates, 1960〜2004," (with Tamaki Morita), *The Japanese Economic Rwview*, Vol.60, No.4, Dec., 2009. 佐藤隆三著作集第7巻第10章に収録

"Discussion with Professor Samuelson on New Era of US-Japan Relations," Shizuoka Shimbun Oct. 21, 2009 (「政権交代：日米変革の時代 サミュエルソン教授との対談」(2009年12月に死去した教授の最後の対談) 静岡新聞2009年10月21日付)

"American Economics in 50 Years: My Experience," Series of Essays on American Economics, *Keizai Seminar*, 「私が体験した米国経済学の50年」『経済セミナー』連載, Oct. 2007（No.631）〜Oct. 2009（No.650), Nippon Hyoron Sha.

"Capitalism with Warm Heart," Nihon Keizai Shimbun, Keizai Kyoshitsu, 「温かい資本主義復権の時」Oct. 27, 2009.

* "The Stability of the Solow-Swan Model with Biased Technical Change," chapter 2 of *Biased Technical Change and Economic Conservation Laws*, by Ryuzo Sato, Springer, 2006.

"Macroeconomic Performance and Labor-Saving Innovation as an Alternative to Population Growth," (with Tamaki Morita), Working Paper Series, Stern School of Business, 2006.

* "Evaluating Corporate Performance: Empirical Tests of a Conservation Law," (with Mariko Fujii), *Japan and the World Economy*, Vol.18, No.2, 2006.

* "Economic Consevation Laws as Indices of Corporate Performance," *Japan and the World Economy*, August, 2004.

* "Optimal Economic Growth: Test of Income-Welth Conservation Laws in OECD Countries," *Macroeconomics Dynamics*, 2002.

* "Hartwick's Rule and Economic Conservation Laws," *Journal of Economic Dynamics and Control*, 2001.

* "Technical Change and International Competition," *Japan and the World Economy*, Vol.13(3), 2001, pp.217-233.

* "Optimal Growth with Endogenous Technical Progress: Hicksian Bias in a Macro Model," (with Rama V. Ramachandran), *Japanese Economic Review*, Vol.51 (2), June 2000.

* "A Model of Optimal Economic Growth with Endogenous Bias," (with Rama V. Ramachandran and Chengping Lian), *Macroeconomic Dynamics*, Vol.3, 1999.

* "Estimation of Biased Technical Progress," (with Rama V. Ramachandran and Youngduk Kim), *Global Competition and Integration*, Ryuzo Sato, Rama V. Ramachandran and Kazuo Mino (eds.), Kluwer Academic Publishes, 1999.

* "Note on Modeling Endogenous Growth," *Keio Economic Studies*, April, 1996.

"Three Applications of Lie Groups" (with Rama V. Ramachandran), *Organizations, Performance and Equity: Perspectives in Japanese Economy*, Ryuzo Sato, Rama V. Ramachandran and Hajime Hori (eds.), Kluwer Academic Publishers, 1995.

* "Risk-Adjusted Deposit Insurance for Japanese Commercial Banks," (with Rama V. Ramachandran), *International Financial Markets*, Ryuzo Sato and Rama V.

Ramachandran (eds.), Cambridge University Press, 1993.

"Economic Policy in Japan," (with Rama V. Ramachandran), in Comparative Handbook of National Economic Policies, Dominick Salvatore (ed.), Greenwood Publishing Group, 1993.

"Protectionism and Growth of Japanese Competitiveness," (with Rama V. Ramachandran and Shunichi Tsutsui), in *Protectionism and World Welfare*, Dominick Salvatore (ed.), Cambridge University Press, 1993.

"The Role of Strategies and Cultural Factors in International Trade: Experience of Japan" (with Rama V. Ramachandran and Shunichi Tsutsui), in *Recent Developments in Finace*, Anthony Saunders (ed.), Dow Jones Irwin, 1991.

"Dynamic Invariances in Economics," in *Trade & Development*, ICU Press, 1991.

"Nature's Ways are Invariant" in *The Journal of Social Science*, Vol.29, No.2, 1991.

"National Economic Policies in Japan," (with Rama V. Ramachandran and Elias Grivoyannis), in *National Economic Policies*, Dominick Salvatore (ed.), Greenwood Press, 1991.

"Conservation Laws in Continuous and Discrete Models of Economic Dynamics," in *Conservation Laws and Symmetry*, Ryuzo Sato and Rama V. Ramachandran (eds.), Kluwer Academic Publishers, 1990.

"The U.S.-Japan Trade Imbalance," (with John A. Rizzo), in *Unkept Promises, Unclear Consequences: U.S.Economic Policy and The Japanese Response*, Ryuzo Sato and John A. Rizzo (eds.), Cambridge University Press, 1988.

"Domestic and International Mergers: Competition or Cooperation?" (with Richard J. Zeckhauser), in *Beyond Trade Friction*, Ryuzo Sato and Julianne Nelson (eds.), Cambridge University Press, 1989.

"Symmetry in Dynamic Economic Models," (with Rama V. Ramachandran), in *Symmetries in Science III*, Bruno Gruber and Francesco Iachello (eds.), Plenum Publishing Corporation, 1990.

"Estimation of Self-Dual Demand Functions: An International Companion," (with Masahiro Matsushita), in *Developments in Japanese Economics*, Ryuzo Sato and Takashi Negishi (eds.), Academic Press, 1989.

"The Economics of Technical Progress," (with Thomas M. Mitchell), *Eastern Economic Journal*, Vol.XV, No.4, October-December, 1989.

"R & D and Dynamic Comparative Advantage: Application to U. S. -Japan

Competition" in *International Competitiveness*, Andrew Michael Spence and Heather A. Hazard (eds.), Ballinger Press, 1988.

* "Application of Group Theory to Economics," in *The New Palgrave: A Dictionary of Economics*, Macmillan Press, 1987.

* "CES Production Functions," in *The New Palgrave: A Dictionary of Economics*, Macmillan Press, 1987.

"On the Distribution of Wealth and Intergenerational Transfers" (with Yannis M. Ioannides), in *Journal of Labor Economics*, Vol.5, No.3, 1987.

* "Factor Price Variation and the Hicksian Hypothesis: A Microeconomic Model," (with Rama V. Ramachandran), *Oxford Economic Papers*, Vol.39, 1987.

"Information Strategies, Market Barriers and Trade Performance," (with Shunichi Tsutsui), *NBER Conference on International Economic Problems Confronting the U.S. and Japan*, 1986.

"The Invariance Principle and Income-Wealth Conservation Laws: Application of Lie Groups and Related Transformations," *Journal of Econometrics*, Vol.30, 1985. 佐藤隆三著作集第7巻の第9章に修正後再収録

"Measuring the Burden of Property and Income Taxation," (with John A. Rizzo), *Public Sector and Political Economy*, Horst Hanusch (ed.), Gustav Fischer Verlag, 1985.

"Technical Progress, the Schumpeterian hypothesis and market Structure," (with Shunichi Tsutsui), *Journal of Economics, Supplement 4, Entrepreneurship*, Dieter Bos, Abram Bergson and John R. Meyer (eds.), 1984.

"Hidden Symmetries, Lie Groups and Economics Conservation Laws," (with Takayuki Nôno and Fumitake Mimura), in *Oprerations Research and Economic Theory*, Herbert A. Hauptman (ed.), Springer-Verlage, 1984.

"R & D Activities and the Technology Game: A Dynamic Model of the U.S.-Japan Competition," *NBER Working Paper*, 1984.

"An Alternative Model for Accounting for Technical Progress: Theory and Estimation," (with Thomas M. Mitchell), in *Productivity Analysis*, Ali Dogramaci (ed.), Kluwer Academic Publishers, 1984.

* "Unattainability of Integrability and Definiteness Conditions in the General Case of Demand for Money and Goods," (with Paul A. Samuelson), *American Economic Review*, September, 1984. included in Selected Essays of Ryuzo Sato, vol.2, 1999.

"Japanese Environmental Regulations and Their Economic Effects: A Survey," in *Environmental Repercussions on Trade and Investment: Case Studies of Five Countries*, (ILO Sponsored Research), Anthony Y. C. Koo (ed.), Min-Teh Foundation, 1982.

"Comparison of American and Japanese Educational Systems," *Shincho Sha 45 Plus*, October, 1982.

"Keynesian Policy Today," (Panel Discussion with Motoo Kaji and Miyohei Shinohara), *Oriental Economist*, August, 1982.

"Trade Policy and Foreign Exchange Market," (dialogue with Richard M. Cooper), *Modern Economic Series, Oriental Economist*, October, 1982.

"Economic Policy of Modern Times," *Japan Economic Journal*, July, 1982.

"Trade Friction and International Economics," *Tax Bulletin*, Chuo-Keizai Sha, 1982.

"Dynamic Symmetries and Economic Analysis," (with Takayuki Nono and Fumitake Mimura), *Department of Economics*, Brown University, 1982.

"Analysis of the Effects of Basic and Applied Research on Productivity Gains: The U.S.-Japanese Case," *Productivity and Economic Growth*, Manoranjan Dutta (ed.), 1982.

* "A Theory of Endogenous Technical Progress: Dynamic Bohm-Bawerk Effect and Optimal R & D Policy," (with Takayuki Nôno), *Zeitschrift fur Nationalokonomie*, Vol.42, No.1, 1982.

* "Lie Group Methods and the Theory of Estimating Total Productivity," (with Paul S. Calem), in *Developments in Econometric Analyses of Productivity Measurement and Modeling issues*, Ali Dogramaci (ed.), 1982.

"Taste Change and the Stability of Competitive Equilibrium," (with Victor Cholewicki), *Keio Economic Studies*, Vol.18, No.1, 1981.

"Thirty Years of American Economics (in Japanese), *Shakai-Kagaku-no-Hoho*, Vol.14, No.10, 1981.

"Invariance and Economic Laws," Modern Economic Series, *Japan Economic Journal*, October, 1981.

"Estimation of Implicit Utility Models," (with William A. Barnett and Kenneth J. Kopecky), *European Economic Review*, Vol.15, 1981.

"Econometric and Mathematical Models of the Japanese Economic Planning, in

Encyclopedia of Japan, U.S.A., Kodansha, 1981.

"Adjustment Time and Economic Growth Revisited" *Journal of Macroeconomics,* Vol.2, No.3, Summer 1980.

* "The Impact of Technological Change on the Holotheticity of Production Function," *Review of Economic Studies,* Vol.47, 1980.

"Measurement of the Impact of Technical Progress on Demand for Intermediate Goods: A Methodological Survey," (with Rama V. Ramachandran), *Journal of Economic Literature,* September, 1980.

"A Mathematical Model of Technical Change," in *Essays in Honor of Miyohei Shinohara,* Keiso-Shobo Co., 1980.

"Non-homothetic Production Functions Subject to Different Types of Technical Progress," (with Wilhelm E. Krelle), *Keizai Kenkyu,* Vol.29, No.4, 1978.

* "Homothetic and Non-homothetic CES Production Functions," *The American Economic Review,* Vol.67, No.4, 1977.

"Analysis of Production Functions by Lie Theory of Transformation Groups: Classification of General CES Functions," in *Allocation of Resources and Division of Space,* Ryuzo Sato and Takashi Fujii (eds.), Springer-Verlag, 1977.

* "Self Dual Preferences," *Econometrica,* Vol.44, No.5, 1976.

"Economic Growth," Technical Progress and the Production Function (with Martin J. Beckmann), *Jahrbuchern fur Nationalokonomie und Statistik,* Bank 189, Heft 1/2, 1975.

"The Implicit Formulation and Non-homothetic Structure of Utility Functions," *Quantitative Wirtschaftsforschung,* Horst Albach, Ernst Helmstadter and Rudolf Henn (eds.), 1976.

"A Survey of Modern Mathematical Economics," *Mathematical Sciences,* September, 1975.

* "The Most General Class of CES Functions" *Econometrica,* Vol.43, No.5-6, 1975.

"Global Univalence and Stability of Competitive Markets," *Keizai Kenkyu,* Vol.26, No.3, 1975.

"Market Behavior and the Types of Production Functions," (with Tetsunori Koizumi and Benjamin Wolkowitz), *European Economic Review,* Vol.6, 1975.

"Tax Incidence in a Growing Economy," (with Ronald F. Hoffman), in *Essays in Honor of Professor R. Musgrave,* North Holland, 1974.

"Non-homothetic Production Functions and Technical Progress," (with Martin J. Beckmann), in *On the Measurement of Factor Productivities*, Franz-Lothar Altmann, Oldrich Kyn and Hans-Juergen Wagener (eds.), Vandenhoeck & Ruprecht, 1974.

* "On the Class of Separable Non-Homothetic CES Functions," *The Economic Studies Quarterly*, Vol.XXV, No.1, 1974.

* "On the Stability Properties of Dynamic Economic Systems," *International Economic Review*, Vol.14, No.3, 1973.

"Relative Shares and Elasticities Simplified: Reply" (with Tetsunori Koizumi), *The American Economic Association*, Vol.63, No.4, 1973.

"The Production Function and the Theory of Distributive Shares" (with Tetsunori Koizumi), *The American Economic Review*, Vol.53, No.3, 1973.

"On the Elasticities of Substitution and Complementarity" (with Tetsunori Koizumi), *Oxford Economic Papers*, Vol.25, No.1, 1973.

* "The Stability of the Competitive System Which Contains Gross Complementary Goods," *The Review of Economic Studies*, Vol.39, No.4, 1972.

"Alternative Approaches to the Estimation of Production Functions and of Technical Change," (with Martin J. Beckmann and Mark Schupack), *International Economic Review*, Vol.13, No.1, 1972.

"Optimal Strategies in a Developing Economy," *Weltwirtschaftliches Archiv*, No. 4, 1972.

* "Population Growth and the Development of a Dual Economy," (with Yoshio Niho), *Oxford Economic Papers*, Vol.23, No.3, 1971.

"On the Concept of Technological Change," (a survey article), in *Britannica*, September, 1971.

"A Survey of the Theory of Economic Growth," in *Readings in Modern Economic Theory*, Takashi Negishi (ed.), September, 1971.

"Growth and Stability Under Differential Efficiency of Factor Inputs," *Keizai Kenkyu*, Vol.22, No.2, 1971.

* "Optimal Savings Policy when Labor Grows Endogenously," with Eric G. Davis, *Econometrica*, Vol.39(6), November, 1971, 877~97.

* "The Estimation of Biased Technical Progress and the Production Function," *International Economic Review*, Vol.11, No.2, 1970.

* "Substitutability, Complementarity and the Theory of Derived Demand," (with Tetsunori Koizumi), *The Review of Economic Studies,* Vol.37, No.1, 1970.

* "Shares and Growth Under Factor-Augmenting Technical Change," (with Martin J. Beckmann), *International Economic Review,* Vol.11, Oct. 1970.

* "A Further Note on a Difference Equation Recurring in Growth Theory," *Journal of Economic Theory,* Vol.2, 1970.

* "Stability Conditions in Two-Sector Models of Economic Growth," *Journal of Economic Theory,* Vol.1, June 1969.

* "Aggregate Production Functions and Types of Technical Progress: A Statistical Analysis (with Martin J. Beckmann), *American Economic Review,* 59, March 1969.

"On a Class of Production Functions Generated by Log-Linear Relationship," (with Martin J. Beckmann), in *American Economic Review Proceedings, Series 12,* Paper #5, 1969.

"The Theory of Economic Growth," in *Hitotsubashi Ronso,* Vol.62, No.4, 1969.

* "Production Functions with Variable Elasticity of Factor Substitution: Some Analysis and Testing," (with Ronald F. Hoffman), *Review of Economics and Statistics,* Vol.50, Nov. 1968.

"Technical Progress and the Aggregate Production Function of Japan, 1930-1960," *Economic Studies Quarterly,* March, 1968.

* "An Addendum," (with Martin J. Beckmann), *Review of Economic Studies,* Vol. XXXV, July, 1968.

* "Neutral Inventions and Production Functions," (with Martin J. Beckmann), *Review of Economic Studies,* Vol.35, Jan. 1968.

* "A Note on Scarcity of Specific Resources as a Limit to Output: A Correction," *Review of Economic Studies,* Vol.34, Oct. 1967.

* "The Stability of Oligopoly With Conjectural Variations," (with Keizo Nagatani), *Review of Economic Studies,* Vol.34, Oct. 1967.

"Linear Elasticity of Substitution Production Functions," *Metroeconomica,* Vol.19, 1967.

* "The Harrod-Domar Model vs. The Neo-Classical Growth Model," *Economic Journal,* Vol.74, June, 1964.

* "Diminishing Returns and Linear Homogeneity: Comment," in *American Economic*

Review, Vol.54, 1964.

* "Fiscal Policy in a Neo-classical Growth Model: An Analysis of Time Required for Equilibrating Adjustment," *Review of Economic Studies,* Vol.30, No.1, Feb. 1963.

* "Factor Prices, Productivity, and Economic Growth," (with John W. Kendrick), *The American Economic Review,* Vol.53, 1963.

"Models of Input-Output Analysis," in *East-West Center Publication,* 1962.

"Note on Demand for Money," *Hitotsubashi University Review,* December, 1961.

"Economic Growth and the Interaction of Aggregate Supply and Demand," *Economic Studies Quarterly,* April, 1956.

"Economic Implications of Non-Par Value Shares," *Trust,* No.1, 1955.

3. 主たる翻訳

・ポール A. サミュエルソン『経済分析の基礎』，勁草書房，1967年，2004年
・『サミュエルソン経済学大系』全10巻（篠原三代平，佐藤隆三編集および訳），勁草書房，1979〜1997年
・ハル R. ヴァリアン『ミクロ経済分析』（三野和雄と共訳），勁草書房，1986年
・ハル R. ヴァリアン『入門ミクロ経済学』原著9版（佐藤隆三監訳），勁草書房，2015年

●著者紹介

佐藤隆三（さとう りゅうぞう）

ニューヨーク大学 C. V. スター財団冠講座経済学部名誉教授（C. V. Starr Professor Emeritus of Economics）。秋田県湯沢市生まれ（1931年）。一橋大学経済学部卒業（1954年）。フルブライト大学院留学生として渡米（1957年）。ジョンズ・ホプキンス大学大学院卒業（Ph. D. 取得、1962年）。一橋大学より経済学博士号取得（1969年）。*Who's Who in Economics* に、1983年の初版以来世界著名経済学者の一人として名前が掲載されている。［主要著書と論文のリストは第7巻に収録］

主たる勤務先：ニューヨーク大学 C. V. スター財団冠講座経済学部教授、及び同大学日米経営・経済研究センター所長（1985〜2005年）。東京大学大学院経済学研究科客員教授（2003〜2004年、2006〜2008年）。ブラウン大学経済学部教授（1965〜1985年）。ハーバード大学ケネディ行政大学院兼任教授（1983〜2002年）。京都大学工学部招聘教授（1978〜1979年）、一橋大学経済研究所客員教授（1975〜1976年）。独ボン大学経済学部客員教授（1974〜1975年）、英ケンブリッジ大学招聘教授（1970〜1971年）、全米経済研究所（NBER）研究理事（1982〜1990年）、米国グーゲンハイム財団研究フェロー（1975〜1976年）他。

主たる編集活動：*Advances in Japanese Business and Economics* シリーズ Editor-in-Chief（Springer）（2013年〜現在まで）、*Japan and the World Economy: International Journal of Theory and Policy*, Editor（1987〜2005年）, *Journal of Economic Literature* （American Economic Association）, Associate Editor（1975〜1980年）, *Lecture Notes in Economics and Mathematical Systems*（Springer）、Associate Editor（1975〜2005年）、読売新聞客員調査研究員（1990〜2000年）、静岡新聞客員論説委員（1988年〜現在）

佐藤隆三著作集　第7巻　Symmetry and Economic Invariance

2017年1月25日　第1版第1刷発行

著　者——佐藤隆三
発行者——串崎　浩
発行所——株式会社日本評論社
　　　　〒170-8474　東京都豊島区南大塚3-12-4　電話　03-3987-8621（販売）、8595（編集）
　　　　振替　00100-3-16
印　刷——精文堂印刷株式会社
製　本——牧製本印刷株式会社
装　幀——図工ファイブ
検印省略 © R. Sato, 2017
Printed in Japan
ISBN978-4-535-06757-8

JCOPY 〈(社) 出版者著作権管理機構 委託出版物〉
本書の無断複写は著作権法上での例外を除き禁じられています。複写される場合は、そのつど事前に、（社）出版者著作権管理機構（電話03-3513-6969、FAX03-3513-6979、e-mail:info@jcopy.or.jp）の許諾を得てください。
また、本書を代行業者等の第三者に依頼してスキャニング等の行為によりデジタル化することは、個人の家庭内の利用であっても、一切認められておりません。